RSF: The Russell Sage Foundation Journal of the Social Sciences

The Coleman Report and Educational Inequality Fifty Years Later

VOLUME 2 • NUMBER 5 • SEPTEMBER 2016

RSF: The Russell Sage Foundation Journal of the Social Sciences ISSN 2377-8261

The Russell Sage Foundation

The Russell Sage Foundation, one of the oldest of America's general purpose foundations, was established in 1907 by Mrs. Margaret Olivia Sage for "the improvement of social and living conditions in the United States." The foundation seeks to fulfill this mandate by fostering the development and dissemination of knowledge about the country's political, social, and economic problems. While the foundation endeavors to assure the accuracy and objectivity of each book it publishes, the conclusions and interpretations in Russell Sage Foundation publications are those of the authors and not of the foundation, its trustees, or its staff. Publication by Russell Sage, therefore, does not imply foundation endorsement.

Board of Trustees

Sara S. McLanahan, *Chair*
Larry M. Bartels
Karen S. Cook
W. Bowman Cutter III
Sheldon H. Danziger
Kathryn Edin
Lawrence F. Katz
David Laibson
Nicholas Lemann
Martha Minow
Peter R. Orszag
Claude M. Steele
Shelley E. Taylor
Richard H. Thaler
Hirokazu Yoshikawa

Mission Statement

RSF: The Russell Sage Foundation Journal of the Social Sciences is a peer-reviewed, open-access journal of original empirical research articles by both established and emerging scholars. It is designed to promote cross-disciplinary collaborations on timely issues of interest to academics, policymakers, and the public at large. Each issue is thematic in nature and focuses on a specific research question or area of interest. The introduction to each issue will include an accessible, broad, and synthetic overview of the research question under consideration and the current thinking from the various social sciences.

RSF Journal Editorial Board

Elizabeth O. Ananat, Duke University
Annette Bernhardt, University of California, Berkeley
Karen S. Cook, Stanford University
Sheldon H. Danziger, RSF President
Janet C. Gornick, The CUNY Graduate Center
Jennifer Hochschild, Harvard University
Douglas S. Massey, Princeton University
Mary E. Pattillo, Northwestern University
James Sidanius, Harvard University
Mary C. Waters, Harvard University
Bruce Western, Harvard University

Copyright © 2016 by Russell Sage Foundation. All rights reserved. Printed in the United States of America. No part of this publication may be reproduced, stored in a retrieval system, or transmitted in any form or by any means, electronic, mechanical, photocopying, recording, or otherwise, without the prior written permission of the publisher. Reproduction by the United States Government in whole or in part is permitted for any purpose.

Opinions expressed in this journal are not necessarily those of the editors, the editorial board, trustees, the Russell Sage Foundation, or the William T. Grant Foundation.

We invite scholars to submit proposals for potential issues through the *RSF* application portal: https://rsfjournal.onlineapplicationportal.com/. Submissions should be addressed to Suzanne Nichols, Director of Publications.

To view the complete text and additional features online please go to **www.rsfjournal.org**.

Russell Sage Foundation
112 East 64th Street
New York, NY 10065

ISSN (print):	2377-8253
ISSN (electronic):	2377-8261
ISBN:	978-0-87154-036-2

The William T. Grant Foundation

The William T. Grant Foundation supports research to improve the lives of young people ages five to twenty-five in the United States. The foundation's grantmaking centers on research that has the potential to advance theory, build empirical evidence, and improve policy and practice. Throughout its eighty-year history, the foundation has awarded grants to prominent researchers yielding research that has been pivotal in improving outcomes for youth and the systems in which they develop.

Currently, the foundation funds research that increases our understanding of programs, policies, and practices that reduce inequality in youth outcomes, and research that identifies, builds, and tests strategies to improve the use of research evidence in ways that benefit youth.

Adam Gamoran, President
Russell Pennoyer, Chair, Board of Trustees

RSF: The Russell Sage Foundation
Journal of the Social Sciences

The Coleman Report and Educational Inequality Fifty Years Later

ISSUE EDITORS
Karl Alexander, Johns Hopkins University
Stephen L. Morgan, Johns Hopkins University

CONTENTS

The Coleman Report at Fifty: Its Legacy and Implications for Future Research on Equality of Opportunity 1
Karl Alexander and Stephen L. Morgan

Part I. The Legacy of EEO and Current Patterns of Educational Inequality

Is It Family or School? Getting the Question Right 18
Karl Alexander

School Segregation and Racial Academic Achievement Gaps 34
Sean F. Reardon

Racial and Ethnic Gaps in Postsecondary Aspirations and Enrollment 58
Barbara Schneider and Guan Saw

Still No Effect of Resources, Even in the New Gilded Age? 83
Stephen L. Morgan and Sol Bee Jung

First- and Second-Order Methodological Developments from the Coleman Report 117
Samuel R. Lucas

Part II. Looking to the Future

Educational Equality Is a Multifaceted Issue: Why We Must Understand the School's Sociocultural Context for Student Achievement 142
Prudence L. Carter

What If Coleman Had Known About Stereotype Threat? How Social-Psychological Theory Can Help Mitigate Educational Inequality 164
Geoffrey D. Borman and Jaymes Pyne

A New Framework for Understanding Parental Involvement: Setting the Stage for Academic Success 186
Angel L. Harris and Keith Robinson

Necessary but Not Sufficient: The Role of Policy for Advancing Programs of School, Family, and Community Partnerships 202
Joyce L. Epstein and Steven B. Sheldon

Accountability, Inequality, and Achievement: The Effects of the No Child Left Behind Act on Multiple Measures of Student Learning 220
Jennifer L. Jennings and Douglas Lee Lauen

Can Technology Help Promote Equality of Educational Opportunities? 242
Brian Jacob, Dan Berger, Cassandra Hart, and Susanna Loeb

Connecting Research and Policy to Reduce Inequality 272
Ruth N. López Turley

The Coleman Report at Fifty: Its Legacy and Implications for Future Research on Equality of Opportunity

KARL ALEXANDER AND STEPHEN L. MORGAN

July 2016 marked the fiftieth anniversary of the release of *Equality of Educational Opportunity* (hereafter EEO), commonly known as the Coleman Report after the lead investigator of the research team, James S. Coleman (Coleman et al. 1966). *The Coleman Report and Educational Inequality Fifty Years Later* celebrates the occasion. To set the stage for the papers that follow, we take a brief look in this introduction back to the origins of EEO in the 1960s and its immediate impact on scholarship and the policy debate. But this issue, in intent and execution, is decidedly forward-looking. Our contributors include some of the nation's leading authorities on issues at the intersection of schooling, race, and social inequality. They appraise EEO's lasting value, the continuing relevance of the issues it addressed, and the ways in which its research approach has stood the test of time, but their larger contribution is to forge, by way of example, a recast equality of educational opportunity research agenda appropriate to twenty-first-century America. As a bridge between then and now, we conclude our introduction with an overview of educational inequality as it now stands, through the lens of the EEO report. That exercise centers on conditions in Baltimore City, Coleman's home base when leading the EEO team.

BACKGROUND

Commissioned by Congress in the Civil Rights Act of 1964, the EEO report is located at the center of that era's struggle to desegregate America's public schools. Here is the authorizing language from section 402 of the Civil Rights Act:

> The Commissioner [of Education] shall conduct a survey and make a report to the President and the Congress, within two years of the enactment, concerning the lack of availability of equal educational opportunity for individuals by reason of race, color, religion, or national origin in public institutions at all levels in the United States, its territories and possessions, and the District of Columbia.

The Civil Rights Act of 1964 pushed a sometimes reluctant country into a new era in pursuit of civil rights for black Americans. By virtue of its provenance in the act, EEO was destined to achieve landmark status. That has proven to be the case: written in a highly

---

Karl Alexander is director of the Thurgood Marshall Alliance and John Dewey Professor Emeritus of Sociology at Johns Hopkins University. **Stephen L. Morgan** is Bloomberg Distinguished Professor of Sociology and Education at Johns Hopkins University.

We thank Minhyoung Kang and Joel Pally for their programming assistance as well as attendees of the November 2015 gathering at the Russell Sage Foundation for their helpful suggestions. Direct correspondence to: Karl Alexander at karl@jhu.edu, School of Education, 2800 N. Charles St., Johns Hopkins University, Baltimore, MD 21218; and Stephen L. Morgan at stephen.morgan@jhu.edu, Department of Sociology, 3400 N. Charles St., Johns Hopkins University, Baltimore, MD 21218.

charged political climate, the project was the most ambitious deployment to that time of the tools of social science in the service of education policy.

In its 1954 and 1955 *Brown v. Board of Education* decisions, the Supreme Court had ordered that the system of segregated schooling throughout the South be dismantled "with all deliberate speed." A decade of resistance and foot-dragging later, with too much deliberation and not enough speed, not much had changed. The survey that Congress mandated in 1964 was intended to advance the cause by establishing that segregation by race remained widespread throughout the country and that the schools attended by black children were grossly inferior to those attended by white children. These conditions were thought to be self-evident, but having them documented would provide the ammunition—that is, the scientific justification—for a final assault on the edifice of school segregation.

Considering the moment in history and all that was at stake, it is striking how little guidance Congress provided in its enabling language. Indeed, it sketched just the barest outline: a national study encompassing all levels of schooling was to be completed—meaning written up and delivered—in a mere two years. Nothing was said on the most consequential matters of method and substance. What kind of survey, for example, was to be conducted? Even more fundamentally, what was meant by "equal educational opportunity," and what evidence was required to decide whether its availability differed along lines of race, religion, or national origins? These large questions were left to be resolved by the research team in consultation with the commissioner of education.

James Coleman, then on the faculty at Johns Hopkins University, was recruited to lead the effort. Large-scale survey research was uncommon at the time, but Coleman had the requisite experience through his first major project after graduate school, a study published in 1961 as *The Adolescent Society*. That project concluded that the anti-intellectualism characteristic of peer cultures in ten Chicago-area high schools deflected youth's energies from academic priorities. Three years later, Coleman published *An Introduction to Mathematical Sociology* (1964), which put him at the vanguard of those advocating for greater empirical rigor in the social sciences.

Coleman must have seemed the ideal candidate to lead the effort. *The Adolescent Society* had brought him standing as a leading authority on conditions of schooling, and his bona fides in research methods were second to none. But how exactly was he to proceed? He began by accepting that the time frame and scope obliged his team to pursue breadth over depth. The EEO was a massive national survey and testing program involving more than half a million students in thousands of schools. Its empirical analysis used what were then state-of-the-art statistical methods to sketch the conditions extant in the nation's public schools, with special attention to the experience of poor minority children and the contrasts between their experience and that of majority whites.

Considering the time constraints, the fractious political climate, and the primitive computer technology available to the research team, it is hardly surprising that the implementation of the study design was imperfect. For example, many school districts, including some large city school districts and many Southern districts, declined to participate; only a handful of items on family conditions were procured (such as the educational level of the parents, whether there were two parents coresident in the household, the number of siblings in the home, an index of household possessions, and the parents' interest in their child's education), and then through highly fallible student reports; and the project's information about conditions at school was superficial. Data on per-pupil expenditures, for example, were collected at the district level, not the school level, and they were not disaggregated in any way. Likewise, information on school facilities was compiled by way of a checklist, with little detail and no nuance.

Nor was there much theoretical or conceptual depth to the report's analysis. The effort was little more than an empirical parsing of the association between children's test scores at various grade levels, on the one hand, and measures of family background and school resources, on the other. The focus on school resources and family background was aimed at identifying the relative weight of possible causative factors, but the design and framing were poorly suited to the task. The data, and so the analyses, were cross-sectional, not longitudinal, and so not well suited to causal attributions, while at the level of ideas, the EEO lacked an account of how children's school performance developed over time in response to conditions at home and at school, and it had even less to say about how children's performance developed in response to *changes* in conditions at home and at school, as would have been the ideal.

It is fair in retrospect to say that the report's methodology was limited in these and other respects, and critiques were advanced following its publication. Indeed, the report itself acknowledged many of its limitations, although those cautions were not especially evident in the way its conclusions were presented. Rather, the weight of sentiment seemed to be that the mere force of numbers would override research design limitations and the anticipated stark differences in facilities and resources between schools attended by black children and those attended by white children would be of such magnitude as to be undeniable.

We now know that "big" will not always carry the day; nevertheless, the report's key conclusions held up fairly well against thoroughgoing critical scrutiny. The best evidence of their strength is found in the papers produced by some of the country's leading academic researchers for a yearlong Harvard conference convened in 1967–1968 by two distinguished academics, then-policy-analyst Daniel Patrick Moynihan (later elected to the Senate from New York) and the distinguished statistician Frederick Mosteller (Mosteller and Moynihan 1972).

The EEO indeed warranted such close and critical scrutiny. By virtue of its provenance in the Civil Rights Act of 1964, EEO was central to policy and political debates about whether and how to advance the cause of school desegregation—a compelling issue then, and a compelling issue still.

Today much has changed, but much also has yet to change. After considerable progress in the 1970s and 1980s, levels of segregation in our public schools have risen sharply, rivaling those extant in the 1960s (Brown 2016). The achievement gap across social lines, achievement gap reduction, and accountability have been elevated to focal concerns in the education policy and reform arenas. They always have been large challenges, but today we recognize them as such. That recognition was largely latent in the mid-1960s when planning for EEO commenced. It probably claims too much to credit today's attention to these topics to the legacy of EEO, but certainly the report helped elevate them.

THE PRIMARY FINDINGS OF EEO

The thinking at the time was that school quality inhered in a school's facilities and resources, such as modern science laboratories, a well-stocked school library, and highly qualified teachers, all of which were regarded as "school inputs," in the language of the report. It was expected that the segregated schools attended by black children would be found to be badly lacking in the inputs thought to be educationally important. From that vantage point, gauging "equality of opportunity" would be revealed in comparisons of school resources, black against white. For that part of the agenda, no fancy statistics were needed.

EEO presented evidence on this point, but evidence that many found hard to believe. The report concluded that school resource disparities revolving around race *distinctively* were not large. There were differences, to be sure—the South lagged behind the rest of the country, and rural areas behind urban—but differences by race within the same geographic space generally were small, too small to account for what today we call the black-white achievement gap.

This is one of several conclusions that made the EEO report controversial, and for many a disappointment. Other significant conclusions trace to the expansive view of equal educational opportunity that was introduced by the research team. Their reformulation shifted attention from disparities in schooling "inputs" as problematic in themselves to disparities in inputs that had bearing on educational "outcomes"—notably achievement test scores—and to achievement differences across social lines as markers of unequal opportunity. These radical reframings of the issue are undoubtedly among the report's most profound and lasting contributions.

Pursuing this line of inquiry, the report compared test scores across racial and ethnic lines, across dimensions of family background (for example, parents' educational level), by grade level, and across different regions and community contexts (urban or rural). In a more analytical vein, it examined variations in test scores and test score gaps in relation to school resources, focusing on average resource differences *across* schools. The school resources examined included teacher qualifications, curricular coverage, and facilities and expenditures, along with compositional characteristics of the student body (such as the percentage of minority enrollment and the percentage of families of low socioeconomic background).

These aspects of the report's work were truly groundbreaking, and very likely not at all by congressional intent. Here, too, EEO's main conclusions were both surprising and, for many, disappointing. These conclusions are addressed in detail in several of the papers in this issue. In thumbnail, EEO concluded that

1. differences across schools in average achievement levels were small compared to differences in achievement levels within schools;
2. the differences in achievement levels detected did not align appreciably with differences in school resources other than the socioeconomic makeup of the student body; and
3. family background factors afforded a much more powerful accounting of achievement differences than did any and all characteristics of the schools that children attended.

THE LEGACY OF EEO

The report's focus on academic achievement (test scores) to assess equality of educational opportunity was revolutionary. Reliance on achievement tests for monitoring and accountability is now routine, and many volumes have been written on how to do such assessments well. But that was not the case a half-century ago.

The report also was transformative in directing attention to the broader social context of children's academic development. If school resources were the sole engine, then evaluating the performance of schools in isolation would be fine. But Coleman's research team understood that resources provided by families and neighborhoods contributed to children's initial school readiness, their achievement levels, and their learning trajectories. That, too, is taken for granted today—there is much interest, for example, in out-of-school time learning (OTL) opportunities—but at the time education policy was inward-looking: education reform meant school reform. Today it is also routine to pose questions about the social factors in children's learning and the determinants of the achievement gap across social lines by asking: is it family or it is school? In the 1960s, when the report posed that question, it was not routine.

The report also established that racial segregation remained the norm throughout the United States, a finding that proponents of school desegregation embraced and used to advance their agenda. The same cannot be said of its conclusions regarding the near-irrelevance of school resources for advancing the cause of educational equity and the imbalance of family and school in children's learning.

EEO's approach was simultaneously informative and limiting. The thinking at the time directed attention to differences between the schools attended by black children and other schools. With school segregation the animating issue, and with segregated schooling the norm throughout the United States, not just in the Southern states, the case for comparing schools could certainly be made. However, not only did that focus neglect conditions within those schools, but the report itself established that roughly 80 percent of the variability in children's test scores was located in achievement differences between children attending the very same school, not in average achievement differences across schools. One implication of this realization, which was not understood until EEO established the point, is that EEO was looking in the wrong place for the root causes of children's unequal school performance. That is no warrant to ignore the average differences across schools that were the report's focus, but certainly a comprehensive accounting would require a more encompassing approach.

And the same holds for methods. With today's standards, any analysis of differences and patterns in learning trajectories that uses only data on school inputs and student outcomes measured at a single point in time is certain to be judged incomplete. If the questions of interest are developmental in nature—and many of the most important questions raised by EEO were—it is understood now that our research must model those trajectories with precision, using measures of outcomes collected over time.

Likewise, today the call for mixed-methods research is de rigueur, but back in the day it was either-or—quantitative or qualitative. The congressional enabling legislation used the word "survey," but it is doubtful that Congress meant that to be taken literally. Still, Coleman's background was in survey research, and the time constraints imposed by Congress ensured that the exercise would have to opt for breadth over depth. Surveys are good for quick broad coverage, and not always so good for drilling down. Qualitative studies done well can yield valuable insights not easily gained using survey methods, but qualitative research is labor-intensive, typically can involve no more than a handful of schools, and is rarely implemented in a way that allows for generalization to a well-defined larger population of interest. Still, as a complement to broad-based, large-scale survey research, qualitative data can be invaluable. The EEO did include a small set of qualitative case studies, but they were conducted in parallel to the survey analyses rather than in conjunction with them. Lacking was a richly textured assessment of the conditions "on the ground" in the schools attended by minority children and the ways in which they contrasted with those in the schools attended by white children. One suspects that had it done that sort of assessment, EEO would have uncovered larger resource differences across this school divide.

These critical observations notwithstanding, it would be hard to overstate the importance of EEO. It stood at the center of policy debates around schooling and equity at a time in our nation's history when the struggle to undo the legacy of 200 years of racial oppression was just beginning to gain momentum. Even today, more than a half-century later, EEO continues to be invoked as an authoritative account of conditions of schooling—not just conditions we see in looking back, as might be expected, but conditions we can see in looking around at schools today.

With that in mind, the next section offers a "looking around" application of EEO's issues and approach to current conditions in Baltimore, Maryland. Not only was Baltimore the venue for the conference associated with this set of papers, but the city was also Coleman's home base when EEO was written. As we show next, a vast inequality of educational outcomes persists in Baltimore, very likely for many of the same reasons highlighted by EEO five decades ago.

EDUCATION AND INEQUALITY IN BALTIMORE FIFTY YEARS LATER

For the first two figures published in EEO (see Coleman et al. 1966, 4–5), Coleman and his colleagues looked at the student racial composition of elementary schools in the nation and then considered regional variations. Figure 1 here presents histograms for the proportion of students identified by their schools as black or African American across the 327 regular elementary schools in the four school districts that encompass the Baltimore metropolitan area—Baltimore City and the three adjacent counties.[1] The pattern of segregation—fifty years after EEO—is dramatic. The median Baltimore City school is 97 percent black. In contrast, the median schools in Anne Arundel County, Baltimore County, and Howard County are 14, 25, and 16 percent black, respectively, although Baltimore County has a larger diver-

---

1. In Maryland, school districts are coterminous with counties, and Baltimore City itself is a county. In figure 1 and all other results reported here, special education schools, vocational education schools, and "alternative/other" schools for federal reporting are excluded.

Figure 1. Proportion of Students Identified as Black or African American in Regular Elementary Schools in the Four School Districts That Encompass the Baltimore Metropolitan Area, 2012

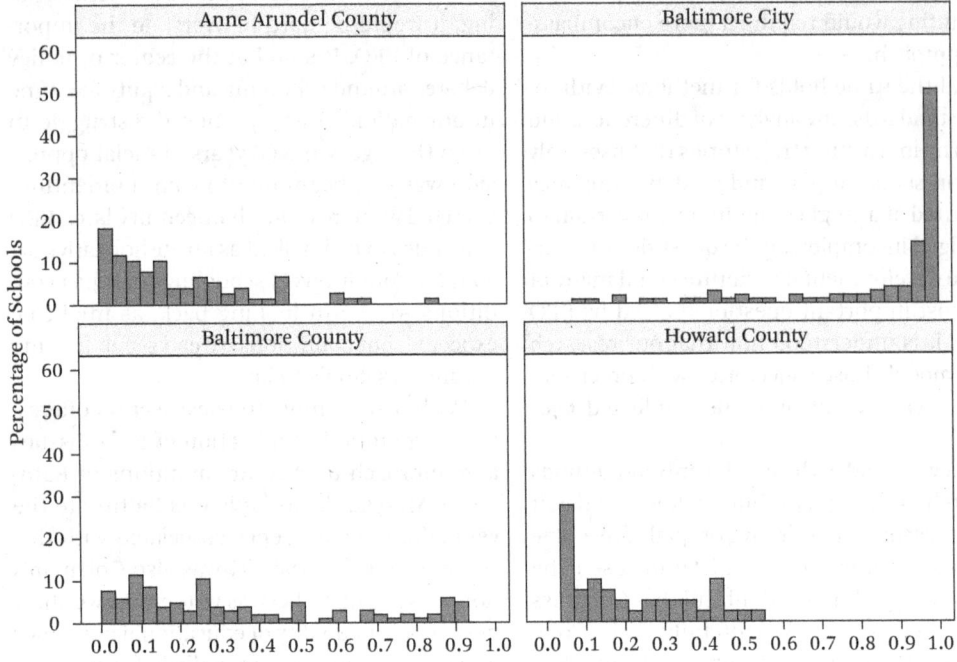

Source: Authors' calculations based on NCES, CCD, 2012 School Universe File (Keaton 2014).
Notes: The number of regular elementary schools is 327 (77 for Anne Arundel County, 105 for Baltimore City, 105 for Baltimore County, and 40 for Howard County). To make the four subgraphs comparable, the vertical axis is the percentage of schools in each school district with the corresponding proportion of black or African American students in the bins listed on the horizontal axis.

sity of racial composition across its schools than both Anne Arundel and Howard.

Table 1 presents basic characteristics of elementary school students in these four school districts. As shown in the first row, the student populations of each district are large, and each district should be able to capture the cost-efficiencies afforded by size. However, student mobility into and out of Baltimore City schools is substantially higher, as shown in the second and third rows of the table. And of particular importance for a consideration of educational opportunity (see Coleman 1968/1990), the last two rows of the table reveal a large difference in proficiency levels for the performance of third-graders on Maryland's official standardized test.[2] Among Baltimore City third-graders, 53 and 44 percent are not proficient in reading and mathematics, respectively. The gaps with the next-closest school district—Baltimore County—are 34 and 24 percent, respectively.

To begin to understand these differences, EEO's approach would direct attention to the geography of Baltimore to determine the extent to which residential patterns structure these differences. We are able to do that today by taking advantage of the geographic information systems now enabled by administrative data collection, supplemented by the Census Bureau's American Community Survey (ACS). These resources were not available to Coleman and his team. To convey a wider regional perspective, figure 2 presents a map of central Maryland with two sets of information displayed simultaneously. First, census tracts are shaded on a gray scale by the proportion of the

---

2. District-level differences for tests in other grades are similar.

Table 1. Elementary School Students in the Four School Districts of the Baltimore Metropolitan Area, 2013–2014

	Baltimore City	Anne Arundel County	Baltimore County	Howard County
Number of elementary school students	39,767	36,749	50,999	23,458
New student transfers	16.9%	12.6%	10.8%	7.3%
Students withdrawn	15.3%	7.2%	7.4%	5.6%
Proficiency in third grade				
Not proficient in reading	53.0%	13.9%	18.9%	15.6%
Not proficient in math	44.1%	14.2%	19.9%	13.5%

Source: Authors' calculations based on data available from the Maryland State Department of Education for the 2013–2014 academic year.
Note: The percentage "not proficient" is the category of "basic" on the Maryland State Assessment in 2014.

Figure 2. Locations of Regular Elementary Schools in Central Maryland, Displayed with a Heat Scale for the Percentage of Students Identified as Neither White nor Asian and Plotted on Top of Census Tracts Shaded by the Percentage of Residents Estimated to Be Neither White nor Asian

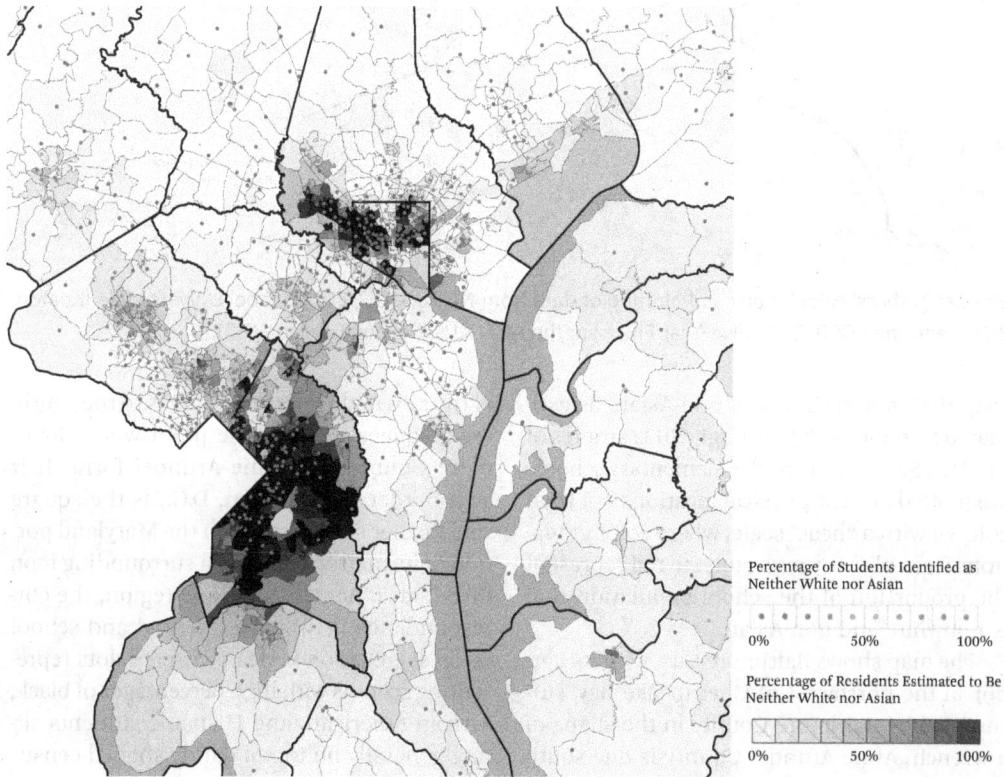

Source: Authors' calculations and plotting of data from NCES, CCD, 2012 School Universe File (Keaton 2014), and the 2009–2013 Five-Year File from the ACS (U.S. Census Bureau 2013).

Figure 3. Locations of Regular Elementary Schools in the Baltimore Metropolitan Area, Displayed with a Heat Scale for the Percentage of Students Identified as Black or African American and Plotted on Top of Census Block Groups Shaded by the Percentage of Residents Estimated to Be Black or African American

Source: Authors' calculations and plotting of data from NCES, CCD, 2012 School Universe File (Keaton 2014), and the 2009–2013 Five-Year File from the ACS (U.S. Census Bureau 2013).

tract that is nonwhite and non-Asian, as estimated by pooled 2009 through 2013 samples of the ACS. Second, all regular elementary schools are plotted at their physical locations but then colored with a "heat" scale, where color gradations from blue through violet to red represent the proportion of the school population that is nonwhite and non-Asian.[3]

The map shows Baltimore City, with its harbor in the northwest of Chesapeake Bay, surrounded by Baltimore County in the shape of a wrench. Anne Arundel County is due south of the city, and Howard County is to the southwest, squeezing in to the point where Baltimore County and Anne Arundel form their own border. Washington, D.C., is the square void farther southwest, with the Maryland portion of its metropolitan area surrounding it on three sides. Across the whole region, the correspondence between residential and school racial segregation is clear, with red dots representing schools with high percentages of black, African American, and Hispanic students sitting generally on top of darkly shaded census

---

3. The optimal way to view these maps is in color. We would refer readers of the print edition of this paper to www.rsfjournal.org/doi/full/10.7758/RSF.2016.2.5.01 to view the color version.

Figure 4. The Persistence of de Facto Segregation for Regular Elementary Schools in the Four School Districts That Encompass the Baltimore Metropolitan Area, 2002 and 2012

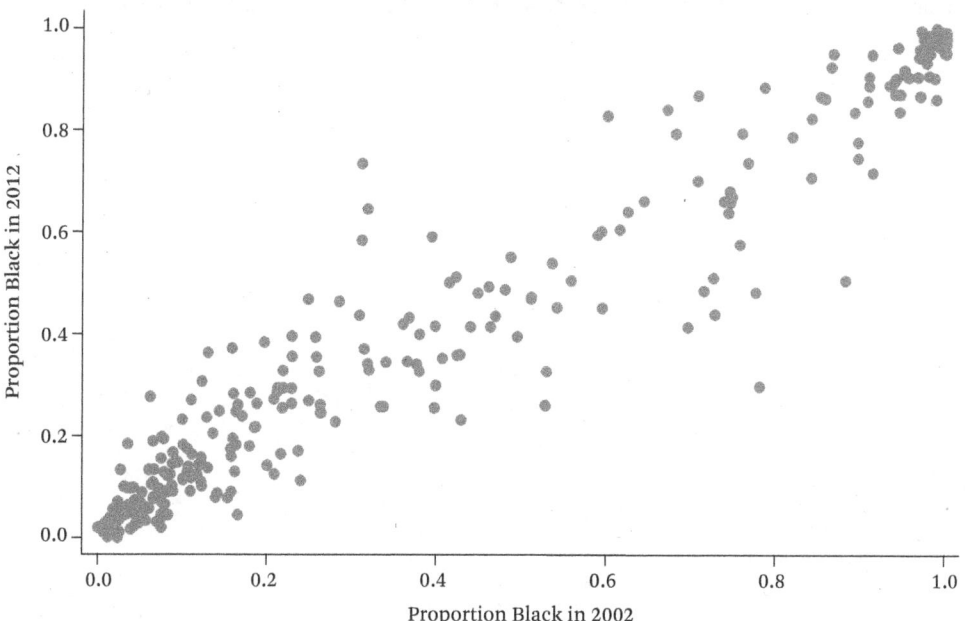

Source: Authors' calculations based on data from NCES, CCD, 2002 and 2012 School Universe Files (Keaton 2014).
Notes: The estimated correlation for the underlying scatterplot is 0.97. The number of elementary schools with valid and available data in both years is 311 (75 for Anne Arundel County, 101 for Baltimore City, 99 for Baltimore County, and 36 for Howard County).

tracts with high proportions of black, African American, and Hispanic residents.[4]

Zooming in on the Baltimore metropolitan area, figure 3 overlays the proportion of each elementary school that is black or African American on top of the proportion of residents of census block groups that are black or African American. The comparatively small Hispanic population in Baltimore ensures a close correspondence between the patterns in figures 2 and 3 in the Baltimore metro area, and the census block groups of this map bring local residential variation into greater relief. In either representation, the overall pattern is clear. Baltimore's black population is concentrated in a distinct V-shaped pattern, mostly within Baltimore City but also extending into Baltimore County, especially to the northwest. Elementary school segregation mirrors the residential pattern very closely. We suspect that it would have been much the same during the 1960s, indeed perhaps even more strikingly so, but the data sources and technology for such a perspective were not available to Coleman and his colleagues.

Next, we consider the stability of the racial segregation of schools to examine whether there has been a trend toward greater integration. Figure 4 offers a scatterplot of the proportion of students designated as black or African American in 311 of the 327 elementary schools for which data are available in both 2002 and 2012. The stability of the pattern over a decade is dramatic, and the correlation coefficient for the ten-year scatter is a staggering 0.97. Thus, although the Baltimore metro area has certainly changed over the past fifty years in many ways, since 2000 at least the racial segregation

---

4. In maps available in the supplementary appendix, we show that the Hispanic population is substantial in the metro D.C. area but not in the metro Baltimore area.

Figure 5. The Proportion of Students Who Fell Below the Reading Proficiency Cutoff in Third Grade in 2013 in Regular Elementary Schools in the Four School Districts That Encompass the Baltimore Metropolitan Area, Plotted Against the Percentage of Each School Identified as Black or African American in 2012

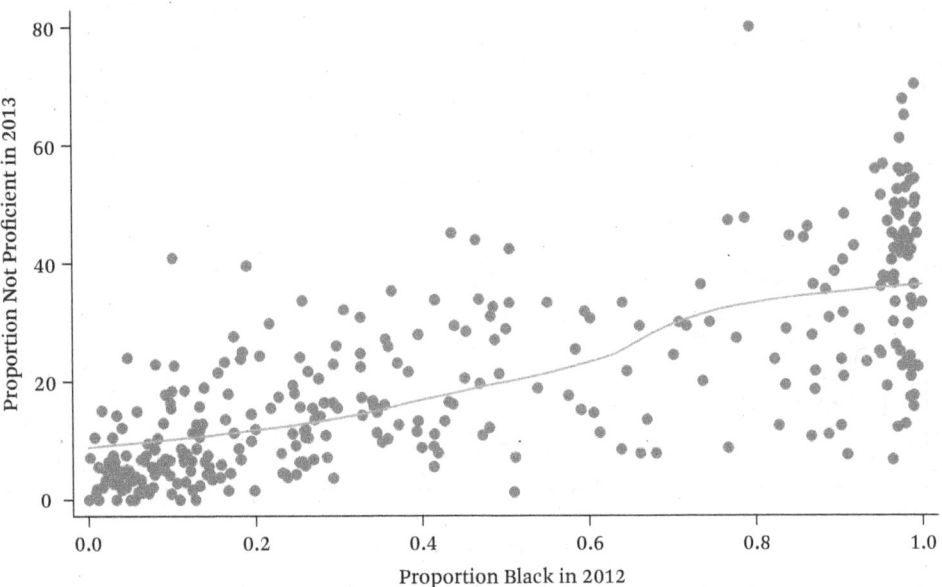

Source: Authors' calculations based on NCES, CCD, 2012 School Universe File (Keaton 2014), merged with publicly available data from the Maryland State Department of Education for 2013.
Notes: The red line is a kernel-smoothed local regression prediction, which is interpretable as the smoothed average proficiency for each value of racial composition. The estimated correlation for the underlying scatterplot is 0.73. The number of elementary schools with valid and available data for the proportion black in 2012 and the percentage not proficient in 2013 is 323 (77 for Anne Arundel County, 101 for Baltimore City, 105 for Baltimore County, and 40 for Howard County).

of elementary schools has looked fixed in place.

The demographic pattern in Baltimore of differences in school performance is taken up next to revisit whether, as in EEO, family background differences remain paramount. Recalling the district differences in proficiency documented already in the last two rows of table 1, we first examine the relationship between a school's African American enrollment (proportion black) and its proportion not proficient. Figures 5 and 6 present scatterplots with schools as the unit of analysis and with reading and math test scores for third-graders. For both figures, the correlation coefficient exceeds 0.7 for the relationship between the proportion not proficient in the subject of the test and the proportion of students identified as black or African American. The nonparametric regression line, presented in red, suggests a threshold in the relationship as the proportion of the school that is black or African American approaches and exceeds two-thirds.

Of course, the relationship between test scores and racial composition at the school level is a surface representation of deeper structural determinants of educational outcomes. Indeed, EEO, probably more than any other piece of research, established clearly why such comparisons have limited value. So, to probe, we might follow EEO's lead and first look for notable differences in school inputs.

Table 2 presents selected input characteristics that are available from administrative reporting, and these do reveal a substantial difference for Baltimore City. The level of instructional staff is lower, and the rate of advanced certification for this staff is lower as well. Yet,

Figure 6. The Proportion of Students Who Fell Below the Mathematics Proficiency Cutoff in Third Grade in 2013 in Regular Elementary Schools in the Four School Districts That Encompass the Baltimore Metropolitan Area, Plotted Against the Percentage of Each School Identified as Black or African American in 2012

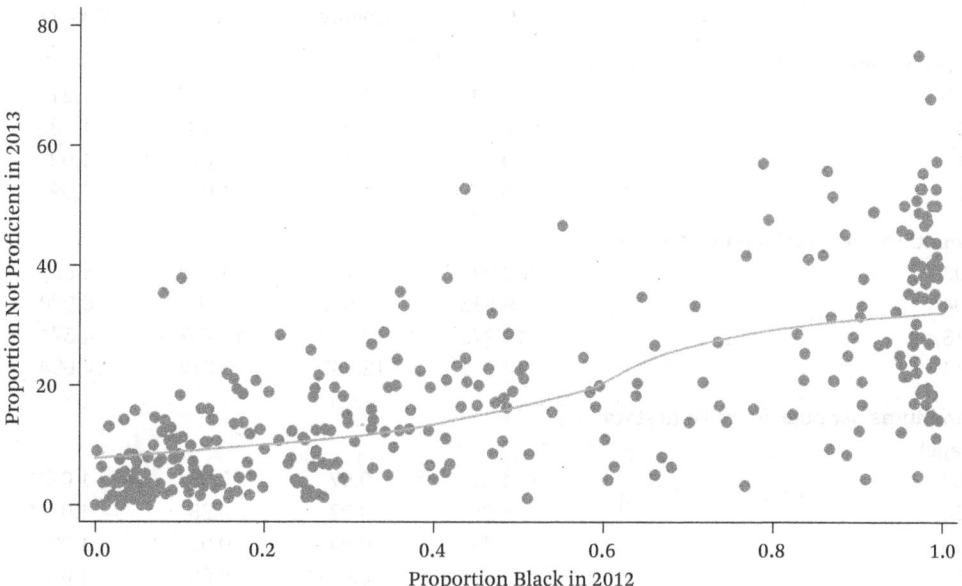

Source: Authors' calculations based on NCES, CCD, 2012 School Universe File (Keaton 2014), merged with publicly available data from the Maryland State Department of Education for 2013.
Notes: The red line is a kernel-smoothed local regression prediction, which is interpretable as the smoothed average proficiency for each value of racial composition. The estimated correlation for the underlying scatterplot is 0.71. The number of elementary schools with valid and available data for the proportion black in 2012 and the percentage not proficient in 2013 is 323 (77 for Anne Arundel County, 101 for Baltimore City, 105 for Baltimore County, and 40 for Howard County).

Table 2. Selected Inputs for the Four School Districts in the Baltimore Metropolitan Area, 2011–2012 and 2013–2014

	Baltimore City	Anne Arundel County	Baltimore County	Howard County
District staff, 2013–2014				
Instructional staff per 1,000 students	62.2	68.6	68.7	73.3
Instructional assistants per 1,000 students	16.1	11.6	9.7	24.9
Advanced certification	47.6%	66.1%	66.4%	65.3%
Distribution of revenue, 2011–2012				
Local	18.7%	57.9%	51.7%	65.6%
State	67.4	37.0	42.6	31.7
Federal	14.0	5.1	5.8	2.7

Source: For district staff, Maryland State Department of Education 2013; for the distribution of revenue, NCES, CCD (Keaton 2014).

Table 3. Wealth and Expenditures per Pupil in the Four School Districts in the Baltimore Metropolitan Area, Before (2003 and 2004) and After (2013 and 2014) Full Implementation of Maryland's Revised Funding Formula for State Expenditures

	Baltimore City	Anne Arundel County	Baltimore County	Howard County
Wealth per pupil (relative to state average)				
2003	0.54	1.20	1.12	1.21
2004	0.53	1.22	1.10	1.18
2013	0.58	1.24	1.01	1.08
2014	0.59	1.24	1.02	1.09
Expenditures per pupil (nominal dollars)				
2003	8,926	8,104	8,138	8,957
2004	9,585	8,522	8,562	8,970
2013	14,973	12,519	12,752	14,571
2014	14,631	12,687	13,012	14,694
Expenditures per pupil (relative to state average)				
2003	1.07	0.97	0.98	1.07
2004	1.09	0.97	0.98	1.02
2013	1.12	0.94	0.95	1.09
2014	1.08	0.93	0.96	1.08

Source: Authors' calculations based on data from the Maryland State Department of Education (2013).
Note: Relative wealth and expenditures per pupil in each year were calculated by dividing the district-specific nominal dollar amount in each year by the Maryland state average across all districts in each year.

without a comprehensive analysis of educational programming and how it varies across districts, differences such as these are hard to interpret. Looking at the distribution of revenue reveals, in contrast, a large and clear difference that sets Baltimore City apart. Only 18.7 percent of Baltimore City's funding is from local sources, in comparison to 51.7 percent for Baltimore County and even higher shares for Anne Arundel and Howard. Unlike the other three districts, far and away the largest portion of Baltimore City's funding is from the state of Maryland. Its funding from federal sources is much larger as well, as most federal funding for K–12 schooling is targeted at high-poverty school districts.

The explanation for these differences is partly revealed in table 3, which shows annual wealth and expenditures per pupil for each of the four districts in two periods, 2003 and 2004, and then 2013 and 2014. For the first time period, Maryland had only just begun to implement a new state program to compensate for variation in low levels of local funding and demonstrated need for better educational performance across the state. For the latter time period, 2013 and 2014, this new funding formula for state expenditures had been fully implemented.

With the goal of better understanding variation in the local capacity to fund schooling, for the first panel per-pupil wealth is tabulated in each year relative to the state average. In both time periods, Baltimore City has dramatically less wealth per pupil, thereby generating much lower local funding from analogous taxation mechanisms.[5] Between the two periods, Baltimore City's wealth per pupil grew slightly

---

5. In fact, Baltimore's property tax rate is much higher than that of its neighboring counties but yields much less revenue owing to these wealth disparities.

more, benchmarked against the state average, than wealth per pupil in the other three school districts, and narrowing a substantial amount on the wealth of Baltimore County.

The story for expenditures is similar, and some subtle patterns drive the results. State and federal funding for Baltimore City kept the district on par with the other three school districts before full implementation of the state's new funding formula. By 2013 and 2014, Baltimore City (and Howard County) had pulled ahead of both Anne Arundel and Baltimore counties in nominal dollars. But in part because per-pupil funding increases from the state program were large in some other districts in the state, the relative positions of all four school districts were little changed, as shown in the third panel. Overall, implementation of these changes in funding affected Baltimore City only modestly, relative to its nearest two school districts, Baltimore and Anne Arundel Counties.

Tables 2 and 3 represent two bedeviling realities of school effects research since EEO was published. First, direct measures of inputs, such as staffing characteristics, are hard to interpret given the wide variation in programming across districts, especially variation due to differences in the number of special needs students. Second, gross district-level funding differences do not line up with common expectations for seemingly resource-poor urban schooling; instead, this research tends to show that urban districts with low tested performance do not lack for funding, at least on paper.

The EEO researchers gathered data about children's families, and those data were central to the report's analyses comparing the relative influence of school and home resources. Today, to conduct like analyses, there would be a similar need for data on students' families, but despite the large increase in resources devoted to accountability measurement in the past two decades, most school districts still collect very little such information. Figures 7 and 8 consider the role of family background inputs as best we can do without data on students' parents to match directly to students' test scores. Each figure plots the same regular elementary schools displayed in figure 3 in the Baltimore metropolitan area, but now with the heat scale set by the percentage of third-graders not proficient on the state tests for math. (The results for reading, provided in the supplementary appendix, show an even more dramatic pattern.) For figure 7, census tracts are shaded dark on a gray scale proportional to the average years of education for residents in the tract who were twenty-five years or older. For figure 8, the shading is for median income among civilians age eighteen or older who reported any income.

Paralleling, again, the EEO report's results, there is a close correspondence between aggregate family background characteristics in census tracts and the levels of student proficiency in the regular elementary schools located within and near to them. With reference to figure 3, within-race variation in family background appears to have a clear relationship with proficiency levels. For example, census tracts outside of Baltimore City that are predominantly black have higher levels of education and income and higher levels of tested proficiency as well.[6]

While undoubtedly there are local communities and particular schools with unique stories of success and failure, the broad pattern across Baltimore is simple. Racial segregation remains dramatic, and historic patterns of family disadvantage, which have changed too little across the decades, convert this segregation into a clear geography of varied school performance. Elementary schools situated in affluent areas test well, but performance falls off steadily and regularly as the local prevalence of family disadvantage increases. Large portions of Baltimore City are deserts of educational performance, dotted with too few oases of distinction.

---

6. In additional figures available in the supplementary appendix, we show that the pattern appears even more starkly when the map is zoomed out to show the entirety of all four counties. Virtually all of the schools in the exurban zones on the fringe of the Baltimore metro area are solidly blue, and none are in or near census tracts with the low levels of education and income characteristic of many areas of Baltimore City.

Figure 7. Locations of Regular Elementary Schools in the Baltimore Metropolitan Area, Colored with a Heat Scale for the Percentage of Third-Graders Not Proficient in Math in 2013 and Plotted on Top of Census Tracts Shaded by Levels of Education for Residents

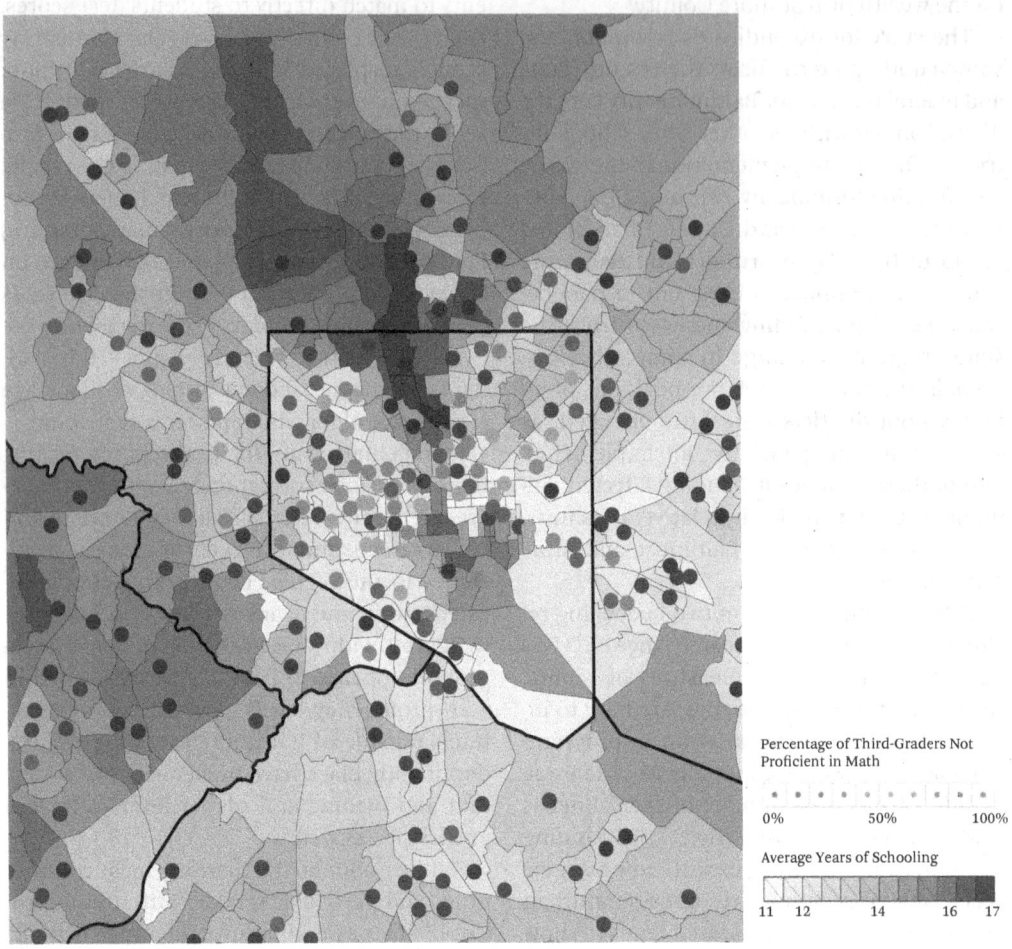

Source: Authors' calculations based on the 2009–2013 Five-Year File from the ACS (U.S. Census Bureau 2013), merged with publicly available data from the Maryland State Department of Education for 2013.

THE HOPKINS CONFERENCE AND THE PRESENT ISSUE

These data from Baltimore and its neighboring school districts instruct us that EEO's agenda is no less relevant today than it was during the civil rights era and the decades that followed: how are we as a nation to *understand* and *moderate* large and troublesome achievement gaps along lines of race-ethnicity and family background? Questions remain as well about the debates and advances that the report set in motion: Are our approaches to accountability sensible? Do a school's resources matter for its students' learning? And what about the balance between in-school and out-of school resources?

Motivated by EEO's prominence in the annals of social science research and mindful of the large questions that remain, we concluded that a thoroughgoing stocktaking was in order on the occasion of the report's fiftieth anniversary. Our goal was to respect the report's role in history, but not defer to it, to take a necessary look back, but also to be forward-looking. That is what prompted us to convene a conference at Johns Hopkins University, Coleman's

Figure 8. Locations of Regular Elementary Schools in the Baltimore Metropolitan Area, Colored with a Heat Scale for the Percentage of Third-Graders Not Proficient in Math in 2013 and Plotted on Top of Census Tracts Shaded by Levels of Income for Residents

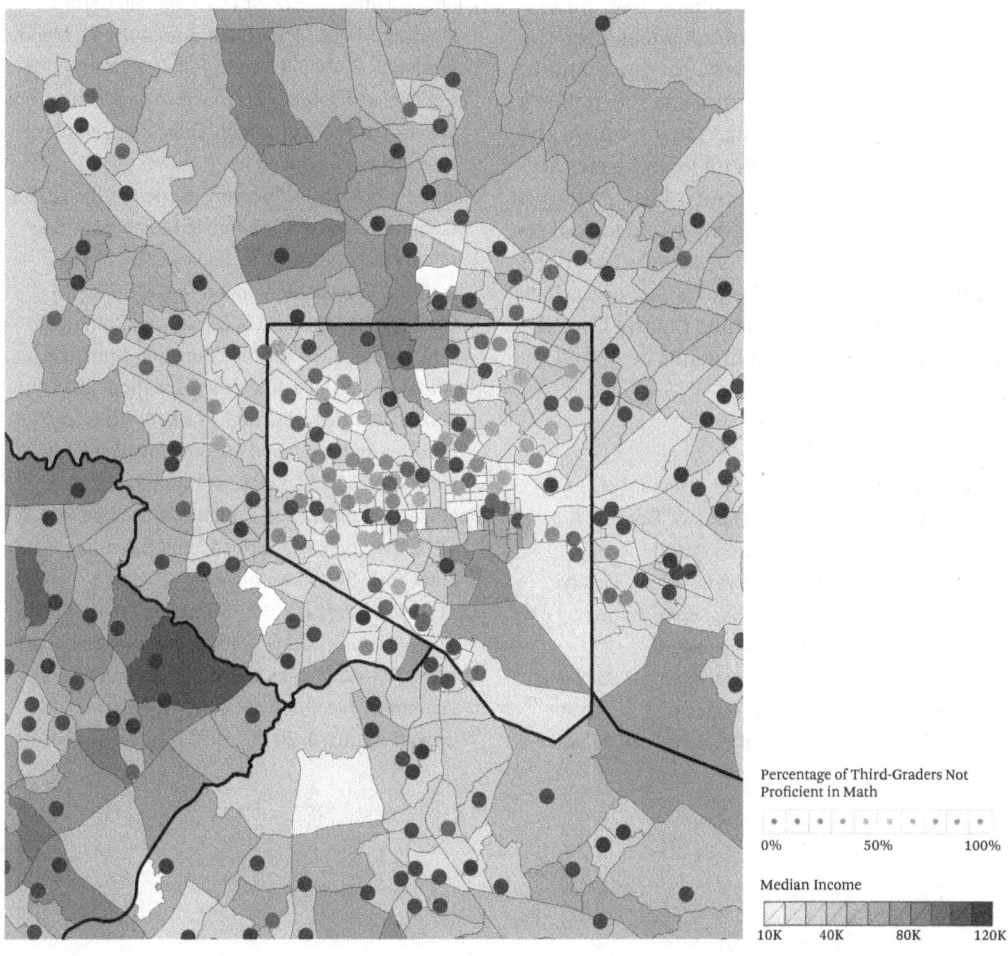

Source: Authors' calculations based on the 2009–2013 Five-Year File from the ACS (U.S. Census Bureau 2013), merged with publicly available data from the Maryland State Department of Education for 2013.

home base while writing EEO. The papers prepared for that conference are shared in this issue of *RSF: The Russell Sage Foundation Journal of the Social Sciences*.

Prominent scholars from several disciplines were invited to offer their reflections on the report's legacy. In our letter inviting their contributions, we explained that "the intent is not simply to valorize the exercise. Rather, it is . . . to be forward-looking and agenda setting." We noted that "the Report's conclusions regarding what today would be called the achievement gap across social lines" would be the conference's most obvious frame of reference, but then reminded invitees that the report's "legacy includes as well the development of a modern social science research infrastructure and advances in how insights from research are used to inform practice."

A truly distinguished set of contributors accepted our invitation to consider how well EEO's insights have held up and to explore their continuing relevance to today's educational and social policy debates. Some of the contributors are quite senior and were on the scene at the time; others are younger and engaged with the report's issues using today's methods and understandings.

The papers that follow address the EEO report's approach and its substantive conclusions through the lens of advances over the past half-century in research methods and in the knowledge base bearing on the report's substantive contributions. They address the balance of family and school in children's academic development, school racial isolation and segregation, school climate and school reform, standards and assessments, and the methodology of school effects research. It is an ambitious agenda, but one that we hope the readers of this issue will find has been well executed.

REFERENCES

Brown, Emma. 2016. "On the Anniversary of Brown v. Board, New Evidence That U.S. Schools Are Resegregating." *Washington Post,* May 17.

Coleman, James S. 1961. *The Adolescent Society: The Social Life of the Teenager and Its Impact on Education.* New York: Free Press.

———. 1964. *Introduction to Mathematical Sociology.* New York: Free Press of Glencoe.

———. 1990. "The Concept of Equality of Educational Opportunity." (1968). In *Equality and Achievement in Education,* edited by James S. Coleman. Boulder, Colo.: Westview Press.

Coleman, James S., Ernest Q. Campbell, Carol J. Hobson, James McPartland, Alexander M. Mood, Frederick D. Weinfeld, and Robert L. York. 1966. *Equality of Educational Opportunity.* Washington: U.S. Department of Health, Education, and Welfare, Office of Education.

Keaton, Patrick. 2014. "Documentation to the NCES Common Core of Data Public Elementary/Secondary School Universe Survey: School Year 2012–13 Provisional Version 1a (NCES 2015-009)." Washington: U.S. Department of Education, National Center for Education Statistics.

Maryland State Department of Education. 2013. "2013 Data Report Card." Available at: http://reportcard.msde.maryland.gov/downloadindex.aspx?K=99AAAA (accessed August 1, 2015).

Mosteller, Frederick, and Daniel P. Moynihan, eds. 1972. *On Equality of Educational Opportunity.* New York: Random House.

U.S. Census Bureau. 2013. "Summary File." *2009–2013 American Community Survey.* Available at: http://www2.census.gov/programs-surveys/acs/summary_file/2013/data/5_year_by_state/ (accessed August 1, 2015).

PART I
The Legacy of EEO and Current Patterns of Educational Inequality

Is It Family or School? Getting the Question Right

KARL ALEXANDER

Much research has tried to parse the school's contribution to children's learning apart from the family's and the family's contribution apart from the school's as though they were discrete and separable. The 1966 Equality of Educational Opportunity report helped launch this agenda, finding in favor of family. In this essay I argue that the framing of the issue as "family versus school" is fundamentally flawed. Rather, family and school (and neighborhood) together shape children's academic development. I argue that the strong effect associated with school socioeconomic composition in the original report, and stronger still in more recent studies, is in fact an expression of family influence: family determines where children live and the schools they attend. But it is a school influence as well. When properties of family, neighborhood, and school overlap, as they do under conditions of extreme neighborhood and school segregation, poor children's profile has them triply disadvantaged. The same ecological perspective on children's learning implies that by reducing the degree of overlap across these "overlapping spheres of influence," school socioeconomic context can function instead to offset family disadvantage. Relevant literatures are reviewed and the concluding section considers the potential of socioeconomic integration at the school level as a policy lever for improving poor children's educational prospects.

Keywords: educational inequality, achievement gap, school socioeconomic integration, school effects, family effects

What are the social forces that govern children's academic development? This question arguably has been, and remains, the core problematic for the sociology of education as a field of inquiry, with the achievement gap across social lines a particular focus. In pursuit of answers, studies typically attempt to parse the school's contribution to children's learning apart from the family's and the family's contribution apart from the school's. Which of the two has the greater weight? James S. Coleman's *Equality of Educational Opportunity* report (Coleman et al. 1966; hereafter Coleman Report), which helped launch this agenda, found decidedly in favor of family.

In this essay, I argue that framing the issue as "family versus school" asks the wrong question. Rather, family and school, along with neighborhood, *together* shape children's academic development, and in ways that may not always be separable. When we think of family resources in support of children's schooling, it is natural to look to the interior of family life—for example, the family's material well-being, the structural integrity of the family, and the parents' engagement with their children's

---

Karl Alexander is director of the Thurgood Marshall Alliance and John Dewey Professor Emeritus of Sociology at Johns Hopkins University.

Direct correspondence to: Karl Alexander at karl@jhu.edu, School of Education, 2800 N. Charles St., Johns Hopkins University, Baltimore, MD 21218.

learning and their children's schools. But the family's reach extends beyond the confines of the household. Where children live and the schools they attend also are parental decisions, and owing to the deeply entrenched residential and school segregation of life in the United States today, the imperatives of family, neighborhood, and school tend to be mutually reinforcing—privileging those already privileged and disadvantaging those already disadvantaged.

THE COLEMAN REPORT AS BACKDROP

Daniel Patrick Moynihan's *New York Times* obituary (1995) for his good friend James Coleman began by recounting an incident at the Harvard Faculty Club on the occasion of the 1966 release of the Coleman Report. Moynihan tells us that he was approached by Seymour Martin Lipset, another eminent member of the faculty, who excitedly pronounced: "You know what Coleman is finding don't you? . . . All family." A few years later, Godfrey Hodgson (1975) introduced his expansive essay on the Coleman Report with the same story: "Hello Pat," Lipset began, "guess what Coleman found? . . . schools make no difference, families make the difference." Though shaded differently, both renderings convey the large takeaway point at the time of the report's rollout: in the tug of war between family and school in shaping children's academic development, family wins. And it is a decisive victory.

The conclusion that "schools make no difference" was a disheartening revelation for those who believed that poor and minority children suffer under the weight of woefully deficient schools. The Coleman Report was expected to provide scientific justification for school improvement as the remedy for generations of racial injustice. Instead, it implicated the private sphere of family life, seeming to leave little room for school reform as a solution.

Some who were distressed by the report's message dismissed it on technical grounds. Others took what they could from it—for example, the "news" that school segregation remained widespread throughout the United States a decade after the Supreme Court struck down the South's dual school system, that differences in children's educational experiences *within* individual schools counted for more than did average differences across schools (the latter being the report's perspective), and that teacher quality seemed to matter some, as did the socioeconomic makeup of a school's enrollment, such that poor and minority children perform better academically in schools with a diverse student body. But against the weight of family advantage and disadvantage, these were mere crumbs, and the decades that followed offered little relief from the deep malaise that set in:

In 1969, Arthur Jensen began his famous paper in the *Harvard Educational Review* (Jensen 1969, 2) with the assertion that "Compensatory Education has been tried and apparently has failed," following with: "Why has there been such uniform failure of compensatory education programs wherever they have been tried?" (3).

In 1972, Frederick Mosteller, a Harvard statistician, and Daniel Patrick Moynihan published the results of a faculty seminar in which distinguished academics from several disciplines revisited the Coleman Report data, analytic procedures, and conclusions. The result? According to the book's dust jacket: "This study turned understanding of a major area of social policy upside down, as had no comparable event in the history of social science" (Mosteller and Moynihan 1972).

In 1989, Robert Slavin's literature review on the educational effectiveness of small classes concluded that there was little benefit short of one-on-one tutoring.

Also in 1989, and then updated a decade later, Eric Hanushek's (1989, 1997) review of the evidence on school funding concluded that "variations in school expenditures are not systematically related to variations in student performance."

In light of such pronouncements, Barbara Heyns (1978, 186) was moved to elevate education research above economics as the "dismal science," a legacy of the Coleman Report that remains with us still. According to Debra Viadero (2006, 23), writing on the occasion of the fortieth anniversary of the report: "What most people took away from the report . . . was the notion that 'schools don't matter.'" She then followed with a telling quote from David Armor, one of the Harvard seminar participants: "No one has found a way, on a large-scale basis, to overcome the influence of family."

Around the same time, Adam Gamoran and Daniel Long (2007, 23) credited the report with "the seminal finding in U.S. sociology of education."[1] Such acclaim after some forty years is quite remarkable, and not much has changed over the ensuing decade. The Coleman Report and the idea that "schools make no difference" continue to be invoked as authoritative, despite the following four facts that bear on the family-school tug-of-war:

1. The Coleman Report did not conclude that "schools make no difference."

2. Studies since, using more rigorous methods applied to both the same data and to new data, buttress—indeed strengthen—the report's actual conclusions.

3. Conclusions from the other studies cited as reinforcing the view that schools make no difference all have been refuted by scholars of comparable standing.

4. Pitting family against school as a contest between "this" and "that" is a flawed framing of the social forces that drive student learning and has led to much wrongheaded thinking.

I address these several points in the sections that follow, starting with the fourth, as it is fundamental.

THE FRAMING: IS IT "FAMILY OR SCHOOL?" OR "FAMILY AND SCHOOL?"

Richard Jessor's 1993 *American Psychologist* essay sketches an ecological perspective on children's development that is at once familiar and profoundly insightful. It follows in the social ecological tradition of Uri Bronfenbrenner (1979), but absent the obscure language. For Jessor, children's development is governed by experiences in the three institutional settings they encounter daily, up close and personal: family, neighborhood, and school. The resources available to children in these three settings, and how they are deployed, combine to channel youth along different developmental paths, ones that often overlap lines of race, gender, and family background.

At a farther remove, but still relevant, are the broader sociostructural and sociocultural contexts within which family, neighborhood, and school themselves are embedded. In my research (for example, Alexander, Entwisle, and Olson 2014), the background context is deindustrialized Baltimore over the last two decades of the twentieth century into the first decade of the twenty-first. The Annie Casey Foundation (2010, 2) has characterized this span of years as a time of

> crippling trends and tragic events—the dramatic loss of manufacturing jobs and tax base, the ruinous riots of 1967 and 1968; the exodus of first white then African-American, middle class families; the sequential epidemics of heroin, crack cocaine, and HIV; the intensified crime and gang activity that fed and feasted off the drug trade; and the activities of slumlords, property flippers and predatory lenders. The end result has been an ever-deepening cycle of disinvestment and decline.

It is fundamental to the life-course perspective on human development that the life paths children follow and the characteristic differences across social lines in those life paths are historically situated. It is self-evident that the conditions just described pose challenges for the healthy development of many of Baltimore's children. Those challenges play out at the interior of family life, in Baltimore's high-poverty neighborhoods, and in Baltimore's public schools, where enrollment systemwide in 2014

---

1. For Gamoran and Long (2007, 23), the seminal finding is that *"variation between schools* in their resources mattered little for *variation among individual students."*

was 84 percent low-income and 83 percent African American.[2]

There is nothing exceptional in Jessor's rendering to this point. That comes with his insight that family, neighborhood, and school are *overlapping spheres of influence* in children's development. That is to say, children's experience of family life, their neighborhood exposure, and the character of the schools they attend are not isolated silos. Rather, they are experienced holistically, as a mosaic. Children who grow up in poor families, live in high-poverty neighborhoods, and attend schools with high-poverty enrollments are triply disadvantaged. This profile, sadly, is all too common, and children who are burdened by it find themselves disadvantaged at every turn. It does not auger well.

Now to my point: poor children's experiences across these settings are an expression of family disadvantage. In deciding where to live, parents, poor and nonpoor alike, determine the character of their children's neighborhood exposure and of the schools they attend. Family, neighborhood, and school as overlapping spheres of influence in children's development characterize both family advantage (a middle-class experience profile) and family disadvantage (a low-income experience profile).

To speak of school influence as something apart from family influence is a false divide. We might try to force their separation heuristically for analytical purposes, but the counterfactual reality so imagined is just that: imaginary. In children's lived lives, school influence is an expression of family influence. That realization is critical to a proper understanding of the Coleman Report's results.

WHAT THE COLEMAN REPORT REALLY CONCLUDED

To see clearly that school influence is an expression of family influence requires going beyond thumbnail accounts, most of which misconstrue the report's import. Here, then, is the original source material (Coleman et al. 1966, 258):

Of the many implications of the study of school effects on achievement, one appears to be of overriding importance.

This is the implication that follows from the following results taken together:

1. The great importance of family background for achievement;

2. The fact that the relation of family background to achievement does not appear to diminish over the years of school;

3. The relatively small amount of school-to-school variation that is not accounted for by differences in family background . . .

4. The small amount of variation in achievement explicitly accounted for by variations in facilities and curriculum;

5. Given the fact that no school factors account for much variation in achievement, teacher's characteristics account for more than any other . . .

6. The fact that the social composition of the student body is more highly related to achievement, independently of the student's own social background, than is any school factor . . .

Taking all these results together, one implication stands out above all: The schools bring little influence to bear on a child's achievement that is independent of his background and general social context.

The report continues with specific reference to home, neighborhood, and peer environments: "For equality of educational opportunity through the schools must imply a strong effect of schools that is independent of the child's immediate social environment; and that strong independent effect is not present in American schools."

Points 1, 3 and 6 are key, as is the language of "independent effects." Family background is of overriding importance—no one would dispute that.[3] But the fact that school-to-school variation in school achievement closely tracks

---

2. Baltimore City Public Schools, "By the Numbers," available at: http://www.baltimorecityschools.org/about/by_the_numbers (updated July 17, 2015).

3. It also should be noted, however, that the report's assessment of family background is quite limited; it includes

family background precisely exemplifies Jessor's "overlapping spheres of influence" thesis.

In fact, school influence on children's achievement is so deeply embedded in children's family life that they hardly are separable.[4] These tight linkages across institutional contexts additionally imply that the social organization of schooling, as constituted back then and still today, functions mainly to maintain or reproduce children's place in the social order. To illustrate, in 2005 nationally, poor students were in the majority in 84 percent of schools with minority enrollments of 90 to 100 percent; in schools with minority enrollments of 10 percent or less, just 18 percent of schools had majority low-poverty enrollments (Orfield and Lee 2007).

The insight that the social composition of the student body is the strongest school-based correlate of student achievement, independent of the child's family background, pinpoints the particular mechanism that channels family influence through the school: neighborhood residential segregation.

Owing to such segregation, most schools enroll mainly children of like background. High-poverty neighborhoods and high-poverty schools are population aggregates. Their properties do not inhere in any single family, and they have consequences beyond those located at the interior of family life. In that sense, they are independently consequential. But their force derives from the residential decisions of individual families, which are historically grounded and contemporaneously maintained. Change the demographics of neighborhood and school and the entire formula potentially changes: with less overlap across spheres, the evidence suggests that the social composition of the school would reverse function and serve to weaken the link between family background and school achievement. But such a circumstance today is the exception, not the rule.

As the national commitment to school desegregation has waned, segregation at the school level has increased: "Nearly 40 years after the assassination of Dr. Martin Luther King, Jr., we have now lost almost all the progress made in the decades after his death in desegregating our schools" (Orfield and Lee 2007, 11). That reversal has been most dramatic in the South, which for a brief period could claim the lowest levels of racial segregation in the country: in 1988 the percentage of black students attending majority-white schools in the South stood at 43.5 percent (up from essentially zero in 1954 and 2.3 percent at the passage of the 1964 Civil Rights Act); by 2005 it had dropped to 27 percent, just a bit above the figure for 1968 (Orfield and Lee 2007, 23).[5]

In an earlier era, the force of law, commercial practices, and, not infrequently, violence maintained segregated schooling and housing and kept neighborhoods separate along lines of race, ethnicity, and income. Today there is formal commitment to "equality of opportunity," but the largely informal practices that maintain such separation are no less powerful than in the past (Bonilla-Silva 1996).

Neighborhood segregation begets school segregation. Consider the parallels in Baltimore, as reported by John Logan (2002): during the 1989–1990 school year, neighborhood and school segregation indices were 79.1 and 76.3, respectively; a decade later, at 74.3 and 79.0, they had barely changed.[6] That the paired fig-

---

just a handful of surface indicators as reported by children and absent a meaningful theory or conceptualization of the processes by which parents and a family's resources are thought to guide children's academic development.

4. Research on summer learning loss, reviewed later in this essay, complicates that conclusion, but for now I let the point stand.

5. The situation for residential segregation is more complicated, as over time segregation by race has decreased while segregation by family income has increased (see, for example, Reardon and Bischoff 2011; Reardon et al. 2009). However, poor blacks specifically remain as isolated as ever (Massey and Brodmann 2014, 7).

6. Segregation indices represent the percentages of children who would have to change their school or neighborhood for every school and neighborhood in the city to have the same percentage African American as the citywide percentage.

ures are similar and high is hardly coincidental.

This degree of alignment reveals why attempting to separate the influence of family from the influence of school as though they are discrete entities serves little purpose. It is not that such a separation cannot be done—the Coleman Report achieved an approximation of it using the tools then available, and an even better job of it can be done today. The problem, rather, is conceptual: focusing on the independent contributions of family and school misses their overlapping contributions. It is not a matter of family *or* school, but of family *and* school.

AMPLIFYING THE "KEY FINDING"

In this section, I review studies from the contemporary literature that add weight to the Coleman Report's conclusions regarding poor and minority children's learning in relation to their school's enrollment mix. These studies instruct us that the report very likely understates the importance of school context, an insight that is startlingly important. I also review studies that compare school-year learning with summer learning, as these comparisons afford a rather different perspective on the contributions of family and school.

Borman and Dowling (2010)

Geoffrey Borman and Maritza Dowling (2010) reanalyze the original Coleman Report data for ninth-graders, acquired through the University of Michigan's Inter-University Consortium for Political and Social Research, a secondary analysis data archive. Some of the original ninth-grade data were missing, but otherwise Borman and Dowling use the same data, predictor set, and variable operationalizations as in the original Coleman Report. Their dependent variable is a test of verbal achievement, a short vocabulary test administered in the original project. The Coleman Report centered on the same test, which it characterized as a test of "verbal ability."

With these parallels to the Coleman analysis, Borman and Dowling's study also suffers the original project's limitations, a large one being its cross-sectional research design. The project did not monitor children's learning over time; rather, it assessed achievement levels at a single point in time and how those covaried in relation to school and family characteristics. Static comparisons across grade levels for different students might look like learning trajectories, but they are not. Still, if the original analysis is accorded credibility, as clearly it has been, then so too should Borman and Dowling's.

In addition to these many parallels, there is one large difference that sets the Borman-Dowling study apart from the original: its mode of analysis. The original report relied on simple correlational and regression analyses. Borman and Dowling instead use an approach that adjusts for the nested data structure that is characteristic of classroom- and school-based research. The methods used in the Coleman Report assume independence of observations, meaning, in this instance, that what happens to one child has nothing to do with what happens to another child. But children who attend the same school or are enrolled in the same classroom share many experiences, including some that no doubt have bearing on their learning.

Owing to this shared experience, the forces that impinge on children's learning vary less across persons than they would if, for example, each child attended a different school. As a result, there is a strain toward homogeneity in the data collected from them and about them. This nesting can be multilayered—for example, children within classrooms, within schools, within school districts, or within states—and to ignore that possibility risks getting biased results. The distortion can be large or small, but since the extent of bias usually is unknown, it looms large as a concern.

Borman and Dowling use hierarchical linear modeling (HLM) to adjust for the fact that observations are nested and not independent, and this does indeed affect the results. We know this because they also report results using the report's original mode of analysis. Here is what they conclude:

> Going to a high-poverty school or a highly segregated African American school has a profound effect on a student's achievement outcomes, above and beyond the effect of his or her individual poverty or minority status.

Specifically, both the racial/ethnic and social class composition of a student's school are more than 1¾ times more important than a student's individual race/ethnicity or social class for understanding educational outcomes. In dramatic contrast to previous analyses of the Coleman data, these findings reveal that school contexts dwarf the effects of family background. (Borman and Dowling 2010, 1239)

All family? Schools don't matter? That hardly seems the case.

Rumberger and Palardy (2005)
Russell Rumberger and Gregory Palardy (2005) pose similar questions using a different data source: the National Educational Longitudinal Survey of 1988, which affords national coverage. This project began in 1988 with a large, representative sample of eighth-grade students and their schools and tracked their educational progress through twelfth grade. Because it monitored the learning of the same students over time, Rumberger and Palardy are able to evaluate *changes* in test scores in relation to characteristics of children's families and schools and in relation to experiences at school. They analyze learning in several achievement domains: math, science, reading, social science, and a composite of all four via HLM, the same mode of analysis used by Borman and Dowling.

Their results are complicated and nuanced, with comparisons across testing domains, different kinds of students (classified by race-ethnicity and family socioeconomic status), and different kinds of schools (for example, low-, mid-, and high-SES). Still, the results of most immediate interest are straightforward:

> The results of this study confirm a widely held belief of many parents: that whom you go to school with matters. But what appears to matter most is the socioeconomic, not the racial composition of schools. . . . While students' own social backgrounds were related to their achievement, so too were the average social class backgrounds of all the students in their school. In fact, the effects of school SES were almost as large, and sometimes much larger, than the effects of student SES. (Rumberger and Palardy 2005, 2020)

Rumberger and Palardy continue by noting that their results confirm the original conclusions of the Coleman Report, although with much closer balance between the influence of school and the influence of family.

Here too, then, the school's enrollment mix—its socioeconomic makeup in particular—emerges as highly consequential for children's learning. For poor and minority children, attending a school with a diverse student body boosts achievement and attending a school with mainly others of like background depresses achievement; thus, when poor children live in high-poverty neighborhoods and attend high-poverty schools, their learning suffers. The original Coleman Report suggested this; these studies strengthen the point.

Schwartz (2010)
Heather Schwartz (2010) focuses on a single community, Montgomery County, Maryland, comparing the school performance of poor children who live in predominantly middle-class neighborhoods against other poor children who live in less affluent communities. This uncommon circumstance is afforded by the county's inclusionary housing policy, which requires real estate developers to set aside a portion of homes to be rented or sold at below market rates. There were 12,000 such units in wealthy Montgomery County at the time of Schwartz's project, one-third of which had been acquired for public housing.

Public housing applicants were randomly selected for placement. Schwartz (2010, 5) examines the experience of 850 children so placed who, as she puts it, "attended elementary schools and lived in neighborhoods that fell along a spectrum of very-low-poverty to moderate-poverty rates." With 40 percent to 85 percent the range of low-income enrollments, Montgomery County has few schools with extreme levels of concentrated poverty. This contrasts sharply with the experience in Baltimore, where most black children attend hypersegregated schools with African American enrollments of 90 percent or more. Still, these differences in Montgomery County are large, and potentially meaningful. Additionally, most of the higher-poverty schools there received supplemental resources not provided to schools with low-poverty enrollments: funding for full-day as opposed to half-day kindergarten, staffing to reduce class size (from twenty-five to seventeen), extra staff professional development, and an enhanced literacy curriculum. Schwartz takes advantage of these resource differences to compare the benefits of income integration to resource enhancement in higher-poverty settings, two very different approaches to addressing needy children's educational challenges.

Assigning families to neighborhoods and children to schools by a random draw effectively eliminates any self-selection of more highly motivated parents into stronger schools. At the time of the Coleman Report, with near-universal segregation by race, one has to wonder whether the small number of black children in schools with diverse enrollments would have done equally as well if they had attended the high-poverty, segregated schools typically attended by other black children. If family is all that matters, then perhaps so, and with residential and school segregation still high, the same uncertainty prevails today. But not in Montgomery County. Taking parental choice out of the picture shows that *school differences* are likely to signify *school effects*. And what are those schools effects? According to Schwartz:

> School-based economic integration effects accrued over time. After five to seven years, students in public housing who were randomly assigned to low-poverty elementary schools significantly outperformed their peers in public housing who attended moderate-poverty schools in both math and reading. Further, by the end of elementary school, the initial large achievement gap between children in public housing who attended the district's most advantaged schools and their non-poor students in the district was cut in half for math and one-third for reading. (Schwartz 2010, 6)

Imagine that—improved performance by poor students compared to other poor students attending resource-enhanced schools and a greatly diminished achievement gap compared to nonpoor students. These gains took time to materialize, with economic integration in children's neighborhoods and schools both implicated (the latter in larger measure). Schwartz adds that these impressive results are probably a lower bound to the benefits that poor children could realize by attending low-poverty schools: she notes that fewer than 1 percent of Montgomery County's elementary schools have high-poverty enrollments, compared to 40 percent of urban elementary schools nationwide.

These results also accord with Coleman's conclusions. Indeed, to this point, we have encountered no contradictions to the Coleman Report, although the school context effects documented in these more recent studies are vastly larger than those in the report. These studies thus add force to the report's conclusions, help establish their contemporary relevance, and suggest, in a way that the report analysis could not, a path to school improvement for poor children: reduce the degree of overlap in the "overlapping spheres of influence" that impedes their academic development.

THE SEASONALITY OF LEARNING

Interest in summer learning as distinct from school-year learning extends back to the first decade of the twentieth century (see Cooper et al. 1996). The modern era of research on the topic was launched by Barbara Heyns in her remarkable book *Summer Learning and the Effects of Schooling* (1978). Her great insight was that comparing children's summer learning to their school-year learning affords leverage for disentangling the influence of school from the influence of family.

It is clear that the overlap of school characteristics with family characteristics poses challenges for poor children, but that same overlap also poses challenges for researchers. Observational (that is, non-experimental) data oblige the separation of family influence from school influence by statistical means, yet the social forces combined by nature do not yield easily to artificial devices. When the overlap is severe the separation is uncertain, and confounds such as parental self-selection into schools with diverse enrollments cloud interpretation. Random assignment, as in Montgomery County, is uncommon, but the school-year calendar affords the same kind of contrast in a natural experiment that is near-universal.

Children are in their families and neighborhoods throughout the year but are in school intermittently. The long summer break, typically three months in the United States, isolates the school's contribution to children's learning: if achievement gains track differently over the summer months, when children are not in school, than during the school year, then time out from school must be implicated. This also eliminates the parental self-selection confound, as the school calendar applies to everyone.[7]

Heyns analyzes achievement gains by family income level and race-ethnicity (African American or white) for a large sample (nearly 3,000) of Atlanta middle school students over an eighteen-month period bracketing two school years and the summer between. Her findings are both expected and unexpected. Among the former is that children, regardless of their background, learn more and learn more efficiently when they are in school—thank goodness for that! Among the latter findings is that poor children and African American children come close to keeping up academically during the school year. That is to say, their learning from fall to spring is nearly at parity with that registered by whites and children from higher-income families. But these children are not performing at the same level at year's end, and the reason why is revealing: they fall behind during the summer months owing to a dearth of learning resources in their families and neighborhoods.

Heyns's study thus reveals that the achievement gap across social lines traces substantially to differences in out-of-school learning opportunities over the long summer break.[8] On this basis, she concludes that school—regular school—is compensatory education for poor and disadvantaged minority children (Heyns 1978, 188).

We find much the same in our Baltimore research (Alexander, Entwisle, and Olson 2001; Entwisle, Alexander, and Olson 1997; Entwisle, Alexander, and Olson 2001). Our summer learning studies track test score gains for a representative sample of children who began first grade in twenty Baltimore City public schools in the fall of 1982, with seasonal comparisons through the end of elementary school (five school years and the four summers between).[9]

In reading comprehension (assessed via the California Achievement Test battery), low-income and middle-class children's scores differed by a half-grade equivalent in the fall of first grade; by the end of fifth grade the gap had increased to three grade equivalents.[10] To be reading at a third- or fourth-grade level when poised to transition to middle school is hardly what we would want for our children, but in Baltimore, just as in Atlanta, most of the gap increase over this span of years happened during the summer months. During the summer, middle-class children's reading skills continued to improve, but low-income children's did not, a pattern known as "summer slide" or "summer setback." The school-year pattern was altogether different, as then low-income children and middle-class children registered similar progress.

In the late 1990s, the Early Childhood Longitudinal Study-Kindergarten cohort (ECLS-K), national in scope, yielded broadly similar results for learning over kindergarten, first grade, and the summer in between (Downey, von Hip-

---

7. Heyns also monitors summer school attendance, another facet of the "in school" versus "not in school" comparison.

8. This is not apparent under the more common accountability regime that tracks testing from spring to spring, blurring together school year and summer learning.

9. The city schools at the time were doing twice-annual achievement testing, in the fall and spring. It is this schedule that allows for the separation of school-year learning (fall to spring) from summer learning (spring to fall across successive school years).

10. A similar pattern maintained for math concepts and applications.

pel, and Broh 2004; Burkam et al. 2004). This was clearest for disparities along lines of family socioeconomic level, which paralleled the patterns seen in Atlanta and Baltimore:

> Past seasonal researchers have argued that inequality in cognitive skills emerges primarily when school is not in session, and that it likely is a function of different family and neighborhood experiences.... With substantially better data than previous researchers, we provide the strongest support to date for this position.... With respect to socioeconomic status, the primary source of inequality lies in children's disparate non-school environments. (Downey, von Hippel, and Broh 2004, 632)

"Better data" here refers to the ECLS-K's national coverage and large sample size. Also, with testing dates and school-year starting and ending dates known, ECLS-K analyses more accurately bracket the relevant seasonal intervals (in-school or summer).[11]

The patterning of learning disparities along lines of family socioeconomic background is consistent across these several studies, despite their many differences.[12] They span three decades, cover different student populations in different localities at different grade levels, and monitor different domains of achievement using different instruments. Overriding these differences of detail are two profound insights: (1) poor children are capable learners in that they come close to keeping up when they are in school; (2) it is mainly family disadvantage, not school disadvantage, that holds children back.

From the literature on summer learning we see that when the influences of family and school are convincingly separated, both emerge as powerful forces in children's learning. And what of David Armor's assertion that "no one has found a way, on a large-scale basis, to overcome the influence of family"? Research into the seasonality of learning gives the lie to any such claim. School—and better still, a high-quality school experience—is the key to counteracting family disadvantage.

REGARDING THE NAYSAYERS

And what of those "dismal science" voices proclaiming the irrelevance of educational resources? After examining the relevant literatures, expanded to include trends in test performance over time and international comparisons, the economist Alan Krueger (1998, 30) had this to say: "The ... widely held belief that American schools have failed ... is not supported by the evidence. The evidence suggests that the perceived crisis in education has been greatly exaggerated, if indeed there is a crisis at all."

And Krueger was hardly alone. Other voices from around the same time also pushed back against the assertion that America's schools are in decline and ineffectual (see, for example, Bracey 2004; Berliner and Biddle 1995; Rothstein 1995), including mine (Alexander 1997). And what of the naysayers' specific assertions? In each area, there have been countervailing voices, also highly regarded and with supporting evidence:

1. Against Jensen's (1969) assertion that compensatory education has been tried and failed is evidence of impressive benefits of the Perry Preschool, ABECEDARIAN, and other early education programs that extend beyond achievement effects to include reduced risk of grade retention and high school dropout and, in young adulthood, lower levels of criminality and unemployment; see Barnett (2008, 2011), Heckman (2008), and Schweinhart and Weikart (1997) for small-scale studies that extend over many years. Large-scale studies, but of shorter duration, have demonstrated effectiveness for academic outcomes specifically—for example, in Oklahoma (Gormley

---

11. Having these dates provided an important technical check. Such adjustments might have altered estimates of school-year and summer learning gains, as well as of differences in the seasonal patterning of gains along social lines, but those details instead proved to be robust.

12. The same does not hold for the achievement gap by race-ethnicity: in the ECLS-K data, that gap expanded during the school year and there was little difference in learning rates summer versus school year.

2013) and New Jersey (Barnett, Jung, and Youn 2013).

2. Against Slavin's (1989) conclusion that smaller class sizes are no more effective than larger enrollments is evidence from the Tennessee class size experiment—a true experiment in which poor and minority children were found to derive substantial and long-lasting benefits from smaller classes in the early elementary grades (for example, Krueger and Whitmore 2002), extending, it seems, even to earnings in young adulthood (for example, Chetty et al. 2010).

3. And against Hanushek's (1989, 1997) assertion that expenditures and the things that expenditures are used to purchase have little bearing on achievement, Larry Hedges, Richard Laine, and Rob Greenwald (1994, 11) conclude, after reviewing the same body of evidence, that effects for per pupil expenditures are "substantially positive" and effects for teacher salary, administrative inputs, and facilities are "typically positive."

There have always been conflicting evidence, conclusions, and claims about the efficacy of schools and schooling in promoting student success, and it seems safe to predict that this will continue. But the extent to which the negative voices have dominated public perceptions—and I would say professional perceptions as well—really is quite striking. Why that is the case is hard to say, although I suspect that the foundation laid by the Coleman Report has played a role.

My pushback against these negative voices should not be construed as a belief that we have arrived at some blissful state of educational nirvana. To the contrary, the challenges we confront, especially for poor children in high-poverty school systems, are daunting and deeply entrenched. They will not yield easily, and the resources that we know can help these children often are in short supply in the schools they attend. One of those resources, the one I take up in my concluding comments, is the opportunity to attend schools not burdened by the drag of concentrated poverty.

CONCLUDING THOUGHTS

My conclusion from the review in this essay of five decades of research is that there indeed are enduring truths to be found in the Coleman Report, but they are not the ones typically touted. Moreover, I can imagine a future in which they no longer maintain; that is to say, though the report's insights remain relevant, they are not immutable. At issue are consequences for children's learning that flow from the overlapping spheres of influence emanating from family, neighborhood, and school. Alter the degree of overlap and the entire formula potentially changes. The Coleman Report instructs us that the surest route to helping poor and minority children keep up academically is to enable them to attend schools that are not just desegregated but authentically integrated —by which I mean that the experience of diversity infuses children's daily experience: As Coleman notes, "School integration is vital . . . because it is the most consistent mechanism for improving the quality of education of disadvantaged children." He continues: "So long as middle-class students remain a majority in a given school they establish the achievement tone . . . and by attending such a school disadvantaged students make more consistent educational gains than by any other mechanism."

This was Coleman in 1970, sharing lessons he learned from the report that bears his name.[13] His conclusion implies that weakening the link between family background and the character of the schools that children attend could well be transformative. School choice has that potential, although at present it is largely unrealized.[14] So too would a renewed commitment to neighborhood and school desegregation along lines of family income (see, for example, Kahlenberg 2010; Semuels 2015); certainly that is what the Montgomery County research indicates. Consider this, from recent

---

13. Jack Rosenthal, "School Expert Calls Integration Vital Aid to Educating the Disadvantaged," *New York Times*, March 9, 1970.

14. See, for example, Diane Ravitch's (2010) critique of the pro-charter school documentary *Waiting for "Superman."*

commentary: "Desegregation is the best way to improve our schools. Racial achievement gaps were narrowest during the height of school integration."[15] And as Nikole Hannah-Jones told Ira Glass, "Integration works.... We have this thing that we know works, that the data shows works, that we know is best for kids, and we will not talk about it.... It's not even on the table."[16]

Hannah-Jones overstates the case, but only somewhat. The Century Foundation has identified ninety-one school districts and individual charter schools throughout the United States that have a purposeful commitment to diversity (Potter, Quick, and Davies 2016). Those include some large school systems, including Hartford, Connecticut (Eaton 2013) and Louisville, Kentucky (Semuels 2015), both of which are pursuing a metropolitan regional approach. And Louisville holds the distinction of being a Southern school system that maintained its commitment to integration even after the court order that forced desegregation was lifted. Hartford and Louisville are exceptions, however, and ninety-one districts and schools is too few altogether—many too few.

If we have known for a half-century that school desegregation works—and not just for disadvantaged minority children[17]—why isn't that the conventional wisdom, rather than the rhetoric of "schools make no difference"? And why the retreat from one of the few demonstrable interventions that is known to work? No doubt there are many considerations, but I suspect that the Coleman Report's "family versus school" framing has played a role, together with the misconstruals of its results and their implications.

As noted by George Theoharis, when the Supreme Court's school desegregation mandate did eventually begin to be enforced vigorously, levels of school segregation nationally declined dramatically.[18] In parallel, and I think not coincidentally, the achievement gap across lines of race-ethnicity also declined dramatically. In a 1997 essay, I wrote: "Would it surprise you to learn that the 'IQ' gap separating black and white youth declined by almost a third between 1970 and 1990?" (Alexander 1997, 1). A year later, Krueger (1998, 31) pointed out that the black-white gap in math National Assessment of Educational Progress (NAEP) scores among seventeen-year-olds declined by nearly half between 1970 and 1990.[19]

Nothing is fixed. Attempts to parse the "whether" of school versus family seek a definitive answer, but this false dichotomy fundamentally misconstrues the backdrop to children's learning. Family matters, to be sure, but school also matters, and it is how the two intersect that sets children on their developmental paths. The consequences that follow when many poor children live in high-poverty communities and attend schools with high-poverty enrollments are easy to anticipate, but are those consequences really removed from family? That the school's enrollment mix emerges consistently in research as the school factor most strongly implicated in children's learning makes it a difficult to case to argue.

In generating opportunity, family and school are indeed in tension, but it is a tension not captured in the "school versus family" framing. Here too Coleman understood the sense of it better than most: what counts is the balance between private family resources and

---

15. George Theoharis, "'Forced Busing' Didn't Fail. Desegregation Is the Best Way to Improve Our Schools," *Washington Post,* October 23, 2015.

16. Nikole Hannah-Jones, "The Problem We All Live With," interview with Ira Glass, *This American Life,* July 31, 2015, available at: http://thisamericanlife.org/radio-archives/episode/562/transcript (accessed June 28, 2016).

17. Anya Kamenetz, "The Evidence That White Children Benefit from Integrated Schools," nprED, October 19, 2015, available at: http://www.npr.org/sections/ed/2015/10/19/446085513/the-evidence-that-white-children-benefit-from-integrated-schools (accessed June 28, 2016).

18. Theoharis, "'Forced Busing' Didn't Fail"; see also Orfield and Lee 2005.

19. Recent NAEP data indicate an upward track in scores since 2000 among whites, Latinos, and African Americans, accompanied by a modest reduction in the gap (Education Trust 2015). This trend, unlike the earlier one, is probably not driven by school desegregation.

public resources in support of children's learning. At present, the private and public resources invested in children's schooling are highly unequal, and they favor families of means. On that basis, Coleman concluded that complete parity across social lines in schooling probably is not feasible. The goal, rather, should be to move toward greater parity or gap reduction, which he believed was both feasible and desirable (Coleman 1975).

The resources at issue are not just material, as important as those are. In our Baltimore research, the typical "urban disadvantaged" parent, white or African American, had not finished high school; many were single parents weighed down by the so-called feminization of poverty. These parents themselves struggled at school, and many suffered a low literacy level and a weak command of formal English (see, for example, Farkas and Beron 2004; Hart and Risley 1995).

Given that it is hard for these parents to model and support the kinds of learning that are valued in school and to provide the enriching experiences so critical to children's healthy development, is it realistic to expect that their children will arrive at school as well prepared as the children of middle-class and professional parents? The consequences of family resource inequality for children's schooling are apparent at kindergarten entry (Lee and Burkam 2002). And because those inequalities are ever-present in children's lives, so too is their drag (Alexander, Entwisle, and Olson 2007; Entwisle, Alexander, and Olson 1997)—absent, that is, an effective counterbalance to them.

The public resources invested in children's schooling could be that counterbalance, but these resources are less abundant than the private resources commanded by some families. Moreover, public investments in children do not always, or even usually, favor the disadvantaged. Parents of means understand that a good school matters, and they see to it that their children attend one, either by paying a premium to purchase a home in a community that maintains good schools or by enrolling their children in a private school. Schools in wealthier communities serve the interests of their residents, and when those communities are isolated by race and family income, as is typical, the interests they serve are those of the well-to-do.

But it also needs to be said that schools do not simply reinforce patterns of family advantage and disadvantage. Rather, poor children fall behind when their learning depends on the sparse resources available to them at home and in their communities. Their schools, even those burdened by concentrated poverty, help them to keep up academically. From research on summer learning loss we learn that the portion of school influence that is separable from family serves to lift up poor children, not hold them back.

The key insight here is that the "overlap" of these overlapping spheres of influence is not perfect. Schools are at the very same time agents of social reproduction, favoring those already favored, *and* agents of social mobility. There is no logical contradiction in this duality, but to achieve greater public resource balance and so tilt the scales more in favor of social mobility, poor children need to have access to the same quality schooling as do the nonpoor.

And what exactly might that look like? Decades of research anchored in the Coleman Report instruct us that the most valuable school resource for poor and minority children inheres in the school's demographic makeup. Poor children do best academically when they attend schools not burdened by concentrated poverty. Resource enhancement in high-poverty schools is a second-best option, as results under that approach are less impressive (Schwartz 2010) and there is little precedent for achieving sustained excellence in such settings on a broad scale.[20]

Richard Kahlenberg (2001, 2012), a leading advocate for school socioeconomic integration, has cataloged the many advantages that accrue to poor children when they attend schools that enroll a solid middle-class core:

---

20. Samuel Casey Carter (2000) identifies a number of individual schools that appear to meet this standard, but his report has received much critical commentary; see, for example, Billing and Bracey (2000) and Schmidt (2001). For a counterargument, see Duncan and Murnane (2013).

beneficial peer influences, such as stronger academic motivation and preparation; a more orderly classroom environment with less student mobility and fewer absences; improvement in parental resources through more effective advocacy and involvement; higher-quality teachers with higher expectations for their students; and a more demanding curriculum. To this list Rumberger and Palardy (2005) add the amount of homework students do and their feelings of safety at school.[21] Meanwhile, Roslyn Mickelson (2005) and Karolyn Tyson (2011), among others, have revealed the harm done to poor and minority children in nominally desegregated schools when they are isolated in low-level remedial programs—internal resegregation through tracking. The goal must be authentic integration; simply having children of different backgrounds in the same building is not enough.

Not every wealthy suburban school provides an optimal learning environment, and not all high-poverty urban schools are distressed. These are tendencies, but as tendencies they are quite real and they matter. They matter for the poor children who are resource-deprived in their homes, their communities, and their schools, and they ought to matter for those of us who wish a brighter future for them.

To advance the cause of socioeconomic integration will not be easy, and certainly the demographic profile districtwide in places like Baltimore poses daunting challenges. But from the experience in those communities and individual schools throughout the country that are committed to this goal (Kahlenberg 2012; Kahlenberg and Potter 2014), we know that it is not impossible. If the Coleman Report helped trigger what I have called a deep malaise, perhaps the time has come to reverse course. From that document, and Coleman's own good counsel, we know "what works." What is needed is the will to follow through.

REFERENCES

Alexander, Karl L. 1997. "Public Schools and the Public Good." *Social Forces* 76(1): 1–30.

Alexander, Karl L., Doris R. Entwisle, and Linda S. Olson. 2001. "Schools, Achievement, and Inequality: A Seasonal Perspective." *Educational Evaluation and Policy Analysis* 23(2): 171–91.

———. 2007. "Lasting Consequences of the Summer Learning Gap." *American Sociological Review* 72(2): 167–80.

———. 2014. *The Long Shadow: Family Background, Disadvantaged Urban Youth, and the Transition to Adulthood.* New York: Russell Sage Foundation.

Annie Casey Foundation. 2010. *The East Baltimore Revitalization Initiative: A Case Study of Responsible Redevelopment.* Baltimore: Annie E. Casey Foundation.

Barnett, W. Steven. 2008. "Preschool Education and Its Lasting Effects: Research and Policy Implications." Tempe: Arizona State University, Education Policy Research Unit.

———. 2011. "Effectiveness of Early Educational Intervention." *Science* 333(6045): 975–78.

Barnett, W. Steven, Kwanghee Jung, and Min-Jong Youn. 2013. "Abbott Preschool Program Longitudinal Effects." Rutgers, N.J.: National Institute for Early Education Research.

Berliner, David C., and Bruce J. Biddle. 1995. *The Manufactured Crisis: Myths, Fraud, and the Attack on America's Public Schools.* Reading, Mass.: Addison-Wesley.

Billing, Bruce, and Gerald Bracey. 2000. "No Excuses, Lots of Reasons: A Response to *No Excuses: Lessons from 21 High-Performing, High-Poverty Schools.*" Education Policy Project (July 1).

Bonilla-Silva, Eduardo. 1996. "Rethinking Racism: Toward a Structural Interpretation." *American Sociological Review* 62(3): 465–80.

Borman, Geoffrey D., and Maritza Dowling. 2010. "Schools and Inequality: A Multilevel Analysis of Coleman's Equality of Educational Opportunity Data." *Teachers College Record* 112(5): 1201–46.

Bracey, Gerald. 2004. *Setting the Record Straight: Responses to Misconceptions About Public Education in the U.S.* Portsmouth, N.H.: Heinemann.

Bronfenbrenner, Urie. 1979. *The Ecology of Human Development: Experiments by Nature and Design.* Cambridge, Mass.: Harvard University Press.

Burdick-Will, Julia, Jens Ludwig, Stephen W. Raudenbush, Robert J. Sampson, Lisa Sanbonmatsu, and Patrick Sharkey. 2011. "Converging Evidence

---

21. Many high-poverty schools are located in high-crime neighborhoods. Trauma surrounding exposure to violence affects children's school performance (see Burdick-Will et al. 2011; Sharkey 2010), yet another way in which outside conditions filter into the school.

for Neighborhood Effects on Children's Test Scores: An Experimental, Quasi-experimental, and Observational Comparison." In *Whither Opportunity? Rising Inequality, Schools, and Children's Life Chances*, edited by Greg J. Duncan and Richard J. Murnane. New York: Russell Sage Foundation.

Burkam, David T., Douglas D. Ready, Valerie E. Lee, and Laura F. LoGerfo. 2004. "Social-Class Differences in Summer Learning Between Kindergarten and First Grade: Model Specification and Estimation." *Sociology of Education* 77(1): 1–31.

Carter, Samuel Casey. 2000. *No Excuses: Lessons from 21 High-Performing, High-Poverty Schools*. Washington, D.C.: Heritage Foundation.

Chetty, Raj, John N. Friedman, Nathanial Hilger, Emmanuel Suez, Diane Whitmore Schanzenbach, and Danny Yagen. 2010. "How Does Your Kindergarten Classroom Affect Your Earnings? Evidence from Project STAR." Working Paper 16381. Cambridge, Mass.: National Bureau of Economic Research.

Coleman, James S. 1975. "What Is Meant by 'an Equal Educational Opportunity'?" *Oxford Review of Education* 1(1): 27–29.

Coleman, James S., Ernest Q. Campbell, Carol J. Hobson, James McPartland, Alexander M. Mood, Frederick D. Weinfeld, and Robert L. York. 1966. *Equality of Educational Opportunity*. Washington: U.S. Department of Health, Education, and Welfare, Office of Education.

Cooper, Harris, Barbara Nye, Kelly Charlton, James Lindsay, and Scott Greathouse. 1996. "The Effects of Summer Vacation on Achievement Test Scores: A Narrative and Meta-analytic Review." *Review of Educational Research* 66(3): 227–68.

Downey, Douglas B., Paul T. von Hippel, and Beckett Broh. 2004. "Are Schools the Great Equalizer? Cognitive Inequality During the Summer Months and the School Year." *American Sociological Review* 69(5): 613–35.

Duncan, Greg, and Richard J. Murnane. 2013. *Restoring Opportunity: The Crisis of Inequality and the Challenge for American Education*. Cambridge, Mass.: Harvard Education Press.

Eaton, Susan. 2013. "Years After a Landmark Court Decision, Connecticut's Solution to School Segregation Shows Promise: Can It Inform Action in Baltimore?" *The Abell Report* (Abell Foundation, Baltimore) 26(5, June).

Education Trust. 2015. "Trends in Achievement and Attainment Since We've Had Annual Testing, Transparency, and Serious Accountability for All Groups of Children." Washington, D.C.: Education Trust.

Entwisle, Doris R., Karl L. Alexander, and Linda S. Olson. 1997. *Children, Schools, and Inequality*. Boulder, Colo.: Westview Press.

———. 2001. "Keeping the Faucet Flowing: Summer Learning and Home Environment." *American Educator* 25(3): 10–15, 47.

Farkas, George, and Kurt Beron. 2004. "The Detailed Age Trajectory of Oral Vocabulary Knowledge: Differences by Class and Race." *Social Science Research* 33(3): 464–97.

Gamoran, Adam, and Daniel A. Long. 2007. "Equality of Educational Opportunity: A Forty Year Retrospective." In *International Studies in Educational Inequality, Theory, and Policy*. The Netherlands: Springer.

Gormley, William T., Jr. 2013. "Oklahoma's Universal Preschool Program: Better Than OK." *Georgetown Public Policy Review* (May 6).

Hanushek, Eric A. 1989. "The Impact of Differential School Expenditures on School Performance." *Educational Researcher* 18(4): 45–65.

———. 1997. "Assessing the Effects of School Resources on Student Performance: An Update." *Educational Evaluation and Policy Analysis* 19(2): 141–64.

Hart, Betty, and Todd R. Risley. 1995. *Meaningful Differences in the Everyday Experience of Young American Children*. Baltimore: Paul H. Brookes Publishing.

Heckman, James J. 2008. "Early Childhood Education and Care: The Case for Investing in Disadvantaged Young Children." *DICE* (University of Munich, Ifo Institute for Economic Research) 6(2): 3–8.

Hedges, Larry V., Richard D. Laine, and Rob Greenwald. 1994. "Does Money Matter? A Meta-analysis of Studies of the Effects of Differential School Inputs on Student Outcomes." *Educational Researcher* 23(3): 5–14.

Heyns, Barbara. 1978. *Summer Learning and the Effects of Schooling*. New York: Academic.

Hodgson, Godfrey. 1975. "Do Schools Make a Difference?" In *The "Inequality" Controversy: Schooling and Distributive Justice*, edited by Donald M. Levine and Mary Jo Bane. New York: Basic Books.

Jensen, Arthur R. 1969. "How Much Can We Boost IQ and Scholastic Achievement?" *Harvard Educational Review* 39(1): 1–123.

Jessor, Richard. 1993. "Successful Adolescent Development Among Youth in High-Risk Settings." *American Psychologist* 48(2): 117–26.

Kahlenberg, Richard D. 2001. *All Together Now: Creating Middle-Class Schools Through Public School Choice.* Washington, D.C.: Brookings Institution Press.

———.2010. "Housing Policy Is School Policy." *Education Week*, October 15. Available at: http://www.edweek.org/ew/articles/2010/10/20/08kahlenberg_ep.h30.html (accessed June 22, 2016).

———. 2012. *The Future of School Integration: Socioeconomic Diversity as an Education Reform Study.* New York: Century Foundation Press.

Kahlenberg, Richard D., and Halley Potter. 2014. *A Smarter Charter: Finding What Works for Charter Schools and Public Education.* New York: Teachers College Press.

Krueger, Alan B. 1998. "Reassessing the View That American Schools Are Broken." *Federal Reserve Bank of New York Economic Policy Review* 4(1): 29–43.

Krueger, Alan B., and Diane M. Whitmore. 2002. "Would Smaller Classes Help Close the Black-White Achievement Gap?" In *Bridging the Achievement Gap*, edited by John E. Chubb and Tom Loveless. Washington, D.C.: Brookings Institution Press.

Lee, Valerie, and David T. Burkam. 2002. *Inequality at the Starting Gate: Social Background Differences in Achievement as Children Begin School.* Washington, D.C.: Economic Policy Institute.

Logan, John R. 2002. "Choosing Segregation: Racial Imbalance in American Public Schools, 1990–2000." Albany, N.Y.: University at Albany, Lewis Mumford Center for Comparative Urban and Regional Research.

Massey, Douglas D., and Stefanie Brodmann. 2014. *Spheres of Influence: The Social Ecology of Racial and Class Inequality.* New York: Russell Sage Foundation.

Mickelson, Roslyn A. 2005. "How Tracking Undermines Race Equity in Desegregated Schools." In *Bringing Equity Back: Research for a New Era in American Educational Policy*, edited by Janice L. Petrovich and Amy Stuart Wells. New York: Teachers College Press.

Mosteller, Frederick, and Daniel P. Moynihan 1972. *On Equality of Educational Opportunity.* New York: Vintage Books.

Moynihan, Daniel P. 1995. "Moved by Data, Not Doctrine." *New York Times Magazine*, December 31.

Orfield, Gary, and Chungmei Lee. 2005. "Why Segregation Matters: Poverty and Educational Inequality." Cambridge, Mass.: Harvard University.

———. 2007. "Historic Reversals, Accelerating Resegregation, and the Need for New Integration Strategies." Los Angeles: UCLA Civil Rights Project.

Potter, Halley, Kimberly Quick, and Elizabeth Davies. 2016. "Districts and Charters Pursuing Socioeconomic Diversity." New York: Century Foundation (February 9).

Ravitch, Diane. 2010. "The Myth of Charter Schools." *New York Review of Books*, January 13.

Reardon, Sean F., and Kendra Bischoff. 2011. "Growth in the Residential Segregation of Family by Income, 1970–2009." US2010 Project: Brown University and Russell Sage Foundation. Providence, R.I.: Brown University.

Reardon, Sean F., Chad R. Farrell, Stephen A. Matthews, David O'Sullivan, and Kendra Bischoff. 2009. "Race and Space in the 1990s: Changes in the Geographic Scale of Racial Residential Segregation, 1990–2000." *Social Science Research* 38(1): 55–70.

Rothstein, Richard. 1995. "The Myth of Public School Failure." *The American Prospect* 13 (Spring): 20–34.

Rumberger, Russell W., and Gregory J. Palardy. 2005. "Does Segregation Still Matter? The Impact of Student Composition on Academic Achievement in High School." *Teachers College Record* 107(9): 1999–2045.

Schmidt, George. 2001. "No Excuses for No Excuses." *Phi Delta Kappan* 83(3): 194.

Schwartz, Heather. 2010. "Housing Policy Is School Policy: Economically Integrative Housing Promotes Academic Success in Montgomery County, Maryland." New York: Century Foundation.

Schweinhart, Lawrence J., and David P. Weikart. 1997. "The High/Scope Preschool Curriculum Comparison Study Through Age 23." *Early Childhood Research Quarterly* 12(2): 117–43.

Semuels, Alana. 2015. "The City That Believed in Integration." *The Atlantic*, March 27.

Sharkey, Patrick. 2010. "The Acute Effect of Local Homicides on Children's Cognitive Performance." *Social Sciences* 107(26, June 29): 11733–38.

Slavin, Robert E. 1989. "Class Size and Student Achievement: Small Effects of Small Classes." *Educational Psychologist* 24(1): 99–110.

Tyson, Karolyn. 2011. *Integration Interrupted: Tracking, Black Students, and Acting White After Brown.* New York: Oxford University Press.

Viadero, Debra. 2006. "Race Report's Influence Felt 40 Years Later: Legacy of Coleman Study Was New View of Equity." *Education Week*, June 20.

School Segregation and Racial Academic Achievement Gaps

SEAN F. REARDON

Although it is clear that racial segregation is linked to academic achievement gaps, the mechanisms underlying this link have been debated since James Coleman published his eponymous 1966 report. In this paper, I examine sixteen distinct measures of segregation to determine which is most strongly associated with academic achievement gaps. I find clear evidence that one aspect of segregation in particular—the disparity in average school poverty rates between white and black students' schools—is consistently the single most powerful correlate of achievement gaps, a pattern that holds in both bivariate and multivariate analyses. This implies that high-poverty schools are, on average, much less effective than lower-poverty schools and suggests that strategies that reduce the differential exposure of black, Hispanic, and white students to poor schoolmates may lead to meaningful reductions in academic achievement gaps.

Keywords: achievement gap, school segregation, residential segregation, school poverty

Does segregation exacerbate racial educational inequality? And if so, through what mechanism? Is it racial segregation per se that matters, or the association of racial segregation with unequal schooling or neighborhood conditions? When the Supreme Court ruled in *Brown v. Board of Education* that "separate educational facilities are inherently unequal," its argument was that legally sanctioned segregation based on race necessarily inflicted on African American children a psychological wound that could not be salved by the provision of materially equivalent schooling facilities and resources. In the Court's view, it was the very act of legal exclusion that created inequality and violated the Fourteenth Amendment. Even if separate schools, in practice, had equivalent material conditions (that is, if the *Plessy v. Ferguson* standard of "separate but equal" were met in strictly material terms), the Court argued, black children would nonetheless be harmed by virtue of their state-sanctioned exclusion from schools enrolling white students.

This argument suggests that there is something explicitly racialized about the effects of segregation, particularly in the context of de jure segregation. The Court's argument does not, however, imply that the race-specific nature of school segregation laws is the only way that segregation may harm children; it merely

Sean F. Reardon is endowed professor of poverty and inequality in education at Stanford University.

The research described here was supported by grants from the Institute of Education Sciences (R305D110018) and the Spencer Foundation (201500058). The paper would not have been possible without the assistance of Ross Santy, who facilitated access to the data. This paper benefited substantially from ongoing collaboration with Andrew Ho, Demetra Kalogrides, and Kenneth Shores. Some of the data used in this paper were provided by the National Center for Education Statistics (NCES). The opinions expressed here are my own and do not represent the views of NCES, the Institute of Education Sciences, the Spencer Foundation, or the U.S. Department of Education. Direct correspondence to: Sean F. Reardon at sean.reardon@stanford.edu, 520 CERAS Building, no. 526, Stanford University, Stanford, CA 94305.

suggests that there would be harm even if the material conditions of racially segregated schools were equalized.

Twelve years after the *Brown* decision, when Coleman wrote his *Equality of Educational Opportunity* report, he was concerned less with the psychological harms of de jure segregation and more with the material inequalities that existed (or were presumed to exist) in both de jure and de facto segregated school systems of the 1960s. By 1966, *Brown* had yet to substantially reduce segregation in the South, and one aim of the Coleman Report was to investigate the extent to which black and white students attended schools of different quality and the relationship between measures of material school quality and academic achievement.

Coleman reported several facts about school segregation in the United States. First, unsurprisingly, racial segregation was very high. Two-thirds of black students attended schools that were 90 to 100 percent black; 80 percent of white students attended schools that were 90 to 100 percent white. More importantly, he found that the academic achievement of both white and black students was higher in predominantly white schools than in predominantly minority schools. In addition, black students who had spent more time in desegregated schools had modestly higher average scores than others, a pattern that held when controlling for individual student socioeconomic background (Coleman et al. 1966, 331–32). Little of the association of test scores with school racial composition could be explained, however, with the set of school quality measures available to him. Instead, Coleman wrote, "the higher achievement of all racial and ethnic groups in schools with greater proportions of white students is largely, perhaps wholly, related to effects associated with the student body's educational background and aspirations" (307). In other words, the negative association of segregation with academic achievement disparities appears to have been largely driven by the differences in the socioeconomic composition of the schools where black and white students were enrolled.

Geoffrey Borman and Maritza Dowling (2010), in their reanalysis of Coleman's data, likewise find that both the racial and socioeconomic composition of schools are strongly related to student outcomes (as have numerous other studies). These findings, although correlational rather than causal in nature, suggest that any effects of racial segregation on achievement patterns are at least partly driven by factors associated with school socioeconomic composition rather than by racial composition per se. These factors might include material resources, instructional focus and quality, parental social and economic capital, social norms, and peer effects. The Coleman data (and other subsequent studies) have not, however, convincingly identified if and how such mechanisms link school segregation to unequal outcomes.

In this paper, I use new data based on over 100 million test score records from all grade 3 through 8 students in public schools from 2009 to 2012 in over 300 metropolitan areas to further investigate the association between racial segregation and racial academic achievement gaps. In particular, I assess whether it is differences in the racial or socioeconomic composition of schools that drives the persistent association between segregation and achievement inequality. A better understanding of the mechanisms driving the effects of segregation may be useful in counteracting those effects.

This paper proceeds in four parts. I first describe four related but conceptually distinct dimensions of segregation, each of which might affect academic achievement gaps. These four dimensions yield sixteen different measures of segregation, each of which I use in this analysis. I next describe the data and measures used in the paper. These are measures of academic achievement gaps and segregation patterns in roughly 320 metropolitan areas in the United States. The third section of the paper describes the analyses and results. Here I demonstrate that all sixteen measures of segregation are correlated with racial achievement gaps, but that one in particular—the disparity in average school poverty rates between white and black students' schools—is consistently the strongest correlate of achievement gaps, a pattern that holds in both bivariate and multivariate analyses. In the final section of the paper, I discuss the implications of these findings.

Table 1. Dimensions of Metropolitan Area Segregation

	School Segregation		Residential Segregation	
	Between-School	Between-District	Between-Tract	Between-District
Black students' exposure to				
Black neighbors or schoolmates	x	x	x	x
Poor neighbors or schoolmates	x	x	x	x
Difference between black and white students' exposure to				
Black neighbors or schoolmates	x	x	x	x
Poor neighbors or schoolmates	x	x	x	x

Source: Author.

DIMENSIONS OF SEGREGATION

One of the challenges in understanding the potential effect of segregation on academic achievement patterns is that there are many different aspects of segregation, each of which might affect achievement through a different set of mechanisms. In this paper, I consider four dimensions of segregation. First is the distinction between *residential and school segregation* (which I call here the *context* dimension). Second, is the distinction between *between-district and between-school or between-neighborhood segregation* (the *scale* dimension). Third is the distinction between *absolute and relative segregation* (the *exposure/unevenness* dimension). And fourth is the distinction between *racial and socioeconomic composition* as the key population characteristics through which segregation affects students (the *composition* dimension). In this section, I discuss these different dimensions in some detail.

Table 1 illustrates that the intersection of these four dimensions give rise to sixteen possible features of segregation that may affect students. The columns of table 1 distinguish the context (school or residential) and scale (between-school or between-district) dimensions; the rows distinguish the exposure/evenness (exposure or differences in exposure) and composition (racial or socioeconomic composition) dimensions. It is worth noting that Coleman and his colleagues (1966) focused on the segregation dimensions represented in the far upper left of the table—measures of student exposure to black and poor schoolmates.

The Coleman Report did not attend to residential segregation, to the distinction between between-school and between-district segregation, or to measures of unevenness.

The Context Dimension: Residential and School Segregation

Both residential and school segregation might independently affect students. If, in segregated school systems, schools' racial composition and quality are correlated, then school segregation will lead to racial achievement gaps. Certainly there is considerable evidence indicating that white, black, and Hispanic students' schools often differ in important ways (Hanushek and Rivkin 2007; Johnson 2011; Kozol 1991; Lankford, Loeb, and Wycoff 2002). Owing to residential segregation—by which I mean the patterns of where children live, as opposed to which school they attend—white and black or Hispanic children live in different neighborhoods. Because neighborhood conditions appear to affect children's cognitive development and long-term educational outcomes (Burdick-Will et al. 2011; Chetty, Hendren, and Katz 2016; Sampson, Sharkey, and Raudenbush 2008; Sharkey 2010; Wodtke, Harding, and Elwert 2011), residential segregation may lead to achievement gaps and other forms of educational disparities if it causes children of different races to live in systematically higher- and lower-quality neighborhoods.

Because school and residential segregation are linked (many children attend schools near their homes) and because school and neighborhood quality are linked (schools in communities with abundant resources can draw on those resources in ways that schools in poor communities cannot), it is not clear whether school or residential segregation patterns are most important in shaping achievement gaps. If school quality is the key factor shaping schooling outcomes, then residential segregation may matter only to the extent that it leads to school segregation. On the other hand, if neighborhood conditions in early childhood lead to hard-to-change patterns of inequality in school readiness, then school segregation may matter little, net of residential segregation. Or it may be that both neighborhood and school segregation contribute independently to academic achievement gaps.

The Scale Dimension: Distinguishing Between-School and Between-Neighborhood Segregation from Between-District Segregation

The overall residential or school segregation of a population (a metropolitan area, for example) can be thought of as the sum of two distinct organizational and geographic components: between- and within-district segregation. Most metropolitan areas contain multiple school districts (sometimes only a few, but often dozens or more). In the average metropolitan area, roughly two-thirds of between-school racial segregation is due to differences in the racial composition of school districts (Reardon, Yun, and Eitle 2000; Stroub and Richards 2013); the same is true of residential segregation (Bischoff 2008). There is considerable variation, however, in the proportions of both school segregation and residential segregation that lie between districts.

It is not clear how the scale of segregation is related to patterns of educational outcomes. Consider two metropolitan areas with the same level of total between-school segregation; suppose that in one all of the segregation is due to between-district segregation (within each district, all schools have equal racial composition), while in the other all of the segregation is due to within-district segregation (all districts have an equal racial composition but are internally segregated). Depending on the processes that link segregation to students' opportunities to learn, we might expect one or the other to have larger achievement gaps.

Between-district segregation may be particularly consequential for achievement gaps because there are often substantial differences in school and community resources among school districts. If racial between-district segregation is linked to disparities in either the quality of school districts or the availability of other municipal or community resources that benefit children, then between-district segregation may lead to large achievement gaps. And if school resources and learning opportunities are relatively evenly distributed within school districts (for example, if a district provides equal funding for all schools and randomly assigns teachers to schools, and if municipalities randomly assign spaces in high-quality publicly funded preschools regardless of where in the city a child lives), then within-district segregation patterns might matter less.

On the other hand, if the effects of segregation are largely driven by processes at the school level—for example, if schools' ability to attract and retain the most skilled teachers is largely driven by their racial and socioeconomic composition, regardless of their district characteristics—then total segregation may be more important in driving achievement patterns than between-district segregation. More generally, if resources are allocated unevenly among schools and neighborhoods in ways that are correlated with racial composition, and if these allocation processes operate within districts as strongly as they do between districts, then the organizational scale of segregation will be less important than total segregation.

Exposure and Unevenness

Segregation is generally measured in one of two ways. First are exposure measures (sometimes called isolation measures), which describe the average racial or socioeconomic composition of the schools or neighborhoods of children of a given race. For example, the average proportion of students in a black student's school (or neighborhood) who are black is a measure of the racial isolation of black children. The average proportion of poor children in the black students' schools or neighborhoods is likewise an exposure measure. Second are evenness (or unevenness) measures, which describe the *difference* in the average racial or socioeconomic composition of schools or neighborhoods between children of different races. That is, exposure measures describe the average contexts of children of a given race, and unevenness measures describe the difference in average contexts between two racial groups: unevenness measures can be thought of as simply differences in exposure measures. For example, if the average black student enrolls in a school where 60 percent of the students are poor, black exposure to poverty will be 0.60—a very high exposure to poverty. But if the average white student in the same school district is also enrolled in a school where 60 percent of students are poor, the unevenness in exposure to poverty will be zero.

If the racial or socioeconomic composition of schools or neighborhoods affects students of all races equally, then unevenness measures of segregation should be more strongly associated with achievement gaps than black or Hispanic exposure measures. But if attending a high-poverty school or living in a high-poverty neighborhood is harmful for black and Hispanic students but not for white students (perhaps because white students have access to other resources that buffer them against any negative effects of high-poverty contexts), then the exposure of black students to poor schoolmates and neighbors may be more strongly associated with achievement gaps than the black-white difference in such exposure. In other words, if school composition (and the factors associated with it) affects white and black students equally, then the composition of black students' schools (exposure) will be associated with achievement gaps only to the extent that black and white students' schools differ, on average, in composition.

The Composition Dimension: Racial and Socioeconomic Contexts
As noted earlier, both the Coleman Report and other studies find that both the racial and socioeconomic composition of schools are strongly related to student outcomes. The distinction between segregation processes that operate through racial composition per se and those that operate through other processes that are correlated with racial composition is important, though difficult to disentangle. Given the correlation between race and socioeconomic status, children in predominantly black or Hispanic schools and neighborhoods are typically exposed to much higher poverty levels than those in predominantly white schools. Indeed, the black-white and Hispanic-white difference in exposure to poverty is generally much greater than would be predicted based on racial differences in family income alone: even middle-class black and Hispanic children live in neighborhoods and attend schools with higher poverty rates than most poor white children (Reardon, Fox, and Townsend 2015; Saporito and Sohoni 2007). As a result, schools with high proportions of black students tend also to be schools with high proportions of poor students. Nonetheless, the correlation is not perfect, and it would be useful to know whether it is exposure to minority students or exposure to poverty that is more strongly predictive of achievement gaps.

ANALYTIC STRATEGY
This discussion suggests that many or all of the sixteen types of segregation defined in table 1 may be related to achievement patterns. The goal of this paper is to investigate which of these dimensions are most strongly predictive of racial achievement gaps. My strategy will be to measure achievement gaps and each of the sixteen types of segregation in metropolitan areas of the United States and then to assess the correlation of each measure with achievement gaps, both with and without a set of control variables. This analysis cannot determine the *effect* of any specific dimension of segregation (nor their aggregate effect). It does, nonetheless, provide detailed descriptive information about the relative strength of association between segregation measures and achievement gaps and so is useful for guiding future analyses and providing a set of stylized facts that a model of segregation's effects should be able to explain.

The one study I am aware of that is similar to this is David Card and Jesse Rothstein's (2007) study of the relationship between achievement gaps on the SAT and patterns of residential and school segregation. That study finds that residential segregation is at least as strong a predictor of racial achievement gaps as school segregation, or even stronger. Moreover, the analyses suggest that the association between residential segregation and achievement gaps is driven largely by black-white differences in neighborhood income levels: in metropolitan areas where black children live in much poorer neighborhoods than white children, achievement gaps tend to be larger. The Card and Rothstein (2007) study is quite valuable but has several shortcomings relative to my purpose here. First, it relies on SAT tests, which are not taken by all students. Although Card and Rothstein use a selection model to adjust for differences in SAT-taking rates, this relies on a set of assumptions that cannot be verified and so may be subject to bias. Second, the Card and Rothstein analysis does not examine all the dimensions of segregation that I do here. In particular, they do not consider between-district segregation or exposure measures of segregation. And third, I examine both black-white and Hispanic-white segregation and achievement gap patterns; their analysis is restricted to black-white achievement gaps.

DATA

Achievement Gap Data

I use students' state accountability test scores in grades 3 through 8 in the years 2009 to 2012 in every public school district in the United States. These data were provided by the National Center for Education Statistics under a restricted data use license. The data include, for each public school district in the United States, counts of students scoring at each of several academic proficiency levels (often labeled something like "Below Basic," "Basic," "Proficient," and "Advanced"). These counts are disaggregated by race (here I use counts of non-Hispanic white, non-Hispanic black, and Hispanic students), grade (grades 3 to 8), test subject (math and English language arts), and year (school years 2008–2009 through 2011–2012). I combine the proficiency counts in charter schools with those of the public school district in which they are formally chartered or, if not chartered by a district, in the district in which they are physically located. Thus, a "school district" includes students in all local charter schools as well as in traditional public schools.

There are 384 metropolitan areas and roughly 12,200 school districts serving grades 3 to 8 in the United States. To construct metropolitan area achievement gaps, I aggregate data from all public school districts (including their charter schools) within a given metropolitan area, so long as the metropolitan area falls entirely within a single state. Because districts in different states use different achievement tests, proficiency categories in different states are not comparable, so I cannot construct aggregated data for the 45 (of 384) metropolitan areas that cross state boundaries. The 339 metropolitan areas that do not cross state boundaries include 81 percent of black and 92 percent of Hispanic public school students in grades 3 to 8 in metropolitan areas (and 69 percent and 79 percent of black and Hispanic students in the United States).

The data span six grades, two subjects, and four years, making a total of 16,272 possible metropolitan area–grade–subject–year combinations (in the 339 metropolitan areas). Several states do not have sufficient data to compute achievement gaps in some years. (Nebraska and Wyoming are both missing one or more years of data.) In addition, some metropolitan areas have too few minority students to reliably estimate achievement gaps: I exclude cells with fewer than 20 white or 20 black/Hispanic students. After excluding cells with too few students, I am able to estimate white-black and white-Hispanic achievement gaps in at least one grade-year-subject for all but a few metropolitan areas. In total, the sample includes roughly 14,200 white-black and white-Hispanic metropolitan area achievement gaps, an average of roughly 42 gaps per area.

I estimate achievement gaps in each metropolitan area using the methods described by Andrew Ho and myself (Ho and Reardon 2012; Reardon and Ho 2015). The achievement gaps are measured using the V-statistic, which measures the difference between two distributions in pooled standard deviation units. The advantage of V is that it relies only on the ordered nature of test scores, which allows comparability of gap estimates across tests that measure achievement in on different scales. Given that the data include achievement measured on roughly 600 different standardized tests (typically one for each state-grade-subject combination, sometimes with variation across years), this comparability is a key feature of the *V*-statistic for measuring gaps.

Measures of Segregation

I compute thirty-two measures of segregation for each metropolitan area (sixteen for white-black segregation and sixteen for white-Hispanic segregation), corresponding to the sixteen cells of table 1. School segregation measures are computed from 2008–2009, 2009–2010, and 2010–2011 enrollment data from the Common Core of Data (CCD), which includes racial composition and counts of students by free- or reduced-price-lunch eligibility status for every public school and district in the United States. Residential segregation measures are computed from 2006–2010 American Community Survey (ACS) data, which include racial composition and poverty rates for each census tract in the United States.

The exposure measures are computed by averaging school, district, or census tract racial composition or poverty rates within each metropolitan area, weighting by the number of black or Hispanic students in the school, district, or tract, as appropriate. The unevenness measures are simply the difference in black (or Hispanic) and white students' exposure-relevant measures. Because the ACS and CCD data are based on full population counts (in CCD) or on large samples pooled every five years (in ACS), the segregation measures are very precise.

Not surprisingly, the sixteen segregation measures are correlated, often quite highly, with one another (see appendix tables A1 and A2). Nonetheless, in some cases the correlations are quite modest, suggesting that we may be able to distinguish their associations with achievement gaps.

Additional Covariates

I include a set of additional variables as controls in some of the models shown here. The controls are constructed from CCD data and School District Demographic System (SDDS) data. The SDDS is a special tabulation of the 2006–2010 ACS data that includes tabulations of the demographic characteristics of the families living in each school district who have children enrolled in the public schools. I aggregate these to the metropolitan-area level and construct measures of family socioeconomic characteristics (income inequality, median family income, parental educational attainment, occupational status, poverty rates, unemployment rates, single-parent household rates, home value and median rent, racial disparities in family socioeconomic characteristics, and racial composition); in each case these measures apply to families in the metropolitan area with children enrolled in public schools. From the CCD, I construct a measure of metropolitan-area school district fragmentation. This is the Herfindahl index applied to school district enrollment; it measures the degree to which students are concentrated in a small number of large districts or dispersed among many small districts, and it has been shown to be related to between-district segregation patterns (Bischoff 2008; Reardon and Yun 2001). From the CCD, I also include a measure of metropolitan-area average per-pupil public school spending. These variables are used in controls in some of the models shown here. Because some of the SDDS-based measures are not available for all metropolitan areas, I limit all analyses here to those with complete data on all measures: 311 metropolitan areas for white-black gap analyses and 318 for the white-Hispanic gap analyses.

BIVARIATE AND PARTIAL CORRELATIONS BETWEEN SEGREGATION AND ACHIEVEMENT GAPS

To begin, I examine the bivariate correlations among various segregation measures and racial achievement gaps. Table 2 reports the correlation of each of the sixteen segregation measures with the white-black achievement gap. Note that almost all of the segregation measures are positively correlated with the achievement gap. However, the correlations range from 0.013 to 0.628. Table 2 makes clear several patterns. First, each measure of school segre-

Table 2. Bivariate Correlations Between the White-Black Achievement Gap and Various Dimensions of Segregation, 311 Metropolitan Areas, 2009–2012

	School Segregation		Residential Segregation	
	Between-School	Between-District	Between-Tract	Between-District
Black students' exposure to				
Black neighbors or schoolmates	0.386***	0.344***	0.352***	0.325***
Poor neighbors or schoolmates	0.217***	0.155**	0.191***	0.013
Difference between black and white students' exposure to				
Black neighbors or schoolmates	0.429***	0.340***	0.401***	0.314***
Poor neighbors or schoolmates	0.628***	0.459***	0.461***	0.354***

Source: Author's calculations.
Note: Each cell is the bivariate correlation between the pooled white-black achievement gap and a measure of segregation.
*p < .05; **p < .01; ***p < .001

Table 3. Bivariate Correlations Between the White-Hispanic Achievement Gap and Various Dimensions of Segregation, 318 Metropolitan Areas, 2009–2012

	School Segregation		Residential Segregation	
	Between-School	Between-District	Between-Tract	Between-District
Hispanic students' exposure to				
Hispanic neighbors or schoolmates	0.395***	0.342***	0.318***	0.308***
Poor neighbors or schoolmates	0.134*	−0.041	0.023	−0.118*
Difference between Hispanic and white students' exposure to				
Hispanic neighbors or schoolmates	0.600***	0.515***	0.519***	0.532***
Poor neighbors or schoolmates	0.678***	0.515***	0.450***	0.381***

Source: Author's calculations.
Note: Each cell is the bivariate correlation between the pooled white-Hispanic achievement gap and a measure of segregation.
*p < .05; **p < .01; ***p < .001

gation is more highly correlated with achievement gaps than the corresponding measure of residential segregation. Second, in every case, segregation among schools or census tracts is more correlated with achievement gaps than is segregation between school districts. Third, racial differences in exposure to black or poor schoolmates or neighbors are more strongly related to achievement gaps than is simple exposure, though this pattern holds more consistently for exposure to poverty than for racial exposure. Fourth, although achievement gaps are more highly correlated with black students' exposure to other black students or neighbors than with exposure to poor schoolmates or neighbors, this pattern is reversed when we consider the association between achievement gaps and racial *differences* in exposure to black or poor peers. The bottom panel of table 2 shows that differences in exposure to poverty are more strongly correlated with achievement gaps than are differences in exposure to same-race peers.

Table 3 shows the corresponding correla-

Table 4. Partial Correlations Between the White-Black Achievement Gap and Various Dimensions of Segregation, 311 Metropolitan Areas, 2009–2012

	School Segregation		Residential Segregation	
	Between-School	Between-District	Between-Tract	Between-District
Black students' exposure to				
Black neighbors or schoolmates	0.348***	0.294***	0.306***	0.267***
Poor neighbors or schoolmates	0.156**	0.105	0.109	−0.079
Difference between black and white students' exposure to				
Black neighbors or schoolmates	0.299***	0.214***	0.266***	0.180**
Poor neighbors or schoolmates	0.509***	0.452***	0.406***	0.348***

Source: Author's calculations.

Notes: Each cell is the partial correlation between the pooled white-black achievement gap and a measure of segregation, conditional on metropolitan-area characteristics. The top panel (partial correlations with exposure measures) includes controls for racial disparities in family socioeconomic status and metropolitan-area fragmentation. The bottom panel (partial correlations with differential exposure measures) includes the same covariates as the top panel plus additional controls for metropolitan-area racial and socioeconomic composition as well as per-pupil average spending. See text for details.
*p < .05; **p < .01; ***p < .001

tions between white-Hispanic achievement gaps and the measure of Hispanic students' segregation. The magnitude of the correlations is roughly similar to those in table 2, except for the correlations with differences in exposure to Hispanic neighbors and schoolmates, where the correlations with white-Hispanic gaps are larger than those in table 2. Likewise, the general pattern of correlations is similar.

With only a few exceptions then, the bivariate correlations follow a clear pattern: achievement gaps are more highly correlated with school segregation than residential segregation; more highly correlated with segregation among schools and tracts than among districts; and more highly correlated with differences in exposure to poor or same-race schoolmates or neighbors than with simple exposure measures. The measure of segregation most highly correlated with the metropolitan-area achievement gap is the racial difference in students' exposure to poor schoolmates (white-black $r = 0.628$; white-Hispanic $r = 0.678$).

I next examine the partial correlations between achievement gaps and measures of segregation, conditional on a set of metropolitan-area characteristics. For the exposure measures, I control for racial differences in family socioeconomic characteristics in the metropolitan area and the fragmentation of the metropolitan area. I do not include measures of the racial or socioeconomic composition of the metropolitan area because these are mechanically related to the exposure measures (all else being equal, black students will have more black schoolmates in a predominantly black metropolitan area); their inclusion in the model would change the interpretation of the coefficient on the exposure measure to be similar to that of the differential exposure measures. The coefficients would indicate the extent to which achievement gaps are larger, on average, in metropolitan areas where black students attend schools with more black schoolmates than would be expected given the racial composition of the metropolitan-area public school population. This is essentially what the evenness segregation measures capture. To preserve the interpretation of the exposure measure coefficients, then, I do not include covariates indicating the racial or socioeconomic composition of the metropolitan area in computing the partial correlations in the top panels of tables 4 and 5.

Table 5. Partial Correlations Between the White-Hispanic Achievement Gap and Various Dimensions of Segregation, 318 Metropolitan Areas, 2009–2012

	School Segregation		Residential Segregation	
	Between-School	Between-District	Between-Tract	Between-District
Hispanic students' exposure to				
Hispanic neighbors or schoolmates	0.046	−0.009	−0.015	−0.036
Poor neighbors or schoolmates	−0.145*	−0.206***	−0.207***	−0.360***
Difference between Hispanic and white students' exposure to				
Hispanic neighbors or schoolmates	0.213***	0.120*	0.111	0.120
Poor neighbors or schoolmates	0.357***	0.259***	0.202**	0.235***

Source: Author's calculations.

Notes: Each cell is the partial correlation between the pooled white-Hispanic achievement gap and a measure of segregation, conditional on metropolitan-area characteristics. The top panel (partial correlations with exposure measures) includes controls for racial disparities in family socioeconomic status and metropolitan-area fragmentation. The bottom panel (partial correlations with differential exposure measures) includes the same covariates as the top panel plus additional controls for metropolitan-area racial and socioeconomic composition as well as per-pupil average spending. See text for details.
*$p < .05$; **$p < .01$; ***$p < .001$

I do include such measures, however, in the models for the bottom panels. Here the segregation measures are not mechanically related to composition (that is the virtue of the evenness measures), so the composition measures can be used as controls without altering the interpretation of the coefficients on the segregation measures. Therefore, the estimates in the bottom panels control for metropolitan-area racial composition, family socioeconomic characteristics, racial differences in these characteristics, metropolitan fragmentation, and metropolitan-area average per-pupil public school spending.

Table 4 reports these partial correlations for the white-black achievement gaps. In general, the partial correlations are weaker than the bivariate correlations. This is particularly true in the second row of table 4: after controlling for racial differences in family socioeconomic characteristics, measures of black students' exposure to poor schoolmates or neighbors are at best only very weakly correlated with achievement gaps. The correlations with the unevenness measures of segregation are generally about 10 to 30 percent smaller than the uncontrolled correlations in table 2. They are modest in size but not trivial, ranging from roughly 0.18 to 0.51. Just as in table 2, the largest correlation is the correlation with racial differences in exposure to poor schoolmates ($r = 0.509$).

Table 5 reports the analogous correlations of the segregation measures and the white-Hispanic achievement gap. Here the partial correlations with exposure to Hispanic schoolmates or neighbors are not statistically different from zero. Interestingly, white-Hispanic achievement gaps are negatively correlated with Hispanic students' exposure to poor peers and neighbors. This correlation reverses, however, in the bottom panel of the table once the models include metropolitan-area racial and socioeconomic composition measures. Thus, the negative correlations with exposure to poverty may simply reflect a correlation between achievement gaps and overall poverty rates.

In the bottom panel of table 5, white-Hispanic achievement gaps remain correlated with differences in exposure to poverty after controlling for metropolitan socioeconomic characteristics and composition in addition to racial socioeconomic disparities. Nonetheless, the correlations are only modest in size and are considerably smaller than their counterparts in table 4.

Tables 4 and 5 together reveal a clear pattern: net of a set of key covariates, achievement gaps are more highly correlated with school segregation than residential segregation; they are more highly correlated with segregation among schools and tracts than among districts; and they are generally more highly correlated with differences in exposure to poor or same-race schoolmates and neighbors than with simple exposure measures (though the last point is not true of exposure to black students or neighbors in table 4). Net of the set of covariates in the models, the racial difference in students' exposure to poor schoolmates remains the measure of segregation most highly correlated with metropolitan-area achievement gaps (white-black $r = 0.509$; white-Hispanic $r = 0.357$).

DISENTANGLING MULTIPLE ASPECTS OF SEGREGATION

The bivariate and partial correlations in tables 2 through 5 are useful for assessing whether segregation measures are associated with achievement gaps, net of a vector of metropolitan-area socioeconomic conditions and disparities. But because the segregation measures are correlated with one another (see appendix tables A1 and A2), the individual correlations do not indicate which of the segregation dimensions are most important.

To investigate the relative importance of the different dimensions of segregation, I regress achievement gaps on various measures of segregation, controlling for the full set of metropolitan-area covariates included in the bottom panels of tables 4 and 5. In these models, I include various combinations of the differential exposure segregation measures; I exclude the simple exposure measures because, as noted earlier, they are mechanically related to the other measures once racial and socioeconomic composition are included in the models.

Tables 6 and 7 display selected coefficients from a series of models designed to isolate the primary dimensions of segregation driving the general association between segregation and achievement gaps. Each model includes the metropolitan-area covariates described earlier. The first column (model 0) simply reports the R-squared statistic from the model that includes the covariates but none of the segregation measures ($R^2 = 0.66$ in the white-black model; $R^2 = 0.72$ in the white-Hispanic model). Model 1 includes the four between-district segregation measures; model 2 includes the four total segregation measures (between-school enrollment segregation and between-tract residential segregation); model 3 includes all eight measures.

Below the coefficients are the p-values from a set of hypothesis tests. The first tests the null hypothesis that the coefficients on the residential segregation terms in the model are all equal to zero (that is, the coefficients in the rows labeled b, d, f, and h in the table are all zero). The second tests the hypothesis that the school segregation terms are all nonsignificant. The third and fourth test the hypotheses that the four between-district terms are all nonsignificant and that the four total segregation terms are all nonsignificant, respectively. The fifth tests that the coefficients on the four racial exposure terms are zero; the sixth tests that those on the four poverty exposure terms are all zero. The seventh tests the hypothesis that all of the terms other than the two describing the differential exposure to poor school- or districtmates are zero. The final tests the null hypothesis that all the coefficients except that on the differential exposure to poor schoolmates are zero. This effectively tests whether that one measure of segregation contains all the predictive power of the full set of eight measures.

The coefficients and hypothesis tests in tables 6 and 7 tell a very consistent story. In each model, we cannot reject the null hypothesis that the residential segregation terms are not predictive of achievement gaps, conditional on the school segregation terms. We can, however, reject the opposite hypothesis (that school segregation is uninformative, conditional on residential segregation). In other words, the segregation of schools is predictive of achievement gaps; net of that, variation in neighborhood segregation patterns is not correlated with achievement gaps.

In the Hispanic-white models (table 7), we

Table 6. Coefficient Estimates and Hypothesis Tests from Multivariate Regression Models of the Association Between the White-Black Achievement Gap and Segregation, 311 Metropolitan Areas, 2009–2012

	Model 0	Model 1	Model 2	Model 3	Model 4	Model 5
Difference between black and white students' exposure to						
a. District enrollment proportion black		-0.046		-0.025		
		(0.295)		(0.321)		
b. District residential proportion black		-0.312		-0.470		
		(0.314)		(0.319)		
c. District enrollment proportion poor		0.897***		0.501*	0.147	
		(0.160)		(0.230)	(0.148)	
d. District residential proportion poor		0.203		-0.106		
		(0.562)		(0.580)		
e. School enrollment proportion black			-0.159	0.195		
			(0.161)	(0.224)		
f. Neighborhood residential proportion black			-0.025	-0.053		
			(0.159)	(0.167)		
g. School enrollment proportion poor			0.793***	0.358	0.638***	0.759***
			(0.132)	(0.213)	(0.145)	(0.079)
h. Neighborhood residential proportion poor			0.365	0.481		
			(0.283)	(0.300)		
Adjusted R-squared	0.566	0.664	0.678	0.686	0.676	0.676
N	311	311	311	311	311	311
Hypothesis tests (p-values)						
Residential exposure = 0 (b = d = f = h = 0)		0.609	0.433	0.283		
Educational exposure = 0 (a = c = e = g = 0)		0.000***	0.000***	0.000***		
District composition = 0 (a = b = c = d = 0)				0.045*	0.320	
School or neighborhood composition = 0 (e = f = g = h = 0)				0.000***	0.000***	
Exposure to racial composition = 0 (a = b = e = f = 0)		0.010**	0.184	0.032*		
Exposure to poverty = 0 (c = d = g = h = 0)		0.000***	0.000***	0.000***	0.000***	
Only educational exposure to poverty ≠ 0 (a = b = d = e = f = h = 0)		0.020*	0.248	0.045*		
Only school exposure to poverty ≠ 0 (a = b = c = d = e = f = 0)				0.053		

Source: Author's calculations.
*$p < .05$; **$p < .01$; ***$p < .001$

Table 7. Coefficient Estimates and Hypothesis Tests from Multivariate Regression Models of the Association Between the White-Hispanic Achievement Gap and Segregation, 318 Metropolitan Areas, 2009–2012

	Model 0	Model 1	Model 2	Model 3	Model 4	Model 5
Difference between Hispanic and white students' exposure to						
a. District enrollment proportion Hispanic		−0.098		−0.116		
		(0.236)		(0.307)		
b. District residential proportion Hispanic		−0.115		−0.051		
		(0.332)		(0.323)		
c. District enrollment proportion poor		0.409*		−0.190	−0.185	
		(0.189)		(0.250)	(0.163)	
d. District residential proportion poor		0.553		0.591		
		(0.734)		(0.776)		
e. School enrollment proportion Hispanic			0.245	0.370		
			(0.227)	(0.288)		
f. Neighborhood residential proportion Hispanic			−0.486	−0.478		
			(0.284)	(0.285)		
g. School enrollment proportion poor			0.590***	0.657**	0.720***	0.568***
			(0.151)	(0.219)	(0.162)	(0.091)
h. Neighborhood residential proportion poor			−0.014	−0.115		
			(0.332)	(0.366)		
Adjusted R-squared	0.720	0.738	0.756	0.754	0.755	0.755
N	318	318	318	318	318	318
Hypothesis tests (p-values)						
Residential exposure = 0		0.754	0.180	0.399		
(b = d = f = h = 0)						
Educational exposure = 0		0.070	0.000***	0.000***		
(a = c = e = g = 0)						
District composition = 0				0.710	0.256	
(a = b = c = d = 0)						
School or neighborhood composition = 0				0.000***	0.000***	
(e = f = g = h = 0)						
Exposure to racial composition = 0		0.511	0.188	0.499		
(a = b = e = f = 0)						
Exposure to poverty = 0		0.000***	0.000***	0.001***	0.000***	
(c = d = g = h = 0)						
Only educational exposure to poverty ≠ 0		0.578	0.267	0.572		
(a = b = d = e = f = h = 0)						
Only school exposure to poverty ≠ 0				0.531		
(a = b = c = d = e = f = h = 0)						

Source: Author's calculations.
*p < .05; **p < .01; ***p < .001

cannot reject the null hypothesis that between-district segregation (whether residential or school segregation) is nonpredictive once we include measures of total between-school and between-tract segregation in the model. In the black-white models (table 6), however, the hypothesis test suggests some association between between-district segregation and gaps, net of total segregation ($p = 0.045$). In both tables, however, we reject the opposite hypothesis: total district segregation measures are predictive of achievement gaps, net of between-district segregation ($p < 0.001$). Although there is some evidence that between-district segregation is independently associated with white-black achievement gaps, the magnitude of this association is small relative to the association with total segregation.

The p-values from the fifth and sixth hypothesis tests show that differential exposure to same-race schoolmates and neighbors is not predictive of white-Hispanic achievement gaps ($p = 0.499$) and is modestly associated with white-black gaps ($p = 0.032$), conditional on differential exposure to poverty. Differential exposure to poor schoolmates and neighbors is predictive, however, conditional on racial exposure patterns ($p < 0.001$).

Together the first six hypothesis tests strongly suggest that differential exposure to poor schoolmates is the key dimension of segregation associated with racial achievement gaps. The seventh hypothesis test indicates whether excluding the four residential segregation measures and the two measures of exposure to same-race schoolmates reduces the fit of the model. In the white-Hispanic models (table 7), we fail to reject the hypothesis that all six of those terms can be excluded from model 3 ($p = 0.572$). In the white-black models (table 6), however, these six terms do carry a very small amount of predictive power ($p = 0.045$); a comparison of the adjusted R-squareds from models 3 and 4 in table 6, however, shows that adding these six terms to the model increases the R-squared by only 0.01.

In both the white-black and white-Hispanic models, we also fail to reject the hypothesis (hypothesis 8) that seven of the eight terms can be excluded (all but the measure of differential exposure to school poverty) from the model. Models 4 and 5 include only the differential exposure to poor school- and districtmates measures. The district-level measure is not significant in model 4, leaving model 5 as the preferred model.

DISCUSSION

The results of these descriptive analyses are unequivocal. Racial segregation is strongly associated with racial achievement gaps, and the racial difference in the proportion of students' schoolmates who are poor is the key dimension of segregation driving this association. Conditional on that measure, the other measures in tables 6 and 7 collectively explain no additional variance in achievement gaps. The adjusted R-squareds are nearly identical in model 5 and model 3 (which includes seven additional measures of segregation).

The coefficients on the difference in exposure to poor schoolmates in model 5 in tables 6 and 7 are relatively large. To get a sense of their magnitude, consider figure 1, which shows that in some metropolitan areas there is no difference in exposure to poor schoolmates between black or Hispanic and white students, while in others the difference is as high as 40 percent. The coefficients in tables 6 and 7 imply that a 40 percent difference in exposure to poverty corresponds to a roughly 0.30- or 0.23-standard-deviation increase in the white-black and white-Hispanic achievement gap, respectively, relative to a metropolitan area where there is no racial difference in exposure to poverty. In the average metropolitan area, the racial difference in exposure to poverty is roughly twenty percentage points, corresponding to an achievement gap of 0.12 to 0.15. This implies that racial segregation—specifically racial differences in exposure to poverty—accounts for roughly one-fifth of the average racial achievement gap.

What should we make of these findings? First, it is important to reiterate that the coefficients in tables 4 to 7 should not be interpreted causally. They do not imply that reducing segregation will reduce achievement gaps. The models here simply provide evidence that segregation—specifically segregation that produces racial differences in exposure to poor schoolmates—is strongly correlated with

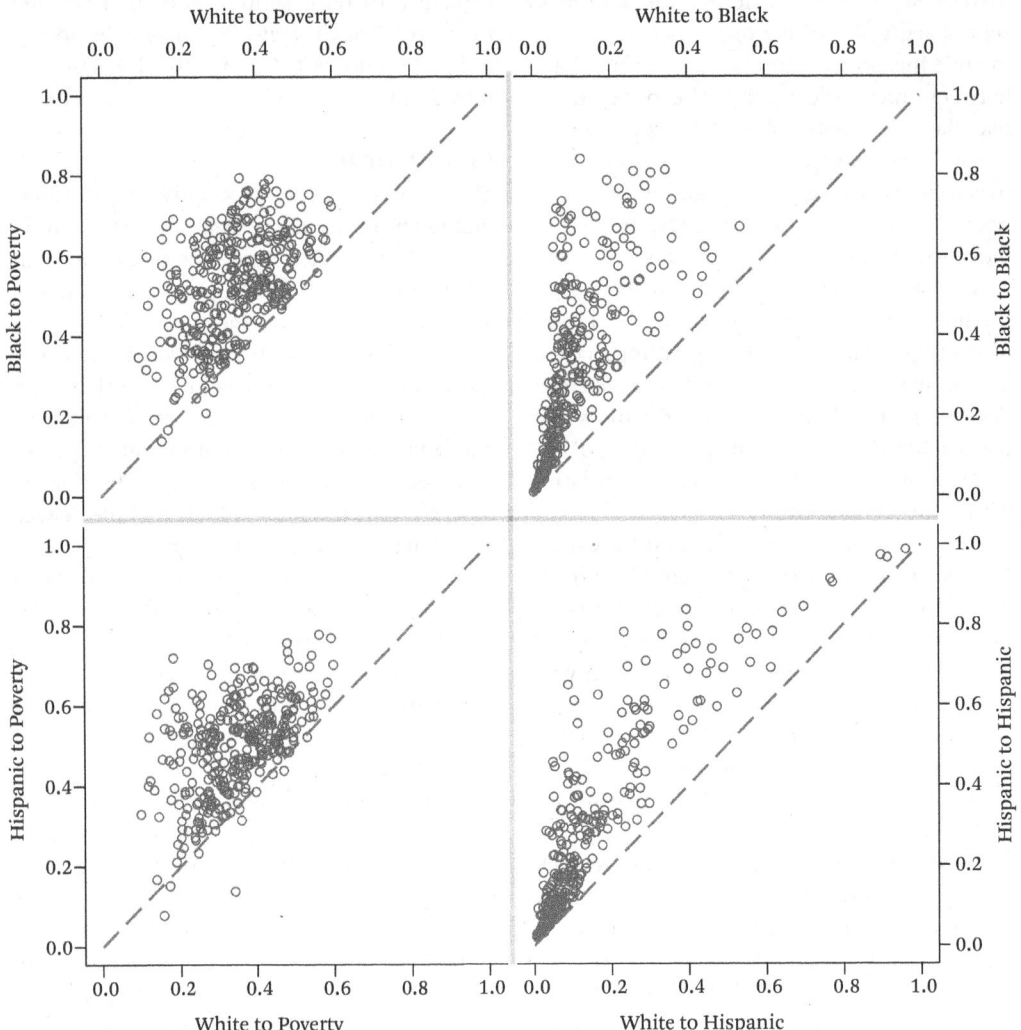

Figure 1. Exposure to Poor and Minority Schoolmates, by Race, U.S. Metropolitan Areas, 2009–2012

Source: Author's calculations.

achievement gaps net of a wide range of covariates that are strongly related to achievement gaps, including racial disparities in family income, poverty rates, unemployment rates, and parental education. In metropolitan areas where racial segregation is higher than predicted from racial disparities in socioeconomic conditions, achievement gaps are, on average, significantly larger. While that is certainly suggestive of a causal link between segregation and achievement gaps, the correlation might arise from mechanisms other than segregation. One might imagine, for example, that metropolitan areas that are more segregated than expected are those in which racial prejudice and discrimination are particularly high in general; if such discrimination affects students' opportunity through some mechanism other than segregation, this might explain the observed association between segregation and achievement gaps. Additionally, there may be racial-ethnic differences in family background —such as differences in wealth, immigration history and experiences, or English fluency— that are not captured by our measures of socioeconomic status but that lead to both segregation and to differences in academic achievement patterns. Again, this might account for the observed correlation of segregation with achievement gaps. The association between segregation and achievement gaps is large, however, even after controlling for a number of measures of socioeconomic disparities, so such alternative pathways would need to lead to sizable effects on achievement gaps. Thus, the results presented here are suggestive of powerful effects of segregation, but are not definitive.

Second, the pattern of results here strongly suggests that the mechanisms through which segregation is related to achievement gaps are related to differences in students' exposure to poor schoolmates. The greater the difference in poverty rates in white and black students' schools, the larger the achievement gap, on average. There are a number of potential explanations for this pattern. One is that a school's poverty rate is a proxy for general school quality—quality of instruction and opportunities to learn. High-poverty schools may have fewer resources, a harder time attracting and retaining skilled teachers, more violence and disruption, and poorer facilities. Additionally, the parents of students in such schools generally have fewer resources—economic, social, and political—that can be used to benefit their children's schools.

Another possibility is that exposure to poor schoolmates affects students' learning and academic performance through some direct or indirect form of peer influence. For example, high-poverty schools, because they typically have more low-performing students than do schools with fewer poor students, may typically offer less advanced curricula than low-poverty schools. In a classroom where most students' skills are well below grade level, students—even those whose skills are at grade level—are therefore unlikely to encounter challenging curricula and instruction. In this way, having low-performing schoolmates may limit one's own learning because it alters instructional and social processes in the classroom. The data here do not speak to which, if any, of these processes drive the association between school poverty and academic achievement, of course; there are clearly many such potential mechanisms. Nonetheless, the estimates imply a strong association between school poverty and school quality (where school quality is understood to encompass the full set of instructional, parental, and peer resources in a school).

Indeed, another way of assessing the magnitude of the coefficients in tables 6 and 7 is to think of them simply as estimates of the association between school poverty rates and average achievement levels, controlling for students' family socioeconomic background and race. To see this, note that my estimates here are akin to those that would be obtained from a metropolitan-area fixed-effects model that estimates the average within-race and within-metropolitan-area association between academic achievement and average exposure to poverty, controlling for other measures of family socioeconomic status and school composition.[1] The results here therefore are consistent with a model in which high-poverty schools are, on average, less effective at promoting achievement than lower-poverty schools. The coefficient of 0.75 on the racial difference in exposure to poverty measure in model 5 of table 6, then, implies that a ten-percentage-point difference in school poverty rates is associated with an average difference of 0.075 standard deviations of student achievement. In metropolitan areas where black or Hispanic students disproportionately attend high-poverty schools, then, achievement gaps tend to be larger.

Third, the results here suggest that residential segregation is not associated with racial achievement gaps, once we take into account family socioeconomic characteristics

---

1. To see this, note that a metropolitan-area fixed-effects model of the form $Y_{mi} = \alpha(WHITE_i) + \beta(SCHPOV_i) + \mathbf{X}_i\Gamma + \Delta_m + e_{mi}$ (where m indexes metropolitan areas, i indexes individuals, $SCHPOV_i$ is the poverty rate in student i's school, and $\mathbf{X}_i$ is a vector of socioeconomic covariates) is the same as the model $\overline{Y}_{mw} - \overline{Y}_{mb} = \alpha + \beta(\overline{SCHPOV}_{mw} - \overline{SCHPOV}_{mb}) + (\overline{\mathbf{X}}_{mw} - \overline{\mathbf{X}}_{mb})\Lambda + u_m$ (where the subscripts mw and mb indicate white and black populations in metropolitan area m). My models are similar to the latter form (though they differ in that they include additional metropolitan-area covariates). In either model, β is interpreted as the association between exposure to poverty and academic achievement.

and school segregation patterns. This appears somewhat at odds with Card and Rothstein's (2007) finding that black-white differences in poor neighbors were the key mechanism driving the association between segregation and racial achievement gaps. However, Card and Rothstein did not include differential exposure to both poor schoolmates and poor neighbors in their models simultaneously. When I include both in the model (see model 2 in tables 6 and 7), I find that school differences in exposure to poverty are strong predictors of achievement gaps, while residential differences in exposure to poverty are not statistically significant predictors. (In models not shown, I replicate the Card and Rothstein models; I find that neighborhood differential exposure to poverty is a strong predictor of achievement gaps if school differential exposure to poverty is not in the model, consistent with their results.) This suggests that Card and Rothstein's conclusion might have been different had they included both terms in their models. Nonetheless, both their findings and mine here suggest that racial segregation may matter most when coupled with large differences in white and minority students' exposure to poverty.

Does this mean that residential segregation is inconsequential for academic achievement? No. Residential segregation may contribute to achievement gaps primarily through its effect on school segregation patterns. As tables A1 and A2 show, racial differences in exposure to poor schoolmates are strongly correlated (0.78 and 0.72, respectively, in the black-white and Hispanic-white cases) with racial differences in poor neighbors. This is not surprising, given that most students attend schools relatively close to home; residential segregation is a key factor shaping school segregation patterns. Thus, residential segregation—particularly racial differences in exposure to neighborhood poverty—may affect achievement patterns (for evidence that neighborhood poverty affects long-term educational outcomes, see, for example, Chetty, Hendren, and Katz 2016), but it may do so primarily by leading to differences in school quality.

Finally, does the importance of racial differences in exposure to poverty imply that we should not worry about racial segregation per se? One might read tables 6 and 7 and conclude that racial differences in exposure to white and minority schoolmates and neighbors do not appear to affect achievement gaps. Does this mean that we should abandon *Brown* and efforts toward racial integration and focus instead on the socioeconomic integration of schools, as some have suggested (see Kahlenberg 2006)?

It does not. The data clearly show an association between racial school segregation and achievement gaps, net of many socioeconomic differences between white and minority families (see row 3 of tables 4 and 5). Tables 6 and 7 do not undermine this; rather, they show that the association between racial segregation and achievement gaps is driven by the strong association between racial segregation per se and racial differences in school poverty. Indeed, the correlation between racial differences in exposure to minority schoolmates and racial differences in exposure to poor schoolmates is roughly 0.80 (see appendix tables A1 and A2, row 14, column 10); in metropolitan areas where black and Hispanic students disproportionately attend schools with same-race schoolmates, they also disproportionately attend schools with poor schoolmates. This is a result of (a) the fact that poverty rates are much higher among black and Hispanic students; (b) patterns of residential segregation that concentrate black and Hispanic students in much poorer neighborhoods than even equally poor white students (Logan 2011; Pattillo 2013; Reardon, Fox, and Townsend 2015; Sharkey 2014); and (c) school assignment and school choice policies that further isolate poor and minority students (Saporito and Sohoni 2006, 2007). Given the large differences in poverty rates between white and black families and patterns of residential segregation, there is no feasible way of eliminating racial disparities in school poverty without substantially reducing racial segregation per se. Moreover, race-specific integration policies may be the most effective way of eliminating racial disparities in school poverty. Income integration policies are rare in the United States and have produced little racial integration even in the few instances where they have been implemented (Reardon, Yun, and Kurlaender 2006; Reardon and Rhodes

2011). In sum, racial integration policies remain essential for reducing racial disparities in school poverty rates.

Moreover, racial segregation per se may affect outcomes other than academic achievement gaps. In *Brown,* the Court was concerned about the psychological harms of racial segregation, not about its effects on academic achievement. Nothing in the results presented here should be construed as demonstrating that there are no direct harms from racial isolation. It is certainly possible that de facto racial segregation, even in the absence of de jure segregation and differences in exposure to poverty, may damage minority students' self-concept in the ways documented by Kenneth and Mamie Clark and others cited in the *Brown* decision (Clark and Clark 1939a, 1939b, 1950; Deutscher, Chein, and Sadigur 1948). It may also lead to lower between-group understanding and empathy and increased prejudice (Pettigrew and Tropp 2006). It may degrade students' ability to collaborate in diverse settings and hamper the collective functioning of a democratic society (Page 2008). It may lead to segregated social networks that persist long beyond high school and create unequal opportunities in the labor market and unequal access to social and political capital. My finding here that racial segregation per se is not independently associated with academic achievement gaps, net of racial differences in exposure to poverty, does not rule out these many other potential consequences of racial isolation.

This study is not new in identifying a strong association between racial segregation and academic achievement gaps. It does, however, provide a much sharper description of the features of segregation patterns that are most strongly predictive of academic achievement gaps. The evidence here very clearly shows that racial differences in exposure to poor schoolmates is linked to achievement gaps. Black and Hispanic students' test scores, relative to whites', are much lower when black and Hispanic students attend schools with more poor schoolmates. Reducing school segregation—in particular, reducing racial disparities in exposure to poor schoolmates—may therefore be an effective means of improving the equality of students' access to high-quality educational opportunities.

APPENDIX

Table A1. Correlation Matrix of Metropolitan-Area Black-White Segregation Measures, 311 Metropolitan Areas, 2009–2012

	Exposure to...							
	Black				Poor			
	Students in...		Neighbors in...		Students in...		Neighbors in...	
	District (1)	School (2)	District (3)	Tract (4)	District (5)	School (6)	District (7)	Tract (8)
(1)	1.00							
(2)	0.97	1.00						
(3)	0.99	0.97	1.00					
(4)	0.94	0.97	0.95	1.00				
(5)	0.64	0.62	0.63	0.63	1.00			
(6)	0.61	0.64	0.61	0.65	0.93	1.00		
(7)	0.52	0.47	0.51	0.46	0.77	0.71	1.00	
(8)	0.55	0.55	0.53	0.53	0.70	0.71	0.75	1.00
(9)	0.81	0.74	0.78	0.70	0.61	0.52	0.57	0.53
(10)	0.89	0.92	0.88	0.89	0.64	0.63	0.52	0.58
(11)	0.79	0.73	0.79	0.71	0.59	0.50	0.57	0.51
(12)	0.85	0.90	0.86	0.94	0.64	0.64	0.48	0.56
(13)	0.53	0.47	0.50	0.45	0.59	0.48	0.54	0.41
(14)	0.60	0.62	0.58	0.60	0.60	0.62	0.47	0.48
(15)	0.54	0.47	0.52	0.44	0.55	0.44	0.66	0.52
(16)	0.61	0.63	0.59	0.62	0.64	0.65	0.56	0.80

Source: Author's calculations.

	Black-White Difference in Exposure to...							
	Black				Poor			
	Students in...		Neighbors in...		Students in...		Neighbors in...	
	District (9)	School (10)	District (11)	Tract (12)	District (13)	School (14)	District (15)	Tract (16)
	1.00							
	0.88	1.00						
	0.98	0.87	1.00					
	0.79	0.94	0.79	1.00				
	0.82	0.66	0.79	0.58	1.00			
	0.74	0.78	0.72	0.72	0.87	1.00		
	0.81	0.66	0.81	0.57	0.89	0.76	1.00	
	0.69	0.74	0.68	0.71	0.67	0.78	0.72	1.00

Table A2. Correlation Matrix of Metropolitan-Area Hispanic-White Segregation Measures, 318 Metropolitan Areas, 2009–2012

	Exposure to ...							
	Hispanic				Poor			
	Students in ...		Neighbors in ...		Students in ...		Neighbors in ...	
	District (1)	School (2)	District (3)	Tract (4)	District (5)	School (6)	District (7)	Tract (8)
(1)	1.00							
(2)	0.99	1.00						
(3)	1.00	0.98	1.00					
(4)	0.98	0.98	0.98	1.00				
(5)	0.19	0.22	0.18	0.21	1.00			
(6)	0.37	0.42	0.36	0.38	0.89	1.00		
(7)	0.31	0.29	0.31	0.33	0.66	0.57	1.00	
(8)	0.35	0.35	0.35	0.38	0.50	0.48	0.77	1.00
(9)	0.63	0.63	0.60	0.57	0.30	0.41	0.26	0.26
(10)	0.70	0.76	0.66	0.68	0.32	0.51	0.20	0.26
(11)	0.37	0.38	0.35	0.30	0.27	0.29	0.21	0.22
(12)	0.79	0.83	0.76	0.80	0.33	0.51	0.27	0.31
(13)	0.19	0.22	0.15	0.15	0.44	0.41	0.27	0.24
(14)	0.35	0.42	0.31	0.34	0.43	0.56	0.19	0.23
(15)	0.04	0.06	0.01	0.02	0.38	0.28	0.44	0.36
(16)	0.39	0.43	0.37	0.41	0.45	0.48	0.50	0.68

Source: Author's calculations.

	Hispanic-White Difference in Exposure to . . .							
	Hispanic				Poor			
	Students in . . .		Neighbors in . . .		Students in . . .		Neighbors in . . .	
	District (9)	School (10)	District (11)	Tract (12)	District (13)	School (14)	District (15)	Tract (16)
	1.00							
	0.89	1.00						
	0.88	0.74	1.00					
	0.82	0.94	0.63	1.00				
	0.74	0.64	0.78	0.51	1.00			
	0.71	0.80	0.69	0.69	0.87	1.00		
	0.54	0.43	0.70	0.32	0.86	0.68	1.00	
	0.60	0.62	0.61	0.62	0.69	0.72	0.72	1.00

REFERENCES

Bischoff, Kendra. 2008. "School District Fragmentation and Racial Residential Segregation: How Do Boundaries Matter?" *Urban Affairs Review* 44(2): 182-217.

Borman, Geoffrey D., and Maritza Dowling. 2010. "Schools and Inequality: A Multilevel Analysis of Coleman's Equality of Educational Opportunity Data." *Teachers College Record* 112(5): 1201-46.

Burdick-Will, Julia, Jens Ludwig, Stephen W. Raudenbush, Robert J. Sampson, Lisa Sanbonmatsu, and Patrick Sharkey. 2011. "Converging Evidence for Neighborhood Effects on Children's Test Scores: An Experimental, Quasi-Experimental, and Observational Comparison." In *Whither Opportunity? Rising Inequality and the Uncertain Life Chances of Low-Income Children*, edited by Greg J. Duncan and Richard J. Murnane. New York: Russell Sage Foundation.

Card, David, and Jesse Rothstein. 2007. "Racial Segregation and the Black-White Test Score Gap." *Journal of Public Economics* 91(11): 2158-84.

Chetty, Raj, Nathaniel Hendren, and Lawrence F. Katz. 2016. "The Effects of Exposure to Better Neighborhoods on Children: New Evidence from the Moving to Opportunity Experiment." *American Economic Review* 106(4): 855-902.

Clark, Kenneth B., and Mamie K. Clark. 1939a. "Segregation as a Factor in the Racial Identification of Negro Preschool Children: A Preliminary Report." *Journal of Experimental Education* 8(2): 161-63.

———. 1939b. "The Development of Consciousness of Self and the Emergence of Racial Identification in Negro Preschool Children." *Journal of Social Psychology* 10(4): 591-99.

———. 1950. "Emotional Factors in Racial Identification and Preference in Negro Children." *Journal of Negro Education* 19(3): 341-50.

Coleman, James S., Ernest Q. Campbell, Carol J. Hobson, James McPartland, Alexander M. Mood, Frederick D. Weinfeld, and Robert L. York. 1966. *Equality of Educational Opportunity*. Washington: U.S. Department of Health, Education, and Welfare, Office of Education.

Deutscher, Max, Isidor Chein, and Natalie Sadigur. 1948. "The Psychological Effects of Enforced Segregation: A Survey of Social Science Opinion." *Journal of Psychology* 26(2): 259-87.

Hanushek, Eric A., and Steven G. Rivkin. 2007. "School Quality and the Black-White Achievement Gap." Working Paper 12651. Cambridge, Mass.: National Bureau of Economic Research.

Ho, Andrew D., and Sean F. Reardon. 2012. "Estimating Achievement Gaps from Test Scores Reported in Ordinal 'Proficiency' Categories." *Journal of Educational and Behavioral Statistics* 37(4): 489-517.

Johnson, Rucker C. 2011. "Long-Run Impacts of School Desegregation and School Quality on Adult Attainments." Working Paper 16664. Cambridge, Mass.: National Bureau of Economic Research.

Kahlenberg, Richard D. 2006. "A New Way on School Integration." New York: The Century Foundation.

Kozol, Jonathan. 1991. *Savage Inequalities: Children in America's Schools*. New York: Crown.

Lankford, Hamilton, Susanna Loeb, and James Wycoff. 2002. "Teacher Sorting and the Plight of Urban Schools: A Descriptive Analysis." *Educational Evaluation and Policy Analysis* 24(1): 37-62.

Logan, John R. 2011. "Separate and Unequal: The Neighborhood Gap for Blacks, Hispanics, and Asians in Metropolitan America." US2010 Project: Brown University and Russell Sage Foundation. Providence, R.I.: Brown University.

Page, Scott E. 2008. *The Difference: How the Power of Diversity Creates Better Groups, Firms, Schools, and Societies*. Princeton, N.J.: Princeton University Press.

Pattillo, Mary. 2013. *Black Picket Fences: Privilege and Peril Among the Black Middle Class*. Chicago: University of Chicago Press.

Pettigrew, Thomas F., and Linda R. Tropp. 2006. "A Meta-analytic Test of Intergroup Contact Theory." *Journal of Personality and Social Psychology* 90(5): 751.

Reardon, Sean F., Lindsay Fox, and Joseph Townsend. 2015. "Neighborhood Income Composition by Race and Income, 1990-2009." *Annals of the American Academy of Political and Social Science* 660(1): 78-97.

Reardon, Sean F., and Andrew D. Ho. 2015. "Practical Issues in Estimating Achievement Gaps from Coarsened Data." *Journal of Educational and Behavioral Statistics* 40(2): 158-89.

Reardon, Sean F., and Lori Rhodes. 2011. "The Effects of Socioeconomic School Integration Policies on Racial School Segregation." in *Integrating Schools in a Changing Society*, edited by Erica

Frankenberg and Elizabeth DeBray. Chapel Hill: University of North Carolina Press.

Reardon, Sean F., and John T. Yun. 2001. "Suburban Racial Change and Suburban School Segregation, 1987–1995." *Sociology of Education* 74(2): 79–101.

Reardon, Sean F., John T. Yun, and Tamela McNulty Eitle. 2000. "The Changing Structure of School Segregation: Measurement and Evidence of Multi-racial Metropolitan Area School Segregation, 1989–1995." *Demography* 37(3): 351–64.

Reardon, Sean F., John T. Yun, and Michal Kurlaender. 2006. "Implications of Income-Based School Assignment Policies for Racial School Segregation." *Educational Evaluation and Policy Analysis* 28(1): 49–75.

Sampson, Robert J., Patrick Sharkey, and Stephen W. Raudenbush. 2008. "Durable Effects of Concentrated Disadvantage on Verbal Ability Among African-American Children." *Proceedings of the National Academy of Sciences* 105(3): 845–52.

Saporito, Salvatore, and Deneesh Sohoni. 2006. "Coloring Outside the Lines: Racial Segregation in Public Schools and Their Attendance Boundaries." *Sociology of Education* 79(2): 81–105.

———. 2007. "Mapping Educational Inequality: Concentrations of Poverty Among Poor and Minority Students in Public Schools." *Social Forces* 85(3): 1227–53.

Sharkey, Patrick. 2010. "The Acute Effect of Local Homicides on Children's Cognitive Performance." *Proceedings of the National Academy of Sciences* 107(26): 11733–38.

———. 2014. "Spatial Segmentation and the Black Middle Class." *American Journal of Sociology* 119(4): 903–54.

Stroub, Kori J., and Meredith P. Richards. 2013. "From Resegregation to Reintegration: Trends in the Racial/Ethnic Segregation of Metropolitan Public Schools, 1993–2009." *American Educational Research Journal* 50(3): 497–531.

Wodtke, Geoffrey T., David J. Harding, and Felix Elwert. 2011. "Neighborhood Effects in Temporal Perspective: The Impact of Long-Term Exposure to Concentrated Disadvantage on High School Graduation." *American Sociological Review* 76(5): 713–36.

Racial and Ethnic Gaps in Postsecondary Aspirations and Enrollment

BARBARA SCHNEIDER AND GUAN SAW

One major finding of the Equality of Educational Opportunity (EEO) report was that a smaller proportion of African Americans than whites reported "wanting to go no further than high school in each region of the country." Blacks in the 1960s had high college aspirations, and those aspirations have continued, but today, as then, fewer blacks than whites attend four-year colleges. Since the EEO report, the U.S. population has become increasingly diverse, and postsecondary aspirations and enrollment now vary considerably among racial and ethnic groups. Whereas the EEO report focused on the significant role of students' concrete knowledge about college in postsecondary attendance, it paid limited attention to variation in postsecondary preparation activities. This study contrasts earlier indicators of student college knowledge with college preparation activities to understand variations in college enrollment among different racial and ethnic groups. Results indicate that concrete knowledge has less impact on minority postsecondary enrollment than taking more-advanced academic courses.

Keywords: educational aspirations, college enrollment, high school college preparation activities, Equality of Educational Opportunity report

Measuring educational aspirations in the 1960s was commonly viewed as the single most important factor in determining how adolescents made sense of their future plans and whether such plans were realistic or not. The sociologist James S. Coleman, one of the leading scholars of the time, along with other researchers viewed aspirations as having lifelong significance, influencing both career choices and future earnings (Alexander, Bozick, and Entwisle 2008; Andrew and Hauser 2011; Coleman et al. 1966; Morgan 2005). Aspirations were also perceived as an early predictor of social mobility for students whose parents had less than a college degree and worked in low-skilled jobs. As the amount of required schooling has increased for many occupations, researchers have had to adapt their understanding and the predictive value of that once highly valued question: how far beyond high school graduation did a student expect to continue his or her education? Today aspirations in and of themselves are especially less predictive of future outcomes in relation to college enrollment for

Barbara Schneider is John A. Hannah Distinguished Professor at Michigan State University. **Guan Saw** is assistant professor at the University of Texas at San Antonio.

This work is supported by the U.S. National Science Foundation (NSF), through Grant DRL-1316702, and the U.S. National Institutes of Health (NIH), through Grant 1R01GM102637-01 (Principal Investigator: Barbara Schneider). Any opinions, findings, and conclusions or recommendations expressed in this material are those of the author(s) and do not necessarily reflect the views of the organizations. Direct correspondence to: Barbara Schneider at bschneid@msu.edu, Michigan State University, 516B Erickson Hall, East Lansing, MI 48824; and Guan Saw at guan.saw@utsa.edu, University of Texas at San Antonio, Department of Educational Psychology, 501 W. Cedar E. Chavez Blvd., San Antonio, TX 78207.

multiple reasons, including financial constraints (Dynarski and Scott-Clayton 2013), inadequate academic preparation (Riegle-Crumb and Grodsky 2010), and lack of information regarding the college admission process (Hoxby and Avery 2012).

Although there are clear limits to the predictive value of aspirations, they are still considered an index of one's knowledge of education pathways and occupational choices, which are modified in turn by family, peer groups, and schooling experiences. More recently, models that use measures of aspirations to predict college status take into account a variety of high school factors, including students' achievement and subjective values, their exposure to and familiarity with college information, and their academic preparation while in high school. This focus on the contextualization of aspirations can be traced to Coleman's view, as articulated in *The Adolescent Society* (1961) and the *Equality of Educational Opportunity* report (1966), that adolescents' education plans are the consequence of the socialization process they experience in the family and during high school. This perspective has, in part, driven the analysis for this study.

In contrast to the 1960s, the transition from high school to college for today's students is a very complicated process; there are a wide range of postsecondary institutions to which a student can apply, multiple fields in which to study, and numerous financial aid programs to select from to support his or her ambitions. Furthermore, an increasingly influential societal norm—reinforced by policymakers and often referred to as "college for all"—suggests that everyone needs to receive some type of postsecondary education (Rosenbaum 1997). Most adolescents in high school believe that attending and graduating from college will make them more viable job applicants in an increasingly competitive labor market. A college degree is seen as the signal of employability and considered the minimum qualification needed for later financial as well as social success. Students rarely think about being overqualified or too educated for positions that require little of their knowledge, skills, or prior work experiences (National Center for Education Statistics 2015a). The college diploma could be thought of as the twenty-first-century driver's license that is flashed to travel, obtain money, and participate in civic life (for an analysis of civic participation among young adults, see Nie, Junn, and Stehlik-Barry 1996).

One of the major findings of the EEO report was that, in the 1960s, African Americans did not enroll in college at the same rate as whites. Although educational aspirations have continued to rise since the 1960s, these aspirations have not translated into actual postsecondary enrollment, especially for some racial and ethnic groups. Why is this so, especially since many high schools have significantly altered their programs and now offer more opportunities for students to learn about and be prepared for college? To answer this question, we compare EEO findings with results from analyses using the most recent national longitudinal data set, the High School Longitudinal Study of 2009 (HSLS:09), taking into account individual characteristics as well as concrete knowledge about college and academic preparation, which we suspect may influence postsecondary enrollment. Unlike the EEO report, which focused on black-white comparisons, our analysis examines the differences in college aspirations, preparation, and enrollment among the more diverse populations that now attend U.S. high schools.

COMPARING EEO FINDINGS WITH RECENT NATIONAL LONGITUDINAL STUDIES

It has now been fifty years since the EEO report, and reviews of its major findings suggest that many of the same problems that beset secondary school students then have continued. Despite high educational aspirations, black enrollment in postsecondary school continues to be proportionately lower than it is for whites. In 2012, only 36.4 percent of the black population between the ages of eighteen and twenty-four were enrolled in degree-granting postsecondary institutions, whereas for whites and Asians the numbers are 42.1 percent and 59.8 percent, respectively (NCES 2015b). Blacks are not the only minority group that proportionately fails to enroll in college. Hispanics and multiracial groups also enroll in postsecondary institutions in numbers lower than their proportion in the population would indicate —37.5 percent and 39.4 percent, respectively (NCES 2015b). To understand why this enrollment pattern has continued, we compare some of the student and school factors that were studied in the EEO report with similar items found in the most recent HSLS:09. Additionally, we include several factors that research has demonstrated to influence college preparation, such as taking advanced courses, to determine the relative importance of these factors in explaining variation in racial and ethnic postsecondary enrollment.

For example, a number of items in the EEO report tend to be overlooked but have recently been suspected of influencing college attendance. These lesser-known items comprise a set of subjective constructs that includes academic commitment, self-concept, effort, and resistance. Similar items can also be found in HSLS:09, and they are included in our multivariate models predicting postsecondary destinations. With respect to postsecondary knowledge, we also have comparable information regarding reading college materials, meeting with guidance counselors, and preparing for college entrance exams. One major difference between the two data sets is a measure of advanced-course taking, which in the EEO report is limited to students' high school program (college, general, or vocational), whereas in HSLS:09 we have access to the restricted transcript file that identifies the actual courses students took in high school. Although HSLS:09 is clearly not identical to the EEO sample, many of the items in both surveys provide enough of an overlap to justify making comparisons.

Several unique characteristics of the HSLS:09 data set make it different from other national longitudinal data sets and from the EEO sampling frame. First, HSLS:09 began early in the students' high school careers (the fall of ninth grade) and obtained a series of baseline information (for example, key covariates such as sex, race and ethnicity, and family background) that we use in our analytic models. In previous longitudinal studies—such as the Education Longitudinal Study of 2002 (ELS:2002)—each follow-up wave of respondent populations had its cohorts freshened so that the retained sample for each wave could be generalized to the population as a whole.[1] That is not the case with the HSLS:09, in which no sample freshening has occurred. Our analytic estimates are therefore only generalizable to the ninth-grade student populations in 2009 in the United States.

Second, the first follow-up of HSLS:09 was conducted in the spring of students' eleventh-grade year. The EEO sample was collected when the students were in twelfth grade. One of the reasons for the change in the HSLS:09 sampling period from prior national longitudinal studies was the ability to collect more accurate and earlier information on postsecondary plans and enrollment. Surveying in the eleventh grade makes it possible to obtain a more definite estimate of students' actual aspirations and plans without the confounding effect of the college application plans and outcomes typically occurring in the junior and senior years. Administering a second follow-up over the summer after high school graduation and in the early fall of that same year captures more precise measures of actual destinations immediately after high school graduation.

Third, this updated post–senior year survey from June to November following high school graduation identifies a wide range of categories for enrollment in various types of postsecondary institutions and schooling and training opportunities. Over the past thirty years, distinctions between pathways after high school have typically been reduced to more simplified categories, primarily focusing on two- and four-year college attendance (see, for example, Perna and Titus 2005; Rouse 1994). This new set of post–high school classifications consists of enrollment in: (1) a four-year institution; (2) a two-year institution; (3) a certificate or diploma program; (4) courses in a nonspecific

---

1. A freshened sample includes new participants added to a longitudinal sample plus the retained participants from the longitudinal sample used to produce cross-sectional estimates of the population of a given student cohort for each subsequent wave of a longitudinal data collection.

Table 1. Educational Aspirations of Eleventh-Grade Students, by Race-Ethnicity, 2012

	All	White	Black	Hispanic	Asian	Multiracial
High school or less	0.109	0.095	0.114	0.147	0.042	0.105
	(0.312)	(0.294)	(0.318)	(0.354)	(0.200)	(0.307)
Certificate/other training	0.063	0.056	0.066	0.076	0.050	0.072
	(0.242)	(0.230)	(0.249)	(0.265)	(0.217)	(0.259)
Associate's degree	0.103	0.103	0.084	0.121	0.057	0.104
	(0.303)	(0.304)	(0.378)	(0.326)	(0.232)	(0.305)
Bachelor's degree	0.274	0.303	0.224	0.232	0.263	0.288
	(0.446)	(0.460)	(0.417)	(0.422)	(0.440)	(0.453)
Graduate school	0.345	0.345	0.408	0.296	0.449	0.328
	(0.475)	(0.475)	(0.491)	(0.457)	(0.498)	(0.470)
Don't know	0.109	0.098	0.104	0.128	0.140	0.104
	(0.311)	(0.298)	(0.305)	(0.334)	(0.347)	(0.305)

Source: HSLS:09.
Notes: The entries are means and standard deviations (in parentheses) of individual-level data for HSLS:09 students who participated in both base-year and first follow-up surveys. Data are weighted to be generalizable to the population of ninth-grade students in 2009 in the United States. The racial status of a small number of students is identified as "other," including non-Hispanic American Indian, Alaska Native, Native Hawaiian, and Pacific Islander. They are included in the "all" category but not shown in the table as a separate group.

program; and (5) "other." Similar to the categories used in EEO, the third option is an increasingly important post–high school destination, particularly for students with limited financial resources. Often offered in two- and four-year colleges, these training programs (for example, early childhood education, computer technology, laboratory technician) can also give students the opportunity to take other college courses offered in person or online. This third option constitutes a category distinct from the first two options in our college outcome measure.

ASPIRATIONS AND COLLEGE ENROLLMENT

Since the 1960s, studies have shown that aspirations change over time and tend to edge downward as they become more realistic (Jacob and Wilder 2011). This would suggest that what Coleman found, at least for black twelfth-graders in 1960s, may have been confounded by macro-societal conditions at the time. There is some evidence to suggest this was the case, as Coleman argued that acquiring additional education beyond high school was an important mechanism for blacks to achieve social mobility. During the 1960s, a number of employment opportunities opened up for black graduates following the Civil Rights Act of 1964 (Chay 1998), including the teaching profession (Freeman 1977) and jobs within the federal government (Heckman and Payner 1989). These societal changes may have inspired twelfth-grade black students to aspire to a college degree at considerably higher levels than found in previous studies (Schneider and Stevenson 1999).

In the 1960s, 84 percent of all students expected to obtain some postsecondary education and would have been satisfied with any college degree, not necessarily a four-year or graduate degree (see Coleman et al. 1966, 283, table 3.13.6). Today the situation is quite different. The majority of eleventh-grade high school students within various racial and ethnic groups aspire not only to attend college but eventually to enroll in graduate or professional school (see table 1). Comparing aspirations across racial and ethnic groups, nearly half of Asians expect to attend graduate school (45 percent), followed by blacks (41 percent), whites

Table 2. College Enrollment in the Fall of 2013, by Race-Ethnicity

	All	White	Black	Hispanic	Asian	Multiracial
Not in school	0.306	0.272	0.365	0.365	0.115	0.338
	(0.461)	(0.445)	(0.482)	(0.481)	(0.319)	(0.473)
Certificate/other training	0.090	0.084	0.082	0.107	0.084	0.146
	(0.286)	(0.417)	(0.274)	(0.309)	(0.278)	(0.354)
Associate's degree	0.233	0.224	0.229	0.261	0.231	0.155
	(0.423)	(0.417)	(0.421)	(0.439)	(0.422)	(0.363)
Bachelor's degree	0.293	0.368	0.208	0.160	0.501	0.161
	(0.455)	(0.482)	(0.406)	(0.366)	(0.500)	(0.368)
Don't know	0.078	0.053	0.116	0.108	0.069	0.180
	(0.267)	(0.224)	(0.321)	(0.310)	(0.253)	(0.385)

Source: HSLS:09.

Notes: The entries are means and standard deviations (in parentheses) of individual-level data for HSLS:09 students who participated in base-year, first follow-up, and 2013 update surveys. Data are weighted to be generalizable to the population of ninth-grade students in 2009 in the United States. The racial status of a small number of students is identified as "other," including non-Hispanic American Indian, Alaska Native, Native Hawaiian, and Pacific Islander. They are included in the "all" category but not shown in the table as a separate group.

(35 percent), multiracial groups (33 percent), and Hispanics (30 percent).[2] Just as they did in the 1960s, blacks continue to have higher college aspirations than whites.

One major difference between the 1960s and today is that blacks were previously only more likely than whites to *expect* to attend college but in actuality did not enroll in college at the rate that their aspirations suggested. Coleman, using college admissions data from the Higher Education Branch of the Office of Education, showed that only 2 percent of the total postsecondary enrollment (including two- and four-year colleges and other types of higher education institutions) were black, whereas whites made up 95 percent of that enrollment and other nonwhites totaled 3 percent.

The proportion of blacks who enter college immediately after high school graduation has grown dramatically since Coleman's time and now has caught up to the rates for whites but not those for Asians (NCES 2016).[3] The situation is somewhat different when we examine four-year college enrollment. Four-year college enrollment patterns captured in HSLS:09 indicate that blacks (21 percent), Hispanics (16 percent), and multiracial students (16 percent) in 2013 are much less likely than whites (37 percent) and Asians (50 percent) to attend these types of postsecondary institutions (see table 2). There does not seem to be a racial or ethnic difference in two-year college enrollment, with the exception of Hispanics, who are more likely to enroll in a two-year college.

In contrast to the EEO study, which was a cross-sectional study, HSLS:09 tracks students' educational aspirations and enrollment over time. Figure 1 presents a longitudinal perspective on educational aspirations from high school (ninth and eleventh grades) to college enrollment status in the year after high school graduation for HSLS:09 respondents. Nearly 60 percent of high school students aspired to ob-

---

2. All comparisons in tables 1 to 5 have been tested for statistical significance, using Bonferroni adjustments, and are significant at the 0.05 level.

3. While these rates seem to suggest that race may not be an important indicator of inequality of educational opportunity, it is important to point out that blacks and Hispanics are more likely to attend two-year institutions, to enroll in remedial courses, and to have higher dropout rates and lower completion rates in these institutions than whites and Asians (Saw 2016a).

Figure 1. Educational Aspirations in Ninth and Eleventh Grades, and College Enrollment in the Year After Graduation.

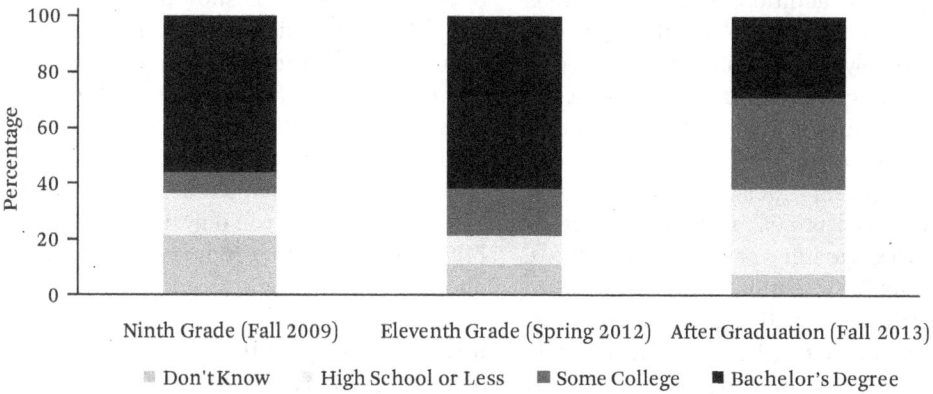

Source: HSLS:09.

tain at least a bachelor degree when they were in ninth grade and eleventh grade; however, only about 30 percent of them enrolled in a four-year college in the fall immediately after their high school graduation. Today the greatest mismatch between aspirations and actual enrollment occurs in four-year college enrollment (Roderick, Coca, and Nagaoka 2011).

In his analysis of the aspirations and postsecondary enrollment of black students, Coleman argued that the failure of blacks to matriculate could be traced to the fact that they lacked concrete knowledge about college, especially information on college requirements and programmatic offerings. Is this the case today? Recent studies have focused on randomized trials to study the impact of imperfect information and suggested that this may be the reason for lower college enrollment (see, for example, Castleman, Arnold, and Wartman 2012; Hoxby and Turner 2013). In the following analysis, we examine the issue of concrete college knowledge or imperfect college information and distinguish it from college academic preparation. We argue that academic preparation has become a major stratification mechanism, especially for low-income minority students, as nearly all high schools have instituted some types of programs to assist students in acquiring college knowledge and admission information.

COLLEGE KNOWLEDGE

Coleman did not view aspirations as the sole determinant of college attendance; he argued that, when determining behavioral choices, it is imperative to examine both objective and subjective measures (Coleman 1990).[4] Objective measures are those actions that demonstrate an individual's interest in and performance toward a particular outcome, such as grades. Subjective measures are individuals' perceptions about themselves regarding their actions and the actions taken by others, such as feeling good about oneself and feeling in control. Both of these types of measures are evident in the EEO items that were used to frame Coleman's analysis.

Coleman contended that certain "concrete" actions taken by students were critical for actualizing college attendance, including having ever read a college catalog, having ever written to or talked to a college official about going to college, and having definite education plans for the fall following high school graduation. Coleman showed that whites and Asians were more likely to have ever read a college catalog, regardless of their regional location, than blacks and Hispanics (who were the least likely to have read a college catalog). He also found this pattern to hold with respect to having conferred with a college official about attending college: here again, whites and Asians were the

---

4. This point is made throughout many of Coleman's writings and most clearly articulated in *Foundations of Social Theory* (1990).

most likely to have talked to college officials, and blacks and Hispanics the least likely to have done so. In addition, compared to whites and Asians, blacks and Hispanics were one-third less likely to report having definite plans to attend college in the fall following senior year (see Coleman et al. 1966, 284, table 3.13.7).

One of the major differences today is that students across all racial and ethnic groups have more exposure to college knowledge, including access to information on eligibility requirements for attending a four-year college and to advice regarding postsecondary options. Early in their high school careers, nearly 90 percent of HSLS:09 respondents talked to a parent, friend, teacher, or school counselor about attending college (see table 3). Blacks (93 percent) tend to do this more so than all other groups.

With respect to college eligibility—that is, taking advanced courses, having high grades, taking college admission tests, and receiving college recommendations from teachers or others—a higher proportion of blacks and Asians than whites and others *recognize the importance* of taking high school courses and college entrance exams, even if they do not actually participate in these preparatory activities (see table 3). With respect to actual participation, eleventh-grade black, Asian, and multiracial students are more likely than whites and Hispanics to report having attended a college tour, searched the Internet, talked to a counselor, or taken a course to prepare for college admission. Asians are the most likely to have taken a college entrance exam course and to have sat in a college class, both of which are highly related to four-year college enrollment.

What these types of measures fail to consider are the differences in resources that make such college exposure items translate into actual enrollment. For example, one of the most complex issues is securing financial resources to pay for college. Without proper information about the responsibility for and sufficiency of loans and scholarships, students may easily misunderstand how much college is going to cost. When receiving tuition and room and board information, students are often overwhelmed by the costs and sometimes have difficulty even understanding when their financial commitments are due. Another problem is Internet searches. Recent data released by the Pew Foundation show that low-income and minority students are less likely than whites to have access to computers, both in and out of school (Lenhart 2015). While students can search the Internet through their phones, unless they have access to computers to complete and submit college applications, surfing the Internet can only do so much. It is difficult to apply to a four-year college on a phone.

SUBJECTIVE MEASURES OF SOCIAL BELONGING AND ACADEMIC COMMITMENT

One of the major markers of adolescence is an increasing awareness of one's social and emotional feelings. Most adolescents experience to some extent increased feelings of stress, self-consciousness, and loneliness in high school, coupled with a general decrease in interest in school subject matter (Eccles and Roeser 2010, 2011). This is not, of course, the situation for all students. Both Coleman's analysis and most current surveys contain abbreviated measures of social and emotional learning. Some social psychologists maintain that blacks and other minority students feel a threat to their identity and feel that they do not belong at school (Owens and Lynch 2012; Steele and Aronson 1995). Coleman developed a set of key subjective measures on these points; for example, one item that could be construed as a belonging measure was "whether the student wanted to come to school." Other subjective items that could be viewed as measuring academic commitment included "if something happened and you had to stop school now, how would you feel?" and "[do] you [want] to be a good student?"

Using items that measured self-concept, Coleman found that blacks and Hispanics were more likely to have a higher overall sense of self than whites. Similar patterns are found today. Some consider this to be a racial paradox—that students who may do poorly in school still have a high self-concept—and some have suggested that these results may be directly tied to low teacher expectations (Ulrich, Wilhelm, and Hanna 2014). Teachers may

Table 3. College Eligibility Knowledge of Ninth- and Eleventh-Grade Students, by Race-Ethnicity, 2009 and 2012

	All	White	Black	Hispanic	Asian	Multiracial
Advice seeking (ninth-graders)						
Father/mother	0.815	0.824	0.831	0.785	0.806	0.837
	(0.388)	(0.381)	(0.375)	(0.411)	(0.395)	(0.370)
Teacher/school counselor	0.293	0.273	0.371	0.278	0.288	0.350
	(0.455)	(0.446)	(0.482)	(0.448)	(0.453)	(0.480)
Friends	0.526	0.539	0.497	0.490	0.592	0.578
	(0.499)	(0.498)	(0.500)	(0.500)	(0.492)	(0.494)
Parent/teacher/counselor/friends	0.899	0.896	0.930	0.887	0.902	0.906
	(0.301)	(0.305)	(0.255)	(0.317)	(0.298)	(0.293)
Knowing the importance of eligibility for getting into a typical four-year college (eleventh-graders)						
High school courses	0.640	0.605	0.710	0.669	0.725	0.626
	(0.480)	(0.489)	(0.454)	(0.471)	(0.447)	(0.484)
High school grades	0.870	0.852	0.893	0.894	0.868	0.872
	(0.336)	(0.355)	(0.309)	(0.308)	(0.339)	(0.334)
SAT/ACT	0.849	0.842	0.905	0.831	0.881	0.845
	(0.357)	(0.365)	(0.294)	(0.375)	(0.324)	(0.362)
Recommendations	0.535	0.489	0.602	0.592	0.562	0.556
	(0.499)	(0.500)	(0.490)	(0.492)	(0.496)	(0.497)
Exposure to college education (eleventh-graders)						
Attended a college tour	0.500	0.504	0.526	0.459	0.541	0.545
	(0.500)	(0.500)	(0.499)	(0.498)	(0.498)	(0.498)
Sat in on or took a college class	0.251	0.250	0.251	0.237	0.325	0.258
	(0.434)	(0.433)	(0.434)	(0.425)	(0.468)	(0.438)
Searched the Internet or read guides to research college options	0.796	0.813	0.827	0.724	0.852	0.820
	(0.403)	(0.390)	(0.378)	(0.447)	(0.355)	(0.384)
Talked to a counselor hired to prepare for college admission	0.125	0.101	0.185	0.140	0.160	0.121
	(0.331)	(0.301)	(0.389)	(0.347)	(0.366)	(0.326)
Took a course to prepare for a college admission exam	0.404	0.410	0.455	0.334	0.547	0.415
	(0.491)	(0.492)	(0.499)	(0.472)	(0.498)	(0.491)

Source: HSOLS:09.

Notes: The entries are means and standard deviations (in parentheses) of individual-level data for HSLS:09 students who participated in both base-year and first follow-up surveys. Data are weighted to be generalizable to the population of ninth-grade students in 2009 in the United States. The racial status of a small number of students is identified as "other," including non-Hispanic American Indian, Alaska Native, Native Hawaiian, and Pacific Islander. They are included in the "all" category but not shown in the table as a separate group.

provide messages to these students that they are doing fine and their work is acceptable when in fact that is not the case.

In terms of *academic* self-concept, Coleman used "how bright do you think you are in comparison to other students in your grade?" "feeling whether one can learn or not," and "would do better if the teachers did not go as fast." In general, responses to these questions were the same for blacks and whites; however, Asians and Hispanics had lower levels of academic self-concept (see Coleman et al. 1966, 288, tables 3.13.12 and 3.13.13). With respect to objective behavioral measures of academic engage-

Table 4. Subjective and Behavioral Measures of Eleventh-Grade Students, by Race-Ethnicity, 2012

	All	White	Black	Hispanic	Asian	Multiracial
Academic commitments						
School is often a waste of time	1.718	1.728	1.633	1.719	1.603	1.828
	(0.748)	(0.740)	(0.748)	(0.745)	(0.703)	(0.802)
Students with bad grades often get good jobs after high school	1.974	1.939	2.049	2.006	1.881	2.002
	(0.710)	(0.667)	(0.815)	(0.715)	(0.722)	(0.731)
Studying in high school rarely pays off later with a good job	2.170	2.038	2.411	2.324	2.072	2.187
	(0.939)	(0.876)	(1.036)	(0.953)	(0.956)	(0.941)
People can do okay even if they drop out of high school	2.197	2.156	2.301	2.198	2.146	2.317
	(0.841)	(0.836)	(0.849)	(0.842)	(0.822)	(0.832)
Academic self-efficacy						
Math self-efficacy (composite)	0.000	−0.016	0.150	−0.056	0.127	−0.055
	(0.998)	(1.011)	(0.964)	(0.958)	(0.931)	(1.067)
Science self-efficacy (composite)	0.000	0.022	0.123	−0.144	0.072	0.020
	(0.995)	(1.011)	(0.911)	(0.981)	(0.922)	(1.059)
Academic effort						
Hours spent on studying (per school day)	4.675	4.987	3.802	4.245	6.989	4.436
	(4.655)	(4.725)	(4.095)	(4.555)	(5.786)	(4.366)
Resistance (number of times in last six months)						
Late for school	2.755	2.418	3.067	3.282	2.446	2.935
	(3.205)	(3.007)	(3.172)	(3.527)	(3.150)	(3.257)
Absent from school	3.509	3.584	3.024	3.748	2.200	3.714
	(3.156)	(3.105)	(2.977)	(3.334)	(2.584)	(3.245)
Cut or skipped classes	0.754	0.602	0.708	1.116	0.566	0.806
	(2.090)	(1.842)	(1.931)	(2.572)	(1.821)	(2.232)
In class without homework done	3.262	3.371	2.715	3.280	2.819	3.611
	(3.495)	(3.543)	(3.100)	(3.537)	(3.163)	(3.744)
In class without note-taking supplies	1.292	1.314	1.336	1.205	0.978	1.415
	(2.634)	(2.635)	(2.610)	(2.607)	(2.402)	(2.796)
In class without books or reading material	1.097	1.122	1.060	1.068	0.917	1.151
	(2.264)	(2.280)	(2.199)	(2.268)	(1.954)	(2.362)
Put on in-school suspension	0.335	0.273	0.558	0.352	0.101	0.387
	(1.204)	(1.128)	(1.379)	(1.241)	(0.772)	(1.298)

Source: HSLS:09.

Notes: The entries are means and standard deviations (in parentheses) of individual-level data for HSLS:09 students who participated in base-year, first follow-up, and 2013 update surveys. Data are weighted to be generalizable to the population of ninth-grade students in 2009 in the United States. The racial status of a small number of students is identified as "other," including non-Hispanic American Indian, Alaska Native, Native Hawaiian, and Pacific Islander. They are included in the "all" category but not shown in the table as a separate group.

ment, the EEO items were fairly limited and included such questions as the number of books a student had read and if the student studied outside of school.

Today blacks remain highly motivated in school (see table 4). Asians and blacks are the least likely, compared to other racial and ethnic groups, to perceive school as a waste of time. Yet there is a major inconsistency: blacks are the most likely to feel that individuals with bad grades can get good jobs after high school, that studying hard rarely pays off with a good job, and that people can do okay without graduating from high school. These responses suggest that while blacks may not view school as a waste of time, their view of working hard academically rarely translates into better career opportunities. This may be related to their views on discriminatory hiring practices as well as misinformation on the benefit of receiving a high school diploma.

Blacks also have a higher sense of self-efficacy in math and science, but they are the least likely to report putting forth considerable effort in the hours they spend studying compared to all other racial and ethnic groups (see table 4). Similar inconsistencies between self-efficacy and effort are also found among multiracial students. Hispanic students generally show a lower level of self-efficacy on all of these items and report the least amount of time spent on studying. Regrettably, these findings are similar to ones in earlier national longitudinal studies (for example, Hafner et al. 1990).

HSLS:09 has multiple measures that could be viewed as indicators of a lack of school commitment and general resistance to positive school behaviors. These school resistance measures include: cutting or skipping classes; being placed on in-school suspension; being late for school; being absent from school; and attending class without completing homework assignments or with no note-taking supplies or reading materials. Hispanics and other multiracial groups appear to exhibit more resistant behaviors, including cutting classes, being in class without homework, and not being prepared for class, whereas blacks, Asians, and whites report fewer incidences of such behaviors. Asians consistently demonstrate the least resistance to school protocols and expectations and a greater tendency to avoid negative school behaviors.

WHAT IS MISSING?
These descriptive statistics suggest that the reasons why minority students fail to enroll in college are not entirely clear. For example, blacks have concrete knowledge of college admissions, have high self-efficacy, engage in relatively low levels of misbehavior, and value the importance of college entrance exams, yet do not proportionally enroll in college compared to whites, who sometimes do not show these same positive patterns. Looking back at ninth grade, blacks, Hispanics, and multiracial students are less likely to plan to take advanced courses in mathematics and to find it useful for college admission (see table 5).[5]

The value of college preparatory coursework has become a major policy lever for increasing college readiness at state and district levels. Many states and large school districts are identifying and requiring more advanced-level coursework, especially in science and mathematics (Jacob et al. 2015). The problem with this policy is that poorly resourced schools—those most likely to serve low-income and minority students—are often less likely to have teachers with the necessary qualifications to teach advanced courses in science, mathematics, and other core academic subjects. Additionally, many students lack the fundamental knowledge base to succeed in courses where the material requires earlier knowledge and skill proficiency (Covay Minor et al. 2015).

Using high school transcript data from HSLS: 09, we find that Asians and whites are more likely to be in highly concentrated academic courses than other racial and ethnic groups (see table 5). Blacks, Hispanics, and multiracial students take lower-level courses in mathematics. In fact, ninth-grade blacks are the most likely to be in math classes below algebra. And similarly, blacks are also less likely to have taken courses above Algebra I (25.6 percent) in comparison to whites (38.8 percent) and Asians (62.6 percent). Hispanics, while not the lowest in math level at ninth grade, fail to complete more than a second year of algebra through high school. At the very highest end, we find that blacks are the least likely to earn Advanced Placement (AP) or International Baccalaureate (IB) credits (earned by 23.7 percent

---

5. This same avoidance of math in forming college plans can be found in the first follow-up (calculations available from authors by request). These responses are particularly troublesome given that taking advanced mathematics in high school continues to show positive effects on earnings (Rose and Betts 2004) and, more recently, on mortality (Warren et al. 2015).

Table 5. College Preparation of Ninth- and Eleventh-Grade Students, by Race-Ethnicity, 2009 and 2012

	All	White	Black	Hispanic	Asian	Multiracial
College plan (in early ninth grade)						
Number of years of math courses expects to take in high school	0.613 (0.487)	0.687 (0.464)	0.491 (0.500)	0.519 (0.500)	0.731 (0.443)	0.573 (0.495)
Plans to take more math because will help to get into college	0.534 (0.499)	0.571 (0.494)	0.444 (0.497)	0.471 (0.499)	0.706 (0.456)	0.553 (0.497)
Plans to take more math because will be useful in college	0.483 (0.500)	0.511 (0.500)	0.424 (0.494)	0.431 (0.495)	0.621 (0.485)	0.491 (0.500)
Academic preparation (transcript data)						
College preparatory program	0.348 (0.476)	0.383 (0.486)	0.311 (0.463)	0.278 (0.448)	0.575 (0.495)	0.295 (0.456)
Highest-level math course taken by the end of ninth grade						
Below Algebra I (for example, no math, basic math, pre-Algebra)	0.150 (0.357)	0.138 (0.345)	0.201 (0.401)	0.149 (0.356)	0.041 (0.199)	0.166 (0.372)
Algebra I	0.504 (0.500)	0.474 (0.499)	0.543 (0.498)	0.574 (0.495)	0.333 (0.472)	0.518 (0.500)
Above Algebra I (for example, Geometry, Algebra II)	0.347 (0.476)	0.388 (0.487)	0.256 (0.437)	0.276 (0.447)	0.626 (0.484)	0.316 (0.465)
Highest-level math course taken by high school graduation						
Below Algebra II (for example, Algebra I, Geometry)	0.193 (0.395)	0.162 (0.369)	0.218 (0.413)	0.266 (0.442)	0.062 (0.241)	0.202 (0.402)
Algebra II	0.228 (0.420)	0.218 (0.413)	0.236 (0.425)	0.238 (0.426)	0.117 (0.322)	0.279 (0.449)
Above Algebra II (for example, calculus, AP/IB math)	0.579 (0.494)	0.620 (0.485)	0.546 (0.498)	0.496 (0.500)	0.821 (0.383)	0.519 (0.500)
Ever earned credits in AP/IB	0.364 (0.481)	0.395 (0.489)	0.237 (0.425)	0.329 (0.470)	0.712 (0.453)	0.339 (0.474)
Credits earned in AP/IB combined	1.170 (2.065)	1.250 (2.246)	0.634 (1.635)	1.015 (2.070)	3.315 (3.521)	1.091 (2.164)
Ever earned credits in college subjects	0.117 (0.321)	0.144 (0.351)	0.058 (0.234)	0.093 (0.291)	0.135 (0.342)	0.098 (0.297)
Credits earned in college subjects	0.224 (0.860)	0.280 (0.917)	0.103 (0.564)	0.166 (0.703)	0.223 (0.714)	0.246 (1.267)

Source: HSLS:09.

Notes: AP = Advanced Placement; IB = International Baccalaureate. The entries are means and standard deviations (in parentheses) of individual-level data for HSLS:09 students who participated in base-year, first follow-up, and 2013 update surveys. Data are weighted to be generalizable to the population of ninth-grade students in 2009 in the United States. The racial status of a small number of students is identified as "other," including non-Hispanic American Indian, Alaska Native, Native Hawaiian, and Pacific Islander. They are included in the "all" category but not shown in the table as a separate group.

of black students on average, whereas the average for all students is 36.4 percent).

It would seem that, even though minority students are receiving college information, that information alone is not enough to help them make a successful postsecondary transition. We argue that course preparation and information are key to college enrollment but have differential effects on the type of postsecondary institution a student attends. We argue that how college information is acted upon with respect to course-taking and other behaviors provides significant insights into how educational inequalities continue to manifest themselves at the postsecondary level. In the next set of analyses, we disentangle concrete college knowledge from academic preparation to understand how the allocation of resources may be undermining equality of educational opportunities for minority groups.

MODELING COLLEGE ENROLLMENT

The following multivariate analysis uses data from the ninth grade, eleventh grade, and 2013 update to predict college enrollment. Our analytic sample contains the 15,237 students who participated in all three waves. The outcome measure is both anticipatory and actual enrollment as of November 2013 in a four-year bachelor's program, in a two-year program, or in a certificate or other training program; not engaged in postsecondary education; and a category for those who reported that they didn't know what their status would be as of November 2013. Since the 2013 update survey was conducted from June to November 2013, we have included in our model a covariate for the timing of the students' responses. We include this category recognizing that some of those who responded with "don't know" might have been considering multiple options for their future plans. In the next follow-up survey, we will be able to unpack and determine a status designation for those in the "don't know" category. These students tended to be poor and minority, from non-intact families, and limited in their college knowledge, which may explain why they responded "don't know" (see table 6).

Another important category is enrollment in certificate and training programs; these students tend to have higher aspirations than those who are not attending any type of schooling after high school. For example, 25.6 percent of students in certificate or training programs reported that they wanted to attend graduate school when they were in eleventh grade, whereas only 16.6 percent of their non-college-going peers had that aspiration. These individuals had better academic preparation than those who stopped their education after high school. However, they had limited college knowledge (see table 6).

In our first analysis, we conduct a multinomial logistic regression with the omitted category "those students who do not expect by November 2013 to be in any school program (n = 3,877)."[6] The models contain demographic information, aspirations at eleventh grade, and subjective and behavioral measures. The two major dimensions we focus on are college knowledge (by which we mean exposure to college education) and college academic preparation. For those covariates with missing values (ranging from 0.1 percent to 4.6 percent), we created indicators to identify missingness patterns. Regression models are weighted using panel weights.

Examining raw differences among racial

---

6. We also conducted an ordered logistic regression that took into account the ordered categories of postsecondary education programs, from the lowest-ranked category ("not in school") to "certificate or other training" and "associate's degree," to the highest-ranked category ("bachelor's degree program"), excluding the category of "don't know." The results (reported in appendix table A1) basically do not change our main conclusions from the multinomial logistic regression reported in table 7. We chose to use results from multinomial logistic regression for two major reasons. One assumption of ordered logistic regression is that the relationship between predictors and ordered (ranked) outcomes is linear. That is not the case in our data as shown in multinomial logistic regression. For example, being Hispanic (as compared to being white) or aspiring to get an associate's degree (as compared with aspiring to obtain no more than a high school diploma) are not linearly correlated with the ordinal category of college enrollment. Second, multinomial logistic regression estimates allow for a more nuanced understanding of the association between individual or contextual factors and a particular postsecondary education group.

Table 6. Descriptive Statistics for HSLS:09 Respondents, by College Enrollment

Variables	Non-College (n = 3,877)		Don't Know (n = 1,001)		Certificate or Other Training (n = 1,269)		Associate's Degree (n = 3,420)		Bachelor's Degree (n = 5,670)	
	Mean	Standard Deviation	Mean	Standard Deviation	Mean	Standard Deviation	Mean	Standard Deviation	Mean	Standard Deviation
Demographics										
White	0.466	0.499	0.352	0.478	0.484	0.499	0.494	0.500	0.643	0.479
Black	0.164	0.370	0.204	0.403	0.125	0.331	0.136	0.343	0.098	0.297
Hispanic	0.253	0.435	0.312	0.464	0.254	0.435	0.249	0.432	0.124	0.329
Asian	0.014	0.117	0.031	0.173	0.035	0.183	0.035	0.184	0.060	0.237
Multiracial	0.089	0.285	0.074	0.261	0.087	0.282	0.078	0.269	0.069	0.254
Other race	0.014	0.118	0.027	0.162	0.016	0.124	0.008	0.089	0.007	0.081
Female	0.410	0.492	0.547	0.498	0.513	0.500	0.540	0.498	0.531	0.499
Socioeconomic status (composite)	−0.416	0.595	−0.336	0.680	−0.173	0.695	−0.101	0.670	0.134	0.340
Intact family	0.422	0.494	0.534	0.499	0.573	0.495	0.574	0.495	0.708	0.454
Non-intact two parents/guardians	0.242	0.429	0.169	0.375	0.171	0.377	0.180	0.385	0.125	0.330
Single parent	0.311	0.463	0.276	0.447	0.236	0.425	0.230	0.421	0.156	0.363
Other family structure	0.025	0.155	0.021	0.145	0.020	0.142	0.016	0.124	0.111	0.105
Education aspiration (eleventh grade)										
Don't know	0.128	0.334	0.179	0.383	0.108	0.310	0.093	0.291	0.062	0.241
High school or less	0.250	0.432	0.113	0.317	0.109	0.311	0.029	0.168	0.006	0.079
Certificate or other training	0.116	0.321	0.061	0.240	0.083	0.276	0.036	0.186	0.010	0.100
Associate's degree	0.130	0.336	0.120	0.325	0.159	0.365	0.122	0.327	0.030	0.170
Bachelor's degree	0.210	0.408	0.255	0.436	0.286	0.452	0.317	0.465	0.323	0.468
Graduate school	0.166	0.372	0.271	0.445	0.256	0.437	0.403	0.491	0.569	0.495

	Mean	SD	Mean	SD	Mean	SD	Mean	SD	Mean	SD
Subjective/behavioral measures (eleventh grade)										
Academic orientations (composite)	−0.359	0.989	−0.141	0.964	−0.139	1.014	0.057	0.974	0.282	0.926
Math self-efficacy (composite)	−0.154	1.028	−0.039	0.969	−0.060	0.990	0.040	0.973	0.222	0.965
Science self-efficacy (composite)	−0.099	1.014	−0.117	1.013	−0.031	0.924	0.046	0.997	0.179	0.984
Hours spent on homework/studying	3.428	3.826	3.781	4.068	4.073	4.197	4.636	4.410	6.725	5.324
Resistance (composite)	0.301	1.171	−0.031	1.010	0.003	0.928	−0.135	0.815	−0.260	0.786
Exposure to college education										
Attended a college tour	0.386	0.487	0.475	0.500	0.454	0.498	0.500	0.500	0.667	0.471
Sat in on or took a college class	0.156	0.363	0.216	0.412	0.208	0.406	0.292	0.455	0.363	0.481
Searched for or read college guides	0.673	0.469	0.800	0.400	0.799	0.401	0.861	0.346	0.932	0.252
Talked to a college admission counselor	0.116	0.320	0.149	0.356	0.111	0.314	0.131	0.338	0.113	0.317
Took a preparation course for college exam	0.294	0.456	0.358	0.480	0.375	0.484	0.407	0.491	0.549	0.498
Academic preparation										
College preparation program	0.113	0.316	0.283	0.450	0.256	0.436	0.357	0.479	0.626	0.484
Low-math pipeline (below Algebra II)	0.401	0.490	0.196	0.397	0.241	0.428	0.127	0.332	0.018	0.135
Mid-math pipeline (Algebra II)	0.281	0.450	0.280	0.449	0.286	0.452	0.267	0.442	0.111	0.315
High-math pipeline (above Algebra II)	0.318	0.466	0.525	0.500	0.474	0.499	0.607	0.489	0.870	0.336
Math standardized score (eleventh grade)	45.095	8.573	48.602	8.916	48.039	9.291	50.663	8.615	57.595	8.885
Earned credits in AP/IB courses	0.207	0.781	0.685	1.541	0.640	1.525	1.001	1.977	2.583	2.955
Earned credits in college subjects	0.075	0.463	0.112	0.521	0.145	0.556	0.277	0.993	0.394	1.139

Source: HSLS:09.

Notes: N = 15,237. AP = Advanced Placement; IB = International Baccalaureate. The entries are means and standard deviations (in parentheses) of individual-level data for HSLS:09 students who participated in base-year, first follow-up, and 2013 update surveys. Data are weighted to be generalizable to the population of ninth-grade students in 2009 in the United States. The racial status of a small number of students is identified as "other," including non-Hispanic American Indian, Alaska Native, Native Hawaiian, and Pacific Islander. They are included in the "all" category but not shown in the table as a separate group.

Figure 2. Predicted Probability of Any Postsecondary Enrollment (Including Certificate or Training Program) for White and Black Ninth- and Eleventh-Grade Students

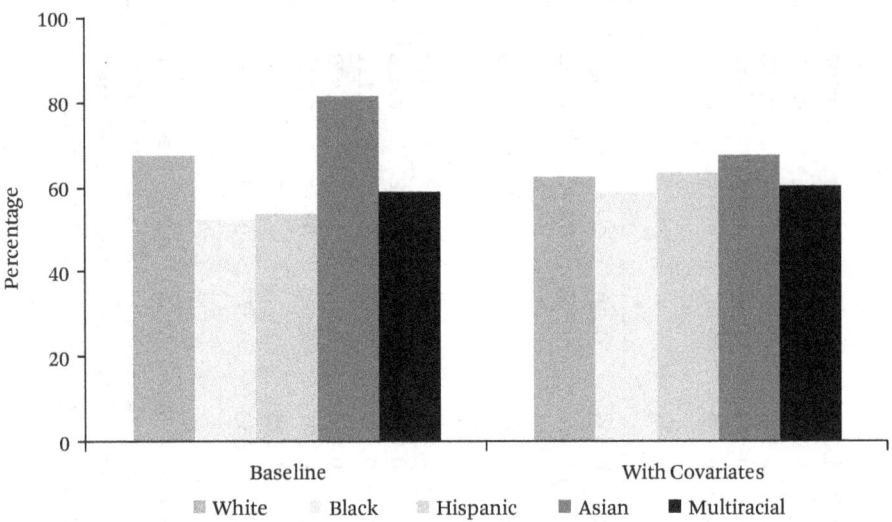

Source: HSLS:09.
Note: Models with covariates are the full models reported in table 7.

Figure 3. Predicted Probability of Two-Year College Enrollment for White and Black Ninth- and Eleventh-Grade Students

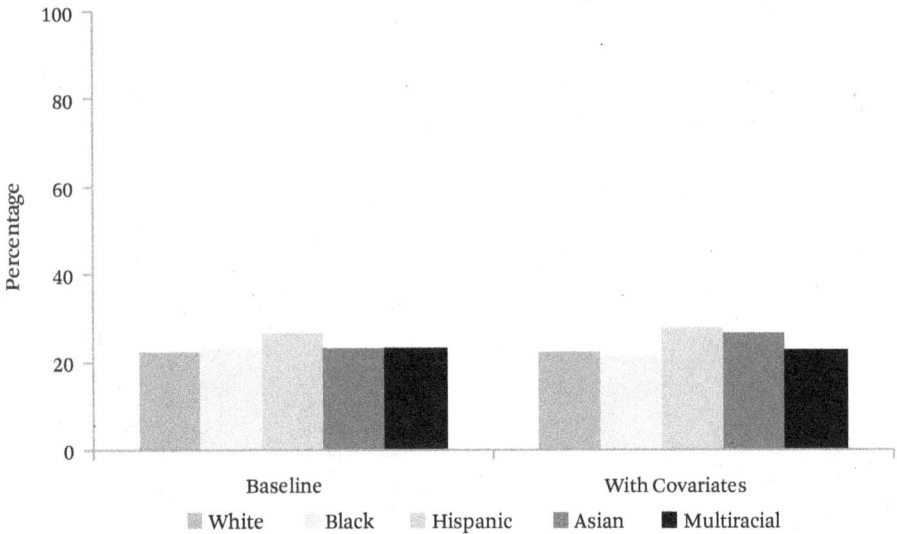

Source: HSLS:09.
Note: Models with covariates are the full models reported in table 7.

groups, blacks and Hispanics are less likely to attend four-year colleges. Approximately 21 percent of blacks would attend a four-year college, whereas for whites that figure is 36 percent (see figures 2 through 4). As shown in figure 4, the baseline difference in four-year college enrollment between blacks and whites is about fifteen percentage points. When adding demographic covariates, the difference is reduced to about 3.6 percentage points, sug-

Figure 4. Predicted Probability of Four-Year College Enrollment for White and Black Ninth- and Eleventh-Grade Students

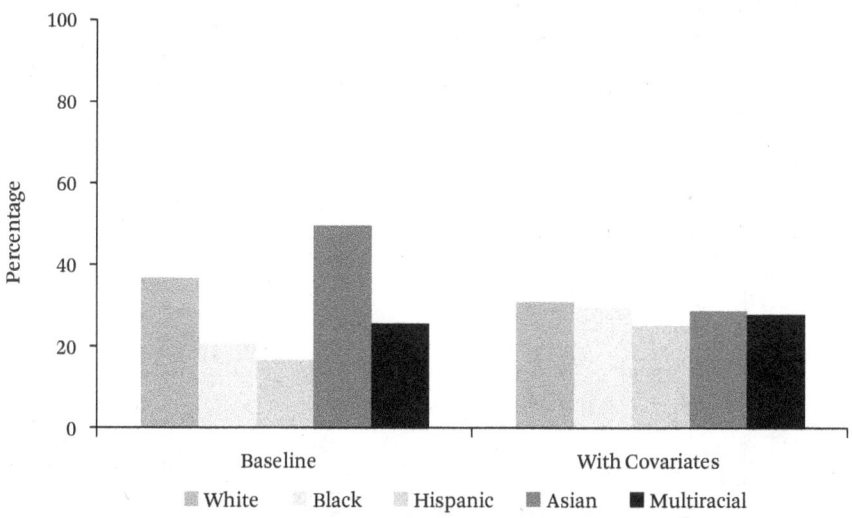

Source: HSLS:09.
Note: Models with covariates are the full models reported in table 7.

gesting that the black-white gap in four-year college attendance can largely be explained by individual and family characteristics. Similar patterns are observed for the outcome measure of any postsecondary enrollment (including certificate or training programs, two-year programs, and four-year programs).

It is important to recognize these baseline differences because, when we include covariates, essentially we are homogenizing individual and contextual factors that previously have been shown to be distinctive. For example, only 10 percent of black students are in advantaged families (the highest quintile of the socioeconomic status composite score in HSLS: 09), whereas 28 percent of whites are.

Table 7 shows results from our complete analytic model. When we estimate educational aspirations, exposure to college education, subjective and behavioral measures, and college preparation, then blacks are as likely as whites to attend four-year colleges. A similar pattern can be found for Hispanics. Overall, those who enroll in four-year colleges tend to have families with more advantaged resources and to reside in two-parent households.

With respect to aspirations, not unexpectedly those in more advantaged families tend to have higher ambitions. Those who aspired to attend a four-year college when they were in eleventh grade were nearly twice as likely to expect to attend graduate school. Four-year-college-goers are also more likely than students in the other categories to be academically oriented, although they tend to have low feelings of efficacy in math and science and they are less likely to misbehave. As for exposure to college, we find that students in four-year colleges are more likely to have taken college tours, searched college guides, or taken a college entrance preparation course. For example, compared with high school graduates who never went on a college tour, the predicted probability of enrolling in a four-year college for those who did go on a college tour increases from 26.5 percent to 31.7 percent (odds ratio = 1.628, $p < 0.001$). Students in associate's degree programs tend to have taken a college class; we suspect that this may be the consequence of dual enrollment opportunities in all types of high schools and that these classes were not necessarily rigorous in their content (Marken et al. 2013). However, it is students in two- and four-year college programs who are the most academically prepared, who took more academic courses in high school, and who took at least one advanced math course and received college

Table 7. Odds Ratios for Multinomial Logit Models Predicting College Enrollment for HSLS:09 Respondents

	Don't Know (n = 1,001)		Certificate or Other Training (n = 1,269)		Associate's Degree (n = 3,420)		Bachelor's Degree (n = 5,670)	
Demographics								
Black (reference = white)	1.921***	(0.346)	0.967	(0.176)	1.109	(0.137)	1.183	(0.224)
Hispanic (reference = white)	1.849***	(0.329)	1.332†	(0.212)	1.396*	(0.183)	0.867	(0.138)
Asian (reference = white)	1.946*	(0.548)	1.924*	(0.530)	1.607*	(0.322)	1.305	(0.279)
Multiracial (reference = white)	1.148	(0.307)	1.058	(0.185)	0.972	(0.121)	0.848	(0.123)
Other race (reference = white)	3.271*	(1.555)	1.283	(0.514)	0.720	(0.265)	0.703	(0.370)
Female (reference = male)	1.449**	(0.187)	1.304*	(0.139)	1.269**	(0.101)	1.165†	(0.095)
Socioeconomic status	1.131	(0.103)	1.525***	(0.150)	1.524***	(0.102)	2.497***	(0.168)
Non-intact two parents/guardians (reference = intact)	0.641**	(0.095)	0.624***	(0.080)	0.723**	(0.075)	0.650**	(0.098)
Single parent (reference = intact)	0.804	(0.133)	0.776*	(0.095)	0.836†	(0.079)	0.812†	(0.087)
Other family structure (reference = intact)	1.081	(0.403)	0.877	(0.349)	0.815	(0.223)	0.675	(0.176)
Education aspiration (reference = high school or less)								
Don't know	2.255***	(0.554)	1.369	(0.326)	3.760***	(0.690)	5.232***	(1.547)
Certificate or other training	0.855	(0.238)	1.305	(0.334)	1.797**	(0.392)	1.550	(0.557)
Associate's degree	1.425	(0.381)	2.052**	(0.494)	4.935***	(1.008)	3.349***	(1.065)
Bachelor's degree	1.541*	(0.328)	1.784**	(0.405)	5.391***	(0.985)	8.559***	(2.474)
Graduate school	1.758***	(0.366)	1.881**	(0.454)	7.463***	(1.374)	11.708***	(3.463)

Subjective/behavioral measures								
Academic orientations	1.067	(0.064)	1.069	(0.060)	1.176***	(0.052)	1.289***	(0.062)
Math self-efficacy	0.982	(0.059)	0.994	(0.053)	0.958	(0.047)	0.915†	(0.046)
Science self-efficacy	0.864†	(0.071)	0.945	(0.047)	0.915†	(0.044)	0.869**	(0.039)
Hours spent on homework/studying	0.978	(0.016)	0.993	(0.013)	0.991	(0.011)	1.015	(0.012)
Resistance	0.843*	(0.059)	0.877**	(0.042)	0.827***	(0.036)	0.803***	(0.041)
Exposure to college education								
Attended a college tour	1.144	(0.138)	1.074	(0.111)	1.124	(0.091)	1.628***	(0.162)
Sat in on or took a college class	1.070	(0.157)	1.018	(0.124)	1.274*	(0.131)	1.201†	(0.130)
Searched for or read college guides	1.166	(0.199)	1.246	(0.172)	1.291*	(0.151)	1.571***	(0.202)
Talked to a college admission counselor	1.250	(0.254)	0.920	(0.168)	1.180	(0.150)	1.175	(0.170)
Took a preparation course for college exam	1.016	(0.130)	1.136	(0.153)	1.053	(0.097)	1.423***	(0.135)
Academic preparation								
College preparation program	1.619**	(0.274)	1.592***	(0.213)	1.699***	(0.205)	2.267***	(0.281)
Low-math pipeline (reference = Algebra II)	0.629**	(0.111)	0.761†	(0.118)	0.510***	(0.069)	0.248***	(0.054)
High-math pipeline (reference = Algebra II)	1.023	(0.165)	0.908	(0.120)	0.964	(0.100)	1.237	(0.164)
Math standardized score (eleventh grade)	1.024**	(0.009)	1.002	(0.007)	1.021***	(0.006)	1.058***	(0.006)
Log(AP/IB credits)	1.563***	(0.194)	1.553***	(0.197)	1.539***	(0.174)	2.266***	(0.242)
Log(college credits)	0.962	(0.199)	1.296	(0.266)	1.566**	(0.245)	1.494*	(0.244)

Source: HSLS:09.

Notes: N = 15,237. AP = Advanced Placement; IB = International Baccalaureate. "High school or less" is the reference group (n = 3,877). In addition to the predictors, indicators for participants with missing values on each covariate and dummy variables indicating the timing of the students' responses on college enrollment status (by month from June to December 2013) are included in the regressions. Standard errors clustered by school are reported in parentheses.

†$p < .10$; *$p < .05$; **$p < .01$; ***$p < .001$ (two-tailed tests)

credit.[7] The predicted probability of attending a four-year college increases from 26.9 percent to 32.5 percent (odds ratio = 2.267, $p < 0.001$) for those students who graduated from a college preparation program in high school (that is, they completed four English credits, three math credits, three science credits, three social studies credits, and two foreign language credits).

In our final analysis, turning back to Coleman's findings comparing the college knowledge of whites and blacks and employing a model of both college exposure and preparation, we find that exposure is beneficial for blacks compared to whites. We also find, however, that the major determinant of college enrollment for blacks is preparation (see table 8). Table 5 shows that blacks are less likely to take more advanced math courses. When blacks have completed a college class in high school, they do not seem to gain the same benefit that whites do from this experience. Blacks are more likely to attend a two-year institution (the predicted probability increases from 23.5 percent to 32.8 percent; odds ratio = 2.535, $p < 0.01$), not a four-year institution.

What might be the problem here? One explanation could be that blacks have less access to financial resources and two-year colleges are less expensive, so they are more likely to attend these less selective institutions even though they have taken advanced classes in high school. However, we suspect that the reason lies with the quality of the courses that the students are taking. Recent analyses of high school transcripts have shown that black students are more likely to enroll in advanced-level courses that in actuality are less rigorous than their course title would suggest (Kim 2015). They also are more likely to fail these courses and take them again the first semester in college (Saw 2016a).

DISCUSSION

This study compares EEO findings on the postsecondary aspirations, preparation, and enrollment of young students in the 1960s with the most recent national cohort of high school students who participated in the HSLS:09. Similar to the EEO report, our results show that today's black students, along with their Asian peers, have higher college aspirations than white, Hispanic, and multiracial students. However, despite major reforms in the past five decades, we continue to find gaps between whites and Asians and blacks and other minority groups (Hispanic and multiracial) regarding four-year college enrollment. While one-third of whites and half of Asians enroll in four-year colleges in the fall following high school graduation, that number is only about one-fifth for blacks, Hispanics, and multiracial students.

To investigate the factors influencing postsecondary enrollment, we build on and extend Coleman's ideas of examining the variation in college knowledge and subjective measures of social belonging and academic commitment among racial and ethnic groups. The multivariate models we conduct analyze HSLS:09 survey and transcript data, including measures of academic preparation, which were omitted in the EEO study. Results from our models show that school interventions designed to increase students' knowledge about postsecondary education, such as meeting a college admission counselor and taking a college class while in high school, have little impact on college enrollment. Instead, we find that academic preparation, such as completing a set of college preparation curricula or earning AP and IB credits, is a powerful predictor for college matriculation. Given the importance of academic preparation in determining postsecondary enrollment, we also find that black, Hispanic, and multiracial students, who are underrepresented in higher education, appear to have completed fewer of these academic preparation activities. These results suggest that it is the stratification of the learning opportunities that students experience in school rather than their personal effort that is the major factor impacting their transition from high school to college.

---

7. The findings are consistent with another set of important studies by Coleman and his colleagues (Coleman and Hoffer 1987; Coleman, Hoffer, and Kilgore 1982) and later work by other scholars (Bryk, Lee, and Holland 1993; Lee et al. 1998) showing that the advantages of Catholic schooling can primarily be attributed to its constrained academic organization and more rigorous curriculum.

Table 8. Interaction Effects: Odds Ratios for Multinomial Logit Models Predicting College Enrollment for HSLS:09 Respondents

	Don't Know (n = 1,001)		Certificate or Other Training (n = 1,269)		Associate's Degree (n = 3,420)		Bachelor's Degree (n = 5,670)	
Demographics								
Black (reference = white)	0.956	(0.957)	5.608	(6.178)	1.342	(1.342)	0.745	(0.745)
Exposure to college education								
Attended a college tour	1.156	(0.156)	1.151	(0.130)	1.116	(0.091)	1.537***	(0.148)
Attended a college tour-by-black	1.003	(0.303)	0.569	(0.226)	1.043	(0.239)	1.904†	(0.682)
Sat in on or took a college class	0.874	(0.148)	0.922	(0.118)	1.057	(0.110)	1.055	(0.116)
Sat in on or took a college class-by-black	2.155†	(0.856)	1.505	(0.661)	2.535**	(0.741)	1.778†	(0.568)
Searched for or read college guides	1.221	(0.228)	1.203	(0.174)	1.252†	(0.148)	1.410*	(0.196)
Searched for or read college guides-by-black	0.814	(0.290)	0.948	(0.559)	1.098	(0.434)	2.144	(1.004)
Talked to a college admission counselor	1.379	(0.315)	0.982	(0.209)	1.223	(0.172)	1.273	(0.202)
Talked to a college admission counselor-by-black	0.735	(0.316)	0.736	(0.290)	0.798	(0.261)	0.600	(0.247)
Took a preparation course for college exam	0.936	(0.127)	1.117	(0.128)	0.972	(0.083)	1.402***	(0.135)
Took a preparation course for college exam-by-black	1.525	(0.507)	1.136	(0.707)	1.696†	(0.480)	0.906	(0.290)
Academic preparation								
College preparation program	1.715**	(0.316)	1.591***	(0.217)	1.603***	(0.194)	2.108***	(0.274)
College preparation program-by-black	0.699	(0.331)	0.819	(0.346)	1.117	(0.439)	1.476	(0.585)
Low-math pipeline (reference = Algebra II)	0.603**	(0.117)	0.739†	(0.118)	0.500***	(0.069)	0.285***	(0.056)
Low-math pipeline (reference = Algebra II)-by-black	1.284	(0.598)	1.615	(0.783)	1.587	(0.567)	0.565	(0.347)
High-math pipeline (reference = Algebra II)	0.908	(0.168)	0.806	(0.106)	0.833†	(0.089)	1.412**	(0.171)
High-math pipeline (reference = Algebra II)-by-black	1.597	(0.703)	2.119	(0.970)	2.419**	(0.748)	0.334*	(0.183)
Math standardized score (eleventh grade)	1.024**	(0.009)	1.009	(0.007)	1.027***	(0.006)	1.063***	(0.006)
Math standardized score (eleventh grade)-by-black	1.009	(0.023)	0.956*	(0.022)	0.972†	(0.016)	0.999	(0.019)
Log(AP/IB credits)	1.487***	(0.200)	1.532***	(0.194)	1.561***	(0.175)	2.261***	(0.236)
Log(AP/IB credits)-by-black	1.435	(0.550)	1.207	(0.572)	1.001	(0.353)	1.088	(0.368)
Log(college credits)	1.188	(0.244)	1.463†	(0.293)	1.835***	(0.264)	1.670**	(0.264)
Log(college credits)-by-black	0.134*	(0.119)	0.232*	(0.147)	0.296**	(0.132)	0.369*	(0.181)

Source: HSLS:09.

Notes: N = 15,237. AP = Advanced Placement; IB = International Baccalaureate. "High school or less" is the reference group (n = 3,877). All other covariates used in table 7 are included in the model. In addition to the predictors, indicators for participants with missing values on each covariate are included in the regressions. Standard errors clustered by school are reported in parentheses.

†$p < .10$; *$p < .05$; **$p < .01$; ***$p < .001$ (two-tailed tests)

Similar to prior studies, our models estimating college enrollment control for a comprehensive set of individual, family, and school factors. Such a multivariate modeling strategy can provide empirical evidence on the relative importance of certain factors in influencing college-going outcomes. However, homogenizing individual and contextual factors that have been shown to be different across racial and ethnic groups runs the risk of overlooking the inequality in college enrollment based on social and racial status. Hence, we highlight the baseline differences in postsecondary attendance, which show that at the group level the gap in college enrollment between advantaged groups (white and Asian) and disadvantaged groups (black, Hispanic, and multiracial) persists.

With or without controls, our findings need to be interpreted with some cautionary limitations. The college outcome measure used in this study is limited to the immediate postsecondary enrollment status following high school graduation. It does not capture the delayed college-going behaviors that tend to be found among students from minority groups and low-income families. Our analyses do not include outcome measures on college persistence and graduation. Racial and ethnic gaps in college completion could be larger than the gaps assessed at initial postsecondary enrollment. Another data limitation is that HSLS: 09 lacks measures of family wealth (such as household assets and debts), which might be an important confounder of our models. Prior studies have shown that family wealth has a strong impact on college enrollment, net of income and other measures of socioeconomic background (Conley 2001; Jez 2014). Dalton Conley's (2001) study shows that, when controlling for parental wealth, black students have a net advantage in the likelihood of college attendance.

Many interventions have been implemented to ease the transition from high school to college, especially for low-income and minority students (Schneider, forthcoming). These interventions tend to be of the college exposure type. And while many states have mandated that students take more advanced courses for high school graduation, somehow the implementation of these policies has not reduced the inequities in college enrollment among blacks and whites, as well as among Hispanics and multiracial groups. Why is this the case? Over the past several years, we have been examining differences in the course-taking patterns of students (Kim 2015), school characteristics that can undermine the implementation of policies (Saw 2016b), and larger macroeconomic conditions that have had significant impacts on schools serving low-income and minority students (Covay Minor et al. 2015).

We have found that in many low-income and minority schools, there are fewer teachers who are able to teach the more advanced courses in subjects such as math and science. To meet state requirements, teachers have to be shifted around, and sometimes the teachers in these courses are only provisionally certified. Moreover, teachers in these schools are more likely to be inexperienced and to leave after one or two years, creating an unstable school environment. Additionally, larger state financial crises have reduced general funds for education, and enrollment patterns in high schools tend to be quite unstable, with considerable movement of students throughout the academic year. Unfortunately, all of these conditions, which have implications for preparing students to transition from high school into college, have been more common for a considerable proportion of low-income blacks and Hispanics, who are more likely to live in racially and ethnically concentrated areas that are ridden with high levels of poverty and have limited social and economic resources.

Coleman had foresight in recognizing the importance of college exposure in explaining postsecondary attainment, but he overlooked the possibility that the curriculum would become so diversified by race and social class, with everyone now in the college track. College exposure is now a mechanism that one can find in nearly every type of high school regardless of race and ethnicity. What Coleman did not foresee was that variation in school quality, especially on issues of college preparation, would continue to remain so stratified among schools serving predominantly low-income black students and those serving mostly middle- and upper-class whites. We continue to have racial and ethnic gaps in college enrollment despite decades of reform primarily because those reforms have failed to focus on the core objective and subjective learning experiences that are crucial for transitioning to postsecondary education.

APPENDIX

Table A1. Odds Ratios for Ordered Logit Models Predicting College Enrollment for HSLS:09 Respondents

	Baseline Model		Full Model	
Demographics				
Black (reference = white)	0.642***	(0.073)	1.063	(0.121)
Hispanic (reference = white)	0.571***	(0.045)	0.923	(0.089)
Asian (reference = white)	1.999***	(0.245)	1.029	(0.119)
Multiracial (reference = white)	0.702***	(0.062)	0.840*	(0.075)
Other race (reference = white)	0.426***	(0.711)	0.783	(0.238)
Female (reference = male)			1.075	(0.057)
Socioeconomic status			1.736***	(0.076)
Non-intact two parents/guardians (reference = intact)			0.776**	(0.066)
Single parent reference = intact)			0.916	(0.061)
Other family structure (reference = intact)			0.819	(0.145)
Educational aspiration (reference = high school or less)				
Don't know			2.887***	(0.397)
Certificate or other training			1.441*	(0.257)
Associate's degree			2.593***	(0.390)
Bachelor's degree			4.069***	(0.557)
Graduate school			5.089***	(0.746)
Subjective/behavioral measures				
Academic orientations (composite)			1.150***	(0.038)
Math self-efficacy (composite)			0.955	(0.030)
Science self-efficacy (composite)			0.920**	(0.026)
Hours spent on homework/studying			1.012	(0.008)
Resistance (composite)			0.847***	(0.026)
Exposure to college education				
Attended a college tour			1.346***	(0.086)
Sat in on or took a college class			1.124†	(0.078)
Searched for or read college guides			1.245*	(0.109)
Talked to a college admission counselor			1.081	(0.093)
Took a preparation course for college exam			1.238***	(0.077)
Academic preparation				
College preparation program			1.617***	(0.126)
Low-math pipeline (reference = Algebra II)			0.528***	(0.062)
High-math pipeline (reference = Algebra II)			1.157†	(0.091)
Math standardized score (eleventh grade)			1.036***	(0.004)
Log(AP/IB credits)			1.653***	(0.096)
Log(college credits)			1.185*	(0.102)

Source: HSLS:09.
Notes: N = 14,236. AP = Advanced Placement; IB = International Baccalaureate. "High school or less" is the reference group (n = 3,877). In addition to the predictors, indicators for participants with missing values on each covariate are included in the regressions. Standard errors clustered by school are reported in parentheses.
†$p < .10$; *$p < .05$; **$p < .01$; ***$p < .001$ (two-tailed tests)

REFERENCES

Alexander, Karl, Robert Bozick, and Doris Entwisle. 2008. "Warming Up, Cooling Out, or Holding Steady? Persistence and Change in Educational Expectations After High School." *Sociology of Education* 81(4): 371–96.

Andrew, Megan, and Robert Hauser. 2011. "Adoption? Adaptation? Evaluating the Formation of Educational Expectations." *Social Forces* 90(2): 497–520.

Bryk, Anthony S., Valerie E. Lee, and Peter B. Holland. 1993. *Catholic Schools and the Common Good*. Cambridge, Mass.: Harvard University Press.

Castleman, Benjamin L., Karen Arnold, and Katherine L. Wartman. 2012. "Stemming the Tide of Summer Melt: An Experimental Study of the Effects of Post–High School Summer Intervention on Low-Income Students' College Enrollment." *Journal of Research on Educational Effectiveness* 5(1): 1–17.

Chay, Kenneth. 1998. "The Impact of Federal Civil Rights Policy on Black Economic Progress: Evidence from the Equal Employment Opportunity Act of 1972." *Industrial and Labor Relations Review* 51(4): 608–32.

Coleman, James. 1961. *The Adolescent Society: The Social Life of the Teenager and Its Impact on Education*. New York: Free Press.

———. 1990. *Foundations of Social Theory*. Cambridge, Mass.: Harvard University Press.

Coleman, James S., Ernest Q. Campbell, Carol J. Hobson, James McPartland, Alexander M. Mood, Frederick D. Weinfeld, and Robert L. York. 1966. *Equality of Educational Opportunity*. Washington: U.S. Department of Health, Education, and Welfare, Office of Education.

Coleman, James S., and Thomas Hoffer. 1987. *Public and Private High Schools: The Impact of Communities*. New York: Basic Books.

Coleman, James S., Thomas Hoffer, and Sally Kilgore. 1982. *High School Achievement: Public, Catholic, and Private Schools Compared*. New York: Basic Books.

Conley, Dalton. 2001. "Capital for College: Parental Assets and Postsecondary Schooling." *Sociology of Education* 74(1): 59–72.

Covay Minor, Elizabeth, Guan K. Saw, Kenneth A. Frank, Barbara L. Schneider, and Kaitlin Obenauf. 2015. "External Contextual Factors, Teacher Turnover, and Student Achievement: The Case of Michigan High Schools." Unpublished paper, Michigan State University, East Lansing.

Dynarski, Susan, and Judith Scott-Clayton. 2013. "Financial Aid Policy: Lessons from Research." *The Future of Children* 23(1): 67–91.

Eccles, Jacquelynne S., and Robert W. Roeser. 2010. "An Ecological View of Schools and Development." In *Handbook of Research on Schools, Schooling, and Human Development*, edited by Judith L. Meece and Jacquelynne S. Eccles. New York: Routledge.

———. 2011. "Schools as Developmental Contexts During Adolescence." *Journal of Research on Adolescence* 21(1): 225–41.

Freeman, Richard B. 1977. "Political Power, Desegregation, and Employment of Black Schoolteachers." *Journal of Political Economy* 85(2): 299–322.

Hafner, Anne, Steven Ingels, Barbara L. Schneider, and David Stevenson. 1990. "A Profile of the American Eighth Grader: NELS:88 Student Descriptive Summary." NCES Publication 90-458. Washington: U.S. Government Printing Office.

Heckman, James J., and Brook S. Payner. 1989. "Determining the Impact of Federal Antidiscrimination Policy on the Economic Status of Blacks." *American Economic Review* 79(1): 138–77.

Hoxby, Caroline, and Christopher Avery. 2012. "The Missing 'One-offs': The Hidden Supply of High-Achieving, Low-Income Students." Working Paper 18586. Cambridge, Mass.: National Bureau of Economic Research.

Hoxby, Caroline, and Sarah Turner. 2013. "Expanding College Opportunities for High-Achieving, Low-Income Students." Discussion Paper 12-014. Stanford, Calif.: Stanford Institute for Economic Policy Research.

Jacob, Brian, Susan Dynarski, Kenneth A. Frank, and Barbara Schneider. 2015. "Success for All? Estimating the Effect of a Mandatory College-Prep Curriculum in Michigan." Working paper. Ann Arbor: Michigan Consortium for Educational Research.

Jacob, Brian, and Tamara Wilder. 2011. "Educational Expectations and Attainment." In *Whither Opportunity? Rising Inequality and the Uncertain Life Chances of Low-Income Children*, edited by Greg J. Duncan and Richard J. Murnane. New York: Russell Sage Foundation.

Jez, Su Jin. 2014. "The Differential Impact of Wealth Versus Income in the College-Going Process." *Research in Higher Education* 55(7): 710–34.

Kim, Soobin. 2015. "Essays on Labor Market and Education." PhD diss., Michigan State University, East Lansing.

Lee, Valerie E., Todd K. Chow-Hoy, David T. Burkam, Douglas Geverdt, and Becky A. Smerdon. 1998. "Sector Differences in High School Course Taking: A Private School or Catholic School Effect?" *Sociology of Education* 71(4): 314–35.

Lenhart, Amanda. 2015. *Teens, Social Media, and Technology Overview 2015.* Washington, D.C.: Pew Research Center.

Marken, Stephanie, Lucinda Gray, Laurie Lewis, and John Ralph. 2013. "Dual Enrollment Programs and Courses for High School Students at Postsecondary Institutions: 2010–11." Washington: U.S. Department of Education.

Morgan, Stephen L. 2005. *On the Edge of Commitment: Educational Attainment and Race in the United States.* Stanford, Calif.: Stanford University Press.

National Center for Education Statistics (NCES). 2015a. "Digest of Education Statistics. Table 502.30. Median Annual Earnings of Full-time Year-round Workers 25 to 34 Years Old and Full-time Year-round Workers as a Percentage of the Labor Force, by Sex, Race/Ethnicity, and Educational Attainment: Selected Years, 1995 Through 2013." Available at: https://nces.ed.gov/programs/digest/d14/tables/dt14_502.30.asp (accessed December 28, 2015).

———. 2015b. "Digest of Education Statistics. Table 302.60. Percentage of 18- to 24-Year-Olds Enrolled in Degree-Granting Institutions, by Level of Institution and Sex and Race/Ethnicity of Student: 1967 Through 2012." Available at: http://nces.ed.gov/programs/digest/d13/tables/dt13_302.60.asp (accessed December 28, 2015).

———. 2016. "Digest of Education Statistics. Table 302.20. Percentage of Recent High School Completers Enrolled in 2- and 4-Year Colleges, by Race/Ethnicity: 1960 through 2012." Available at: http://nces.ed.gov/programs/digest/d13/tables/dt13_302.20.asp (accessed May 26, 2016).

Nie, Norman H., Jane Junn, and Kenneth Stehlik-Barry. 1996. *Education and Democratic Citizenship in America.* Chicago: University of Chicago Press.

Owens, Jayanti, and Scott M. Lynch. 2012. "Black and Hispanic Immigrants' Resilience Against Negative-Ability Racial Stereotypes at Selective Colleges and Universities in the United States." *Sociology of Education* 85(4): 303–28.

Perna, Laura W., and Marvin A. Titus. 2005. "The Relationship Between Parental Involvement as Social Capital and College Enrollment: An Examination of Racial/Ethnic Group Differences." *Journal of Higher Education* 76(5): 485–519.

Riegle-Crumb, Catherine, and Eric Grodsky. 2010. "Racial-Ethnic Differences at the Intersection of Math Course-Taking and Achievement." *Sociology of Education* 83(3): 248–70.

Roderick, Melissa, Vanessa Coca, and Jenny Nagaoka. 2011. "Potholes on the Road to College: High School Effects in Shaping Urban Students' Participation in College Application, Four-Year College Enrollment, and College Match." *Sociology of Education* 84(3): 178–211.

Rose, Heather, and Julian Betts. 2004. "The Effect of High School Courses on Earnings." *Review of Economics and Statistics* 86(2): 497–513.

Rosenbaum, James. 1997. "College for All: Do Students Understand What College Demands?" *Social Psychology of Education* 2(1): 55–80.

Rouse, Cecilia E. 1994. "What to Do After High School: The Two-Year Versus Four-Year College Enrollment Decision." In *Choices and Consequences: Contemporary Policy Issues in Education,* edited by Ronald G. Ehrenberg. New York: ILR Press.

Saw, Guan K. 2016a. "Reducing or Reinforcing Inequality? Evaluating the Impact of Postsecondary Remediation on College Attainment." Unpublished paper, Michigan State University, East Lansing.

———. 2016b. "The Impact of High School Mathematics and Science Course Graduation Requirements: School Academic and Social Organizational Factors." Unpublished paper, Michigan State University, East Lansing.

Schneider, Barbara. Forthcoming. "The College Ambition Program: A Realistic Transition Strategy for Traditionally Disadvantaged Students." *Educational Researcher.*

Schneider, Barbara, and David Stevenson. 1999. *The Ambitious Generation: America's Teenagers, Motivated but Directionless.* New Haven, CT: Yale University Press.

Steele, Claude M., and Joshua Aronson. 1995. "Stereotype Threat and the Intellectual Test Performance of African Americans." *Journal of Personality and Social Psychology* 69(5): 797–811.

Ulrich, Boser, Megan Wilhelm, and Robert Hanna. 2014. "The Power of the Pygmalion Effect: Teacher Expectations Strongly Predict College Completion." Washington, D.C.: Center for American Progress.

Warren, John R., Robert A. Hummer, Melissa Humphries, Chandra Muller, and Eric Grodsky. 2015. "What Aspect of Education Matters for Early Mortality? Evidence from the High School and Beyond Cohort." Paper presented to the 2015 American Sociological Association conference. Chicago (August 24).

Still No Effect of Resources, Even in the New Gilded Age?

STEPHEN L. MORGAN AND SOL BEE JUNG

The Coleman Report argued that family background is a fundamental cause of educational outcomes, while demonstrating the weak predictive power of variation in expenditures and facilities. This paper investigates the effects of family background, expenditures, and the conditions of school facilities for the public high school class of 2004, first sampled in 2002 for the Education Longitudinal Study and then followed up in 2004, 2006, and 2012. The results demonstrate that expenditures and related school inputs have very weak associations not only with test scores in the sophomore and senior years of high school but also with high school graduation and subsequent college entry. Only for postsecondary educational attainment do we find any meaningful predictive power for expenditures, and here half of the association can be adjusted away by school-level differences in average family background. Altogether, expenditures and facilities have much smaller associations with secondary and postsecondary outcomes than many scholars and policy advocates assume. The overall conclusion of the Coleman Report—that family background is far and away the most important determinant of educational achievement and attainment—is as convincing today as it was fifty years ago.

Keywords: family background, resources, expenditures, student achievement, educational attainment

In *Equality of Educational Opportunity* (EEO), James S. Coleman and his colleagues offered empirical results that continue to shape our understanding of schooling five decades later. Yet the structure of inequality has not stood still since the Coleman Report was published in 1966. In the interim, we have seen a growth of labor market inequality, including a soaring college-to–high school wage premium, and now a related explosion of wealth inequality. Both developments have altered the resource distribution available to educate new cohorts of children, and some evidence now exists that gaps in educational achievement have grown between the rich and the poor. At the same time, the intense concern with racial differences, which was the axis of inequality that gave rise to EEO, has receded somewhat, even though most of the differences considered then remain distressingly large now. Finally, changing patterns of family formation and immigration have created new patterns of racial differences in educational outcomes, demanding more refined analysis than can be motivated by templates from the past.

Atop this shifting terrain, the conclusion of EEO that was immediately most controversial remains in a similar position. Many scholars

Stephen L. Morgan is Bloomberg Distinguished Professor of Sociology and Education at Johns Hopkins University. **Sol Bee Jung** is a doctoral candidate at the School of Education at Johns Hopkins University.

We thank Joel Pally for his assistance in graphing the faux ELS. Direct correspondence to: Stephen L. Morgan at stephen.morgan@jhu.edu, Department of Sociology, 3400 N. Charles St., Johns Hopkins University, Baltimore, MD 21218; and Sol Bee Jung at sjung26@jhu.edu, School of Education, 2800 N. Charles St., Johns Hopkins University, Baltimore, MD 21218.

and policy advocates accept the conclusion that school expenditures and other inputs that are comparatively easy to change do not determine educational outcomes to a substantial degree (see, for example, Hanushek 1994, 1996, 2001). Other scholars and alternative policy advocates continue to doubt this primary conclusion, as well as most of the research that has generated more recent support for it, and rely on arguments first constructed in the 1960s and 1970s (for example, Baker 2012). These counterarguments are typically based on two primary claims. First, school expenditures and facilities measured at aggregate levels do not closely map onto the schooling inputs delivered to individual pupils. As a result, measures of district-level characteristics cannot, by their very nature, compete effectively for explanatory power with family background measures that reflect the circumstances of each student.[1] Second, even if such measurement concerns could be addressed comprehensively through a granular accounting of inputs into each classroom in the nation, statistical models estimated with observational data cannot deliver clear results on relative impact. Regression adjustments cannot solve the identification challenge produced by an empirical regularity known all too well: pupils who attend schools with the best facilities are the same pupils most advantaged in the home.[2]

Both sides in this debate can claim, without too much hyperbole, that policy has responded to their conclusions. The accountability movement, which culminated in and may well have been destroyed by the No Child Left Behind legislation, is consistent with the position that it is school management and school performance, not school resources and facilities, that must be fixed (see Hanushek and Jorgenson 1996). The accountability movement's recent transmutation into a campaign to incentivize teacher effectiveness is supported by the same arguments, ratcheted down from school performance to classroom performance (see Hanushek and Lindseth 2009).

Yet policy responsiveness has not been all on the side of the education reform movement. A corresponding movement to narrow resource and input differentials can also claim many victories, often in response to court rulings that have prompted state legislatures to act to ensure higher levels of base funding for schools, through so-called foundation programs. The success of this funding movement, which began before most observers date the successes of the accountability movement, has expanded the amount of funding from state tax revenue that is delivered to local school districts, complementing the growth of federal spending.[3] Many courts have now accepted the position that schools with the most disadvantaged students must be provided with substantially more resources than other schools in order to give their pupils a fair shot, through an adequate education, to meet the standards promulgated in legislative responses to the accountability movement (see Baker and Green 2009; West and Peterson 2007). State legislatures have been slow to implement policies in recognition of this new wave of funding decisions, but we may see new increases now that states are no longer able to delay the implementation of remedies because of weak tax revenues in the wake of the Great Recession.

The net result of all of this scholarly contestation and policy change has been a changing set of standards and inputs into schools.

1. See Carver (1975) for an early version of the argument, as well as Jencks (1972) for an early attempt to evaluate it. For the most widely read account, see Kozol (1992), which almost completely ignores the extant literature. See Archibald (2006) and Odden et al. (2008) for newer pieces in line with this argument, although motivated by the important goal of developing viable school-level resource measures.

2. For an early explanation of the argument, see Cain and Watts (1970) as well as the response by Coleman (1970). See Card and Krueger (1992, 1996) for discussion of the most heavily regarded attempt to support it by adopting an alternative design using state-level variation. See Nguyen-Hoang and Yinger (2014) for a recent attempt to sustain it by adopting a related approach.

3. See figure 21.1 in Corcoran and Evans (2015), which depicts real growth in expenditures from local, state, and federal sources. While expenditures from all sources have increased substantially since the 1960s, the growth of state funding is the most substantial.

School resource differences across particular districts and schools have fluctuated over time (see Corcoran and Evans 2015), but overall levels of resources have increased substantially. At the same time, the monitoring of students, teachers, and school performance is more intrusive than ever. It is reasonable to wonder, therefore, whether the claim that resources and inputs appear to matter surprisingly little has more or less support than in the past. And it is of particular importance if empirical support is accumulating that differences in educational outcomes are growing between the children of the rich and the children of the poor.

RECONSIDERATION OF THE EEO CONCLUSIONS

Initial replications of the EEO results, using what data were available in the years following its publication, were largely supportive of the claim that family background is vastly more important than school resources and facilities (see Jencks 1972, Smith 1972, and other chapters in Mosteller and Moynihan 1972a). Because the literature from the 1980s and 1990s did not substantially alter the support for the EEO conclusions, overview pieces in sociology that have reflected on the report have typically interpreted its conclusions as valid, while then considering the vast literature that has accumulated since its publication to document plausible mechanisms for the overwhelming predictive power of basic family background measures (see, for example, Gamoran 2001; Gamoran and Long 2007; Sørensen and Morgan 2000). Among the lines of scholarship that are particularly valuable for explaining within-school variance, which was perhaps first highlighted most carefully by Frederick Mosteller and Daniel Patrick Moynihan (1972b), a large literature has emerged to explain how effectively, and sometimes unjustly, public schools sort students into structural positions that either support or undermine their life prospects by distributing opportunities for learning differentially. The literature on curriculum tracks alone runs to hundreds of articles, chapters, and books.

Perhaps unsurprisingly, sociologists of education, who are the group of social scientists most heavily influenced by Coleman, have not given much attention to differences in expenditures and facilities in recent decades. This territory has been dominated by a different breed of social scientist: economists and school of education faculty who specialize in educational finance. Much of the conventional wisdom of this subfield is available in Ladd and Goertz (2015), where it can be seen that many of the same debates of the past live on, although at a much higher level of sophistication. (For example, compare Burtless 1996 and Ladd, Hansen, and National Research Council 1999 to Ladd and Goertz 2015.) Working sometimes as consultants in court cases and to state legislatures, some of these scholars have participated in the development of new funding formulas for real-world implementation.

Among the most recent attempts to reconsider the EEO conclusions, the results are a bit more variegated, leaving scholars such as Bruce Baker (2012) some scope to attempt to argue that school resources do matter a lot and always have. Norton Grubb (2009), through a book-length treatment analyzing the high school class of 1992 but using data from the eighth grade in 1988 through follow-ups stretching to 2000, shows that standard measures of expenditures continue to have weak associations with school outcomes, as in EEO. While developing this result, Grubb also asserts that school differences in practices and policies, such as the prevalence of curriculum tracking and innovative teaching, should be labeled school resources as well. And because these sorts of school resources have far more predictive power than dollar-denominated financial resources, he argues that his properly broad conception of school resources demonstrates that school resources matter a great deal. In particular, he writes, "Overall, these results firmly reject the simplistic notion that schools don't make a difference. School resources increase the explanatory power more than any other set of variables" (Grubb 2009, 69).[4]

---

4. Grubb's (2009) expanded resource categories are divided into what he calls compound, complex, and abstract resources. Some of his choices are, we think, nonsensical. For example, he demonstrates how students' cur-

Geoffrey Borman and Maritza Dowling (2010) reanalyzed a subset of the original EEO data, although without the crucial direct measure of expenditures from EEO that is no longer available. With a full deployment of multilevel models developed two decades after EEO was written, they make the case that between-school differences in the test performance of high school students are larger than was recognized for the original analysis as well as for the early replications, such as Jencks (1972) and Smith (1972). Still, Borman and Dowling do not substantially challenge the original conclusions, even though other scholars, such as Baker (2012), interpret their piece as claiming otherwise.[5]

Finally, not all sociologists have left the core controversy to economists and their colleagues in education schools. Jennifer Jennings and her colleagues (2015) have developed the case for an old counterargument to the possibly apocryphal "all family" conclusion of EEO. They argue that the effects of schools—and presumably resources and related inputs—are much stronger for levels of educational attainment than for performance assessed by standardized tests given in high school. This argument is most common in efforts to modify conclusions on the apparently weak effects of desegregation remedies, where short-run associations are downplayed in light of long-run benefits (see, for example, Wells and Crain 1994), but the argument is also present in the core controversy over the effects of resources (see Card and Krueger 1992, 1996).

If there is a consensus position now among that group of scholars not prone to over-interpretation, it is a decidedly begrudging one. Neighborhoods, families, schools, and diverse environments are all thought to matter, and resource inputs to schools can matter. Many articles take such a nested-spheres-of-influence approach to support the first point (for example, Altonji and Mansfield 2011). But it is the second point that is supported by perhaps the best four-page book chapter written in the field, which is the account by Richard Murnane and Frank Levy (1996) of a modest intervention in Austin, Texas, to boost resources and which shows how money can matter, but often does not.[6] And this is perhaps where the debate now stands, as shown in review pieces such as Plecki and Castaneda (2009): interventions to increase funding and resources can matter, and the task of future research is to determine when and how this can be made to be the case more frequently. With this fragile peace, the debate on policy reform can be continued, with the battle lines drawn between those who advocate for increased funding without substantial reforms and those who advocate for reforms to make existing funding matter more.

Although we have no fundamental objections to this consensus opinion, it does leave, we think, important empirical questions on the table, and ones that ought to be answered in a collection of papers that celebrate the enduring value of EEO. What the consensus does not resolve is whether an analysis, fashioned much as in the original work but taking advantage of the data now at our disposal, would still

---

riculum track placements strongly predict many educational outcomes (see his table B1), and he takes the position that track placements should be labeled a compound resource for a school. Decades of research demonstrate that family background strongly predicts track placement. Putting the predictive power of track placement in the column of a school resource effect rather than a mechanism for family background advantage or disadvantage is puzzling. In general, Grubb's semantic shift does not change the associations for expenditures, nor the endogeneity of his additional types of resources relative to family background.

5. Baker (2012, 1) appears to argue that their claim about the presence of larger school effects in the EEO data supports the inference that the effects of resource differences were larger than Coleman and his colleagues inferred. He cites a sentence from the abstract of Borman and Dowling (2010), without follow-up, and without noting that Borman and Dowling lack the expenditures measure that EEO and the early replications utilized. In fact, Borman and Dowling show that the "school" differences they reveal are largely due to average family background differences across schools.

6. The intervention is clearly in line with the call for experimentation, perhaps first issued by John Gilbert and Frederick Mosteller (1972).

show weak associations between expenditures and outcomes. A resolution cannot be found in reanalyses of the 1965 EEO data (such as Borman and Dowling 2010); in convincing studies that demonstrate that recent school effects, whatever their source, are larger for educational attainment than for test performance (for example, Jennings et al. 2015); in quasi-experimental assessments of state-adjusted studies that cannot cleanly separate changes in financing from other aspects of reform that occurred at the same time (Card and Krueger 1992; Nguyen-Hoang and Yinger 2014); or in innovative studies that are nonetheless geographically limited and lack information on students and their families beyond recorded eligibility for free and reduced-price lunch (Archibald 2006).

What we offer in this paper is a more deliberate approach to the analysis of the data at our disposal, casting aside the false claim that Coleman and his colleagues were primitive analysts whose work would not pass peer review in our current journals. In the empirical analysis to follow, we address two unabashedly EEO-style questions:

1. Across a categorization of race-ethnicity that can motivate an assessment of educational opportunity in 2015, what are the disparities in resources and facilities across regular public high schools in the United States?
2. Can these disparities account for differences in educational outcomes, measured during and after high school, or is it still the case, as in EEO, that family background appears to be of preeminent importance?

Although these questions are familiar, we have better data than ever before, and more perspective on what established methods can deliver.

DATA

For our analysis, data for students and their parents are drawn from the Education Longitudinal Study (ELS), 2002 to 2012. The base-year ELS sample is representative of all tenth-grade students in the United States enrolled in public and private schools in the spring of 2002. Additional school-level and district-level data, sourced from the Common Core of Data (CCD) for the 2000–2001 through 2003–2004 school years, were matched to the ELS data records, with the years for the match chosen to correspond to the four years in which the modal ELS student was enrolled in high school. (Note, as already implied by our two questions, that we will not be utilizing a data source that contains information on school differences before the tenth grade. We discuss the implications of this restriction in the discussion section.)

Analytic Sample

Among the original 2002 base-year ELS students, 84 percent participated in the 2012 third follow-up survey. Our models include the respondents for whom third follow-up educational attainment data are available, weighted to adjust for base-year participation, attrition across the waves, and item-specific nonresponse for educational attainment.

We exclude some additional students based on their schools. First, we exclude all students sampled in private high schools because the focus of this paper is the legacy of EEO for K–12 public schooling (and because we have no data on the finances of private schools with which to mount an analysis). Second, we exclude students in four public schools that did not have valid school finance data in the CCD. Third, following our own first-stage data quality assessment, we decided to exclude students in four additional public schools. One of these schools, we believe, was mistakenly included in the sample universe and should have been ruled out of scope.[7] The other three schools had what we regarded as implausible data for per-pupil expenditures from the CCD. Students from the first of this latter group of excluded public high schools were simply struck from the sample, since our retrospective decision was that they were not part of the universe of interest, as defined by the National Center for Education Statistics (NCES). Students from the

---

7. It is a school that when sampled was revealed to be a school solely in a local education agency (LEA) for special needs students, with very large per-pupil expenditures but medium-to-low educational performance.

other seven excluded public schools were dropped from the core analytic sample on which models of inputs and outcomes are based, but because they were part of the universe, they were retained for the construction of the analytic weight and made part of the underlying ratio adjustment for participation in the full panel sample. Our resulting weight therefore generalizes the results to these students as well.

With these school exclusions, our analytic sample is composed of 8,037 students, attending 559 regular public high schools. When weighted, the analytic sample is representative of all sophomores in public high schools for the universe selected by NCES, which excludes high schools that cater solely to vocational education students or special needs students.

Measures

Our outcome variables are standardized tests in reading (tenth grade in 2002) and mathematics (tenth grade in 2002 and two years later in 2004), on-time high school graduation in 2004, enrollment in any type of postsecondary education at any point between 2004 and 2012, and receipt of a bachelor's degree by 2012. We utilize family background measures constructed from responses to the parent questionnaires, which were completed by 85 percent of students' parents or legal guardians. When missing, we utilize available reports from the students' questionnaires and regression imputation for a small number of cases. The school survey administrator questionnaire yields ratings of school facilities, and the CCD supplies the student racial composition of each school as well as finance data at the district level. We introduce the details of particular measures in the course of presenting the results.

RESULTS

Racial Segregation in the ELS

What is the pattern of racial segregation in ELS schools? Table 1 presents a cross-tabulation of racial segregation where the eight rows represent a reductive, yet reasonable, categorization of self-identified race-ethnicity, as well as one embedded dimension of ancestry. It is the primary categorization of interest at the time of EEO, but now tuned to engage the growing interest in the educational prospects of the different types of students who claim Mexican ancestry.[8] (For readers interested in a less reductive categorization, we offer elaborated tables with twenty categories in supplementary appendix tables S1–S4. For readers interested in a broader discussion of segregation, see Sean Reardon's contribution to this issue.) The columns of the cross-tabulation are then the percentage of each student's school that is designated either "black/African American" or "Hispanic," calculated from the administrative reporting encoded in the school universe files of the CCD.

Subject to some measurement qualifications to be discussed later, table 1 reveals pronounced but unsurprising racial segregation. White non-Hispanic students attended high schools that on average were only 9.3 percent black and 6.3 percent Hispanic.[9] Asian students, who were disproportionately enrolled in urban schools and in the West, attended schools that were slightly more diverse: 13.7 percent of students were black, and 15.8 percent were Hispanic. In contrast, black students attended high schools that on average were 47.2 percent black, while Hispanic students attended high schools that on average were between 36 and 58 percent Hispanic (varying across the categories in the fourth through seventh rows of table 1).

8. The race-ethnic categories used for EEO were "Mexican American," "Puerto Rican," "Indian American," "Oriental American," "Negro," and "Majority or white" (see Coleman et al. 1966, 10, table 1, and throughout).

9. Non-Hispanic American Indian and Alaskan Native students attended schools that, on average, appeared similar to those attended by white non-Hispanic students. However, there are additional measurement complications for these students, owing to their clustering within a few schools in the ELS as well as the complex multiple racial identities expressed by students not in these few schools. We will therefore devote comparatively little attention to interpreting the patterns for these students.

Table 1. Racial Composition of ELS High Schools by Respondents' Self-Identified Race-Ethnicity and Immigrant Generational Status If Claiming Mexican Ancestry

	Mean Percent Black of School Attended	Mean Percent Hispanic of School Attended	N
White non-Hispanic, all generations	9.3%	6.3%	4,476
Asian or NHOPI non-Hispanic, all generations	13.7	15.8	986
Black or African American non-Hispanic, all generations	47.2	10.4	1,216
Mexican, Mexican American, or Chicano, first and 1.5th generation	11.7	51.4	183
Mexican, Mexican American, or Chicano, second generation	8.3	58.0	232
Mexican, Mexican American, or Chicano, third and third-plus generation	6.8	43.5	314
Hispanic ethnicity other than Mexican, all generations	18.4	36.0	430
American Indian or Alaskan Native non-Hispanic, all generations	7.5	6.1	156
Missing race, all generations	24.7	15.1	44
All	16.0	13.6	8,037
(Standard deviation)	(22.8)	(22.0)	

Source: ELS, 2002–2012, and CCD, 2001–2004.
Notes: NHOPI = Native Hawaiian and Other Pacific Islander. Data are weighted by the panel weight constructed by the data distributors (f2pnlwt), which adjusts for base-year nonparticipation and subsequent attrition, multiplied by an adjustment weight that we created to account for missing data on educational attainment.

Because of the importance of these patterns and their role in debates over the implications of EEO, we need to offer additional details of measurement. All ELS students who began the race-ethnicity battery of questions by self-identifying as "Hispanic or Latino/Latina" were then asked their ancestry. Those who selected "Mexican, Mexican American, or Chicano" were allocated to three immigrant generation groups, based on parental and student nativity as well as immigration history. Full details of the coding of immigrant generation are available in Morgan and Gelbgiser (2014). In brief, first- and 1.5th-generation immigrants are those born outside of the United States, with first versus 1.5th irrelevant for this paper but based on the age at which the student entered the United States. Second-generation immigrants are those who were born in the United States and have at least one parent born outside of the United States. Third-plus-generation immigrants are those who were born in the United States and whose parents were born in the United States as well. Finally, self-identified Hispanics who did not select the ancestry of "Mexican, Mexican American, or Chicano" were placed in a fourth group composed of seven separate ancestry groups, with no distinction made by immigrant generation, largely because of sample size constraints (see supplementary appendix table S1).

ELS students who did not self-identify as "Hispanic or Latino/Latina" were categorized by self-reported racial identity and sorted into the remaining categories in table 1, which, for the sake of brevity, we typically characterize in the text of this paper as white, black, Asian, and American Indian.[10] None of these groups are sorted by immigrant generation, and they are all reductive in ways that hide important variation in self-identification and lived experiences. Furthermore, it should be kept in mind, when interpreting the results that follow, that Hispanic self-identification receives coding dominance. Thus, all four groups of Hispanic respondents include heterogeneity in self-identified race, including a substantial number of respondents who selected "Black/African American" for racial self-identification.[11]

The percentages defined for the two columns of table 1 are simpler, based on each school district's counting of the number of students in each ELS high school, designated for reporting purposes as "black" or "Hispanic," and then as compiled and adjusted by NCES for dissemination through the CCD. According to the documentation for the data source, the category of "black" is meant to be used for black or African American non-Hispanic students, which aligns with our choice of coding dominance for Hispanic ethnicity with the ELS data. However, it is unclear how well schools and their controlling agencies effectively sorted their own pupils into the same categories that their students would have chosen if given the opportunity that ELS respondents received.

Equality of Opportunity and Inequality of Outcomes

As Coleman explained long ago, a pronounced shift occurred in the latter half of the twentieth century toward a conceptualization of equality of opportunity reliant on measurable equality of outcomes, not simply equality of inputs (see Coleman 1968/1990). This shift has continued, and it now constitutes the most important rationale for the adequacy movement. Table 2 presents mean differences in six measures of educational outcomes available for ELS students.

With white non-Hispanic students as the largest group, and serving as the traditional baseline against which other groups are compared, gaps in test scores are substantial. For tenth-grade reading test scores, for example, the black-white achievement gap is 0.8 standard deviations ([32.19 − 24.30]/9.77). For the math tests, the analogous gaps are 0.9 standard deviations in both the tenth grade and two years later. For another important between-group comparison, note that first- and 1.5th-generation Mexican immigrant students had the lowest test scores among all groups for all of the tests.

For educational attainment patterns, similar gaps are present. These differences are particularly large for receipt of a bachelor's degree by 2012 (eight years after modal high school graduation). The rate of bachelor's degree attainment was more than twice as high for white and Asian students in comparison to black students and all four groups of Hispanic students.

As with the clarification of categories for table 1, we need to offer one clarification of the outcome distributions for table 2. Recognizing the substantial recent attention to the dropout "crisis," we note that the corresponding result in the last row of the table may be surprising. The column for on-time high school graduation reveals that 87 percent of ELS respondents graduated from high school on time in 2004, which is high relative to the rates that others have reported based on other data sources. Recall, however, that the ELS is a sample of high school sophomores, and it includes only those who were enrolled in the spring of their sophomore year, when the ELS survey was fielded. Students who dropped out of school before the

---

10. The acronym NHOPI, which applies to some respondents in the broad category we label "Asian" in the text, is the U.S. 2000 census label for "Native Hawaiian or Other Pacific Islander."

11. Of particular importance for comparisons to EEO, many Hispanic respondents who self-identified as black or African American are embedded within our category "Hispanic ethnicity other than Mexican, all generations." "Puerto Ricans" were their own category for EEO, alongside "Mexican Americans." One wonders about the definitions of these groups for EEO, as well as the heterogeneity within them (and within the "Majority or white" group as well).

Table 2. Standardized Test Results and Subsequent Patterns of Educational Attainment for Groups Defined by Race–Ethnicity and Immigrant Generational Status If Claiming Mexican Ancestry

	Reading Test in 2002 (Tenth Grade)	Math Test in 2002 (Tenth Grade)	Math Test in 2004 (Typically Twelfth Grade)	On-Time High School Graduation in 2004	Any Postsecondary Education by 2012	Bachelor's Degree by 2012	N
White non-Hispanic, all generations	32.19	46.35	51.46	0.91	0.86	0.39	4,476
Asian or NHOPI non-Hispanic, all generations	29.76	46.42	52.09	0.91	0.89	0.49	986
Black or African American non-Hispanic, all generations	24.30	33.79	38.50	0.83	0.83	0.20	1,216
Mexican, Mexican American, or Chicano, first and 1.5 generation	21.46	32.30	36.96	0.73	0.67	0.13	183
Mexican, Mexican American, or Chicano, second generation	24.03	35.77	40.69	0.77	0.81	0.19	232
Mexican, Mexican American, or Chicano, third and third-plus generation	26.88	37.25	41.50	0.80	0.78	0.19	314
Hispanic ethnicity other than Mexican, all generations	24.81	35.77	40.77	0.76	0.83	0.19	430
American Indian or Alaskan Native non-Hispanic, all generations	27.56	38.51	44.12	0.78	0.71	0.17	156
Missing race, all generations	27.06	39.98	44.99	0.86	0.77	0.38	44
All	29.48	42.42	47.45	0.87	0.84	0.33	8,037
(Standard deviation)	(9.77)	(14.06)	(14.80)				

Source: ELS, 2002–2012, and CCD, 2001–2004.

Notes: NHOPI = Native Hawaiian and Other Pacific Islander. Data are weighted by the panel weight constructed by the data distributors (f2pnlwt), which adjusts for base-year nonparticipation and subsequent attrition, multiplied by an adjustment weight that we created to account for missing data on educational attainment.

Table 3. Staffing and Funding Profile by Race-Ethnicity and Immigrant Generational Status If Claiming Mexican Ancestry

	Pupil-to-Teacher Ratio	Percent Teachers with a Master's Degree or Higher	Percent Total Funding from Federal Sources	Percent Free or Reduced-Price Lunch	N
White non-Hispanic, all generations	16.3	47.6%	6.6%	22.2%	4,476
Asian or NHOPI non-Hispanic, all generations	18.3	48.9	7.2	39.8	986
Black or African American non-Hispanic, all generations	16.8	47.1	10.2	28.3	1,216
Mexican, Mexican American, or Chicano, first and 1.5th generation	20.4	37.1	9.3	41.4	183
Mexican, Mexican American, or Chicano, second generation	20.9	33.7	9.3	43.7	232
Mexican, Mexican American, or Chicano, third and third-plus generation	18.5	36.7	9.2	47.2	314
Hispanic ethnicity other than Mexican, all generations	18.5	48.3	8.1	38.0	430
American Indian or Alaskan Native non-Hispanic, all generations	16.7	40.0	11.2	27.8	156
Missing race, all generations	17.4	50.5	8.1	32.0	44
All	17.0	46.2	7.7	28.8	8,037
(Standard deviation)	(4.3)	(24.2)	(4.7)	(20.3)	

Source: ELS, 2002–2012, and CCD, 2001–2004.
Notes: NHOPI = Native Hawaiian and Other Pacific Islander. Data are weighted by the panel weight constructed by the data distributors (f2pnlwt), which adjusts for base-year nonparticipation and subsequent attrition, multiplied by an adjustment weight that we created to account for missing data on educational attainment. The number of cases for pupil-to-teacher ratio is 8,027 rather than 8,037 for all other variables because of missing data on the full-time equivalent calculation for teaching staff in the CCD. The ten lost cases are scattered throughout the categories and are not reflected in the final column.

administration of the survey are therefore out of the universe of the survey, and we know from other research that a substantial proportion of dropouts leave school before the spring of the sophomore year. An important implication of this pattern should be noted now: the school effects analysis that we offer here is relevant only to a subset of students who entered high school at the beginning of ninth grade. Thus, as we discuss in the concluding section, it is possible that the sophomore-and-beyond universe of the ELS robs schools and their characteristics of some of their total effects.

Group Differences in Inputs and Conditions

Table 3 presents group differences in the basic staffing and financial profiles of the 559 ELS schools. In comparison to all other groups, students who claimed Mexican ancestry attended schools that had the highest pupil-teacher ratios and were staffed by teachers with lower levels of advanced educational certification. These students also attended schools with the highest rates of eligibility for free and reduced-price lunch. Black and American Indian students, however, had slightly higher percentages of expenditures from federal sources,

Table 4. Means of Factor-Scored Scales of Poor Conditions and Maintenance of Facilities by Race-Ethnicity and Immigrant Generational Status If Claiming Mexican Ancestry

	Classrooms	Hallways	Bathrooms	Outside School Area	N
White non-Hispanic, all generations	−0.11	−0.11	−0.15	−0.18	3,472
Asian or NHOPI non-Hispanic, all generations	0.09	0.00	0.09	0.06	812
Black or African American non-Hispanic, all generations	0.21	0.19	0.36	0.41	972
Mexican, Mexican American, or Chicano, first and 1.5th generation	0.14	0.41	0.19	0.34	147
Mexican, Mexican American, or Chicano, second generation	0.22	0.29	0.27	0.21	179
Mexican, Mexican American, or Chicano, third and third-plus generation	0.05	0.04	−0.11	−0.02	252
Hispanic ethnicity other than Mexican, all generations	0.31	0.30	0.38	0.47	331
American Indian or Alaskan Native non-Hispanic, all generations	−0.17	−0.01	−0.12	−0.14	128
Missing race, all generations	−0.15	−0.18	0.25	−0.08	40
All	0.0	0.0	0.0	0.0	6,163
(Standard deviation)	(1.0)	(1.0)	(1.0)	(1.0)	

Source: ELS, 2002–2012, and CCD, 2001–2004.
Notes: NHOPI = Native Hawaiian and Other Pacific Islander. Data are weighted by the panel weight constructed by the data distributors (f2pnlwt), which adjusts for base-year nonparticipation and subsequent attrition, multiplied by an adjustment weight that we created to account for missing data on educational attainment.

which we explain further when we consider the size and composition of total expenditures.

Table 4 presents group differences in scores on standardized scales of the conditions and maintenance of school facilities, constructed from factor models of underlying items. The first column presents mean differences for the classroom scale, which is a standard factor-weighted composite of items recorded by the ELS survey administrator for each school:

- The classroom ceiling was in disrepair.
- Graffiti was present on the classroom walls, ceilings, or doors.
- Graffiti was present on classroom desks.
- Trash was observed on the classroom floor.
- The trash can was overflowing.
- Bars were present on classroom windows.
- Classroom windows were broken.

The scale for hallways is based on seven similar items for the school's front hallway, noting the presence of trash, graffiti, broken lights, chipped paint, or damaged ceilings. The scale for bathrooms is based on five items: four for graffiti and trash, and one for whether students loiter in the bathrooms while others are in class. The scale for the area outside of the school is based on five items: one for trash, one for graffiti, one for the presence of boarded-up buildings in the area around the school, and two for the preponderance of students and nonstudents loitering around the area of the school.

These scales of conditions, maintenance, and general disorganization follow expected patterns, although with some interesting variation that we surmise is produced by differences partly attributable to the locations of some schools in distressed urban areas. In general, and subject to some variation that is probably attributable to sampling, the highest values for poor conditions and maintenance are present for the schools attended by black and Hispanic students of all types, with white students, Asian students, and American Indian students attending schools with more favorable physical conditions measured by these scales. Because of the composites' factor scaling, the group differences have no natural metric interpretation. However, the range of variation across groups is generally within one-half of a standard deviation of the full range of variation for each scale (because each is a standardized scale). What is not reported, but is noteworthy, are the within-group patterns of variation. The standard deviations of the four scales are substantially higher among black and Hispanic students, relative to white non-Hispanic students.[12] As such, the mean differences reported in table 4 do not reveal the scale of the differences that are present for some of the schools with particularly poor conditions and maintenance.

Table 5 presents group differences in the focal input of interest—expenditures at the district level, as matched to each ELS high school. The first two columns present total expenditures, the middle two columns present expenditures for instructional purposes only, and the last two columns present expenditures for the salaries of instructional staff only.[13] All expenditures are averaged over four years of data from 2000–2001 through 2003–2004, which are the four years of high school for a continuously enrolled ELS student. The four-year averages also smooth out year-to-year variation, which may be accentuated by the scale modifications produced by the pupil divisor and the cost adjustment operation discussed later.[14]

---

12. For the comparisons of the conditions of classrooms, hallways, and bathrooms, the differences in the group-specific standard deviations are typically on the order of 1.2 versus 0.8. For the areas around schools, the differences are larger for blacks and Hispanics who did not claim Mexican ancestry relative to non-Hispanic whites (typically 1.6 versus 0.6). For Hispanic students who claimed Mexican ancestry, the differences are smaller (typically 1.0 versus 0.6).

13. The most common measurement approach when assessing expenditure differences is to use total current expenditures to form comparisons. The results of this paper are essentially the same if we use this measure, but we favor the alternatives presented in table 5. Instructional expenditures are the core expenditures for learning within the total current expenditure measure, and instructional expenditures are defined for the CCD as "includes payments from all funds for salaries, employee benefits, supplies, materials, and contractual services for elementary/secondary instruction; excludes capital outlay, debt service, and interfund transfers for elementary/secondary instruction. Instruction covers regular, special, and vocational programs offered in both the regular school year and summer school; excludes instructional support activities as well as adult education and community services" (Berry and Zhou 2007, B-6). Salaries are then a subset of this measure. The more encompassing measure of total current expenditures, which we do not utilize, includes expenditures for instructional support services, expenditures for administrative support services, food services, maintenance services, and others. We see more rationale for moving right past total current expenditures and instead taking all expenditures into account when looking to complement an analysis based only on instructional expenditures and instructional salary expenditures. The CCD measure of total expenditures includes everything in total current expenditures, but also capital outlay, which includes expenses for construction and equipment (including instructional equipment). Thus, we see the total expenditures measure as close to the value that many parents recognize implicitly when choosing schooling options based on residential location, while expenditures on instruction is a targeted measure of the resources allocated to the instruction of the modal pupil in each school district. Finally, we use a four-year average, which smooths out the variation in capital outlay across the years (which is thought to be more volatile than expenditures for instruction). Recall also that the expenditure measures are for each district as a whole, not individual schools, and so the capital outlay in each year is itself averaged across all schools.

14. We do not adjust for price differences across the four years and simply take the average of the slightly escalating values across the four years. We assume that variation attributable to local inflation rates is ignorable, and thus that our four-year averages work well for the level of expenditures experienced by students sampled near to the midpoint of their high school careers (the spring of sophomore year, when the 2002 ELS was fielded).

Table 5. Means of Per-Pupil Expenditures by Race-Ethnicity and Immigrant Generational Status If Claiming Mexican Ancestry

	Total Expenditures		Instructional Expenditures		Salaries for Instructional Staff		
	Per Pupil	Per Pupil and Cost-Adjusted	Per Pupil	Per Pupil and Cost-Adjusted	Per Pupil	Per Pupil and Cost-Adjusted	N
White non-Hispanic, all generations	$9,052	$9,154	$4,706	$4,768	$3,349	$3,393	4,476
Asian or NHOPI non-Hispanic, all generations	9,872	9,385	5,139	4,897	3,643	3,472	986
Black or African American non-Hispanic, all generations	9,298	9,073	4,850	4,737	3,434	3,360	1,216
Mexican, Mexican American, or Chicano, first and 1.5th generation	8,552	8,514	4,291	4,271	3,058	3,046	183
Mexican, Mexican American, or Chicano, second generation	8,489	8,490	4,326	4,336	3,111	3,125	232
Mexican, Mexican American, or Chicano, third and third-plus generation	8,348	8,548	4,145	4,263	3,009	3,097	314
Hispanic ethnicity other than Mexican, all generations	10,251	9,775	5,470	5,220	3,772	3,602	430
American Indian or Alaskan Native non-Hispanic, all generations	8,951	9,173	4,559	4,688	3,234	3,326	156
Missing race, all generations	9,250	8,979	4,694	4,570	3,340	3,256	44
All	9,137	9,122	4,742	4,743	3,368	3,370	8,037
(Standard deviation)	(2,286)	(1,989)	(1,262)	(1,146)	(836)	(753)	

Source: ELS, 2002–2012, and CCD, 2001–2004.

Notes: NHOPI = Native Hawaiian and Other Pacific Islander. Data are weighted by the panel weight constructed by the data distributors (f2pnlwt), which adjusts for base-year nonparticipation and subsequent attrition, multiplied by an adjustment weight that we created to account for missing data on educational attainment.

Figure 1. Cost Adjustment Values, Displayed for Hypothetical ELS High Schools, Calculated from 2002 County Wage and Salary Levels Shrunk to the National Median

Source: Authors' calculations, based on raw rata from the U.S. Bureau of Economic Analysis, Regional Economic Accounts, table CA34, 2002 (Bureau of Economic Analysis 2014), matched to high schools sampled proportional to size from the 2001–2002 CCD

Consider first the raw per-pupil levels of expenditures, ignoring cost adjustments. In contrast to the scales for poor conditions, table 5 reveals in its group differences some patterns that would be quite surprising to readers unaware of debates on school resource levels. For example, for all three measures of expenditures, the levels are higher for schools attended by black non-Hispanic students than for those attended by white non-Hispanic students. The lowest levels are for Hispanic students who claim Mexican ancestry, and the highest levels are for Hispanic students who do not claim Mexican ancestry. As is well documented (see Ladd and Goertz 2015), these differences are produced by a complex set of underlying determinants, the two most important of which are (1) the availability of compensatory funding from federal and state sources for students in poverty and those with special needs, and (2) the higher teacher salaries and other expenses typical of schooling in metropolitan areas, especially in high-wage states, relative to rural areas and all areas in low-wage states.

Inspired by some recent approaches in the literature to adjust for the different costs faced by school districts (see Duncombe, Nguyen-Hoang, and Yinger 2015), we constructed a set of cost adjustment values from the average wage and salary levels of jobs at the county level, calculated by the U.S. Bureau of Economic Analysis for the years 2001 through 2004. Because these county-level wage and salary averages are too dispersed relative to public-sector wages, we shrunk the county wage levels toward the national median using an exponential shrinkage parameter, after which we rescaled the wage and salary levels to a proportional adjustment factor with a mean of 1.

To give a sense of the calculated cost adjustment values, figure 1 presents a hypothetical set of ELS high schools, plotted at their actual physical locations but sampled at random (proportional to size) from the 2001–2002 CCD.[15]

---

15. We cannot offer a map that displays the actual ELS schools, for disclosure reasons, but we assure the reader that the one in figure 1 looks qualitatively similar. Slightly different schools are chosen in each metropolitan area, but they are all represented in about the same proportions as in figure 1. More variation is present, as expected, for nonmetropolitan areas, but the overall pattern for the true ELS schools is qualitatively similar to figure 1 when viewed at the presented scale. The optimal way to view the figures in this article is in color. We refer readers of the print edition of this paper to www.rsfjournal.org/doi/full/10.7758/RSF.2016.2.5.05 to view the color version.

Schools are colored by a weather severity scale, from green through yellow to red, for the size of the cost adjustment value. In particular, the values were binned into five colors for interpretability, as shown in the figure's legend, but the underlying values used for the analysis vary continuously from 0.72 to 1.32.[16]

When nominal expenditures are divided by these cost adjustment values, the effect is to render $13,000 per pupil in red high schools equivalent to approximately $10,000 per pupil in yellow high schools and approximately $7,000 in dark green high schools. At the risk of oversimplifying, the adjustment eliminates expenditure differences attributable to cost differences across high schools in high-wage metropolitan areas like New York City (colored red in figure 1), average-wage metropolitan areas like Toledo (colored yellow in figure 1), and low-wage counties like those in Appalachian Kentucky (colored dark green in figure 1). As we discuss later, this cost adjustment procedure is imprecise and surely inaccurate for many areas, and yet we argue that the adjustment is sufficient to demonstrate how little such cost differences matter for the sorts of models we offer.

To see some of the consequences of our cost adjustment procedures for the expenditures of actual ELS schools, consider the second, fourth, and sixth columns of table 5. After cost adjustments, expenditure differences across groups narrow slightly, with the largest changes being the relative declines in the amount of money spent on the schools attended by non-Hispanic black students (who are more likely to attend urban schools) as well as those attended by Asian students and Hispanic students who do not claim Mexican ancestry (two groups more likely to attend schools in high-wage counties, especially in California and the New York metropolitan area). The expenditure gap between white and black non-Hispanic students is no longer upside down relative to journalistic expectations. The expenditures for Hispanic students who claim Mexican ancestry remain substantially lower than for all other groups.

School Inputs and Family Background as Predictors

Since the publication of EEO, we have had five decades of methodological improvement, yielding many new techniques, as well as a much deeper understanding of the techniques utilized by Coleman and his colleagues. Even so, techniques have not changed so much that it is no longer appropriate to offer an analysis of predictive power by first estimating simple models of the variance explained. Accordingly, table 6 presents estimates of the variance accounted for by predictor variables in ninety different specifications (fifteen each across the same six educational outcomes presented in table 2). For the three test scores, the models are generic ordinary least squares (OLS) regression models. For the three educational transitions models, they are corresponding logistic regression models.

Consider first the models reported in the first three columns for test scores as the outcome variables. Each row of table 6 specifies the predictor variables for each underlying regression model, without any attempts to fashion tighter fits through variable transformations and without any cross-product interaction terms. Just as important, no attempt is made to remove confounding from any "causally prior" variables. Accordingly, all of these models would be regarded as "naive" models in the modern literature on causal inference. With less pejorative labeling from the era of EEO, they would be labeled bivariate or unadjusted regression models.

The specifications are divided into four groups. The first two specifications are labeled "individual" because all predictors are indisputably individual and family characteristics. Consider the first model for the prediction of tenth-grade reading test scores. The eight

---

16. Supplementary appendix figure S1 shows an analogous map for the underlying wage and salary data. Figure S1 is more dispersed by color, with high-wage counties in and near San Francisco and New York City especially pronounced. Shrinking the averages to the national median brings these high-salary metropolitan areas into closer alignment with other metropolitan areas. A similar pattern is present for the other end of the distribution (for example, for Appalachian counties relative to other rural counties).

Table 6. Proportion of Variance Explained for Separate Naive Linear Regression and Logistic Regression Models, Without Any Adjustments for Confounding and with No Effort to Respecify for Any Suspected Nonlinearities

	Reading Test in 2002 (Tenth Grade)	Math Test in 2002 (Tenth Grade)	Math Test in 2004 (Typically Twelfth Grade)	On-Time High School Graduation in 2004	Any Postsecondary Education by 2012	Bachelor's Degree by 2012
Individual						
Race-ethnicity and immigrant generation (eight dummies)	0.136	0.153	0.147	0.026	0.015	0.050
Family background (five variables for socioeconomic status and one variable for living only with mother or female guardian)	0.175	0.184	0.210	0.054	0.078	0.142
Individual and school						
Region and urbanicity (eleven dummies)	0.036	0.040	0.035	0.013	0.008	0.016
Racial composition (two variables for percent black and percent Hispanic)	0.084	0.095	0.086	0.015	0.004	0.020
Percent free and reduced-price lunch	0.096	0.114	0.107	0.020	0.014	0.047
Percent of total funding from federal sources	0.042	0.058	0.054	0.007	0.008	0.026

School						
Teaching corps (two variables for pupil-to-teacher ratio and percent of teachers with a master's degree or higher)	0.014	0.011	0.012	0.004	0.003	0.005
Poor conditions scales (four variables)	0.021	0.019	0.016	0.003	0.001	0.007
School principal scale for learning "hindered by" poor conditions and facilities	0.006	0.009	0.008	0.003	0.001	0.002
District						
Total expenditures per pupil	0.002	0.002	0.003	0.001	0.006	0.008
Total expenditures per pupil and cost-adjusted	0.002	0.001	0.001	0.001	0.001	0.003
Instructional expenditures per pupil	0.002	0.001	0.002	0.001	0.004	0.007
Instructional expenditures per pupil and cost-adjusted	0.001	0.001	0.001	<0.001	0.001	0.001
Salaries for instructional staff per pupil	0.004	0.004	0.005	0.001	0.005	0.010
Salaries for instructional staff per pupil and cost-adjusted	0.003	0.003	0.003	0.001	0.002	0.004

Source: ELS, 2002–2012, and CCD, 2001–2004.

Notes: Data are weighted by the panel weight constructed by the data distributors (f2pnlwt), which adjusts for base-year nonparticipation and subsequent attrition, multiplied by an adjustment weight that we created to account for missing data on educational attainment. Most models were estimated for 8,037 students, but others were estimated for subsets of this full sample because of missing data on the predictor variables: percent free and reduced-price lunch (8,026), teaching corps (6,898), learning "hindered by" (6,555), and scales for poor conditions (6,163).

dummy variables, representing the nine rows used already in tables 1 through 5 for race-ethnicity and immigrant generation, account for 13.6 percent of the variance of reading test scores. The next row is for a model that specifies six variables for family background—mother's education, father's education, mother's occupational standing, father's occupational standing, family income, and living only with one's mother or a female legal guardian. These variables account for 17.5 percent of the variance of tenth-grade reading test scores. Now, looking across the first three columns, there is some small variation in the predictive power across all three test scores, but not enough to merit a detailed accounting.

Consider the second group of specifications, labeled "individual and school." The variables for all four specifications here are characteristics that cannot be cleanly delineated as either individual or school characteristics. The first specification, which includes eleven dummies to parameterize differences across four regions (West, South, Northeast, and Midwest) crossed by urbanicity (rural, urban, suburban), accounts for between 3 and 4 percent of the variance of test scores.[17] The racial composition of schools is measured at the school level, but of course these values are based on individual characteristics, with the compositions shaped themselves to a large extent by the residential decisions of parents and the constraints upon them. Thus, racial composition, which can account for between 8 and 10 percent of the variance of test scores, is not clearly a school-level characteristic either.

This "levels" ambiguity is clearest for the final two specifications—the percentage of a school's students who are eligible for free or reduced-priced lunch and the percentage of a school's funding from federal sources. Each is nominally a school-level measure, but both are based entirely on family background differences across schools, when measured through administrative rules for transfer allocations for compensatory education programs. The percentage of students who qualify for free and reduced-price lunch can account for 10 to 11 percent of the variance of test scores, while the percentage of funding from federal sources can account for 4 to 6 percent of the variance of test scores.

The next group of specifications are for measured characteristics of schools that are much more clearly attributes of schools themselves. First, two variables for the teaching corps of each school—the level of staffing, summarized by the pupil-to-teacher ratio, and the level of advanced educational certification—can account for only about 1 percent of the variance of test scores. The four conditions and maintenance scales presented earlier can account for about 2 percent of the variance of test scores, matching the results of Alex Bowers and Angela Urick (2011), who develop conclusions based on a similar analysis of the predictive power of these items for the ELS data. And finally, a third specification, which is a scale of items reported by the school principal, labeled as a scale for learning "hindered by" poor conditions and facilities, can account for only 1 percent or less of the variance of test scores.[18]

The final group of specifications includes district-level expenditure measures, presented earlier in the six columns of table 5. All of these expenditure measures can account for less than 1 percent of the variance of test scores.

17. Technically, these variables are measured at the school level, and some students live in urban areas but attend schools in suburban areas, and so forth. But these are not separable without students' residence locations, which are not available for the ELS. Nonetheless, most students live in areas that match their schools, when measured at this geographic scale.

18. This scale is a factor-weighted composite of ten items that the school principal rated on a four-point scale from "not at all" to "a lot" in response to the question: "In your school, how much is the learning of tenth-graders hindered by: (a) poor condition of buildings, (b) poor heating, cooling, or lighting systems, (c) inadequate science laboratory equipment, (d) inadequate facilities for fine arts, (e) lack of instructional space (for example, classrooms), (f) lack of instructional material in the library, (g) lack of text books and basic supplies, (h) not enough computers for instruction, (i) lack of multi-media resources for instruction, and (k) inadequate or outdated vocational-technical education equipment or facilities." Item j ("lack of discipline and safety") was excluded from the scale, as it did not fit with the first factor.

Contrary to the expectations of some, focusing on instructional resources only, or even more narrowly on the salaries of instructional staff, does not alter the results much at all. Likewise, adjusting for cost differences, as explained earlier for table 5 and as depicted in figure 1, does not change the results either.

The literature has long recognized that the intradistrict allocation of expenditures across schools is not uniform, given both the indivisibility of salary lines and the operation of specialized programs, some for students with special needs and some for students now labeled "gifted and talented." The ELS, when supplemented by a match from the CCD, does not allow us to examine the importance of these patterns. We can, nonetheless, dispel one concern. When we drop 18 students in charter high schools and 571 students in magnet high schools from the analysis sample of 8,037 students and then reestimate table 6, the results are nearly identical. It is not the case that the 589 students in these schools represent outliers exerting leverage on the estimated regression line that represents the variance explained (as would be the case if students in these high schools all had high performance but comparatively low district-level expenditures that hide higher but unobserved school-specific expenditures).

Now we consider the last three columns of table 6 for models that predict educational transitions. For these models, the notion of variance explained must shift a bit in recognition of the dichotomous outcomes. However, estimation itself is simple, and accordingly we estimate logit models for the outcomes using the same specifications of predictors for the models that predict test scores. In the final three columns of table 6, we offer a measure of the proportion of the variance explained, following the recommendation of Tue Tjur (2009) to compute the difference in predicted probabilities from the model across the two realized values of the outcome. This coefficient of discrimination is a generalization of classification summary statistics, and it is easy to justify as a direct analog to the variance explained in least squares regression.[19]

The pattern for educational transitions differs in some respects from the pattern for test scores. With the shift to dichotomous outcomes (and with different base rates as well), it may feel unnatural to compare the raw values for the variance explained using Tjur's (2009) coefficient of discrimination, and so we will spare the reader. Regardless, for the educational transitions, relative comparisons within columns are easily justified, and these relative comparisons can be considered across rows.

For educational transitions, family background accounts for much more variation than our representation of race-ethnicity and immigrant generation. Likewise, free and reduced-price lunch accounts for more variation than racial composition. For all of the models in the school- and district-level specifications, the models have little predictive power, approaching at most 1 percent of the variation for bachelor's degree attainment. Here, one interpretive complication arises. With variation in unconditional rates for each of the three transitions, the functional form of the logit makes between-outcome comparisons difficult. Partly for this reason, we offer school-level models of attainment rates in table 7 and make the case that expenditures may matter most for bachelor's degree attainment. Nonetheless, the overall conclusion of this section is unaffected by the complications of between-model comparisons. For all of the models in table 6, expenditures are much weaker predictors of the six outcomes than are measures of family background.

A Graphical Explanation of Differences in Predictive Power

Although the weak predictive power of school expenditures may not be surprising to those who have followed school resource debates, it is still important to explain the "why" and

---

19. We offer in supplementary appendix table S5 all models in table 6 estimated with OLS regression. As such, the models for educational transitions become linear probability models. We also report adjusted R-squared values (instead of unadjusted R-squared values for test scores and Tjur's [2009] coefficient of discrimination for the educational transition models). The results are nearly the same, and all of this paper's conclusions would be the same substituting those models into the main text.

Figure 2. Tenth-Grade Math Test Scores by Per-Pupil Expenditures for Instructional Salaries

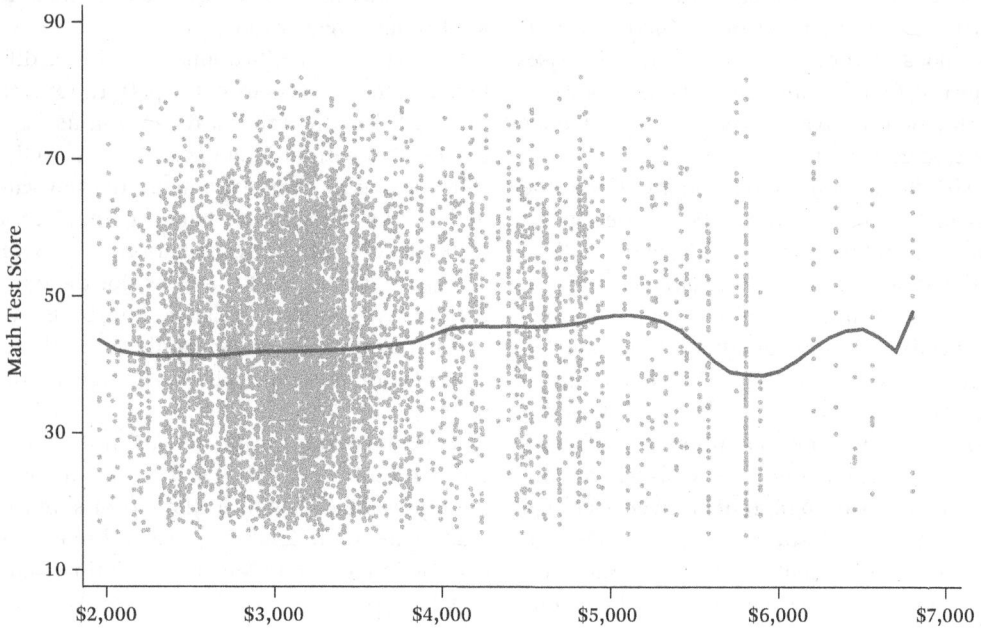

Source: ELS, 2002, and CCD, 2001–2004.

"how" of these results. As a first step, consider figures 2 and 3, which present two scatterplots in which the vertical axis is the math test score in the tenth grade and the horizontal axes are per-pupil salary expenditures and cost-adjusted per-pupil salary expenditures, respectively, in the two figures. Each blue dot is a student, and the red line is a locally smoothed average for the relationship between test scores and salary expenditures.[20]

The vast majority of the variation in test scores appears to be within schools, as shown by the wide variation in test results within each school (that is, each vertical line of blue dots is a single school, since per-pupil expenditures nearly always differ just a little bit from school to school). Figures 2 and 3 appear quite similar, suggesting that rearrangements of the ordering on the horizontal axis to take account of costs are unlikely to matter much for the association. The nonparametric smooth presented as the red line fluctuates at its ends, but largely because these are the regions where the data are sparse. If we engage in some unabashed curve fitting, trimming to the interior range from $2,500 to $4,750, we can generate very slightly more predictive power for expenditures (see our between-school models in table 7). Of course, with similar tweaking for other sets of predictors, we could boost their predictive power as well, and it would be hard to know when to stop. The supplementary appendix provides analogous figures for the other five outcomes (see figures S2, S4, S6, S8, and S10). Only the figure for bachelor's degree receipts suggests a slightly stronger association, as we discuss later.

Now we consider the strong predictive power of family background. For figures 4 through 6, we first created a factor-scored variable for socioeconomic status, which is a standardized composite variable for five underlying items

20. The results in figures 2 and 3, as well as those in figures 4 through 6, do not account for the study design of the ELS; for example, they do not incorporate adjustments for the nested sample design or nonresponse. We offer these figures only to provide a sense of the main patterns in the data that shape the more carefully estimated results in the tables.

Figure 3. Tenth-Grade Math Test Scores by Cost-Adjusted Per-Pupil Expenditures for Instructional Salaries

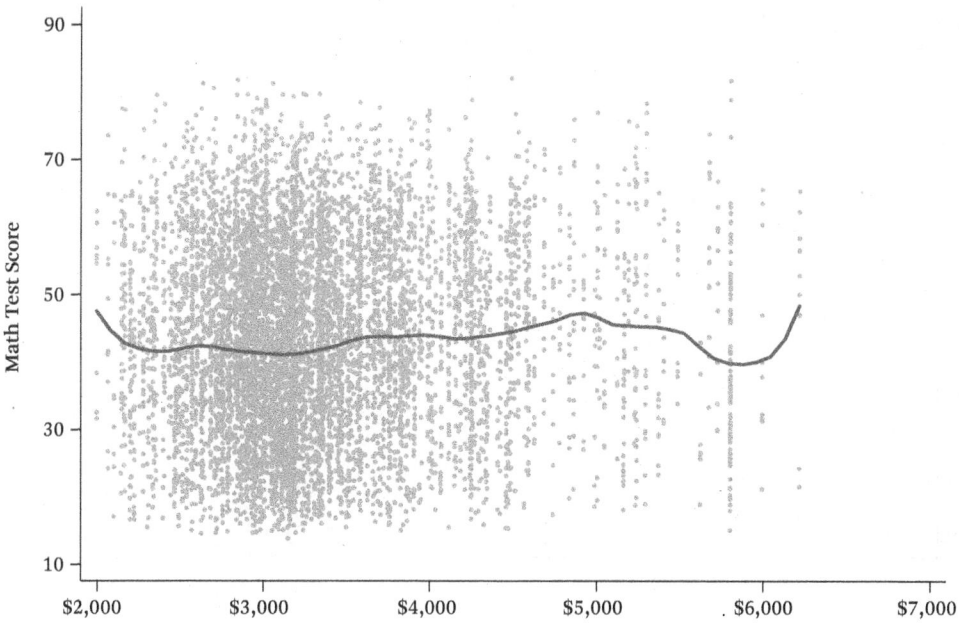

Source: ELS, 2002, and CCD, 2001–2004.

Figure 4. Individual Tenth-Grade Math Test Scores by Individual Socioeconomic Status

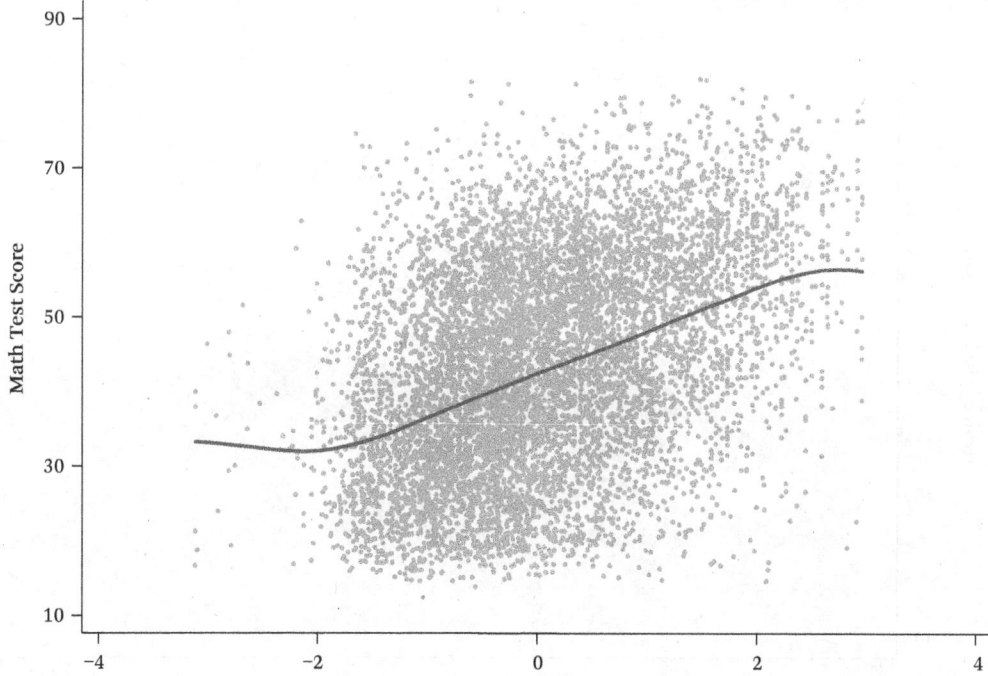

Source: ELS, 2002, and CCD, 2001–2004.

Figure 5. School Mean Tenth-Grade Math Test Scores by School Mean Socioeconomic Status

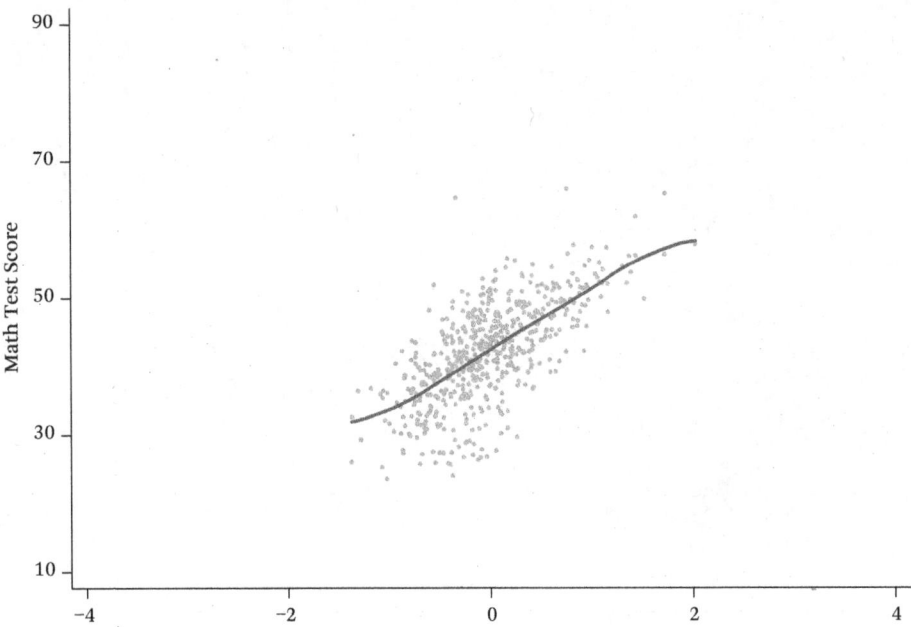

Source: ELS, 2002, and CCD, 2001–2004.

Figure 6. Individual Tenth-Grade Math Test Scores by Socioeconomic Status, Plotted as Individual Deviations from School Means

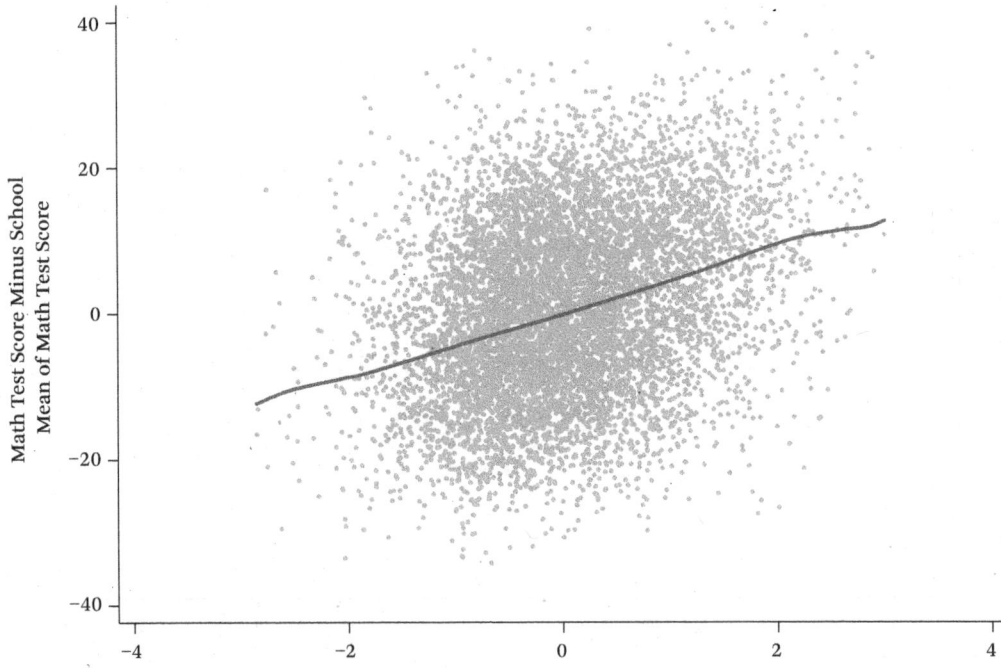

Source: ELS, 2002, and CCD, 2001–2004.

(mother's and father's educational attainment and occupational standing, as well as total family income). For figure 4, socioeconomic status is the variable for the horizontal axis and the tenth-grade math test score is again the variable for the vertical axis. The red line is an analogous local average line, but unlike for expenditures, it now moves relentlessly upward with increases in socioeconomic status.

Figure 5 plots the school math test means against the school socioeconomic status means, and figure 6 plots within-school deviations from these mean values for both variables. Figure 5 is hardly surprising, since it is well known that schools with the most disadvantaged students have the lowest observed levels test performance. Figure 6 shows that the within-school relationship between socioeconomic status and test scores is nearly as strong as the total association shown in figure 4. Accordingly, the within-school variation revealed in figures 2 and 3 is not idiosyncratic variation in test performance; a large portion of it is patterned variation that can be predicted by family background. Thus, the overall relationship between socioeconomic status and test scores has important between-school and within-school components.

Simple Models with Adjustments

Although measurement debates followed the release of EEO, the most withering criticism was based on the modeling assumptions that suggested alternative specifications of adjustment variables. In brief, the primary claim was that the effects of school facilities and resources were not clarified by simultaneous adjustment for family background. Instead, parents with high levels of education and the family income to support a wide range of neighborhood choice were likely to choose to send their children to schools with high expenditures. As a result, some of the expenditure "effect" was said to be picked up by the family background coefficients themselves.[21]

As table 6 shows, this criticism is hard to sustain with the ELS data because the unadjusted relationship between expenditures and educational outcomes is very weak. But a fair critic could reasonably wonder whether some fashion of suppression is in operation and may therefore care to know how models that allow least squares formulae to purge common linear dependence between predictors might generate alternative conclusions. In brief, the answer is: not much at all. Consider just the prediction of tenth-grade math test scores, as for figures 2 and 3. A model that specifies all race-ethnicity, region, urbanicity, and family background variables generates an R-squared value of 0.266, which is smaller than the summation of the separate R-squared values from table 6, which were 0.153, 0.184, and 0.040, respectively. As is well known, these variables share predictive variance for educational outcomes. What is the result when we now add expenditures to this multiple regression specification? Almost nothing. The R-squared value for a model that adds per-pupil salary expenditures remains at 0.266, and the coefficient on expenditures is nonsignificant and substantively trivial. If, instead, we add the student-to-teacher ratio, the percentage of teachers with advanced certification, our four scales of the conditions of facilities, and the principal's learning "hindered by" scale to the model, the R-squared value increases from 0.266 to only 0.269. And this is the common pattern for all outcomes, with all measures of expenditures

---

21. Although Coleman and his colleagues could not deflect this criticism effectively (see Coleman 1970), compelling evidence against the criticism was present in the EEO data all along, as shown in replications such as Smith (1972; see his appendix tables). The unadjusted relationship between expenditures and test scores was very weak, and hence the adjustment for family background inputs was not crucial to the conclusion that the estimated effects of expenditures were surprisingly small. Coleman and his colleagues could have blunted this particular criticism if they had simply shown the bivariate associations between expenditures and outcomes, rather than revealing associations only conditional on family background adjustment. In fact, it is clear to a contemporary reader that one of the main weaknesses of EEO was its overreporting of results in table after table, many of which muddied the waters with variance comparisons across alternative specifications of models that were not always clearly conveyed in the writing.

and all measures of school characteristics. The unadjusted models reported in table 6 are excessively favorable to the assertion that expenditures and facility differences matter.

Multilevel Models

Since the 1990s, it has been customary to call for multilevel regression models in observational educational research whenever student-level data are nested within school-level data. Figures 5 and 6 demonstrate why the separation of an association into a between-school component and a within-school component can offer an illuminating descriptive portrayal of a relationship. Contrary to what other scholars sometimes imply, multilevel modeling does not in general clarify causal inference; estimating between-school effects and within-school effects at the same time does not imbue either with causal power (see also Lucas's paper in this issue for a related critique).

For the ELS, the possibilities for multilevel modeling are limited by our comparatively small within-school sample sizes. As a comparison, Borman and Dowling (2010), in their reanalysis of a subset of the original EEO data with multilevel models, utilized a sample of 30,590 ninth-graders enrolled in 226 schools. In contrast, we have a smaller and more dispersed sample at our disposal, with 8,037 tenth-graders enrolled in 559 schools. As depicted in figures 2 and 3, we typically have between 10 and 20 students per school, but the full range is from 3 to 29 students per school. Although one can induce software to estimate multilevel models with samples like the ELS, too little information is available at the school level to reliably estimate both school-level and student-level associations with enough random components to bring the models into alignment with standards in multilevel modeling. And if one wishes to adjust away potential bias from panel attrition and missing data on outcomes using tailored complete case weights, multiple positions exist on how such weights should or should not propagate to school-level associations. Rather than force software to do what we think is unwise, we instead offer some basic between-school models to explain why such an effort would not sub- stantially elevate the explanatory power of expenditures in the ELS data.

Table 7 presents results from twenty-four school-level regression models in which we show the coefficient for each of our six expenditure measures for the prediction of tenth-grade math test scores. The underlying models are specified to mimic the inferences of multilevel models by utilizing precision weights for each school (that is, scaling the underlying weights by the within-school sample sizes in order to give more weight to schools with more precisely estimated means).

The coefficients in the first column of the top panel are from six separate regression models for all 559 schools, and the coefficients in the third column of the top panel are for a corresponding set of six separate regression models that incorporate adjustments for region, urbanicity, and school means of the six family background measures utilized for the individual-level models in table 6. The second and fourth columns present the R-squared values for the models.

At the school level, the six expenditure measures account for very little of the variance of school means of math test scores, as shown in the second column. The metric coefficients suggest that $1,000 increases are associated with very small increments in test scores, between 0.26 and 0.97 points. The particular amount depends, however, on the measure of expenditure, since $1,000 in total expenditures is less proportionally than for instructional salaries (which is reflected in the standard deviations of $2,310 for per-pupil total expenditures versus $882 for per-pupil instructional salaries). Consider the 0.97 and 0.88 in the last two rows of the first column in the top panel. These are the metric slopes for linear regression lines through study design–modeled analogs to figures 2 and 3. A $1,000 shift is associated with increases of 0.97 and 0.88 on the school mean of math tests, which are 0.13 and 0.12 standard deviations of the school-level standard deviation of test scores (for example, 0.97/7.45 = 0.13, and 0.88/7.45 = 0.12). If 0.13 and 0.12 were warranted estimates of causal effects, then they would be small but nonetheless meaningful effects of what would be a substan-

Table 7. Metric Coefficients for Expenditure Variables for Separate Between-School Models of Tenth-Grade Math Test Scores, With and Without Adjustments for Family Background, Region, and Urbanicity

	Unadjusted		With Adjustments for Family Background, Region, and Urbanicity	
	Coefficient (Standard Error)	R-Squared	Coefficient (Standard Error)	R-Squared
Full sample (559 schools)				
Total expenditures per pupil	0.26 (0.16)	0.007	−0.13 (0.12)	0.568
Total expenditures per pupil and cost-adjusted	0.24 (0.17)	0.004	0.01 (0.14)	0.567
Instructional expenditures per pupil	0.39 (0.30)	0.005	−0.23 (0.25)	0.568
Instructional expenditures per pupil and cost-adjusted	0.30 (0.30)	0.002	0.10 (0.27)	0.568
Salaries for instructional staff per pupil	0.97 (0.46)	0.013	−0.18 (0.34)	0.568
Salaries for instructional staff per pupil and cost-adjusted	0.88 (0.46)	0.009	0.31 (0.37)	0.568
Restricted sample (518 schools)				
Total expenditures per pupil	0.24 (0.16)	0.006	−0.16 (0.12)	0.582
Total expenditures per pupil and cost-adjusted	0.22 (0.17)	0.004	−0.04 (0.15)	0.581
Instructional expenditures per pupil	0.34 (0.32)	0.004	−0.24 (0.26)	0.581
Instructional expenditures per pupil and cost-adjusted	0.25 (0.33)	0.002	0.11 (0.30)	0.581
Salaries for instructional staff per pupil	0.96 (0.50)	0.012	−0.21 (0.36)	0.581
Salaries for instructional staff per pupil and cost-adjusted	0.89 (0.52)	0.008	0.33 (0.40)	0.581

Source: ELS, 2002–2012, and CCD, 2001–2004.

Notes: Expenditure variables are entered in thousands of dollars. Data are weighted by the school mean of the individual-level weight (that is, the panel weight constructed by the data distributors [f2pnlwt], multiplied by an adjustment weight that we created to account for missing data on educational attainment) multiplied by the within-school sample sizes in order to generate the precision weighting that is typical of multilevel models.

tial $1,000-per-pupil intervention for each school.

For the six models summarized by the third and fourth columns in the top panel, the additional variables explain a great deal of the variation, as should not be surprising from inspection of figure 5. The very small coefficients for expenditures from the first column move uniformly closer to zero (and flip sign for all expenditures without cost adjustments). These twelve models suggest that between-school differences in expenditures do not predict between-school differences in test scores much at all, but school means of our six family background measures are very strongly predictive. The true causal effects of expenditures lie somewhere in between the values in columns 1 and 3 of the table, and as such these columns constitute reasonable bounds on the range of likely true effects of interventions. Multilevel models would reveal the same basic patterns, if we were to offer a full presentation of them.

As is clear from the red lines in figures 2 and 3, the nonparametric regression smooth for math test scores becomes unstable and turns upward at low and high values of per-pupil expenditures, both with and without cost adjustments. It is reasonable to wonder whether between-school regression results would suggest different conclusions if we were to declare these schools outliers and trim the sample to the interior of the distribution of expenditures. Accordingly, for the models reported in the second panel of table 7, we dropped 41 of the 559 schools from the analysis because their per-pupil, cost-adjusted salary expenditures were less than $2,500 or greater than $4,750 (see, for reference, figures 4 through 6). The results for expenditures do not change substantially. If anything, the R-squared values suggest that limiting the sample increased the predictive power of family background relative to expenditures. Because we do not have any principled reason for declaring that the 41 schools that we dropped for the bottom panel are outliers worthy of purging from the population, and because their funding levels are themselves plausible, we favor the complete-sample models presented in the top panel of table 7. However, if we had decided otherwise, our basic conclusions would not change.

We noted earlier, when presenting the individual-level results in table 6, that expenditures may have slightly stronger associations with bachelor's degree attainment. To assess whether this difference is present for between-school models as well, table 8 presents twelve models structured analogously to those in table 7, but now for rates of bachelor's degree receipt. The coefficients that are presented have a different scale than for table 7. The outcome variable now varies between 0 and 1 because it is each high school's proportion of sampled students who obtained a bachelor's degree by 2012. Most importantly, the R-squared values suggest that expenditures predict bachelor's degree receipt to a substantial degree.

In particular, for the full sample results in the first panel, a $1,000 shift in salaries for instructional staff is associated with an increase of 6 percent and 4 percent in bachelor's degree receipt, with the difference between the two attributable to cost adjustment. The results in the third column suggest that simultaneous adjustment for family background differences across schools reduces the net associations by half, to 3 and 2 percent, respectively. The bottom panel offers similar conclusions, after dropping the forty-one schools with low and high levels of expenditures.

What are we to make of this last set of results? For context, we should note that we offer results for the other four outcome variables in supplementary appendix tables S6–S9. The results for the other two test score outcomes are very similar to those already presented for tenth-grade math test scores in table 7. The same is true for on-time high school graduation. However, the results for the rate of any postsecondary education suggest that the predictive power of expenditures, just as one would expect, is midway between the patterns revealed by tables 7 and 8. Similar expenditures predict an increase in the attendance rate of 3 and 2 percent, rather than 6 and 4 percent, for bachelor's degree attainment. And again, these coefficients are reduced by about half when simultaneous adjustment for school means of family background are used as adjustment variables.

Now to the substantive question: why do we see slightly more predictive power for expenditures in these between-school models of postsecondary educational attainment? Substantively, there may be good reason to believe narratives that stress why long-run outcomes are influenced by learning environments more than is suggested by the analysis of only short-run, test-based outcomes (see Jennings et al. 2015). However, it is not necessarily the case that expenditures explain the divergence. It

Table 8. Metric Coefficients for Expenditure Variables for Separate Between-School Models of Bachelor's Degree Attainment, With and Without Adjustments for Family Background, Region, and Urbanicity

	Unadjusted		With Adjustments for Family Background, Region, and Urbanicity	
	Coefficient (Standard Error)	R-Squared	Coefficient (Standard Error)	R-Squared
Full sample (559 schools)				
Total expenditures per pupil	0.02 (0.004)	0.056	0.01 (0.003)	0.504
Total expenditures per pupil and cost-adjusted	0.02 (0.004)	0.026	0.01 (0.004)	0.503
Instructional expenditures per pupil	0.03 (0.007)	0.048	0.02 (0.008)	0.505
Instructional expenditures per pupil and cost-adjusted	0.02 (0.008)	0.021	0.01 (0.008)	0.503
Salaries for instructional staff per pupil	0.06 (0.011)	0.066	0.03 (0.011)	0.505
Salaries for instructional staff per pupil and cost-adjusted	0.04 (0.012)	0.031	0.02 (0.011)	0.503
Restricted sample (518 schools)				
Total expenditures per pupil	0.02 (0.004)	0.051	0.01 (0.003)	0.519
Total expenditures per pupil and cost-adjusted	0.01 (0.005)	0.022	0.01 (0.004)	0.518
Instructional expenditures per pupil	0.03 (0.008)	0.045	0.02 (0.008)	0.523
Instructional expenditures per pupil and cost-adjusted	0.02 (0.009)	0.018	0.02 (0.009)	0.520
Salaries for instructional staff per pupil	0.06 (0.012)	0.064	0.03 (0.012)	0.522
Salaries for instructional staff per pupil and cost-adjusted	0.04 (0.014)	0.028	0.02 (0.013)	0.520

Source: ELS, 2002–2012, and CCD, 2001–2004.
Notes: Expenditure variables are entered in thousands of dollars. Data are weighted by the school mean of the individual-level weight (that is, the panel weight constructed by the data distributors [f2pnlwt], multiplied by an adjustment weight that we created to account for missing data on educational attainment) multiplied by the within-school sample sizes in order to generate the precision weighting that is typical of multilevel models.

may be that, even net of family background differences across schools, college-bound youth have parents who choose to send them to more highly resourced schools, under the common belief that schools with more resources are also more likely to prepare their children for college. Students might, in turn, benefit from being surrounded by concentrations of college-bound youth, even if their short-run performance is unaffected (see Wells and Crain 1994). These same parents may also have higher levels of wealth, against which they can borrow to fund their children's postsecondary education through to bachelor's degree completion. Our measures of education, occupation, and income do not fully account for wealth differences between ELS families and hence average levels across their schools.

DISCUSSION

We have offered an analysis of standardized test performance in secondary school and subsequent educational attainment for the high school class of 2004, measured from the sophomore year in 2002 through eight years after typical high school graduation. Setting up the results in ways consistent with the organization and design choices of EEO, we first showed that patterns of achievement and attainment are stratified by race-ethnicity and one dimension of ancestry, using a categorization that is consistent with EEO but also updated for use today. We then showed that the profiles of the high schools attended by ELS students—from patterns of segregation through differences in school facilities and maintenance—are not too dissimilar from those that Coleman and his colleagues considered five decades ago. We also showed what is perhaps surprising to some readers: disparities in expenditures that, without adjustment for the higher costs of schooling in metropolitan areas, imply that some of the groups with the lowest achievement attend schools with some of the highest expenditures.

We then offered models—again following some of the study design choices of EEO—that showed how weakly expenditures and facilities predict achievement and attainment for the ELS students. This weak predictive power remained after adjustments for costs and for family background, as well as after robustness checks that redefined the sample (for example, dropping charter and magnet school students from the individual-level models and dropping schools in the tails of the expenditure distributions from the school-level models). For economy of space, we focused the latter part of our school-level analysis on tenth-grade math test scores and bachelor's degree receipt, but little additional predictive power for expenditures was revealed in our more comprehensive analysis of all six outcome measures analyzed at the individual level, or in additional between-school models presented in the supplementary appendix.

Altogether, the results are mostly in line with the whispered result that has become the apocryphal characterization of EEO: "It's all family." This is certainly what we found for our models of test scores, which were the outcomes studied for EEO. Our between-school models, however, did offer a bit of evidence for expenditure effects on postsecondary educational attainment, especially bachelor's degree receipt. But even here, the associations were dwarfed by the impressive predictive power of between-school means of our measures of family background.

But why? In the remainder of this section, we first discuss contrarian methodological explanations that are plausible. We then consider substantive explanations, based on extant research.

Contrarian Explanations for Why the Results May Be Artifactual

As is always the case in observational research with imperfect data, explanations for the patterns of results exist that justify dismissing them on methodological grounds. These explanations include:

1. Expenditures measured at the district level are a poor indicator of the expenditures relevant to the instruction of individual students, as discussed at the beginning of this paper. As a result, the measured variables we utilized have too little validity to sustain inferences of little or no causation from models that demonstrate little or no association.

2. The ELS sample, and perhaps all of its predecessors since EEO, departs systematically from the target population of regular public high schools in the United States. Schools with students who are harmed by the low expenditures of their districts do not agree to participate in the survey at the same rate as other schools.

3. Because the ELS sample was drawn in the spring of the sophomore year, a disproportionate amount of variation relevant for the

relationships between expenditures and outcomes is absent. Students whose outcomes would generate stronger positive relationships between expenditures and test performance and between expenditures and educational attainment dropped out of high school before the sample was drawn.

Although we concede that these explanations are plausible, we think that they are too extreme, for the following reasons.

For the first explanation, it is undoubtedly the case that there are many school-to-school variations in expenditures. Nonetheless, with nearly fifty years to investigate this possibility since scholars such as Christopher Jencks (1972) first tried, we know of no research that has uncovered stronger effects on achievement for within-district, school-by-school differences in per-pupil expenditures. It is possible that school-to-school variation is not predictive because it is generated mostly by the minor lumpiness of class sizes, slight variation in teacher salaries due to seniority, and other patterns that have little bearing on learning processes. Studies such as Archibald (2006) are largely uninformative because they do not have sufficient measures of students' family backgrounds, and those such as Odden et al. (2008) are focused on the costs of specialized interventions in small numbers of schools—again without sufficient student-level measures of parent characteristics and home environments.

We should also note that some of our results are incompatible with this explanation. The ELS includes ratings of school facilities that capture their condition and maintenance, and these are measured directly at the school level by the relevant ELS survey administrator. Our results match those of Bowers and Urick (2011) in showing that these measures have very small associations with outcomes in the ELS: they explain no more than 2 percent of the student-level variance, even without adjustments for differences in family background. In addition, the ELS elicits items for a scale of whether school principals felt that the learning of tenth-graders was "hindered by" school facilities and their condition. This scale predicts outcomes even more weakly.

These arguments aside, we think that there may well be a relevant hidden dimension across schools that our measures of expenditures cannot pick up: the apparent desire, on average, of many teachers to work in environments, for similar salary levels, where students are easier to teach. We discuss sorting of this type later, because it may be part of a true substantive explanation for our results.

Moving to the second potential methodological explanation, it is possible that patterns of cooperation with NCES vary in ways that undermine the results of longitudinal surveys such as the ELS. The nation's education data collection apparatus does not allow for enough linking of our national samples to universe characteristics of outcome distributions that would permit evaluations of this sort of explanation. Thus, while we know of no evidence that supports this explanation, we also wish that evidence to refute it were available.

More work is needed to conclusively eliminate the third explanation as well. Parallel analyses such as ours for elementary and middle schools would be helpful. Surely more work could be done with national data sources, and we are surprised that we could not find more studies structured just like ours, including some for elementary school students. It is possible that such studies do exist but that they are unpublished because of the "recycling bin" effect that too frequently consigns null findings to the paper mill. Only in celebrations of the EEO, such as this one, are publication goals clearly in line with demonstrating a set of findings that might otherwise be dismissed by journal referees as null results that need not be published.

Positive Substantive Explanations

As much as we find the methodological explanations of the last section unpersuasive, we cannot eliminate them from plausibility. But suppose for this section that they are invalid. And furthermore, suppose that our results are even more extensive, such that they would hold even for measures of standardized test performance and grade progression in elementary and middle school as well. This extended supposition, as we noted earlier, may be incorrect, but too little research has focused on associations between expenditures and educational outcomes in elementary and middle school for us to know. For the sake of argument, suppose that such additional research would come into line with the basic patterns revealed in this paper.

In this case, any substantive explanation can, first and foremost, avail itself of decades of research that suggests why family background is a fundamental cause of educational outcomes. Many of these explanations can account for both between-school and within-school differences in outcomes. We will not review this literature because many pieces already exist that show its connections to the arguments of EEO (see Gamoran and Long 2007; Sørensen and Morgan 2000), as well as other papers in this issue (see Alexander's paper in particular).[22]

Beyond the large explanatory component attributable solely to the pervasive effects of family background, a full substantive explanation of our results would benefit from two additional components, one of which would explain why expenditures have always had weak associations with outcomes and the other of which would explain why those weak associations may have declined over the past five decades.

If one believes the recent research that argues that (a) teacher effectiveness varies a great deal and (b) sorting exists, such that highly effective teachers, at every salary level, are the least likely to be working in regular public schools with the most disadvantaged students, then it follows that instructional quality may have a weak association with average teacher salaries. And because teacher salaries are a large component of differences in expenditures across districts, all measures of expenditures may have correspondingly weak associations with educational outcomes. This structure of teaching effectiveness, generated by the choices of teachers and those who hire them, may have lurked beneath the EEO data as well.

Consider the literature on teacher sorting, which is a prominent theme in decades of research on teacher mobility and teacher attrition. As early as Becker (1952), it has been recognized that many teachers favor work conditions that do not require that they teach students with substantial home disadvantages, or as Howard Becker wrote after studying public schools in Chicago:

> The positions open to a particular teacher in the system at a given time appear, in general, quite similar, all having about the same prestige, income, and power attached to them. . . . Though the available teaching positions in the city schools are similar in formal characteristics, they differ widely in terms of the configuration of the occupation's basic work problems which they present. . . . The greatest problems of work are found in lower-class schools and, consequently, most movement in the system is a result of dissatisfaction with the social-class composition of these school populations. Movement in the system, then, tends to be out from the "slums" to the "better" neighborhoods, primarily in terms of the characteristics of the pupils. Since there are few or no requests for transfer to "slum" schools, the need for teachers is filled by the assignment to such schools of teachers beginning careers in the Chicago system. Thus, the new teacher typically begins her career in the least desirable kind of school. (Becker 1952, 471–72)

Subsequent research in the wake of EEO reinforced Becker's point that salary differences were not the crucial determinant of such moves (see Greenberg and McCall 1974). A consensus position emerged that teachers appeared to demand higher wages to teach in schools with concentrations of students living in poverty, especially if those students were nonwhite (see Antos and Rosen 1975 and Levinson 1988, both of which use EEO as motivating material). More recent research suggests that these patterns remain (see, for example, Clotfelter, Ladd, and Vigdor 2011; Goldhaber, Destler, and Player 2010).

---

22. In addition, we think the support for "school" effects in Grubb (2009) and Borman and Dowling (2010) is also consistent with the extant research because the relevant coefficients in their models are best interpreted as endogenous with respect to family background as well.

If the realities of dysfunction in distressed urban districts are now as dire as scholars such as Charles Payne (2008) claim, then teacher sorting patterns may have strengthened since the 1960s.[23] Moreover, the accountability and standards movement has made it clear to teachers how very risky it is for their career prospects to teach students whose learning is undercut by disadvantages in the home (see Labaree 2010). It would be hard to imagine effective teachers not sorting themselves more than ever in ways that would reinforce any preexisting pattern, even if more teachers are now motivated to enter the profession for altruistic reasons than they were before the challenges of contemporary schooling became widely known and publicly debated.

If one does not believe the recent literature on teacher effectiveness, arguing instead that differences in teacher effects are modest and do not cumulate to the school level, then sorting by teachers may still exist so that salary rates, and hence expenditures, are more similar across districts than would otherwise be the case. And if teachers have comparatively small effects, perhaps because the influences of families are so strong, learning outcomes would then have to be largely determined by support from the home and experiences in residential neighborhoods. In this case, differences in expenditures across districts may reflect sorting by teachers, with higher salaries in more distressed and demoralized districts being necessary simply to staff the classrooms, conditional on differences due to years in the teaching profession.

Regardless of what position one takes on the distribution of effective teachers, it must still be recognized that all of the changes in the structure of inequality and in the policy landscape discussed at the beginning of this paper are in the direction of eliminating any small association between expenditures and outcomes. If Sean Reardon (2011) is correct, and we are witnessing since the 1980s a strengthening of the effects of family background on educational outcomes for a variety of reasons, then both within-school and between-school associations between socioeconomic status and educational outcomes may be rising.[24] But more than this, it is likely that federal funding for compensatory education programs, coupled with states' foundation funding, have delivered funding precisely where it is thought to be needed, so that schools that struggle to generate positive results are also schools that increasingly receive resources that can, it is hoped, help to meet their challenges. But herein has been the opening for the education reform movement. Many of its proponents argue that these additional resources of recent decades have encountered demoralization and dysfunction, which are part and parcel of a preexisting regime of sorting by teachers, and perhaps also by school leaders. If this explanation has merit, then it is the alternative solutions that must continue the debate. Either policy must fundamentally transform schools, or it must deliver an unprecedented amount of money to undo the sorting of effective teachers and school leaders. Either possibility could be successful, although the proponents of each strategy are likely to lock horns.

The more frightening possibility, which we cannot dismiss, is that effective teaching does not line up with the sorting of teachers and all of the most important determinants of educational outcomes remain in the home. In this case—which is probably the default position of many sociologists of education—redistributing teachers and school leaders, by whatever method is feasible, would have small effects

---

23. In addition, some struggling school districts are plagued by dysfunction between state officials, local elected officials, and school administrators. This dysfunction often generates haggling over funding allocations. Such dysfunction can lessen the effectiveness of the available resources that are eventually distributed and recorded as expenditures. In addition to generating staffing uncertainty that undermines program effectiveness, teachers and administrators may be more likely to flee to external opportunities that are more stable and compatible with their long-term career goals.

24. Certainly, we know of no evidence that suggests that these gaps are closing. Results from the long-term assessments for the National Assessment of Educational Progress (NAEP), for example, show remarkable consistency in test score results across levels of parents' education.

on the distribution of outcomes. In this case, only a reduction of the inequality of life conditions into which children are born can generate a meaningful reduction in the inequality of educational outcomes that concerns us all.

REFERENCES

Alexander, Karl. 2016. "Is It Family or School? Getting the Question Right." *RSF: The Russell Sage Foundation Journal of the Social Sciences* 2(5). doi: 10.7758/RSF.2016.2.5.02.

Altonji, Joseph G., and Richard K. Mansfield. 2011. "The Role of Family, School, and Community Characteristics in Inequality in Education and Labor-Market Outcomes." In *Whither Opportunity? Rising Inequality, Schools, and Children's Life Chances*, edited by Greg J. Duncan and Richard J. Murnane. New York: Russell Sage Foundation.

Antos, Joseph R., and Sherwin Rosen. 1975. "Discrimination in the Market for Public School Teachers." *Journal of Econometrics* 3(2): 123–50.

Archibald, Sarah. 2006. "Narrowing in on Educational Resources That Do Affect Student Achievement." *Peabody Journal of Education* 81(4): 23–42.

Baker, Bruce D. 2012. "Revisiting That Age-Old Question: Does Money Matter in Education?" Washington, D.C.: Albert Shanker Institute.

Baker, Bruce D., and Preston C. Green III. 2009. "Conceptions, Measurement, and Application of Educational Adequacy and Equal Educational Opportunity." In *Handbook of Education Policy Research*, edited by Gary Sykes, Barbara L. Schneider, and David N. Plank. New York: Routledge.

Becker, Howard S. 1952. "The Career of the Chicago Public Schoolteacher." *American Journal of Sociology* 57(5): 470–77.

Berry, Chip, and Lei Zhou. 2007. "Documentation for the NCES Common Core of Data School District Finance Survey (F-33), School Year 2003-04 (Fiscal Year 2004) (NCES 2007-391)." Washington: U.S. Department of Education, National Center for Education Statistics.

Borman, Geoffrey, and Maritza Dowling. 2010. "Schools and Inequality: A Multilevel Analysis of Coleman's Equality of Educational Opportunity Data." *Teachers College Record* 112(5): 1–2.

Bowers, Alex J., and Angela Urick. 2011. "Does High School Facility Quality Affect Student Achievement? A Two-Level Hierarchical Linear Model." *Journal of Education Finance* 37(1): 72–94.

Bureau of Economic Analysis. 2014. "Wage and Salary Summary (CA34)." *Local Area Personal Income, 2013*. Washington: U.S. Department of Commerce. Available at: http://www.bea.gov/regional/histdata/releases/1114lapi/index.cfm (accessed August 1, 2015).

Burtless, Gary T. 1996. *Does Money Matter? The Effect of School Resources on Student Achievement and Adult Success*. Washington, D.C.: Brookings Institution Press.

Cain, Glen G., and Harold W. Watts. 1970. "Problems in Making Policy Inferences from the Coleman Report." *American Sociological Review* 35(2): 228–42.

Card, David, and Alan B. Krueger. 1992. "Does School Quality Matter? Returns to Education and the Characteristics of Public Schools in the United States." *Journal of Political Economy* 100(1): 1–40.

———. 1996. "School Resources and Student Outcomes: An Overview of the Literature and New Evidence from North and South Carolina." *Journal of Educational Perspectives* 10(4): 31–50.

Carver, Ronald P. 1975. "The Coleman Report: Using Inappropriately Designed Achievement Tests." *American Educational Research Journal* 12(1): 77–86.

Clotfelter, Charles T., Helen F. Ladd, and Jacob L. Vigdor. 2011. "Teacher Mobility, School Segregation, and Pay-Based Policies to Level the Playing Field." *Education Finance and Policy* 6(3): 399–438.

Coleman, James S. 1970. "Reply to Cain and Watts." *American Sociological Review* 35(2): 242–49.

———. 1990. "The Concept of Equality of Educational Opportunity" (1968). In *Equality and Achievement in Education*, edited by James S. Coleman. Boulder, Colo.: Westview.

Coleman, James S., Ernest Q. Campbell, Carol J. Hobson, James McPartland, Alexander M. Mood, Frederick D. Weinfeld, and Robert L. York. 1966. *Equality of Educational Opportunity*. Washington: U.S. Department of Health, Education, and Welfare, Office of Education.

Corcoran, Sean P., and William N. Evans. 2015. "Equity, Adequacy, and the Evolving State Role in Education Finance." In *Handbook of Research in Education Finance and Policy*, edited by Helen F. Ladd and Margaret E. Goertz. New York: Routledge.

Duncombe, William D., Phuong Nguyen-Hoang, and John Yinger. 2015. "Measurement of Cost Differentials." In *Handbook of Research in Education Finance and Policy*, edited by Helen F. Ladd and Margaret E. Goertz. New York: Routledge.

Gamoran, Adam. 2001. "American Schooling and Educational Inequality: A Forecast for the 21st Century." *Sociology of Education* 74 (extra issue): 135–53.

Gamoran, Adam, and Daniel A. Long. 2007. "Equality of Educational Opportunity: A 40-Year Retrospective." In *International Studies in Educational Inequality, Theory and Policy*, edited by Richard Teese, Stephen Lamb, and Marie Duru-Bellat. Netherlands: Springer.

Gilbert, John P., and Frederick Mosteller. 1972. "The Urgent Need for Experimentation." In *On Equality of Educational Opportunity*, edited by Frederick Mosteller and Daniel Patrick Moynihan. New York: Random House.

Goldhaber, Dan, Katharine Destler, and Daniel Player. 2010. "Teacher Labor Markets and the Perils of Using Hedonics to Estimate Compensating Differentials in the Public Sector." *Economics of Education Review* 29(1): 1–17.

Greenberg, David, and John McCall. 1974. "Teacher Mobility and Allocation." *Journal of Human Resources* 9(4): 480–502.

Grubb, W. Norton. 2009. *The Money Myth: School Resources, Outcomes, and Equity*. New York: Russell Sage Foundation.

Hanushek, Eric A. 1994. *Making Schools Work: Improving Performance and Controlling Costs*. Washington, D.C.: Brookings Institution.

———. 1996. "Measuring Investment in Education." *Journal of Economic Perspectives* 10(4): 9–30.

———. 2001. "Spending on Schools." In *A Primer on America's Schools*, edited by Terry M. Moe. Stanford, Calif.: Hoover Institution Press, Stanford University.

Hanushek, Eric A., and Dale W. Jorgenson. 1996. *Improving America's Schools: The Role of Incentives*. Washington, D.C.: National Academy Press.

Hanushek, Eric A., and Alfred A. Lindseth. 2009. *Schoolhouses, Courthouses, and Statehouses: Solving the Funding-Achievement Puzzle in America's Public Schools*. Princeton, N.J.: Princeton University Press.

Jencks, Christopher. 1972. "The Coleman Report and the Conventional Wisdom." In *On Equality of Educational Opportunity*, edited by Frederick Mosteller and Daniel Patrick Moynihan. New York: Random House.

Jennings, Jennifer L., David Deming, Christopher Jencks, Maya Lopuch, and Beth E. Schueler. 2015. "Do Differences in School Quality Matter More Than We Thought? New Evidence on Educational Opportunity in the Twenty-First Century." *Sociology of Education* 88(1): 56–82.

Kozol, Jonathan. 1992. *Savage Inequalities: Children in America's Schools*. New York: Harper Perennial.

Labaree, David F. 2010. *Someone Has to Fail: The Zero-Sum Game of Public Schooling*. Cambridge, Mass.: Harvard University Press.

Ladd, Helen F., and Margaret E. Goertz, eds. 2015. *Handbook of Research in Education Finance and Policy*. New York: Routledge.

Ladd, Helen F., Janet S. Hansen, and National Research Council (U.S.), Committee on Education Finance. 1999. *Making Money Matter: Financing America's Schools*. Washington, D.C.: National Academy Press.

Levinson, Arik M. 1988. "Reexamining Teacher Preferences and Compensating Wages." *Economics of Education Review* 7(3): 357–64.

Lucas, Samuel R. 2016. "First- and Second-Order Methodological Developments from the Coleman Report." *RSF: The Russell Sage Foundation Journal of the Social Sciences* 2(5). doi: 10.7758/RSF.2016.2.5.06.

Morgan, Stephen L., and Dafna Gelbgiser. 2014. "Mexican Ancestry, Immigrant Generation, and Educational Attainment in the United States." *Sociological Science* 1: 397–422.

Mosteller, Frederick, and Daniel P. Moynihan, eds. 1972a. *On Equality of Educational Opportunity*. New York: Random House.

———. 1972b. "A Pathbreaking Report." In *On Equality of Educational Opportunity*, edited by Frederick Mosteller and Daniel Patrick Moynihan. New York: Random House.

Murnane, Richard J., and Frank Levy. 1996. "Evidence from Fifteen Schools in Austin, Texas." In *Does Money Matter? The Effect of School Resources on Student Achievement and Adult Success*, edited by Gary T. Burtless. Washington, D.C.: Brookings Institution Press.

Nguyen-Hoang, Phuong, and John Yinger. 2014. "Education Finance Reform, Local Behavior, and Student Performance in Massachusetts." *Journal of Education Finance* 39(4): 297–322.

Odden, Allan, Margaret Goertz, Michael Goetz, Sarah

Archibald, Betheny Gross, Michael Weiss et al. 2008. "The Cost of Instructional Improvement: Resource Allocation in Schools Using Comprehensive Strategies to Change Classroom Practice." *Journal of Education Finance* 33(4): 381–405.

Payne, Charles M. 2008. *So Much Reform, So Little Change: The Persistence of Failure in Urban Schools.* Cambridge, Mass.: Harvard Education Press.

Plecki, Margaret L., and Tino A. Castaneda. 2009. "Whether and How Money Matters in K–12 Education." In *Handbook of Education Policy Research,* edited by Gary Sykes, Barbara L. Schneider, and David N. Plank. New York: Routledge.

Reardon, Sean F. 2011. "The Widening Academic Achievement Gap Between the Rich and the Poor: New Evidence and Possible Explanations." In *Whither Opportunity? Rising Inequality, Schools, and Children's Life Chances,* edited by Greg J. Duncan and Richard J. Murnane. New York: Russell Sage Foundation.

———. 2016. "School Segregation and Racial Academic Achievement Gaps." *RSF: The Russell Sage Foundation Journal of the Social Sciences* 2(5). doi: 10.7758/RSF.2016.2.5.03.

Smith, Marshall S. 1972. "Equality of Educational Opportunity: The Basic Findings Reconsidered." In *On Equality of Educational Opportunity,* edited by Frederick Mosteller and Daniel Patrick Moynihan. New York: Random House.

Sørensen, Aage B., and Stephen L. Morgan. 2000. "School Effects: Theoretical and Methodological Issues." In *Handbook of the Sociology of Education,* edited by Maureen T. Hallinan. New York: Kluwer/Plenum.

Tjur, Tue. 2009. "Coefficients of Determination in Logistic Regression Models—a New Proposal: The Coefficient of Discrimination." *The American Statistician* 63(4): 366–72.

Wells, Amy Stuart, and Robert L. Crain. 1994. "Perpetuation Theory and the Long-Term Effects of School Desegregation." *Review of Educational Research* 64(4): 531–55.

West, Martin R., and Paul E. Peterson, eds. 2007. *School Money Trials: The Legal Pursuit of Educational Adequacy.* Washington, D.C.: Brookings Institution Press.

First- and Second-Order Methodological Developments from the Coleman Report

SAMUEL R. LUCAS

Equality of Educational Opportunity *was a watershed for sociological engagement with public policy, yet the questions the project addressed drew attention to several challenging methodological issues. Statistical advances, such as the multilevel model, were important first-order developments from the Coleman Report. Second-order developments, however, may be far less visible but perhaps even more important. Second-order developments of the Coleman Report stem from two sources: (1) social scientists' reactions to proposed resolutions of the statistical challenges that the report navigated, and (2) Coleman's own (perhaps implicit) theoretical response to criticisms of such works as* Equality of Educational Opportunity. *Heightened interest in the challenge of identification serves as an example of the former type of second-order effect, whereas "Coleman's boat" (Coleman 1990)—and the social analytics that adopt, among other approaches, simulation strategies of inquiry consistent with Coleman's typology of causal pathways—serves as an example of the latter. First-order developments take the questions as given and see the challenge as a practical, technical issue; second-order developments explicitly or implicitly reassess the question, treating the challenge as epistemological or social-theoretic. Second-order developments therefore may change the game, upsetting or rejecting routine practice at a fundamental level. I contend that as knowledge of second-order developments and their means of practical implementation in analyses diffuses among social analysts, they will prove of far more value than first-order developments to social understanding, sociology, and social policy.*

Equality of Educational Opportunity (Coleman et al. 1966) constituted arguably the peak moment of sociologists' influence on social, economic, and poverty policy as the national leadership turned to the discipline to contribute fundamental research to help address long-standing racial and socioeconomic inequality. Legislators endeavored to inform policy first and advance social science second. To further this aim Coleman and colleagues administered an ambitious, freestanding, multilevel data collection enterprise. All sampling, in-

Samuel R. Lucas is professor in the Department of Sociology at the University of California, Berkeley.

I thank Stephen Morgan, Karl Alexander, Adam Gamoran, Gary Orfield, Jennifer Jennings, Douglas L. Lauen, William A. Darity Jr., and two anonymous reviewers for comments on an earlier draft, as well as Jan Jacobs, Susan Rachel Schacht (posthumously), H. Sorayya Carr, and participants in the Methods and Epistemology of the Social Sciences (MESS) workshop at Berkeley for continuing helpful conversations on methods. All errors and omissions are the fault of the author. Direct correspondence to: Samuel R. Lucas at lucas@berkeley .edu, Sociology Department, University of California-Berkeley, 410 Barrows Hall, #1980, Berkeley, CA 94720-1980.

strument development, data collection, and report writing was completed in two years—an amazing feat.

The amazement only increases once one realizes the massive nature of the undertaking and the resulting analyses in the Coleman Report. Nearly 100 staff members (Pfautz 1967) used mid-1960s computing power, software, and storage technology to estimate, analyze, and report 500,000 correlations and results of up to 2,000 separate regression equations (Crain 1967, 354)! The multitudinous analyses, the importance of the issues, and the availability of the data combined to motivate and facilitate rigorous reassessments and syntheses, chasing behind findings that reverberated through the halls of Congress and judges' chambers (Bowles and Levin 1968, n. 4) and even the Oval Office (Grant 1973). Thus, by any measure, the Coleman Report was a social scientific watershed.

But as social scientists engage in systematic research, they build on both the notable accomplishments and the stubborn limitations of earlier work. Intriguingly, the Coleman Report is as noteworthy for the advances it has inspired as for those it embodied. Considering the future of research, it will be useful to turn our attention to the former, for those may develop into the foundation on which further comprehension will stand.

To make this turn, I briefly identify a few additional noteworthy aspects of the Coleman Report study design. I then relate key critiques of the Coleman Report. Next, I discuss two exemplary first-order responses to the criticisms, after which I describe a design that takes these responses into account, a "neo–Coleman Report I." As analysts did not enter stasis upon the development of these responses, I next turn to criticisms of the first-order responses. These criticisms motivated additional innovative responses, which are related next. Returning again to the concrete, I describe a design for a "neo–Coleman Report II" that takes account of the second-order response. In the penultimate section, I mention several other efforts that bear the marks of Coleman Report and first- and second-order response influence. Concluding remarks follow. I begin with selected relevant aspects of the Coleman Report.

IMPORTANT DESIGN ELEMENTS OF THE COLEMAN REPORT

As is well known, data collection for the Coleman Report was mandated by the Civil Rights Act of 1964 (Coleman et al. 1966, 549). Data were collected from school superintendents, principals, teachers, and students in grades 1, 3, 6, 9, and 12, with an oversample of schools with high proportions of nonwhites. Multiple tests were administered to students, and a test of verbal achievement was administered to teachers (Ehrenberg and Brewer 1995).

The multistage sampling design nested students in probability-sampled schools and -sampled students such that the students sampled represented their peers at the school. Seventy percent of sampled high school principals responded, and 67 percent of sampled high schools delivered student tests and questionnaires; all told, 59 percent of high schools had both types of data. Seventy-four percent of principals for sixth-grade schools returned both principal and student materials (Coleman et al. 1966, 564). Given the massive target sample sizes, these response rates meant that data were obtained on over 3,000 schools and over 625,000 students, an impressive number given that several large urban school districts (Sewell 1967), including Chicago (Havighurst 1967) and Los Angeles (Grant 1973), refused to participate.

Question-specific nonresponse also occurred. Missing data were addressed by substituting the mean of the valid values for respondents with missing responses. The analysis team conducted several tests to assess the impact of both nonparticipation and question-specific nonresponse, finding the bias to be small and unpatterned.

Parenthetically, what has often gone unnoticed is that the investigation team used mixed methods. Raymond W. Mack directed ten case studies of the education of urban nonwhites, while George William Foster directed an analysis of the legal issues involved in desegregation in seven cities (Sewell 1967, 475). These qualitative analyses were later published (see, for example, Mack 1968), but chapter 7 of the Coleman Report presents highlights of some of those analyses.

The legislation aimed to document resource differences, motivating collection of data on school-level inputs to education. For decades, research had documented racial inequality in number of school days (for example, Norton 1926), teacher qualifications (Norton 1926), per-pupil expenditure (Phillips 1932), teacher-student ratio (Moses 1941), facilities (Moses 1941; Strayer 1949), and curriculum (Strayer 1949; Wallace 1951). Thus, the data collection team focused on such inputs—a task that may have become more difficult with the end of de jure racial segregation. Still, the question of interest was whether nonwhites attended schools with fewer, low-quality, or otherwise substandard resources. Thus, data on these kinds of school factors were obtained because decades of research, while not national in scope, documented racial inequality in these resources.

For all districts, the study team obtained district-level measures on expenditures per student from which school-level expenditures per student were calculated. Data on the size of each school and its library were also obtained. For high schools, data were obtained on whether the school had guidance counselors, a science laboratory, an accelerated curriculum, a comprehensive school curriculum, tracking, and extracurricular activities, as well as the school's location in a city, suburb, town, or rural area. In addition, the study team used aggregate characteristics of the student body to measure the peer environment. The proportion of families owning an encyclopedia, the level of attendance, and the number of student transfers were obtained for all schools. The study team also aggregated elementary school teachers' reports of their perception of the quality of the student body; for high schools, they calculated the average hours of homework and the proportion of students planning to attend college as additional measures of peer environment.

Data were collected on parents' education level, father's occupation, and the presence of several items in the home (television set; telephone; record player, hi-fi, or stereo; refrigerator; dictionary; encyclopedia; automobile; vacuum cleaner; delivered newspaper). Notably, the occupation data seem to have been omitted in indexing students' backgrounds.[1]

The analysis documented high levels of racial segregation. However, it showed general equality in the distribution of school-level resources. Further, in comparing the amount of variance explained by student background and school-level factors, it showed that background factors won the explained variance "horse race." Although students' school peers and some characteristics of teachers explained some of the variance in achievement, the horse-race results were interpreted as indicating that schools had little impact on student achievement.

KEY CRITICISMS OF THE COLEMAN REPORT

Selected Criticisms and Their Implications

The claim that "the schools bring little influence to bear on a child's achievement that is independent of his [sic] background and general social context" (Coleman et al. 1966, 325) was perhaps the most famous and controversial statement from the study. But many of the study's findings were controversial, and these controversies motivated microscopic reexamination of and debate about many aspects of the design (see, for example, Crain 1967; Sewell 1967; Bowles and Levin 1968; Dyer 1968; Pettigrew 1968; Wilson 1968; Aigner 1970; Cain and Watts 1970; Hanushek and Kain 1972; Mosteller and Moynihan 1972).

The low response rates were one immediate concern (Nichols 1966; Sewell 1967; Bowles and Levin 1968; Dyer 1968). Although the number of schools and students participating was impressive, central cities were more likely to opt out; thus, metropolitan *samples* were more suburban than metropolitan *populations*, and impoverished schools with high proportions

---

1. Diane Looker (1989) finds that children are better reporters of their parents' occupation than of their parents' education.

of nonwhites may have been underrepresented. The low response rate and its nonrandom nature threaten the generalizability of the findings and raise the possibility that the variance of school-level variables was artificially deflated, reducing the chance of finding an association between school-level factors, race, and achievement.

Question-specific nonresponse was also a concern (see, for example, Bowles and Levin 1968). Because the solution, mean substitution, lowers the variance of the variable so treated as well as its covariance with other variables, the chance of a discernible association between mean substituted variables and other variables is lowered as well.

Another criticism centered on the school-level data collection. Historic research had shown that under dual systems of education, expenditures per white student exceeded the expenditure per nonwhite student (see Irby 1930; Phillips 1932). That same research had documented the great difficulty in obtaining data that would reveal the disparities, because the records released often combined categories in a way that, purposely or not, masked them (Moses 1941). Such data and difficulties suggest that within-district school-to-school differences might have been an important mechanism through which racial inequality in education was maintained. Alas, the data collection team collected district-level expenditure data and allocated an equal amount of funds to each school in the district (Bowles and Levin 1968, 8–9). Coleman (1968, 239) contended that, owing to the state of financial records in U.S. school systems, the survey team's strategy was the only feasible option, and further, that its use simply transformed the interpretation from one of school-to-school differences into one of system-to-system differences. Yet historic evidence indicates that in some jurisdictions those accounting systems had long masked large within-district racial disparities in expenditure. If such masking had continued, the failure to gather truly school-specific expenditure data in the mid-1960s could underlie the finding of small or even nonexistent differences in resources by race and, by restricting the range of the variables and introducing measurement error, may explain why school-level factors of the period appeared to be of little consequence for racial inequality.

Analysts also questioned the effort to draw causal conclusions (see Bowles and Levin 1968). One version of this criticism (for example, Nichols 1966; Dyer 1968) highlighted the difficulty of using cross-sectional data to draw causal conclusions and called for a longitudinal design to enable statistical controls for prior achievement. Such critics often admitted and lamented that the legislatively imposed time frame precluded a longitudinal study.

A second version of the criticism (for example, Dyer 1968) of the effort to draw causal conclusions focused on the horse-race statistical reporting. This criticism noted that the horse-race approach failed to consider the dynamic production of achievement—that is, it failed to consider a process by which student race and socioeconomic background factors affected peer-level and school-level characteristics and treatment of the student (including the possible differentiating behavior of school personnel), which affect student attitudes and school-provided opportunities, which lead to the opportunities, effort, and gains that eventuate in measured achievement. This criticism implied that the achievement process was so much more complex than the model specified that findings from the model were likely to mislead. Coleman (1968) contended that the limited state of knowledge about the achievement process prevented the use of a more comprehensive and dynamic model. Further, to refrain from research until such a model became possible was to force policymakers to act in the absence of understanding.

While Coleman's response rings true, this criticism raised key questions about the stark, implicit input-output model employed in the achievement analyses. In the intervening decades, analysts have focused intently on this issue, in essence heeding both the criticism *and* Coleman's response, by developing and elaborating theories of the education process and the methodological tools needed to analyze that process. Thus, criticism of the implicit input-output model employed has spurred important advances for contemporary analysts and set the stage for additional advances in the decades to come.

Selected Implications of the Critique of the Input-Output Model

One implication of the criticism of the report's input-output model turns on the specification and "horse-race" assessment of the regression model. Focusing on a horse race between socioeconomic background and school-level variables implied that 100 percent of the variance in achievement could be explained by cross-school differences (often cross-system differences in the Coleman Report case, owing to its measurement strategy). This approach was likely to produce what appeared to be low estimates of school-level effects because individual-level variables, such as socioeconomic background, varied within and between schools. Thus, the maximum variance in an individual-level outcome that could be explained by individual-level variables was the sum of all of the variance that occurred within schools and all of the variance that occurred between schools—in other words, 100 percent of the variance in the outcome. In contrast, school-level variables only varied across schools, not within them; thus, school-level variables could only explain the outcome variance that occurred between schools, which was almost always less—and often a great deal less—than 100 percent of the variance in the outcome. Essentially, a horse race of this character compares the distance covered after allowing one horse to run up to 100 percent of the course while constraining the other horse to stop running long before it can cover most of the course. The Coleman Report horse-race comparison thus unequally calibrated the variance explainable at each level, leading to what can be termed the *calibration critique*.

A second implication of the critique of the input-output model is more theoretical. The critique is that in-school processes were mostly ignored (Dyer 1968; Bowles and Levin 1968). For example, teachers' own cognitive levels as an input to students' learning are admittedly important. Yet, depending on grade level, a teacher with great subject matter knowledge but less (or lower-quality) pedagogical knowledge may produce less student achievement than a teacher with less subject matter knowledge but more (or higher-quality) pedagogical knowledge. Such possibilities change the issue from one of determining which teachers know more to assessing both what teachers know and whether and how they use that knowledge in teaching students. The *education process critique* implies that the Coleman Report's findings may be off or unclear in part because the findings are not grounded in solid prior understanding of how students, teachers, and schools actually work.

These two critiques differ in character. The calibration critique contends that the school effect estimates may be right, but that they have been interpreted incorrectly (and probably understated), whereas the education process critique implies that by missing central aspects of the way learning occurs, the school effects estimates are wrong and are likely to be underestimated.

In the decades following publication of the Coleman Report, many analysts attended to either or both of these critiques, and the resulting dialogue pushed the analysis of education—and other socially important phenomena—to new heights of sophistication and capability. That dialogue can be understood as having occurred in stages. In the original stage, which I term the *first-order response,* analysts resolved the calibration and education process critiques in terms outlined in the original debate. This promising stage ended, however, as compelling criticisms of the first-order responses emerged, criticisms that prevented the easy adoption of the solutions produced by the first-order response. Those criticisms pushed scholars further, inspiring critical, reflective engagement with the foundational issues that were perhaps latent within the original critiques. The responses that followed these criticisms form the *second-order response*. For the remainder of this analysis, I turn attention to all three phases of the developing, multistage, somewhat discontinuous dialogue following from the Coleman Report.

EXEMPLARY FIRST-ORDER RESPONSES

The calibration critique calls for development of means to properly partition the variance across individual and contextual levels. The education process critique calls for better understanding of how schools work to produce learning and other outcomes. The multilevel model was, in part, a response to the calibration critique, while an intensified turn to the differentiating power of in-school and cross-school processes and arrangements was a response to the education process critique.

The Multilevel Model as a Response to the Calibration Critique

The Coleman Report was perhaps the most complex effort to take account of multiple levels of analysis simultaneously, but several analysts of the period were already attempting such work under the label of *contextual analysis* (for example, Bowers 1968). Contextual analysts define contexts by the aggregated values of a single individual-level variable. For example, for contextual analysis schools are placed into categories according to the mean level of parents' education; thus, high schools might be classified as high, medium-high, medium-low, and low parental education contexts. Then analysts assess whether some outcome of interest (such as student test scores) varies by schools' parental education context. Some analysts might compare the power of the education of students' own parents to the power of schools' parental education context.

For several reasons, contextual analysis failed at its appointed task. Robert Hauser (1970a, 1974) persuasively showed that contextual analysis forced researchers to decompose individual outcomes into only two factors: (1) that due to individual-level variation in independent variables, and (2) that due to variation in contexts *defined by an aggregation (mean, proportion) of one other individual-level variable of interest* (for example, the mean level of education in the context). A key basis of the method's failure, therefore, was that it forced analysts to define contexts, which necessarily have multiple traits, in a way that ignored that multiplicity. Further, because contexts are at least somewhat homophilous, an aggregated individual-level characteristic arguably provides an error-corrected version of the individual-level variable (Bowles and Levin 1968). These and other problems in part motivated Hauser's (1970b, 517) call for analysts to "operationalize directly those variables—individual or aggregate—which play a part in the social processes we study." These features imply that a horse race between an individual-level variable and its context-level analog is uninformative as to the relative power of either, whether that race be scored in terms of explained variance or otherwise.

However, some were reluctant to abandon contextual analysis (for example, Farkas 1974), perhaps owing to the undeniable possibility that context matters. Absent an apparatus for simultaneously studying multiple levels, analysts would be forced to adopt one of two ineffective approaches: either (1) reduce all phenomena to the individual level, or (2) aggregate all individual-level factors to a contextual level (Burstein, Linn, and Capell 1978). Thus, contextual analysis joined the alternatives of the period in being unable to satisfy researchers' substantive and theoretical demands.

A more promising line of approach grew in part out of attempts to resolve the reduction/aggregation challenge, an effort that would lead regression coefficients themselves to be conceived as partially random outcomes (see, for example, Zellner 1969; Akkina 1974) and that would eventually produce a method to answer the questions that contextual analysts had sought to address (Boyd and Iverson 1979). William Mason, George Wong, and Barbara Entwisle (1983) note, however, that the breakthrough of Lindley and Smith (1972), built on a Bayesian framework and applying the concept of exchangeability, was not immediately recognized as relevant in part because the statistical, sociological, and economics literatures were pursued largely in isolation. However, advances in computer processing power (Fuchs 2001), software (Bryk et al. 1988), and key didactic works (Bryk and Raudenbush 1992; Hox 1995; Kreft and de Leeuw 1998; Snijders and Bosker 1999; Goldstein 2003; Pinheiro and Bates 2004) eventually brought the model to the wider community.

One can identify at least two types of multilevel models. In *means-as-outcomes models*, the regression equation intercept, b_0, is allowed to vary across contexts. It is an adjusted mean if any other microlevel variables are included in the model. In *slopes-as-outcomes models*, one or more regression slopes for microlevel variables are allowed to vary across contexts.

Appendix A conveys both multilevel models in equation form. An intriguing implication arises upon juxtaposing the means-as-outcomes and slopes-as-outcomes models. In the means-as-outcomes models, macrolevel factors are associated with the outcome only by being associated with context-specific outcome means. Thus, the means-as-outcomes model simply restates the constraints of the original input-output model—that is, school-level variables can only affect between-school differences. However, the slopes-as-outcomes model differs: in that model, macrolevel factors interact (mathematically) with one or more individual-level factors, such that the payoff of one or more individual-level factors depends on the values of macrolevel variables. The major implication of this specification is that *within*-school differences can vary across schools in line with *between*-school factors—that is, the relationships inside the school can be different depending on the value of variables that differ across schools. Thus, the complete inability of cross-school differences to alter within-school effects is no more!

Modelers began by considering interval-level outcomes, but analysts have developed forms of multilevel models for logistic regression (Wong and Mason 1985), ordinal outcomes (Hedeker and Gibbons 1994), time series analysis (Goldstein, Healy, and Rasbash 1994), structural equations (Muthén 1994), event history analysis (Steele, Goldstein, and Browne 2004), and more (for cross-classified data, for example, see Goldstein 1994).

The multilevel model has been used in multiple areas of the social sciences. As the key response to the calibration critique, the multilevel model became an important resource for analysts in multiple areas of inquiry, in part because its application seemed to require few demands. For some, the multilevel model required only a data set that linked individuals to macrolevel contexts (Luke 2004); indeed, even a convenience sample was deemed sufficient (Hox 1995, 1). Still, before the model could be used to deepen our understanding of how schools work, the theoretical and empirical lines that emanated from the Coleman Report needed to mature. It is that development to which I now turn.

Theorizing and Investigating In-School and Between-School Stratification:
Response to the Education Process Critique

The Coleman Report analysis team adopted the input-output model because consensus around a more complex, more faithful-to-the-inner-workings-of-education model did not exist (Coleman 1968, 239–40). Some critics acceded to the proposition that research on the inner workings of schools had not coalesced into, much less provided, a solid enough position to guide the analysis of an endeavor such as the Coleman Report (see, for example, Dyer 1968, 54).

Henry Dyer (1968) used tracking research as an example of an area of study that had been pursued with insufficient coordination and systematicity. The immense number of possible ways of grouping students for multiple subjects or even one subject of study, coupled with a lack of systematicity across the many studies, had harmed analysts' efforts, he argued, to develop consensus understandings of the ubiquitous school practice of grouping.

In a paper titled "Organizational Differentiation of Students and Educational Opportunity," Aage Bøttger Sørensen (1970) provided a major step forward from this state of affairs. Setting aside age-grading—the allocation of students to grades based largely (but not completely) on an age-qualified initiation of formal schooling—Sørensen noted that school systems divide the curriculum horizontally and vertically. Vertical divisions are such that one lesson or course facilitates the next. For example, arithmetic is a precursor to algebra. Horizontal divisions, however, do not build on each other; for example, neither calculus nor matrix algebra is a prerequisite for the other, nor are chemistry and French II prerequisites for each other.

Sørensen identified several dimensions along which systems of curriculum differentiation might vary. For example, systems might allow large, moderate, small, or no incidence of mobility. And the system of allocation to subjects might have wide or narrow scope, with the former meaning that much of a student's day is spent with the same peers. This theoretical development facilitated empirical efforts to determine schools' placement along multiple dimensions, enabling assessment of the complex possibilities and potential effects of different ways of arranging curriculum differentiation.

Given Sørensen (1970), analysts used multiple analytic strategies, comparing students in different curricular locations (Gamoran 1987), schools with and without tracking (Hoffer 1992), students at different levels of schooling (Hotchkiss and Dorsten 1987; Pallas et al. 1994), and schools with different organizational features (Riehl, Pallas, and Natriello 1999) and studying a multiplicity of outcomes (on college entry, see Rosenbaum 1980; on delinquency, see Wiatrowski et al. 1982; on alienation, see Oakes 1982). For reviews of this extensive literature, see, for example, Gamoran and Berends (1987), Slavin (1990), and Lucas (2008).

If Sørensen (1970) outlined the dimensions within which the black box of schooling is located, other analysts began to open that receptacle to detailed study of the learning process. Identifying classrooms and subunits of classrooms as a primary site of learning, Rebeca Barr and Robert Dreeben (1983) plumbed those sites for the processes underlying their effects while simultaneously tracing how the stage for those effects is set by higher-level organizational factors. Sørensen and Maureen Hallinan (1977) specified a process model of student achievement involving students' ability, effort, and opportunity to learn. Through this model, Sørensen and Hallinan established the theoretical finding that under some conditions good schools (defined as those with many opportunities to learn) increase within-school achievement inequality.

On the basis of such work, analysts learned that the resources that schools supply—especially time and materials—affect teachers and thus differentially affect the learning of students in high- and low-track positions (Gamoran and Dreeben 1986); that class size, another determinant of the time available for each students' learning, matters (Krueger and Whitmore 2002); that racial-ethnic and socioeconomic diversity are associated with track rigidity independent of students' prior profiles of achievement (Lucas and Berends 2002); that high school achievement depends in part on students' placement in the structure of curriculum differentiation and what the structure is (Gamoran 1992); and more.

Alongside these research streams, Coleman, Thomas Hoffer, and Sally Kilgore (1981) analyzed school sector differences, finding that students in public schools performed less well than peers at Catholic and private non-Catholic schools. That analysis can be seen as an effort to establish school effects using the vehicle of school sector. Each sector represented different in-school process *regimes,* such that to compare sectors is to compare arguably coherent sets of in-school processes (Chubb and Moe 1988).

However, this effort sparked serious criticisms (see, for example, Goldberger and Cain 1982), some of which applied to the in-school stratification literature as well; the compelling nature of this criticism signaled the beginning of the end of the heyday of the first-order response. Before turning to those criticisms, I first describe a Coleman Report replication design that takes account of the first-order response.

The Neo-Coleman Report I: A First-Order, Critique-Influenced Coleman Report Replication

Replicating the Coleman Report based on the first-order responses would leave some features of the study intact. Notably, the collection of data on students nested in schools and the collection of cognitive test data on teachers would be maintained. And as before, data to allow study of both school outcomes, such as cognitive achievement, grade retention, graduation, and college entry, and factors within the schooling process, such as educational aspirations and other social-psychological factors, would be collected. But major design changes would also follow.

First, simultaneous collection of data on multiple schooling grades would be maintained but reduced to shift study resources to lower the incidence of missing data. Offering participating districts and schools analyses of key relations of interest (for example, anonymized graphs of the relation of sex-gender, socioeconomic background, race-ethnicity, course levels, teaching strategies, and more with achievement) could aid persuasion efforts. In addition, follow-up contacts on missing critical items would be used to reduce missing data for key variables (see, for example, Lucas et al. 1987).

Second, the collection of data would be improved for concepts that were originally measured with proxies. For example, instead of collecting district-specific expenditure data and allocating the expenditures equally across schools, actual school-specific expenditure data would be collected. As another example, instead of calculating a proxy for class size by dividing the number of students by the number of teachers, actual class size (and attendance) data would be collected for each class period.

Data would be collected on students' course-taking in sufficient detail to allow students' placement in the national, differentiated curriculum (Lucas 1999). This part of the design necessitates collecting sufficient data on additional levels of nesting (for example, the classroom) to allow assessment of classrooms inside schools and thus facilitate assessment of within-school differences. And because systems of student allocation to courses may matter as well, data sufficient to score schools on Sørensen-dimensions of curricular stratification would also be collected, facilitating cross-school analyses.

Much of schooling occurs inside classrooms, but knowing no more than which students are within which classrooms addresses only the structural aspects of education processes, not the instructional aspects. In order to fully address the education process critique data on instruction are also needed. For example, instead of stopping the measurement of resources at the level of depth reflected in counting the number of library books, analysts would go further, collecting the textbooks and syllabi used in each class and coding the materials to peg the rigor of each student's classes. Such measures would enable analysts to study both within- and between-school inequalities in resource and instruction quality.

Data would be collected on sampled students for two consecutive academic years, making the design longitudinal, to allow analysts to consider achievement growth from a measured, preexisting level. (Data on their teachers each year would also be collected.) To fully analyze growth, multiple data collections would occur each year (for example, in the fall and spring of each academic year of data collection). The longitudinal design would allow analysts to focus on processes occurring in school by arguably washing out occurrences prior to the school year of interest and enabling the removal of summer learning complexities (Heyns 1979; Alexander, Entwisle, & Olson 2007). Such a design would have the added advantage of allowing analysts to consider the role of both transitory and stable socioeconomic background factors (such as transitory income versus "permanent income").

With such data, analysts would use the multilevel model to estimate coefficients for school-, classroom- (or teacher-), and school-level factors on student outcomes. Analysts would not only use school-level factors, such as the rate of track mobility, and classroom-level factors, such as the rigor of textbooks and syllabi, but also compositional variables, such as the mean level of education of the parents of students in the school or classroom. Using such measures, analysts would attempt to estimate context-level effects on student outcomes. Using the multilevel model with such data addresses the calibration critique. Indeed, the model's ability to properly calibrate context-level effects while allowing coefficients for individual-level factors to vary according to macrolevel factors (for example, allowing socioeconomic background effects on achievement to depend on schools' level of track mobility) renders the stark partition unnecessary and often inappropriate.

Finally, analysts would draw on research on missing data (Little 1992) to systematically employ a better approach than mean substitution. Further, analysts would check the robustness of findings against different assumptions for missing data.

Proponents of the first-order critiques imply that a replication along these lines would alter the Coleman Report results. Alas, we may never know whether using this design in the mid-1960s would have produced the original findings. What could be known, however, is which results from the past would replicate upon using the neo–Coleman Report I design in the contemporary period. Before such an issue is assessed, however, we must recognize that first-order developments were not the final word on the issue. Instead, those developments themselves faced criticisms.

FIRST-ORDER METHODOLOGICAL DEVELOPMENTS CHALLENGED

The Education Process Critique: Questioning the First-Order Response

Many theoretical advances were largely accepted as identifying dimensions or phenomena worthy of study. Yet analysts continued to tighten the focus to discern the key pedagogical factors underlying learning. For example, given the importance of student effort in the production of achievement, David Shernoff and his colleagues (2003) have applied flow theory—a theory of optimal experience—to identify the kinds of pedagogies that maximize student engagement. Martin Nystrand and his colleagues (2003) have studied the emergence of student engagement in the dynamic conditions of classroom dialogue, finding that authentic (teacher) questions, teacher uptake of student contributions, and student questions are important spurs to student engagement. Such work has allowed the visualization of how institutional actors (such as superintendents) and macrolevel factors (for example, socioeconomic residential segregation) might send varying resources (for example, teachers of different skill levels) to different schools, enabling differential teacher-student collaboration in ways that maintain or exacerbate achievement inequality.

However, amid the flurry of empirical research, a long-standing, nagging question became an increasing concern: are outcomes driven by processes allocating students to schools or positions in school, on the one hand, or instead, are outcomes a result of processes occurring inside the schools and the positions to which students are allocated? The question pushed analysts back to consider the determinants of placement and, conditional on those findings, to devise strategies of research to address selection issues that might confound efforts to determine the effects of students' schools or positions in school.

With respect to in-school processes, analysts have found that the higher a student's socioeconomic background (Rosenbaum 1980) or prior achievement (Jones, Vanfossen, and Ensminger 1995), the more likely the student is to enter demanding curricular locations. Findings with respect to race have often been less clear (Garet and DeLany 1988; Mickelson 2001), but later research has reconciled the differences by using the multilevel model to allow black-white differences in probabilities of advanced course-taking to vary across schools. The findings reveal that, net of prior achievement and socioeconomic background, blacks' and whites' probabilities of entering demanding courses differ across schools. Those differences are associated with school diversity, region, and school size (Lucas and Berends 2007). Indeed, the pattern resembles one-for-one substitution of whites for blacks into demanding courses as one traces the graph from less to more diverse schools (see Lucas and Berends 2007, 180, fig. 2).

Findings of differential entry to demanding curricular positions by socioeconomic background and race, even after other determinants (such as achievement) are controlled, have further motivated analysts to attempt to estimate effects of track location that take account of selection on observables. But to purge selection bias from estimates of track effects has required analysts to account not only for observable factors shown to correlate with placement but also for unobservable factors that might nonrandomly allocate students to different tracks.

Analysts have used endogenous switching regression models that can control for selection into tracks on both observable and unobservable factors (Gamoran and Mare 1989; Lucas and Gamoran 2002). Estimates have revealed positive effects of track location on outcomes, indicating that nonrandom allocation to curricular positions does not fully explain prior estimated positive high-track effects. The models address selection bias, but as with all such methods, applications may rely on difficult-to-establish identifying assumptions (Winship and Mare 1992). If those assumptions are faulty, the calculated parameters will not capture the causal effect.

The same conundrum bedevils efforts to estimate school sector effects. The landmark Bryk, Lee, and Holland (1993) study used a mixed-methods approach to investigate the determinants of students' entry into Catholic school and to estimate Catholic school effects. Many aspects of the work are informative and impressive. Yet it is also true that the findings can be explained by selection processes.

For example, key findings conveyed in three figures graph the association between socioeconomic status (SES) and senior-year achievement in public and Catholic schools that resemble: (1) schools with the average social composition of Catholic schools (Bryk, Lee, and Holland (1993, 264–65, fig. 10.6); (2) schools with the average social composition of public schools (fig. 10.7); and (3) schools serving large numbers of disadvantaged students (fig. 10.8). In the first figure, the curve for public schools is lower but steeper than the curve for Catholic schools, a pattern that can be explained by selection on unobservables. Low-SES students with advantaged unobservables (for example, parents especially enabled to find or provide solid educational opportunities for their child) likely have higher achievement than do their unobservably disadvantaged low-SES peers, and they may also be more likely to enter Catholic schools than such peers. The enrollment pattern boosts the achievement of low-SES students in Catholic schools compared to their peers left behind in public school. The Catholic school advantage declines as SES rises, which may occur if selection on achievement-related unobservables declines as SES rises. The boost for lower-SES students in Catholic schools, coupled with less selection on unobservables for higher-SES students, reduces the slope for socioeconomic status in Catholic schools relative to public schools. The same story applies to the second figure, but more mutedly because the comparison is for Catholic and public schools with compositions similar to the average public school.

In the third figure, the curve for Catholic schools is higher and steeper than the curve for public schools. Comparing schools with large numbers of disadvantaged students, unobservables distinguish high-SES students who select into high-disadvantage Catholic schools compared to high-SES students who attend high-disadvantage public schools, leading to higher achievement for the former. Selection on unobservables may be less strong among low-SES students in high-disadvantage schools because the illustrative low-SES parent particularly enabled to find solid educational opportunities for their child may be less able to do so if the relevant Catholic school strongly resembles the nearby public school. But selection may still exist, as reflected in the somewhat higher Catholic school achievement of low-SES students compared to their lower achievement in similar public schools.

Certainly, Bryk, Lee, and Holland (1993) offer plausible interpretations of the patterns that highlight differences in in-school processes. And their mixed-methods analysis does address several criticisms one might articulate. Yet the point of the discussion is not to unequivocally assert that the patterns they document flow from selection; the point is to establish that what appear to be school effects identified through cross-sector comparison could be equally explained as selection effects. And the plausibility of the selection explanation greatly diminishes the utility of the sector comparison strategy for identifying school effects, regardless of whether the method is qualitative or quantitative, unless selection is explicitly addressed.

In this way, in both the effort to consider in-school processes and the effort to look across schools, robust critiques sidelined many empirical elements of the first-order response.

The Calibration Critique: Questioning the Applicability of the Multilevel Model

The multilevel model can be seen as a feasible means to study contexts and thus as an answer to the problems of contextual analysis. Alas, and unbeknownst to many, the multilevel model does not seem to provide the widely applicable escape from many of the problems that have hampered contextual analysis. Problems can be placed into two categories: (1) problems due to common *application* of the multilevel model, and (2) problems *inherent* to the model as a means of decomposing contextual effects.

Application Problems

The application problems are easiest to resolve. One such problem occurs because a high proportion of the research using multilevel models uses secondary data. Analysts collecting their own data might have a chance to ensure sufficient sample size for informative estimation, but the use of secondary data can lead to insufficient level 2 sample size (Bryan and Jenkins 2016), rendering the level 2 estimates unreliable.

Another application problem is that many context analyses capitalize on the higher reliability of aggregated variables, as noted earlier (Bowles and Levin 1968). If we use the mean level of mothers' education in a school as a context-level variable, that variable will be more reliably measured than mother's education is for any single individual student. Such a context-level variable may simply capture variation associated with the individual level that is not captured at the individual level owing to measurement error. A related measurement problem is that inferences are often erroneous because macrolevel factors (for example, the mean level of parents' education in the school) are estimated from the sample rather than known. If analysts treat these estimates as if they are known, standard errors are underestimated (Manski 1995).

An application problem also arises from the common assumption among analysts that processes that allocate entities to contexts can be ignored (Hauser 1974). Ignoring nonrandom selection into contexts, however, can contaminate putative macrolevel causal effects with selection biases. Analysts also often assume that persons know their peers' outcomes, but rarely introduce evidence to support this assumption; the result is yet another application problem (Manski 1995).

A final insidious application problem is that secondary data are often collected with a complex sample design that does not support unbiased estimation of multilevel model parameters. Elsewhere (Lucas 2014), I have proposed the concept of fully multilevel probability (FMP) samples. FMP samples meet three criteria: (1) level 1 entities (for example, students) are probability-sampled to represent the population of level 1 entities (students in the state or nation studied); (2) level 2 entities (for example, elementary schools) are probability-sampled to represent the population of level 2 entities (elementary schools in the state or nation); and (3) level 1 entities (students) are probability-sampled to represent the other level 1 entities (their fellow students) inside their specific level 2 entity (their school). Appendix B provides equations that illustrate the implications of failing on one of those criteria.

Many nationally representative data sets with geocoded data, such as the Panel Study of Income Dynamics (PSID), the General Social Survey (GSS), and the National Longitudinal Study of Adolescent to Adult Health (Add Health), fail to satisfy the criteria of an FMP sample for some research questions. When the criteria are not satisfied, macrolevel parameters are biased to an unknown degree and in an unknown direction (Lucas 2014, 1625–28).

Inherent Problems

The debilitating *inherent* problem of contextual analysis was identification, and as Charles Manski (1995) indicates, the problem remains with the multilevel model. Manski distinguishes: (1) endogenous effects, (2) contextual effects, (3) ecological effects, and (4) correlated individual effects. To fix ideas, consider a cohort of students in several different schools and ask the following question: what factors are associated with a particular student's performance on a standardized achievement test?

If we expect that a student's measured achievement is affected by the measured achievement of other students in the school, then we have posited an *endogenous effect*. Endogenous effects concern the impact of the behavior of others with respect to some phenomenon on a particular person's behavior with respect to the *same* phenomenon; for example, the academic performance of a student's peers may affect that student's academic performance.

In contrast, if we posit that students in schools with a high rate of delinquency will be less likely to have high achievement scores, we have posited a *contextual effect*. In doing so, we are concerned with the question of whether a person's performance varies with the distribution of *other* characteristics in the reference group. Manski (1995) notes that often analysts posit an endogenous effect but investigate several contextual effects (see, for example, Crane 1991). Confusing endogenous and contextual effects impedes effective theorizing of the mechanisms through which contexts might have their effects.

If we expect that schools composed of a large proportion of delinquent students will have other negative characteristics, such as poor facilities or authoritarian discipline practices, then we have posited that students in the same school face similar institutional environments that may account for their similar behavioral response (in this case, their academic performance). Manski regards such effects as *ecological effects*.

Finally, if we believe that students in similar schools share similar unobserved individual characteristics, such as levels of curiosity, and that these individual-level attributes account for their similar behavior, then we have posited *correlated individual effects*. Appendix C develops the difficulty with estimating all four types of effects.

In response to old-style contextual analysis, Hauser (1970a) shows that analysts may often conflate endogenous, contextual, and correlated individual effects. Alas, the same problem can hound multilevel modelers, because, regardless of whether one uses 1960s-era contextual analysis or twenty-first-century multilevel models, there are many ways the analysis can go awry. For example, one may conflate context and correlated individual effects by positing an indefensible individual-level model, inadvertently leaving more unexplained variance that may be captured by context-level variables. That unexplained variance would partially reflect unmeasured individual-level determinants that are correlated across individuals and may be incorrectly assigned to context-level variables. Thus, Hauser contends that the individual-level model must be a defensible baseline.

Manski (1993) demonstrates that even with the introduction of controversial assumptions, contextual and endogenous effects cannot be distinguished. Moreover, even the determination of whether such effects exist is fraught with peril; Manski (1993, 35–36) shows four common scenarios in which important conditions for these results are violated.

The many difficulties that Hauser and Manski identify culminate in a resounding critique of the search for context-level effects even by means of the multilevel model. The inherent problems present serious impediments to obtaining informative estimates of targeted parameters. The application problems escalate the difficulty but have far more tractable solutions. Still, taken together, these complexities establish that the challenge of estimating school effects remains daunting despite popularization of the multilevel model.

Critique of the Neo-Coleman Report I

Key aspects of the ideal first-order replication of the Coleman Report are implicitly criticized, especially the specification of the multilevel model. Data collection for the neo–Coleman Report I would have led several context-level factors to be measured by aggregating student-level variables, running afoul of the aggregation critique discussed earlier. The longitudinal data collection would be seen as helpful but probably insufficient to identify causal effects of context. And the lack of effort to address selection into contexts creates further problems. The existence of information on students' placement in the stratified curriculum would be valuable but, again, insufficient owing to the prospect of the analysis being complicated by unobservable determinants of selection into curricula.

Thus, whether the neo–Coleman Report I design would reproduce the 1966 findings in 1966 or later, or would not do so, the findings would be regarded as indeterminate. More research would be indicated.

SECOND-ORDER METHODOLOGICAL RESPONSES

The criticisms already described set the stage for contemporary second-order responses to the Coleman Report. Those responses are necessary because, as Coleman implied, if solutions to the problems excavated remain elusive, our understanding will simply be limited and policy decisions will be made anyway.

Second-Order Responses to the Calibration Critique

The implications of the criticisms range from limiting to dire. On the limiting side, better sample and questionnaire design and the use of, in principle, macrolevel measures instead of aggregated microlevel factors to measure macrolevel phenomena could readily resolve some of the application limitations. Other application problems, such as the problem of accounting for the process of selection into contexts, are more challenging. Even more challenging yet are efforts to resolve the identification problems inherent in the multilevel model. Indeed, in this area the implications are dire. Advances forward must, as Manski notes, come at the cost of introducing a priori information. There are several ways of introducing such information.

For example, one approach to identifying endogenous and contextual effects is to posit a lag structure. One defense of this alternative is the claim that individual-level factors act contemporaneously but contextual factors act with lag.[2] Although the lag assumption is defensible in general, making it requires not only that one have access to information about the prior performance of others but also (and most important) that one can defend the particular time lag employed. If the time lag employed is simply asserted, then identification again rests on a strong and perhaps unjustified assumption.

In addition, some circumstances conspire to render this strategy ineffective. As Manski notes, the assumption requires our observation of the system in disequilibrium. If the system is in equilibrium, then the lagged value of the context-level variable is a linear function of the other constituent parts of the equation in the same way that a contemporaneous value is, vitiating the identifying power of the time-lag assumption.

A second approach to resolving the identification problem is to restrict some of the parameters; for example, one might assume no endogenous effect and, conditional on this assumption, estimate the contextual effect. This is a common way of identifying effects in the individual-level case. However, one limitation to following this approach is that our knowledge of context-level factors is much less developed than our knowledge of individual-level factors. Thus, an assumption to constrain some types of effects to zero is correspondingly stronger.

These approaches to identifying context-level effects are potentially useful. A general theme of the analysis is that researchers should present an explicit identification analysis that precedes any empirical analysis. In the case of context-level effects, the observations made here set the stage for any empirical analysis attempting to search for contextual effects. In the kind of identification analysis that Manski proposes, the researcher would make plain the assumptions used to identify causal effects. The identification analysis would therefore allow other researchers to determine for themselves whether they accept or reject the assumptions and, in so doing, accept or reject the findings of the analysis.

The introduction of a priori information is a pathway to sustaining the model, but it can come at a high cost. As Manski (1995) argues, often the prior information one can introduce is the very kind of information about which analysts disagree. Thus, the results produced conditional on acceptance of the priors can simply push the debate back one step instead of forward.

A tool that might help break the impasse is needed. Such a tool will make assumptions visible and allow analysts to discern testable implications of their causal hypotheses, if such implications exist. In the contemporary period, such tools are provided by the graphical causal model (GCM) and directed acyclic graphs (DAGs) (Pearl 2010; Elwert 2013).

The ability to determine testable implications, conditional on the posited causal struc-

---

2. To defend the time-lag assumption for standardized test scores, consider that the student is alone during any given test administration. Peers' collective performance on the same test cannot have an effect; however, peers' prior achievement can have an effect.

ture, opens the door to a step-by-step bootstrapping operation by which, over time, causal inferences become tested and certified by cautious and systematic analysis of observational data. Because the posited structure is a precursor to any hypothesis, it is obvious that, if there is disagreement on the set of linkages needed for the causal theory, progress will depend on positing multiple plausible causal structures to determine their testable implications, followed by evaluating those implications with appropriate data. Just as obviously, such a bootstrapping operation may take time.

Second-Order Responses to the Education Process Critique

For DAGs to become more than another rote tool applied quickly and mechanically in the process of churning out text for citation counters to tally, the causal structures posited must be theory-laden (Horan 1978)—that is, they must be based on well-reasoned theoretical positions. Although in many cases observational data have been incredibly suggestive, the selection critique still prevents complete dissolution of analysts' uncertainty as to the mechanisms underlying the parameters estimated. What is needed is a breakthrough that brings into awareness the deeper structure of any claims about individuals in context, as well as an apparatus that can serve as a laboratory for studying the specificities of the claims that flow from that awareness.

Intriguingly, Coleman (1990) provides a candidate resource for the needed structural breakthrough. In *Foundations of Social Theory*, Coleman literally sketches the relation of individuals and the contexts in which they are nested, vis-à-vis any given feature of the latter. The contribution can be interpreted as another in a series of Coleman's own responses to the dialogue that transpired after the Coleman Report. In the public- and private-school work, he makes additional efforts to discern school effects. Here, however, Coleman takes a different tack: the very nature of what it means to talk about contexts having effects becomes the object of study.

Coleman's contribution is suggested by *Coleman's boat*, replicated in figure 1. In one interpretation, nodes A and D represent the

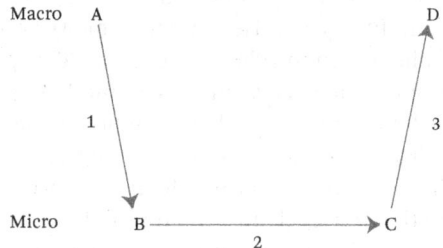

Figure 1. Coleman's Boat

Source: Coleman 1990.

macro level (for example, the school), while nodes B and C represent the micro level (individuals). Any effect of A on D goes through the interaction of individuals in nodes B and C. Further, from interaction between B and C can emerge macrolevel phenomenon D. So, for example, institutional effects are traced by arrow 1. Yet the system is dynamic, such that the individual recipients of that treatment interact with each other at node B, possibly producing endogenous or contextual effects, which would be reflected in node C. Arrow 2 traces the causal path from interaction at node B to microlevel outcomes at node C, outcomes that may be produced by endogenous or contextual processes. Finally, the result of their interaction may have implications for the context level in node D. The causal force of microlevel actors on the macro level is traced by arrow 3.

The framework points analysts toward discerning the microfoundations on and through which all social entities (institutions, norms, extra-individual structures) are based—that is, the mechanisms through which they activate their effects. As they do so, social analysts need to recognize that action can flow from a complex combination of individuals' desires, beliefs, and opportunities (Hedström 2005), and that part of the social analyst's job is to attend to the real motivations of individuals even as analysts may build stark models to test specific, contained mechanisms that might explain patterns and features of the social world. Yet accessing the motivations of real individuals is almost impossible, for multiple technical reasons, including our inability to fully access our own cognition, the tendency of causal claims for the same event to change over time with additional experience and wisdom, the impossibility of resolving the fundamental problem of causal inference on the basis of one case, and finally, the Heraclitian same-river-twice phenomenon (Plato 1921, 402a). Thus, techniques such as agent-based modeling (ABM) (for example, Schelling 1971; Bruch and Mare 2006)—with which analysts can explore whether observed patterns will emerge given certain theoretical claims—hold promise.

However, the concept of mechanisms must not devolve into metaphor, for that would endanger all of the gains in understanding preceding analysts have struggled to develop. By mechanisms what is meant are concrete, identifiable processes, entities, and sets of behaviors. Instead of metaphor, it would be more accurate to view mechanisms as catalytic ingredients of causal recipes for social outcomes—as long as analysts remain epistemological stochasticists regardless of their ontological views (Lucas and Szatrowski 2014, 23–27).

WHAT IS TO BE DONE? HARVESTING THE INSIGHTS OF SECOND-ORDER DEVELOPMENTS

Once we bring together the second-order developments from the calibration and education process critiques, we are left with a perhaps more difficult task. However, we are also left with more possibilities for completing the task than perhaps ever before. As we recognize the threats to proper causal inference (Morgan and Winship 2007), the process of research becomes longer, as should the products of that research as well. Indeed, a subsection on identification (possibly referencing DAGs) should become a routine part of the methods section of articles and the methods appendices of books. Papers and books should grow in length as their numbers decline, for if they remain as constrained and common as now—given the task before us and the need to describe it in sufficient detail for expert readers to evaluate and modify in later work—the counsel to follow is already likely impossible.

The Neo–Coleman Report II: A Second-Order Critique-Influenced Coleman Report Replication

Some changes in the neo–Coleman Report I would be needed to replicate the Coleman Report on the basis of the second-order critique. First, while acknowledging Coleman's (1968) claim that lack of knowledge about the achievement process in 1966 prevented the use of a more comprehensive and dynamic model, the neo–Coleman Report II would be built on the recognition that every analysis requires an implicit or explicit model of the production of its outcome. Ideally, analysts would select a model to guide data collection and analysis, such that the model should be evident prior to data collection.

Thus, in an effort to ensure that the analysis produces results that address the questions of interest while limiting the threats to proper inference, the neo–Coleman Report II would begin by using tools generated by the second-order response, such as DAGs and ABMs, in a complex process of theoretical analysis. In one part of the analysis, researchers would specify a DAG, based largely on previous research, and analyze it to determine which variables to control or not control in models as well as to discern the testable implications of the DAG. In another part of the analysis, they would use ABMs to assess whether context-level patterns can emerge from the posited individual-level factors; if not, then, given the Coleman's boat understanding, they would know that something is missing from the analysis. Further, ABMs might be helpful when a DAG reveals that there are no testable implications of a posited causal structure. Through such theoretical work, analysts will be better placed to identify variables of promise to measure and to determine whether methods as simple as (nonparametric) comparison of group-specific means, methods as complex as marginal structural models (Robins 1999; Robins, Hernán, and Brumback 2000; Sharkey and Elwert 2011), or methods somewhere in the middle are necessary to estimate the causal effects of interest.

After such efforts, data collection would begin. In addition to data collected as described for the neo–Coleman Report I, multiple other data collection methods that collectively capture the processes of interest would be implemented. For example, standardized classroom observations (Nystrand and Gamoran 1991) as well as novel data collection strategies that can capture interaction, such as experience sampling (ES) (for example, Csikszentmihalyi 1990), would be used.[3] Use of such data collection strategies would allow measurement of the quality of pedagogic dialogue specifically, and the pedagogies in general, to which students are exposed, a necessary addition to fully address the education process critique.

Because estimating context-level effects can be simplified if disequilibrium conditions exist, efforts would be made to allow assessment of whether an equilibrium on relevant matters exists for the cohorts and years of study. To facilitate assessment of this issue, some perhaps less extensive data could be collected on multiple adjacent cohorts over multiple years, a task that might force further reduction in the number of grades studied.

To address the aggregation critique specifically, and the general problem of proxy measures in general, analysts would theorize phenomena of interest at their level of existence and ensure that data are collected at the same level. For example, to ascertain whether students in poor schools fare poorly, one would have to measure the sum total of school resources available—public funds as well as any private or endowment funds provided by the wider community—rather than calculate the mean levels of parents' status characteristics in the school.

The Second-Order Response as Determinant of the Contemporary Context

Through the first- and second-order response, the Coleman Report's influence extended far beyond the analysis of inequality in education. Intensified development of the concept of social capital (see, for example, Coleman 1988), more nuanced neighborhood effects research (Sharkey and Elwert 2011), experiment-based efforts to assess discrimination (Pager 2003), the employment of natural experiment data where possible (Heckman and Payner 1989), and close study of intrinsically interesting cases for causal insight (Vaughan 1996) are all, in part, responses to rising awareness of the challenge of estimating effects of interest, an awareness that is perhaps the most general and widespread effect of the responses to the Coleman Report. Intriguingly, it is just such context effects on outcomes that key responses to the Coleman Report have shown are a challenge to establish.

Notably, however, such work, as well as the neo–Coleman Report II, suggests that analysts can be empowered rather than paralyzed by the second-order critiques and developments that flow therefrom. On the basis of those developments, useful steps in research can be identified. The belief that one can estimate causal effects simply from data, without imposing a set of assumptions that make estimation possible and meaningful, has been shown to be in error. Thus, if the aim is to estimate causal effects, the first advice is to conduct theoretical analyses. DAGs and ABMs are useful resources, but as Sørensen and Hallinan (1977) and many others demonstrate (for example, Breen and Goldthorpe 1997; Lucas 2009), just developing and manipulating the theoretical equations implied by various claims can be illuminating and helpful.

Once such theoretical work has created enough clarity for informative empirical analyses to proceed, the next step is to seek out or collect data sufficient to the task. In the case of the multilevel model, data should be used or collected in such a way that it is a fully multilevel probability sample. It is helpful to follow Hauser's advice and measure the factors of interest at the levels at which they occur—and to never aggregate level 1 variables to produce alleged level 2 variables. Parameters of interest should be explicitly identified.

This counsel is where the second-order developments leave us—cautious, committed to a less rote process of evidence generation, and hopeful if not optimistic.

CONCLUDING REMARKS

The Coleman Report, despite its groundbreaking nature, had limitations. Fortunately for those who seek to understand the implications of that report, many of those limitations were

---

3. In ES designs, persons are given beepers that beep at random times. When beeped, the person is to record the requested information about their activities, environment, and state of mind. ES designs were used to establish the concept of flow and its relevance for optimal experience (Csikszentmihalyi 1990).

revealed in the immediate aftermath of the study, owing to the institutional structures and goodwill of the researchers, who made data available and engaged the dialogue forthrightly.

Afterwards, analysts took the trail-blazing nature of the Coleman Report as an inspiration to intensify their efforts to inform our understanding of schools and inequality as well as the methodologies and difficulties of such research. Promising responses to the two criticisms of focus were developed out of those intensified efforts. But key aspects of those responses themselves contained hidden flaws that undermined their success. Many of those flaws were exposed in the transition out of the period of first-order response.

Intriguingly, Coleman's later work in analytic sociology, most notably Coleman's boat, contributed key resources to the second-order response. The second-order developments have been characterized by additional complexity and tools that, if used well, require a measured, cautious, step-by-step process of evidence generation.

Running through the entire dialogue has been a concern with the grounds of causal inference and a desire for analyses to be based in a plausible process understanding of schooling. At this stage of knowledge, we may finally be poised to resolve the critiques originally raised many decades ago and satisfy the desire for solid causal conclusions grounded in and contributing to a developing, accurate understanding of how schools work.

APPENDIX A

The Multilevel Model in Equation Form

A multi-equation specification is perhaps the clearest way to convey the distinct features of the multilevel model. In the following multi-equation specification for an interval-level dependent variable, one individual-level (i) equation contains an outcome variable (Y) and several determinants (X's). If a coefficient (α) for a given X is allowed to vary over J macro-level units, then an equation at the macro level may contain coefficients (λ's) for macrolevel factors (Z's) that may partially determine α_j. So, for example, equations A1–A5 describe a two-level means-as-outcomes model:

$$(A1)\ Y_{ij} = \alpha_{0j} + \alpha_1 X_{1ij} + \alpha_2 X_{2ij} + \alpha_3 X_{3ij} + \varepsilon_{ij}$$

$$(A2)\ \alpha_{0j} = \lambda_{00} + \lambda_{10} Z_{1j} + \lambda_{20} Z_{2j} + \delta_{0j}$$

$$(A3)\ \alpha_1 = \lambda_{01}$$

$$(A4)\ \alpha_2 = \lambda_{02}$$

$$(A5)\ \alpha_3 = \lambda_{03}$$

$$\varepsilon_{ij} \sim N(0, \sigma^2);\ \delta_{kj} \sim N(0, \mathbf{T});\ \rho^{\varepsilon\delta} = 0$$

Equation A1 specifies the level 1 equation, whereas equations A2–A5 specify the macro-level (or level 2) equations. ε_{ij} and δ_{0j} are individual- and macrolevel errors with variance σ^2 and variance-covariance matrix $\mathbf{T}$, respectively. The level 1 coefficient for the intercept varies across macrolevel units, while the other level 1 coefficients do not vary. In equation A1, the variation in α_{0j} is partially associated with macrolevel variables Z_1 and Z_2.

Similarly, equations A6–A10 constitute a slopes-as-outcomes model; for clarity, I switch to β's and γ's for these equations:

$$(A6)\ Y_{ij} = \beta_0 + \beta_{1j} X_{1ij} + \beta_2 X_{2ij} + \beta_3 X_{3ij} + \varepsilon_{ij}$$

$$(A7)\ \beta_0 = \gamma_{00}$$

$$(A8)\ \beta_{1j} = \gamma_{01} + \gamma_{11} Z_{1j} + \gamma_{21} Z_{2j} + \delta_{1j}$$

$$(A9)\ \beta_2 = \gamma_{02}$$

$$(A10)\ \beta_3 = \gamma_{03}$$

$$\varepsilon_{ij} \sim N(0, \sigma^2);\ \delta_{kj} \sim N(0, \mathbf{T});\ \rho^{\varepsilon\delta} = 0$$

In equations A1–A10, note that context-level variation is measured by context-specific coefficients, α_{0j} in equation A1 and β_{1j} in equation A6—that is, the coefficients with j subscripts. Thus, context-level variation can only be explained by macrolevel variables (Z_1 and Z_2) and the error terms associated with that coefficient (δ_{0j} or δ_{1j}). The model partitions the variance across levels and estimates more appropriate standard errors for macrolevel coefficients.

An equivalent specification of the model writes it all as one equation, as in equation A11, which combines equations A1–A5, and equation A12, which combines equations A6–A10:

$$\text{(A11)} \quad Y_{ij} = \lambda_{00} + \lambda_{10}Z_{1j} + \lambda_{20}Z_{2j} + \delta_{0j} + \lambda_{01}X_{1ij} + \lambda_{02}X_{2ij} + \lambda_{03}X_{3ij} + \varepsilon_{ij}$$
$$\varepsilon_{ij} \sim N(0,\sigma^2); \delta_{kj} \sim N(0,T); \rho^{\varepsilon\delta} = 0$$

$$\text{(A12)} \quad Y_{ij} = \gamma_{00} + \gamma_{10}X_{1ij} + \gamma_{11}X_{1ij}Z_{1j} + \gamma_{21}X_{1ij}Z_{2j} + \delta_{1j} + \delta_{1j}X_{1ij} + \gamma_{02}X_{2ij} + \gamma_{03}X_{3ij} + \varepsilon_{ij}$$
$$\varepsilon_{ij} \sim N(0,\sigma^2); \delta_{kj} \sim N(0,T); \rho^{\varepsilon\delta} = 0$$

APPENDIX B

Why Context-Unrepresentative Sampling Fails: An Illustration of the Need for Fully Multilevel Probability Sampling for the Multilevel Model

The discussion here (drawn from Lucas 2014) uses population parameters (for example, α's) rather than sample entities (a's) to underscore that at issue is parameter identification, not simply estimation efficiency.

Consider a probability sample designed to represent a nation with sampled individuals lodged in contexts. Owing to the context-unrepresentative sample design, each context j is composed of two groups of persons: (1) sampling-reachable (r), and (2) sampling-unreachable (u). The proportion of r (p) and u ($1-p$) varies across contexts. By definition, persons' allocation to group r or u is not random. Further, the determinants of assignment are unknown, and the allocation process may vary across contexts. Thus, groups r and u differ in unknown yet systematic ways, such that group r provides no retrievable information on the parameters for group u without heavy assumptions.

Given this design, true context-specific population parameters are actually mixtures:

$$\text{(B1)} \quad \alpha_{0j} = p_j \alpha_{0j,r} + (1-p_j) \alpha_{0j,u}$$

Using the multilevel model (MLM) with such data treats $\alpha_{0j,r}$ as if it is α_{0j}. Expressed as a function of the true population parameter, in reality:

$$\text{(B2)} \quad \alpha_{0j,r} = (p_j \alpha_{0j,u} - \alpha_{0j,u} + \alpha_{0j}) / p_j$$

which is not in general equal to α_{0j}. Using $\alpha_{0j,r}$ as if it is α_{0j} is mistaken, for:

$$\text{(B3)} \quad \alpha_{0j} - \alpha_{0j,r} = p_j \alpha_{0j,r} + \alpha_{0j,u} - p_j \alpha_{0j,u} - \alpha_{0j,r}$$

which is not in general zero. Equation B3 indicates that it will be difficult to establish the magnitude and sign of the difference between $\alpha_{0j,r}$ and α_{0j}. First, to identify magnitude and sign requires information about the unreachable subpopulation in each context. By definition, one has no such information. Second, the unknown bias varies by context as a function of p_j, $\alpha_{0j,r}$, and $\alpha_{0j,u}$, such that large context-specific biases may exist even if the average bias is zero.

The use of $\alpha_{0j,r}$ for α_{0j} causes further problems, for equation A2 becomes:

$$\text{(B4)} \quad \alpha_{0j,r} = (p_j \alpha_{0j,u} - \alpha_{0j,u} + \alpha_{0j}) / p_j = \lambda^*_{00} + \lambda^*_{10}Z_{1j} + \lambda^*_{20}Z_{2j} + \delta^*_{0j}.$$

For equation B4 to produce the sought-after level 2 population parameter:

$$\text{(B5)} \quad \lambda^*_{00} = \lambda_{00}$$
$$\text{(B6)} \quad \lambda^*_{10} = \lambda_{10}$$
$$\text{(B7)} \quad \lambda^*_{20} = \lambda_{20}$$

must be true. But there is little reason to believe that equations B5 through B7 are true, and if they are false, it will be difficult to recover λ_{00}, λ_{10}, and λ_{20} from the model for $\alpha_{0j,r}$.

One of two possible conditions can make r sufficient for estimating α_{0j} unbiasedly. First, if all $p_j = 1.00$, then there is no problem. Of course, if all $p_j = 1.00$, then one has context-representative probability sampling.

Failing this condition, however, one may justify the MLM by assuming:

$$\text{(B8)} \quad \alpha_{0j,r} = \alpha_{0j,u}$$

If equation B8 holds, then there is no problem with using only those in group r to estimate the population parameter(s). There is, however, little reason to suspect that equation B8 will hold in general. Thus, those using the MLM must either use context-representative probability samples ($p_j = 1.00$) or explain why they believe equation B8 holds for the parameters of interest that vary across contexts.

For establishment of the other criteria for an FMP sample, see Lucas (2014).

APPENDIX C

Identification Problems with Estimating Contextual Effects

Equations C1–C3 are drawn directly from Manski (1993); for fuller discussion of these equations and their interrelation, see that work. Manski (1993, equations 42–43) proposes the following equations as a way to distinguish four different effects conceptually:

$$(C1) \; y = \alpha + \beta \, E(y|x) + E(z|x)'\gamma + x'\delta_1 + z'\eta + u$$

$$(C2) \; E(u|x,z) = x'\delta_2$$

where x stands for a set of variables that identify the contexts (for example, a set of dummy variables), z stands for a set of individual-level explanatory variables, β signifies the endogenous effect, γ signifies the contextual effect, $E(y|x)$ stands for the context-specific mean of y, $E(z|x)$ represents the context-specific mean of z, δ_1 signifies the ecological effect, η reflects the effect of z on y, and u captures the error in equation C1. Because $E(u|x,z) \neq 0$ in general, δ_2 reflects the effects of similarity of unobserved attributes for persons in the same context—that is, the correlated individual-level effects. Substituting equation C2 into equation C1 and rearranging the terms reveals that the two equations imply:

$$(C3) \; E(y|x,z) = \alpha + \beta \, E(y|x) + E(z|x)'\gamma + x'(\delta_1 + \delta_2) + z'\eta.$$

Given equation C3, researchers will encounter major difficulty identifying peer effects.

REFERENCES

Aigner, Dennis J. 1970. "A Comment on Problems in Making Inferences from the Coleman Report." *American Sociological Review* 35(2): 249–52.

Akkina, K. R. 1974. "Application of Random Coefficient Regression Models to the Aggregation Problem." *Econometrica* 42(2): 369–75.

Alexander, Karl L., Doris R. Entwisle, and Linda Steffel Olson. 2007. "Lasting Consequences of the Summer Learning Gap." *American Sociological Review* 72(2): 167–80.

Barr, Rebecca, and Robert Dreeben, with Nonglak Wiratchai. 1983. *How Schools Work*. Chicago: University of Chicago Press.

Bowers, William J. 1968. "Normative Constraints on Deviant Behavior in the College Context." *Sociometry* 31(4): 370–85.

Bowles, Samuel, and Henry M. Levin. 1968. "The Determinants of Scholastic Achievement: An Appraisal of Some Recent Evidence." *Journal of Human Resources* 3(1): 3–24.

Boyd, Lawrence H., Jr., and Gudmund R. Iversen. 1979. *Contextual Analysis: Concepts and Statistical Techniques*. Belmont, Calif.: Wadsworth.

Breen, Richard, and John H. Goldthorpe. 1997. "Explaining Educational Differentials: Towards a Formal Rational Action Theory." *Rationality and Society* 9(3): 275–305.

Bruch, Elizabeth E., and Robert D. Mare. 2006. "Neighborhood Choice and Neighborhood Change." *American Journal of Sociology* 112(3): 667–709.

Bryan, Mark L., and Stephen P. Jenkins. 2016. "Multilevel Modelling of Country Effects: A Cautionary Tale." *European Sociological Review* 32(1): 3–22.

Bryk, Anthony S., Valerie E. Lee, and Peter B. Holland. 1993. *Catholic Schools and the Common Good*. Cambridge, Mass.: Harvard University Press.

Bryk, Anthony S., and Stephen W. Raudenbush. 1992. *Hierarchical Linear Models: Applications and Data Analysis Methods*. Newbury Park, Calif.: Sage Publications.

Bryk, Anthony S., Stephen W. Raudenbush, M. Seltzer, and Richard T. Congdon. 1988. *An Introduction to HLM: Computer Program and User's Guide*. 2nd ed. Chicago: University of Chicago Department of Education.

Burstein, Leigh, Robert L. Linn, and Frank J. Capell. 1978. "Analyzing Multilevel Data in the Presence of Heterogenous Within-Class Regressions." *Journal of Educational Statistics* 3(4): 347–83.

Cain, Glen G., and Harold W. Watts. 1970. "Problems in Making Policy Inferences from the Coleman Report." *American Sociological Review* 35(2): 228–42.

Chubb, John E., and Terry M. Moe. 1988. "Politics, Markets, and the Organization of Schools." *American Political Science Review* 82(4): 1065–87.

Coleman, James S. 1968. "Equality of Educational Opportunity: Reply to Bowles and Levin." *Journal of Human Resources* 3(2): 237–46.

———. 1988. "Social Capital in the Creation of Human Capital." *American Journal of Sociology* 94: S95–120.

———. 1990. *Foundations of Social Theory.* Cambridge, Mass.: Harvard University Press.

Coleman, James S., Ernest Q. Campbell, Carol J. Hobson, James McPartland, Alexander M. Mood, Frederick D. Weinfeld, and Robert L. York. 1966. *Equality of Educational Opportunity.* Washington: U.S. Department of Health, Education, and Welfare, Office of Education.

Coleman, James, Thomas Hoffer, and Sally Kilgore. 1981. *Public and Private Schools: Report to the National Center for Education Statistics.* Chicago: National Opinion Research Center.

Crain, Robert L. 1967. "Review of *Equality of Educational Opportunity.*" *American Journal of Sociology* 73(3): 354–56.

Crane, Jonathan. 1991. "The Epidemic Theory of Ghettos and Neighborhood Effects on Dropping Out and Teenage Childbearing." *American Journal of Sociology* 96(5): 1226–59.

Csikszentmihalyi, Mihalyi. 1990. *Flow: The Psychology of Optimal Experience.* New York: Harper & Row.

Dyer, Henry. 1968. "School Factors and Equal Educational Opportunity." *Harvard Educational Review* 38(1): 38–56.

Ehrenberg, Ronald G., and Dominic J. Brewer. 1995. "Did Teachers' Verbal Ability and Race Matter in the 1960s? *Coleman* Revisited." *Economics of Education Review* 14(1): 1–21.

Elwert, Felix. 2013. "Graphical Causal Models." In *Handbook of Causal Analysis for Social Research,* edited by Stephen L. Morgan. New York: Springer.

Farkas, George. 1974. "Specifications, Residuals, and Context Effects." *Sociological Methods and Research* 2(3): 333–63.

Fuchs, Ira H. 2001. "Prospects and Possibilities of the Digital Age." *Proceedings of the American Philosophical Society* 145(1): 45–53.

Gamoran, Adam. 1987. "The Stratification of High School Learning Opportunities." *Sociology of Education* 60(3): 135–55.

———. 1992. "The Variable Effects of High School Tracking." *American Sociological Review* 57(6): 812–28.

Gamoran, Adam, and Mark Berends. 1987. "The Effects of Stratification in Secondary Schools: Synthesis of Survey and Ethnographic Research." *Review of Educational Research* 57(4): 415–35.

Gamoran, Adam, and Robert Dreeben. 1986. "Coupling and Control in Educational Organizations." *Administrative Science Quarterly* 31(4): 612–32.

Gamoran, Adam, and Robert D. Mare. 1989. "Secondary School Tracking and Educational Equality: Compensation, Reinforcement, or Neutrality?" *American Journal of Sociology* 94(5): 1146–83.

Garet, Michael S., and Brian DeLany. 1988. "Students, Courses, and Stratification." *Sociology of Education* 61(2): 61–77.

Goldberger, Arthur S., and Glen G. Cain. 1982. "The Causal Analysis of Cognitive Outcomes in the Coleman, Hoffer, and Kilgore Report." *Sociology of Education* 55(2–3): 103–22.

Goldstein, Harvey. 1994. "Multilevel Cross-Classified Models." *Sociological Methods and Research* 22(3): 364–75.

———. 2003. *Multilevel Statistical Models.* 3rd ed. London: Arnold.

Goldstein, Harvey, M. J. R. Healy, and Jon Rasbash. 1994. "Multilevel Time Series Models with Application to Repeated Measures Data." *Statistics in Medicine* 13(16): 1643–55.

Grant, Gerald. 1973. "Shaping Social Policy: The Politics of the Coleman Report." *Teachers College Record* 75(1): 17–54.

Hanushek, Eric A., and John F. Kain. 1972. "On the Value of 'Equality of Educational Opportunity' as a Guide to Public Policy." In *On Equality of Educational Opportunity,* edited by Frederick Mosteller and Daniel Patrick Moynihan. New York: Random House.

Hauser, Robert M. 1970a. "Context and Consex: A Cautionary Tale." *American Journal of Sociology* 75(4): 645–64.

———. 1970b. "The Author Replies." *American Journal of Sociology* 76(3): 517–20.

———. 1974. "Contextual Analysis Revisited." *Sociological Methods and Research* 2(3): 365–75.

Havighurst, Robert J. 1967. Review. *Journal of the American Statistical Association* 62: 1071–73.

Heckman, James J., and Brook S. Payner. 1989. "Determining the Impact of Federal Antidiscrimination Policy on the Economic Status of Blacks: A Study of South Carolina." *American Economic Review* 79(1): 138–77.

Hedeker, Donald, and Robert D. Gibbons. 1994. "A Random-Effects Ordinal Regression Model for Multilevel Analysis." *Biometrics* 50(4): 933–44.

Hedström, Peter. 2005. *Dissecting the Social: On the Principles of Analytic Sociology.* New York: Cambridge University Press.

Heyns, Barbara. 1979. *Summer Learning and the Effects of Schooling*. New York: Academic Press.

Hoffer, Thomas B. 1992. "Middle School Ability Grouping and Student Achievement in Science and Mathematics." *Educational Evaluation and Policy Analysis* 14(3): 205–27.

Horan, Patrick M. 1978. "Is Status Attainment Research Atheoretical?" *American Sociological Review* 43(4): 534–41.

Hotchkiss, Lawrence, and Linda E. Dorsten. 1987. "Curriculum Effects on Early Post–High School Outcomes." *Research in the Sociology of Education and Socialization* 7(1): 191–219.

Hox, Joop. 1995. *Applied Multilevel Analysis*. Amsterdam: TT-Publikaties.

Irby, Nolan Meaders. 1930. "A Program for the Equalization of Educational Opportunities in the State of Arkansas." PhD diss., George Peabody College for Teachers, Nashville, Tenn.

Jones, James D., Beth E. Vanfossen, and Margaret E. Ensminger. 1995. "Individual and Organizational Predictors of High School Track Placement." *Sociology of Education* 68(4): 287–300.

Kreft, Ita, and Jan de Leeuw. 1998. *Introducing Multilevel Modeling*. Thousand Oaks, Calif.: Sage Publications.

Krueger, Alan B., and Diane M. Whitmore. 2002. "Would Smaller Classes Help Close the Black-White Achievement Gap?" In *Bridging the Achievement Gap*, edited by John E. Chubb and Tom Loveless. Washington, D.C.: Brookings Institution Press.

Lindley, D. V., and A. F. M. Smith. 1972. "Bayes Estimates for the Linear Model" (with discussion). *Journal of the Royal Statistical Society, Series B* 34(1): 1—41.

Little, Roderick J. A. 1992. "Regression with Missing X's: A Review." *Journal of the American Statistical Association* 87(420): 1227–37.

Looker, E. Diane. 1989. "Accuracy of Proxy Reports of Parental Status Characteristics." *Sociology of Education* 62(4): 257–76.

Lucas, Samuel Roundfield. 1999. *Tracking Inequality: Stratification and Mobility in American Schools*. New York: Teachers College Press.

———. 2008. "School Tracking." In *Encyclopedia of the Life Course and Human Development*, edited by Deborah Carr. Farmington Hills, Mich.: Macmillan Reference, USA.

———. 2009. "Stratification Theory, Socioeconomic Background, and Educational Attainment: A Formal Analysis." *Rationality and Society* 21(4): 459–511.

———. 2014. "An Inconvenient Dataset: Bias and Inappropriate Inference with the Multilevel Model." *Quality and Quantity* 48(3): 1619–49.

Lucas, Samuel R., and Mark Berends. 2002. "Sociodemographic Diversity, Correlated Achievement, and de Facto Tracking." *Sociology of Education* 75(4): 328–48.

———. 2007. "Race and Track Location in U.S. Public Schools." *Research in Social Stratification and Mobility* 25(3): 169–87.

Lucas, Samuel R., and Adam Gamoran. 2002. "Tracking and the Achievement Gap." In *Bridging the Achievement Gap*, edited by John E. Chubb and Tom Loveless. Washington, D.C.: Brookings Institution Press.

Lucas, Samuel R., Steven Ingels, Harrison Greene, and Louise Little. 1987. "Student Data Collection." In Steven Ingels et al., *Field Test Report: National Education Longitudinal Study of 1988 (NELS:88)*, prepared for U.S. Department of Education, Center for Education Statistics.

Lucas, Samuel R., and Alisa Szatrowski. 2014. "Qualitative Comparative Analysis in Critical Perspective." *Sociological Methodology* 44(1): 1–79.

Luke, Douglas A. 2004. *Multilevel Modeling*. Thousand Oaks, Calif.: Sage Publications.

Mack, Raymond W. 1968. *Our Children's Burden: Studies of Desegregation in Nine American Communities*. New York: Random House.

Manski, Charles F. 1993. "Identification Problems in the Social Sciences." *Sociological Methodology* 23(1): 1–56.

———. 1995. *Identification Problems in the Social Sciences*. Cambridge, Mass.: Harvard University Press.

Mason, William M., George Y. Wong, and Barbara Entwisle. 1983. "Contextual Analysis Through the Multilevel Linear Model." *Sociological Methodology* 14(2): 72–103.

Mickelson, Roslyn Arlin. 2001. "Subverting Swann: First- and Second-Generation Segregation in Charlotte-Mecklenberg Schools." *American Educational Research Journal* 38(2): 215–52.

Morgan, Stephen L., and Christopher Winship. 2007. *Counterfactuals and Causal Inference: Methods and Principles for Social Research*. New York: Cambridge University Press.

Moses, Earl R. 1941. "Indices of Inequalities in a Dual

System of Education." *Journal of Negro Education* 10(2): 239–44.

Mosteller, Frederick, and Daniel P. Moynihan. 1972. *On Equality of Educational Opportunity*. New York: Random House.

Muthén, Bengt O. 1994. "Multilevel Covariance Structure Analysis." *Sociological Methods and Research* 22(3): 376–98.

Nichols, Robert C. 1966. "Schools and the Disadvantaged." *Science* 154(3754): 1312–14.

Norton, John K. 1926. *The Ability of the States to Support Education*. Washington, D.C.: National Educational Association.

Nystrand, Martin, and Adam Gamoran. 1991. "Instructional Discourse, Student Engagement, and Literature Achievement." *Research in the Teaching of English* 25(3): 261–90.

Nystrand, Martin, Lawrence L. Wu, Adam Gamoran, Susie Zeiser, and Daniel A. Long. 2003. "Questions in Time: Investigating the Structure and Dynamics of Unfolding Classroom Discourse." *Discourse Processes* 35(2): 135–98.

Oakes, Jeannie. 1982. "Classroom Social Relationships: Exploring the Bowles and Gintis Hypothesis." *Sociology of Education* 55(4): 197–212.

Pager, Devah. 2003. "The Mark of a Criminal Record." *American Journal of Sociology* 108(5): 937–75.

Pallas, Aaron M., Doris R. Entwisle, Karl L. Alexander, and M. Francis Stluka. 1994. "Ability-Group Effects: Instructional, Social, or Institutional?" *Sociology of Education* 67(1): 27–46.

Pearl, Judea. 2010. "The Foundations of Causal Inference." *Sociological Methodology* 40(1): 75–149.

Pettigrew, Thomas F. 1968. "Race and Equal Educational Opportunity." *Harvard Educational Review* 38(1): 66–76.

Pfautz, Harold W. 1967. Review. *American Sociological Review* 32(3): 481–83.

Phillips, Myrtle R. 1932. "Financial Support." *Journal of Negro Education* 1(2): 108–36.

Plato. 1921. *Cratylus*. In *Plato in Twelve Volumes*, vol. 12, translated by Harold N. Fowler. Cambridge, Mass.: Harvard University Press; London: William Heinemann Ltd. Available at: http://www.perseus.tufts.edu/hopper/text?doc=Perseus%3Atext%3A1999.01.0172%3Atext%3DCrat.%3Asection%3D402a (accessed June 28, 2016).

Pinheiro, José C., and Douglas M. Bates. 2004. *Mixed-Effects Models in S and S-PLUS*. New York: Springer.

Riehl, Carolyn, Aaron M. Pallas, and Gary Natriello. 1999. "Rites and Wrongs: Institutional Explanations for the Student Course-Scheduling Process in Urban High Schools." *American Journal of Education* 107(2): 116–54.

Robins, James M. 1999. "Association, Causation, and Marginal Structural Models." *Synthese* 121(1): 151–79.

Robins, James M., Miguel Angel Hernán, and Babette Brumback. 2000. "Marginal Structural Models and Causal Inference in Epidemiology." *Epidemiology* 11(5): 550–60.

Rosenbaum, James E. 1980. "Track Misperceptions and Frustrated College Plans: An Analysis of the Effects of Tracks and Track Perceptions in the National Longitudinal Survey." *Sociology of Education* 53(2): 74–88.

Schelling, Thomas C. 1971. "Dynamic Models of Segregation." *Journal of Mathematical Sociology* 1(2): 143–86.

Sewell, William H. 1967. "Review of *Equality of Educational Opportunity*." *American Sociological Review* 32: 475–79.

Sharkey, Patrick, and Felix Elwert. 2011. "The Legacy of Disadvantage: Multigenerational Neighborhood Effects on Cognitive Ability." *American Journal of Sociology* 116(6): 1934–81.

Shernoff, David J., Mihaly Csikszentmihalyi, Barbara Schneider, and Elisa Steele Shernoff. 2003. "Student Engagement in High School Classrooms from the Perspective of Flow Theory." *School Psychology Quarterly* 18(2): 158–76.

Slavin, Robert E. 1990. "Achievement Effects of Ability Grouping in Secondary Schools: A Best-Evidence Synthesis." *Review of Educational Research* 60(3): 471–99.

Snijders, Tom, and Roel Bosker. 1999. *Multilevel Analysis: An Introduction to Basic and Advanced Multilevel Modeling*. Thousand Oaks, Calif.: Sage Publications.

Sørensen, Aage Bøttger. 1970. "Organizational Differentiation of Students and Educational Opportunity." *Sociology of Education* 43(4): 355–76.

Sørensen, Aage B., and Maureen Hallinan. 1977. "A Reconceptualization of School Effects." *Sociology of Education* 50(4): 273–89.

Steele, Fiona, Harvey Goldstein, and William Browne. 2004. "A General Multistate Competing Risks Model for Event History Data, with an Application to a Study of Contraceptive Use Dynamics." *Journal of Statistical Modelling* 4(2): 145–59.

Strayer, George. 1949. *The Report of a Survey of the Public Schools of the District of Columbia*. Washington: U.S. Government Printing Office.

Vaughan, Diane. 1996. *The Challenger Launch Decision: Risky Technology, Culture, and Deviance at NASA*. Chicago: University of Chicago Press.

Wallace, Elsie Hill. 1951. "A Study of Negro Elementary Education in North Alabama." *Journal of Negro Education* 20(1): 39–49.

Wiatrowski, Michael D., Stephen Hansell, Charles R. Massey, and David L. Wilson. 1982. "Curriculum Tracking and Delinquency." *American Sociological Review* 47(1): 151–60.

Wilson, Alan. 1968. "Social Class and Equal Educational Opportunity." *Harvard Educational Review* 38(1): 77–84.

Winship, Christopher, and Robert D. Mare. 1992. "Models for Sample Selection Bias." *Annual Review of Sociology* 18: 327–50.

Wong, George Y., and William M. Mason. 1985. "The Hierarchical Logistic Regression Model for Multilevel Analysis." *Journal of the American Statistical Association* 80(391): 513–24.

Zellner, Arnold. 1969. "On the Aggregation Problem: A New Approach to a Troublesome Problem." In *Economic Models, Estimation, and Risk Programming: Essays in Honor of Gerhard Tintner*, Lecture Notes 15, edited by K. A. Fox, J. K. Sengupta, and G. V. L. Narasimham. New York: Springer-Verlag.

PART II
Looking to the Future

Educational Equality Is a Multifaceted Issue: Why We Must Understand the School's Sociocultural Context for Student Achievement

PRUDENCE L. CARTER

The Coleman Report concluded that if students of color attended schools with more white students, they were likely to garner significantly better achievement results. Several contextual factors should be considered, however, before we make strong conclusions about the strength of the effect of racial and ethnic minority students attending school with white students. This paper makes a case for considering the necessity of both the "material" and "sociocultural" domains of schooling if we are to move toward a more holistic understanding of "school effects" on students' academic well-being. Based on a case-study analysis of four high-performing, diverse schools in different regions, using ethnographic observations and random student surveys, this paper offers evidence that students who hail from similar socioeconomic and family backgrounds but who attend schools with different sociocultural contexts have disparate academic experiences. The findings draw our attention to new directions to consider as we seek to understand how educational outcomes vary depending on the school's organizational culture.

Keywords: race, class, culture, school organizations, social inclusion

What does equality of educational opportunity mean? Does it mean the same opportunity to get an education? Or does it mean an opportunity to get the same education? Or the opportunity to be educated up to the level of one's capabilities and future occupational prospects? Or the opportunity to learn whatever one needs to know to develop one's own peculiar potentialities? Is only racially integrated education equal, irrespective of whether lack of integration is intentional or accidental? Is equality of educational opportunity a moral as well as a mathematical concept? (Thompson 1968).

More than six decades after the landmark Supreme Court decision of *Brown v. Board of Education*, and fifty years since the 1966 publication of the seminal report *Equality of Educational Opportunity* (or the Coleman Report), the United States continues to face the daunting task of equalizing educational opportunity to enhance the life chances of its low-income students and those of its racial and ethnic minority students. Inequality, stubbornly rooted in the foundation of the nation, continues to entrench historically disadvantaged groups at the bottom of the educational and mobility ladders in the United States. Significant dispari-

Prudence L. Carter is dean of the Graduate School of Education at the University of California, Berkeley.

This research was supported by grants from the William T. Grant Foundation (7895), the Spencer Foundation/NAE Postdoctoral Fellowship, and the William F. Milton Fund at Harvard University. I am also grateful for the research assistance of several former graduate and undergraduate students: Grace Atukpawu, Jakeya Caruthers, Jessica Foster, Megan Holland, Rejoice Nsibande, Lazeena Rahman, Lauren Rivera, Carla Shalaby, Graziella da Silva, Kathleen Sullivan, Rebecca Sullivan, Audrey Alforque Thomas, Dana Van Deman, Charnise Virgil, Josh Wakeham, Benita Washington, and Laura Wentworth. Direct correspondence to: Prudence L. Carter at plcarter@berkeley.edu, Graduate School of Education, 1501 Tolman Hall, Berkeley, CA 94720.

ties abound across social class, race, and ethnicity in the United States, affecting low-income and African American, Latino/a, and Native American student populations disproportionately more than other groups (Duncan and Murnane 2011).

The Coleman Report, written by the sociologist James Coleman and his colleagues, found that family background, not school effects, significantly predicted academic achievement. It laid the groundwork for an enduring narrative about the limited effects of between-school differences on student achievement in the presence of the robust effects of family background, concluding that

> schools bring little influence to bear on a child's achievement that is independent of his background and general social context; and that this very lack of an independent effect means that the inequalities imposed on children by their home, neighborhood, and peer environment are carried along to become the inequalities with which they confront adult life at the end of school. For equality of educational opportunity through the schools must imply a strong effect of schools that is independent of the child's immediate social environment, and that strong independent effect is not present in American schools. (Coleman et al. 1966, 325)

Coleman and his team also concluded that the social composition of a school's student body is more highly related than any other school factor to achievement, independently of the student's social background. The Coleman Report therefore yielded two significant takeaways: first, that the advantages and disadvantages conferred by the family context follow students throughout their elementary and secondary schooling; and second, that if disadvantaged students (namely, African Americans, Native Americans, and Mexican Americans) attend schools with more white students, then they are likely to garner significantly better achievement results.

As I elaborate in the following pages, several contextual factors should be considered before we draw our own conclusions about what Coleman and his colleagues reported as a lack of school effects and the strength of the effect of racial and ethnic minority students attending school with white students. First, any analyses of school effects should not be ahistorical; we cannot ignore the near-homogeneous nature of schools for disadvantaged racial and ethnic minority students in the United States in the mid-twentieth century. At the time of publication of the Coleman Report, institutionally sanctioned discrimination and lack of access to a quality education for students of color were as old as the United States itself. Southern states had made it illegal to teach an enslaved person to read, and this policy persisted through the Emancipation and Jim Crow eras; well into the twentieth century, African Americans faced de facto and de jure exclusion from public schools, as did Native Americans and, frequently, Mexican Americans (Kluger 1976; Tyack 1974). Even in the North, problems of exclusion, segregation, and lack of resources were severe for African Americans who migrated from the South to urban areas like Chicago (Neckerman 2007). Therefore, the variation in the proportions of low-poverty and high-poverty schools to which African Americans, Asian Americans, Mexican Americans, and Native Americans were exposed was extremely limited (Anderson 1988; Kluger 1976; Tyack 1974).[1] Finally, as Samuel Lucas (this issue) argues, "failure to gather truly school-specific [as opposed to district-specific] expenditure data in the mid-1960s could underlie the finding of small or even nonexistent differences in resources by race and, by restricting the range of variables and introducing measurement error, may explain why school-level factors of the period appeared to be of little consequence for racial inequality."

The current fiscal and social landscape of schools is similarly dismal for a significant proportion of these students in the second decade of the twenty-first century. The National Center

---

1. Today there are highly visible material disparities and significant variation among the states, with per-pupil expenditures in 2008 ranging from nearly $18,000 in Vermont to just over $6,000 in Utah (Baker, Sciarra, and Farrie 2010).

for Education Statistics (Kena et al. 2015) reports that in the 2012–2013 school year, nearly half of African American and Latina/o students (45 percent for both groups) attended high-poverty schools (schools where more than 75 percent of the students were eligible for free or reduced-price lunch), compared to only 8 and 16 percent of white and Asian students, respectively. Taken altogether, these economic facts should inform the social science community that certain social groups were and continue to be significantly more likely to attend low-quality schools with extremely limited variation in fiscal resources and a concentration of poverty. Arguably, such an enduring material landscape could create an illusion of either limited or absent independent effects of schools.

Second, the Coleman Report points to the positive influences of student composition in a school—namely, the presence of white students. This finding indicates the comparative advantages of diverse schools attended by both students of color and white students. Congruent with Coleman's findings, some newer studies have shown positive effects of desegregated schools, including stronger retention rates, or less dropping out, and better performance of African Americans in these schools than in segregated ones (Guryan 2004; Hanushek, Kain, and Rivkin 2009; Mickelson 2001). In addition, low-income, high-achieving black students in desegregated schools have been found to have a higher chance of getting out of poverty with their high school diplomas (Braddock et al. 1986). We might ask whether these effects stem from (1) students of color sitting next to white students, (2) students interacting in ways that change attitudes and aspirations, or (3) the additional resources that are concomitant with white students' enrollment.

Other studies, in contrast, appear to suggest that school desegregation has no positive influence on the reduction of the racial test-score gap (Vigdor 2011), although data on enrollment in honors courses suggest that within-school segregation increases when schools are more highly diverse, thus potentially offsetting the benefits of school desegregation (Card and Rothstein 2007).[2]

In an assessment of educational outcomes other than test scores, some studies, including that of Geoffrey Borman and Jaymes Pyne (this issue), have shown that racial and ethnic minority students fare better sociopsychologically and culturally in mono-racial and mono-ethnic schools than in desegregated schools (see also Bates 1990). Students of color, according to these studies, feel more attached to school when they attend it with greater proportions of students of their own race or ethnicity (Johnson, Crosnoe, and Elder 2001). In predominantly white higher education settings, black students report problems of cultural alienation, social adjustment, racial discrimination, and strained interpersonal relations with other students, faculty, and staff (Allen 1988, 1992; Bennett 1984; Chavous et al. 2002; Cureton 2003; Hurtado 1998; Kraft 1991; Willie 2003). Fewer studies, however, have explicitly examined the cultures of secondary schools and how they influence the incorporation of specific groups of students.

Persistent achievement differences, in addition to social and cultural challenges, beg the question of whether simply ameliorating a school's "mobility context"—that is, its material or resource conditions—is sufficient to eradicate academic achievement disparities. Researchers—in the intellectual tradition of such scholars as Samuel Bowles and Herbert Gintis (1976) and Pierre Bourdieu (1977)— have suggested that a school's cultural environment affects students' incorporation and their educational behaviors (Delpit 1997; Lareau and Horvat 1999; Soudien 2001). Lucas (this issue) describes the omission of the analysis of in-school processes as a major methodological drawback of the Coleman Report. Instead, the

---

2. The most recent data from the Civil Rights Project at UCLA (Orfield et al. 2014) on segregation shows that although desegregation progress was very substantial for African Americans in the South from the mid-1960s to the late l980s, the South has now lost all of the additional progress made after 1967. Still, the South is the least segregated region for black students. Meanwhile, the growth of segregation has been most dramatic for Latino students, particularly in the West, where there was substantial integration in the l960s. Latinos are also significantly more segregated than blacks in suburban America.

Coleman Report adopted an input-output model, or a material framework (albeit limited in measurement), because consensus around a more complex educational process within schools did not exist (Coleman et al. 1966, 239–40; Lucas, this issue).

Perhaps we social scientists and educational researchers in the United States have not heeded sufficiently the caution of the sociologist W. E. B. Du Bois (1935), who foreshadowed problems that desegregated (and even resource-rich) schools would confront. Placing diverse bodies next to each other would not heighten student achievement, Du Bois argued, since multiracial schools characterized by thick social (that is, racial) boundaries were just as "bad" as segregated schools with limited material resources. In the case of the former, Du Bois suggested, teachers, principals, staff, and students would have to tackle enduring social and symbolic boundaries that compelled individuals and groups to act in ways that reproduced inequality (see also Tilly 1999). And failure to meet the "intangible" goals of integration (see Wells 2000)—that is, bridging the racial, ethnic, and socioeconomic chasms and facilitating cross-cultural communication and relationships among social groups previously isolated from one another—would undermine the goals of equal opportunity within schools.

I argue that to fully understand the school's role in students' incorporation, it is important to differentiate between the school's mobility and sociocultural contexts. The *mobility context* comprises the material or resource conditions of the school. On the one hand, high rates of poverty and other disadvantaged socioeconomic conditions characterize many urban, minority-dominant schools, while greater wealth and improved conditions such as smaller teacher-student ratios, more experienced teachers, more course offerings, more funds and diversity in extracurricular programs, and wider networks of information about college attainment are found in desegregated schools (Crain 1970; Crain and Mahard 1983; McIntire, Hughes, and Say 1982; Orfield 2001). The *sociocultural context,* in comparison, comprises the school's norms of academic achievement, its logic for student conduct and presentations of self, its pedagogical content and practices, and its climate of teacher-student, student-student, and other inter- or intragroup dynamics. The school's cultural environment can also include the meanings that students and educators attach to certain curricular patterns, such as which students belong in specific courses and who plays which sports or participates in particular school activities.

An underlying premise of this paper is that student success, engagement, or well-being is not simply indicated by tests. Several other outcomes that pertain to students' relationships to schooling, including their sense of "engagement" and "incorporation" within their school, are probably related, either directly or indirectly, to students' attainment and achievement. Specifically, I examine the following questions: Are there associations between schools' sociocultural environments—specifically in minority-dominant versus majority-white, multiracial schools—and the incorporation of black and Latino students? If so, what are the features of these environments that enable certain racial and ethnic groups to be incorporated more easily at some schools than at others?

Conceptually, a social group's incorporation within a school entails more than the nature of its members' participation in classes and activities or an individual student's propensity to either stay in school or drop out. Here I use "incorporation" to refer to the reception by an institutional context (a school) of different social groups and that context's ability to move them toward the *center* of the school organization and away from its margins in their social relations and academic participation. That is, I argue that the relational aspects of the school context matter greatly too, and that the nature of educators' and students' social relations— their position, status, and location within the school—can either facilitate or reproduce educational inequality in ways that are masked by a focus only on either the students' family backgrounds or the school's material resources or inputs. To be clear, the objective of this paper is not to present a predictive model of school achievement among social groups across different school contexts (although some test score data comparisons are shown here), but rather to illuminate how the social status of African American and Latino students with similar socioeconomic backgrounds can differ based on the school's sociocultural context and composition. Significant divergences in access and participation in myriad educational activities—which, conceivably, are conducive to greater academic mobility—are found between high-performing majority-minority and majority-white schools.

METHODS

Using a comparative case-study analysis of four schools located in two different regions of the United States, I compare the experiences of students who hailed from similar socioeconomic and family backgrounds but who attended different schools with varying social compositions. Relatively speaking, each school was a high-performing high school (grades 9 through 12) in a metropolitan area, two in a Southern capital city and two in a Northeastern capital city. One school in each city was minority-dominant (one was predominantly black and one was predominantly black and Latino), and one was multiracial and predominantly white. A team of seven researchers (six assistants and I) visited the four schools weekly for six months from January through June 2007. The research team comprised three African Americans, one Egyptian American, and three white Americans. Except at South City Honors, which was visited mainly by two African American researchers, a mixed-race pair of researchers attended an array of classes and extracurricular and lunchroom activities four to five days a week, spending anywhere from three to seven hours at the school.

The four schools in the study shared two main criteria. First, they were all multiracial in terms of student composition, though the racial majority varied in each school. Second, to hold constant the average academic orientation of the schools, the four schools chosen were similar in their state's accountability ratings as it pertained to the No Child Left Behind law: all four schools were relatively high-performing in their district. Also, we selected two cities that were in areas where desegregation struggles had been fraught with racial and ethnic strife (Dalbey and Harris 2001; Eaton 2001) but were also in different areas of the country; thus, regional history might account for variations in the extent of interracial and interethnic contact and the permeability of group boundaries (Farley and Frey 1994). While the four schools were not representative of all schools in their district, they were typical of schools that could be classified as multiracial in their district and metropolitan area.

The data collection began in Southern Capital City (SCC) in January 2007 at South County Prep High School (a pseudonym), a school of grades 9 through 12, with 1,400 students, located at the fringe of a medium-sized, urban Southern capital city (2010 population 175,000).[3] According to the 2010 census, there were 540,000 people residing within the SCC's metropolitan statistical area (MSA). The racial makeup of the MSA was 53 percent white, 45 percent African American, 1 percent Asian, and 1 percent Hispanic or Latino of any race. At South County Prep High School, about 77 percent of the students were racially classified as white, 21 percent as black, 1 percent as Asian, and 1 percent as Hispanic. Sixteen percent of students enrolled qualified for either free or reduced-price lunch.[4] South County Prep's student-teacher ratio was seventeen to one, and all of the teachers and staff, except for three of them, were white. Ten miles west of South County Prep was South City Honors High School, an urban, comprehensive high school of grades 9 through 12 with a notable Advanced Placement (AP) program. South City Honors had 1,300 students, 93 percent of whom were racially classified as black and 6 percent as white. Sixty-four percent of its students were on either free or reduced-price lunch. With a student-teacher ratio of twenty to one, the school was led by a multiracial staff of sixty-eight teachers (see table 1).

Similar school types were selected for ob-

---

3. Pseudonyms are used throughout this paper to protect the identities of the schools, students, and staff and to mask their locations.

4. National Center for Education Statistics (NCES), Common Core of Data (CCD): public schools, 2005–2006 academic year.

Table 1. Demographic Characteristics of the Four Metropolitan High Schools, 2007

	North City Tech High School (Majority-Minority)	North Village Prep High School (Majority-White)	South City Honors High School (Majority-Minority)	South County Prep High School (Majority-White)
Number of students	1,200	1,200	1,300	1,400
Percent Asian students	23	5	0	1
Percent black students	45	6	93	21
Percent Latino students	20	3	0	1
Percent white students	11	84	6	77
Percent students on free or reduced-price lunch	63	2	64	16
Student-teacher ratio	18:1	14:1	20:1	17:1
School NCLB accountability rating	Very high[a]	Very high[a]	Exemplary (4)	Superior (5)[a]

Source: National Center for Education Statistics and the state departments of education for Northern Capital City and Southern Capital City.

[a]Denotes highest performance ranking for the state where South City Honors and South County Prep are located. The performance scale ranged from 1 to 5.

servational, interview, and survey data collection in Northern Capital City (NCC). NCC, a large urban center with a population (2010 population 620,000) that was 54 percent white, 24 percent black, 18 percent Hispanic, and 9 percent Asian, had a public school student population of 60,000. According to the census of 2010, there were about 4 million people who resided within NCC's MSA. The student racial demographics in NCC's public schools did not, however, reflect the residential demographics. With the exception of three exam schools (an organizational structure that attracted a critical percentage of white students), NCC's public schools were highly segregated. Forty-two percent of students were black, 14 percent white, 9 percent Asian, and 35 percent Hispanic.

North City Tech School was one of the three exam schools; in spite of the influx of white students, more than 80 percent of its 1,200 students could be categorized as "minority" or students of color. Although many of these students performed better than the majority of NCC students on their elementary state tests, most North City Tech students had not scored high enough to be accepted to the two other exam schools, which were considered more elite and ranked higher. Out of the four schools in this study, North City Tech was the most racially and ethnically diverse, with about 45 percent black students, 23 percent Asian, 20 percent Hispanic, and 11 percent white. Nearly two-thirds of the students (63 percent) were on free or reduced-price lunch.[5] North City Tech's student-teacher ratio was eighteen to one, and like South City Honors in SCC, its teaching staff and administration of about sixty-five was multiracial.

To find a comparative majority-white school with a critical mass of black and Latino students, I had to look in a suburban, upper-middle-class school district that participated in NCC's metropolitan Voluntary Desegregation Program (VDP).[6] North Village Prep High School, located twenty-three miles northwest of North City Tech High School, had participated in the VDP since 1967 to attract African American or black and Hispanic students,

5. NCES, CCD: public schools, 2005–2006 academic year.

6. VDP is a state-funded program designed to eliminate racial imbalance through the busing of children of color from NCC to public school systems in surrounding suburban communities.

most of whom entered a lottery to attend affluent suburban schools like North Village Prep High School. Of North Village Prep's student population of 1,200, 84 percent were white, 6 percent were black, 5 percent were Asian, and 3 percent were Latino. Only 2 percent of North Village Prep's students were on free or reduced-price lunch. With the exception of one African American and one Asian American teacher, all of North Village Prep High School's eighty-eight teachers were white, and its student-teacher ratio was fourteen to one.

REPORT OF FINDINGS

Variations in Educational Experiences by School Context and Race-Ethnicity

While the Coleman Report documented the positive influences of racial and ethnic minority students attending school with white students, he and his colleagues were unlikely to have anticipated that the potential effects of interracial contact might be mitigated by organizational mechanisms within such schools.[7] There is no shortage of research showing the stratifying and consequential effects of school tracking by race, ethnicity, and social class (Card and Rothstein 2007; Gamoran 1987; Oakes 2005; Tyson 2011). Tracking has begun to be referred to as a form of resegregation because it has evolved into an educational practice that frequently excludes and stratifies on the basis of perceived ability by these social identity categories. Further, from a researcher's perspective, I have seen that the social organization of students within classes and racially demarcated extracurricular activities reinforces the establishment of de facto ethnically and racially segregated spaces.

At North Village Prep, 88 and 71 percent of the Asian and white students, respectively, were enrolled in at least one honors or AP course, compared to 30 percent of their black and Latino peers (see table 2). English and history were not tracked at North Village Prep, but other courses were; we learned that none of the black and Latino students in the school were enrolled in the advanced math and science classes. At South County Prep, 62 percent of the white students surveyed were enrolled in at least one honors or AP course, compared to only 44 percent of the African American students. In contrast, at both South City Honors and North City Tech, surveyed students from all racial and ethnic groups enrolled in such courses at nearly the same rate, ranging from an average of 75 percent at the former and 45 percent at the latter.

Comparing himself to the more privileged students at his school, one fifteen-year-old sophomore, Judah, commented on the academic divide between students participating in the Voluntary Desegregation Program and non-VDP students:

> When I got here, looking at kids my age who are taking trigonometry, and I'm here in geometry ... I'm here in Algebra 2; I'm looking at kids who are in calculus; and I'm still here in Algebra 2, being where I'm supposed to be. And I feel like I have to catch up to them because if I don't, then thirty years down the line, who is going to be the clerk and who is going to be the one who is leading the company?

Judah anticipated a long-term economic impact of tracking in his school, one that would reinforce the socioeconomic class privilege already present at North Village Prep. In his view, different levels of course access and preparation would lead to differential levels of higher education and economic opportunities.

A similar pattern could be seen at South County Prep. Although our research team observed five African American students (out of 302 overall) in several AP and honors courses there, these were usually the same students enrolled in the higher-level classes. Mrs. Spann, one of the three black teachers at South County Prep, gave me her take on the issue of low black representation in the most advanced and demanding classes. I met Mrs. Spann, who taught communications skills, in her first year at South County Prep. I attended one of her classes during the last period of the day and remained after school to talk to her. When I mentioned the low number of high achievers among the African American students, Mrs.

---

7. Some of this section draws heavily on work previously described in Carter (2012).

Table 2. Comparisons of Educational Experiences in Four Metropolitan High Schools, by School Type and Race-Ethnicity, 2007

	Majority-White Affluent High Schools							Majority-Minority, Mixed-Income High Schools						
	North Village Prep				South County Prep			North City Tech				South City Honors		
Selected School Experiences	Asian (26)	Black (33)	Latino (25)	White (58)	Black (103)	White (81)		Asian (48)	Black (60)	Latino (65)	White (38)		Black (68)	White (30)
Percent enrolled in honors classes	89	30**	48**	71	44	62*		40	42	48	50		75	77
Percent enrolled in one or more AP courses	88	30**	48**	71	38	62*		40	42	48	50		75	77
Percent involved in one or more extracurricular activities	77	55*	56*	76	68	73		58	78*	51	40		69	73
Happy with school (percent agree)	89	76*	88	91	55*	69		67	77	65	74		75	86
Feel like part of the school (percent agree)	85	38*	54*	85	59*	67		62	83*	69	66		72	76

Source: Author's tabulations from student survey data set.
*$p < .05$; **$p < .01$

Spann remarked, "There are many more smart students, but you should notice the color of the skin of those who get classified as 'smart.' You'll notice that some of the students, because of the way they look, will never get deemed as smart, even though they are quite competent and intelligent," she continued.

While tracking was also practiced at majority-minority South City Honors and North City Tech, there were significant differences between these two schools and the other two in terms of which students were represented as the "smartest" or the "brightest." On a typical school day in the spring at South City Honors, I sat in on the AP English class of Cate Gilman, a 2007 ACT (American College Test) Star Teacher who was a tall, slender, thirty-something white female with medium-length, fine brown hair and fair skin. Her classroom walls were lined with sketches of the faces of famous authors, including Jane Austen, D. H. Lawrence, and George Orwell. Ms. Gilman had also posted a picture of Toni Morrison on the bulletin board to the right of the door in a collage of other writers' pictures; Morrison was the only writer of color in the mix. Ms. Gilman's second-period class had twenty-two students: fourteen black females, three black males, two white females, and three white males. I was familiar with some of the faces, including Xavier, the African American male who was one of the two National Achievement semifinalists in that year's senior class. Also, there was Benson, a white male who was the high school valedictorian and had obtained a perfect score on the ACT. Ms. Gilman had asked her students to complete an AP practice test exercise, and they worked for about twenty minutes on a difficult prose passage excerpted from a literary work on how a nineteenth-century aristocracy dealt with the virtues of charity and humility. As they worked, Ms. Gilman walked around and passed out cards, each marked with the number of a particular question; as students answered the questions correctly she handed them a card with remarks such as: "You got #1 correct; you're a genius!"

Nearly 1,500 miles away at North City Tech, our research team witnessed similarly diverse classrooms and student and teacher dynamics. The AP physics class of Mr. Jimenez—a thirty-something bald and bespectacled Latino who sported a well-worn University of Northern Capital City sweatshirt embossed with a logo promoting a local youth program at the university—was large (around thirty students), interactive, and lively. It was also racially mixed and fairly balanced in terms of gender. Mr. Jimenez's classroom had the feel of a physics lab: the entire back wall was lined with multiple kinds and sizes of gears, pulleys, and levers and student-made, physics-themed mobiles were hung from the ceiling. Students sat together at tables, interacting across race and gender. On this particular day, for example, a black male, upon entering the room, gave pounds and handshakes to a group of very diverse boys. As they worked the students shared ideas and answers, supporting one another in solving the assigned problems. They moved freely from table to table to help one another, and all conversations between them appeared to be physics-related.

The two classroom observations made at South City Honors and North City Tech High Schools were fairly representative of many of the courses at these schools, especially the ones for high-achieving students. While not all of the classes at these high schools seemed to be as engaging as these, these particular classes for high-achieving students presented a contrast between these two schools—whose predominant groups were characterized as racial and ethnic minorities in the U.S. context—and the two other schools in the study. At South City Honors and North City Tech, it was not a rarity to see the higher-level courses—those considered the most rigorous or even for the "smartest"—filled with significant percentages of black and brown students. In comparison, beyond their class time with white peers in their general comprehensive and college preparatory classes, nearly all of the students of color at North Village Prep—namely, the VDP participants—had limited social contact with white students. Whether they were completing paper assignments, getting tutorial assistance, playing chess, talking politics, or merely hanging out with one another, most VDP students spent at least some time in the "VDP room," away and separate from their white peers.

Other issues threatened to undermine the

initial attention that student leaders and faculty at North Village Prep had given to the social distance and separation between the students. During our first week of research at North Village Prep, I sensed a buzz of eager anticipation in the air: some students and a few fortunate teachers were preparing to head to Japan that spring on a band and orchestra trip for a two-week exchange. While one of only two black teachers at North Village Prep, Mr. Moman, was going on the trip as a chaperone, *none* of the African American and Latino students who participated in the school's VDP were headed to Japan. Yearly, students of this affluent school took trips abroad to Europe, Asia, Latin and Central America—not only after numerous car washes and bake sales but with parental financial support. By contrast, North Village Prep's black and Latino students, the majority of whom were lower-income and voluntarily bused to the school via the VDP, could not afford these trips and were not financially subsidized by the school to participate in them.

Additionally, the school's efforts were challenged by the impact of residential segregation on VDP student participation in non-academic aspects of school life, as well as their social cohesion with schoolmates. Almost all of North Village Prep's VDP students were bused into the district from the urban center and surrounding areas of Northern Capital City. Several voiced their dislike for the lack of neighborhood proximity; they could not fully participate in every aspect of school life, and their principal and teachers had found no easy way around the matter. Although the school did provide a "late" bus, which left at 5:30 PM daily, taking it would have prevented VDP students from participating in any evening programs or early morning meetings that occurred before the bus arrived. One of those students was Neela, who had been on the basketball team and had been able to sleep over at a teammate's house a few evenings when she did not feel like making the long trek back home to the city from the suburbs after the evening practices held from 6:00 to 8:00 PM. Neela did not enjoy having to stay overnight away from her home so often, however, and with no prospect of a late bus, she stopped playing basketball.

"It's a Matter of 'Tastes'": Social Distance and Racial-Ethnic and Class Relations

The school communities of North Village Prep and South County Prep High Schools, the two multiracial, majority-white schools, experienced thick social boundaries (Lamont and Molnár 2002) that endured behind school walls and in classrooms.[8] A stroll through North Village Prep's cafeteria on any given day would reveal this. Filled with vibrant chatter and myriad social dynamics, the school cafeteria is a sociological laboratory for the study of adolescent group relations. The most noticeable and immediate observation at North Village Prep was the sight of the VDP students—nearly all of the African American and Latino students—sitting on the right-hand side near the back door entrance, while the white and Asian students sat on the left-hand side in duos and groups according to clique preferences.

The school's personnel had begun to acknowledge some of its social and cultural difficulties and even attempted to do something about it with the "Challenge Day" program, which would reach at least one hundred students. On an assembly day, as students walked into the auditorium, they had been given randomly assigned, color-coded pieces of paper and told to sit in the area designated by its color. The students had chosen to ignore these directions, not only because they were rebellious adolescents, but also because randomly assigned seating would have taken them out of their comfort zone of sitting with their friends. After they watched video excerpts featuring the Challenge Day program from *The Oprah Winfrey Show*, students were encouraged by two twelfth-grade co-facilitators, an African American female and a white male, to partici-

---

8. Michèle Lamont and Virág Molnar (2002) define "social boundaries" as the lines of demarcation between, or categorizations of, people or practices that are often used to justify the allocation of unequal resources; they define "symbolic boundaries" as the conceptual and cultural tools used to categorize groups to separate the "us" from the "them."

pate in North Village's own upcoming Challenge Day.⁹ While Will, a graduating white male senior, anticipated a positive long-term impact of such a program, he worried about the impact of more immediate practices already in place at his school:

INTERVIEWER: If you were able to change one thing about your school, what would that be?

WILL: I think one thing I would change is I would try to make this school more welcoming for . . . all people. I kind of, I mean, as with any high school, probably, you tend to form . . . tend to break down into groups. I mean, I hang out with people who do a lot of the same activities as me and, you know, get the same grades and are in the same classes, and I think that's one disadvantage of having kind of tracked classes. I'm glad that we don't have them in English or history. I think that helps a little bit, but, yeah, I'm certainly glad that we have the . . . via the [Be the] Change program this year, I think . . . I really think that will make a difference in the school.

INTERVIEWER: You do?

WILL: Yeah. I really do. I mean, I participated in one of the days, and I thought it was an amazing experience, but I think people . . . I think it's . . . if not already, then in the future it will help people to kind of recognize others and not just judge them. It will probably take a while for it to make a really big difference in the school.

How do we make sense of this social distance between students? Like Will, some other students expressed their racial separation as a matter of "interests" and shared understandings. Vonda, an African American sophomore at North Village Prep, explicitly attributed "all the black kids [sitting] together" to their common interests:[10]

I think that people just notice that we sit together because we're a different race or we're different . . . we're like . . . most obviously different from outside than everybody else. [The VDP kids] may very well be a group of basketball players, a group of nerds, a group of hockey players, a group of, you know, ballets or a group of, like, musical. You know what I mean? In the cafeteria they all sit with each other and have cliques, but you can't tell because they all look similar and then we are in the corner over there [*laughs*]. Like obviously different, so people are just like, "Oh, they don't like us." But it's not that. . . . In general people find similarities with other people, and they relate to them and be friends with them and we all understand each other, so we end up doing that. It's the same thing with all the hockey players who understand each other and talk about hockey all day or all the like [*pause*] you know, singers will all sit with each other and sing with each other all day.

Vonda tried to convince me that racial, ethnic, and ostensibly class divisions lead to a sense of shared interests and a social cohesion that presumably would lead any humans with something in common to form groups and distinguish themselves from others spatially in the cafeteria. Unlike their white schoolmates, however, Vonda and her VDP peers did not have the luxury of forming groups according to specific social, extracurricular, academic, or hobby interests. Their low numbers and high visibility precluded that sort of social organization. Still, two obvious and critical questions remain: Why did the other interest groups not include some of these VDP students, who presumably shared their taste for music, sports,

---

9. Founded in 1987, Challenge Day, a program that is part of the Be the Change Movement—which promotes kind and compassionate acts for others and the infusion of humanist tendencies throughout society—was developed by a husband-wife team of motivational speakers. The founders travel to high schools and have students and teachers spend time in one-day retreats discussing and breaking across social boundaries, whether black versus white, poor versus middle-class, popular versus unpopular, overweight versus slim, or bully versus nerd.

10. See Tatum (1997) for social and psychological explanations of why youth in school tend to separate by race and ethnicity.

language, academics, or other interests? And why did Vonda and her VDP peers choose not to integrate those groups?

Similarly, at South County Prep, basketball and step-dancing are to "black" and "black female" as baseball and cheerleading are to "white" and "white female," respectively. There students formed close relationships with those participating in the same activities. Cheerleading, baseball, the Fellowship of Christian Athletes, and the Young Republicans Club had few African American students involved, but these students were well represented in basketball and football. The real and symbolic distinctions students saw mirrored in their social organization within schools were teaching them their places, their boundaries, their "lines" (for more discussion, see Carter 2012). As Ashley, a white female eleventh-grader at South County Prep, noted:

> We have, like, kind of *blurry lines* a lot of the times . . . but like, you know, you have that group and you can't really, like, relate to that group. You can individually but, like, not as a whole group, but a lot of the other groups, just, like, they've learned their *lines* a lot. Like we have a lot of people that are in the AP classes, and they hang out together a lot, and there's, like, theater groups and stuff like that, and they hang out and just, like, random small groups from, like, different . . . just from being in high school together for so long and stuff like that.

Not only did Ashley call out the social "lines" or boundaries between groups of students, but she also distinguished between *interpersonal* and *intergroup* contact and prejudices ("You have that group and you can't really, like, relate to that group. You can individually . . ."). That is, she could cross racial boundaries and relate to an African American peer as a friend, for example, but her friendship with one person did not necessarily allow her to view African Americans as a whole differently. Further, Ashley noted that the social organization of her school influenced her thinking and her relationships with students who differed from her socially. Social psychologists have noted (for example, Pettigrew 1998) that although cross-race friendships may benefit in-group members' perceptions of out-group members, the extent to which the befriended out-group member is perceived to be representative of the out-group actually determines in-group members' ability to change their attitudes about the out-group. Otherwise, the in-group members tend to maintain a "but you're not like the other members of your group" attitude about out-group members.

Thoughts and beliefs like those of Vonda, Ashley, and Will about the consequences of the boundary-making that occurs within schools—the site, we would assume, of deep interracial and ethnic contact—emerged repeatedly in the study. Similarly, at South City Honors and North City Tech, students admitted to having cliques and peer groupings, but the boundaries seemed more permeable at both of these schools. White kids were in the minority at South City Honors. They spoke openly with me about it, and students like Adam and Meredith shared some poignant stories about the consequences of interracial dating in their communities (see Carter 2012). According to Fred, a white male senior, the diminution of racial boundaries at school was undermined by the social climate outside in the communities of his Southern city:

> At South City Honors for . . . [*pause*] you know, people tend to disperse to who they're more related to, and I guess being white and the minority [*laughs*] . . . is, I don't know . . . I guess you can relate maybe a little . . . easier to white people and it's kind of easier to get along with them, but . . . uh . . . and it's kind of how it is, but . . . uh . . . I mean, everyone is cool. Everyone is generous, you know, they're good people, and it's . . . it's kind of like a school friendship but away from school you don't really keep the same friendships and I don't know.

At North City Tech, where more salient ethnic immigrant distinctions arose, students formed ethnic social clubs: at lunch students referred to the Puerto Rican table, the African American table, the Chinese table, the Japanese table, the Haitian table, the Vietnamese table, the "geek" table, and the "loser" table, to name some. Strikingly, the loser table was the most diverse of all the tables in terms of race, ethnicity, and gender. These students would attend each other's programs and events, even if they were not in-group members. We met many cultural boundary crossers, however, at North City Tech. For instance, Cherise, an African American ninth-grader at North City Tech, spoke frankly about why she had decided to enroll in a Chinese language class at school: most of her friends, since seventh grade, had been Asian American—Chinese, to be specific—and she wanted to converse with them in their language. Cherise's was not an exceptional case. Two of her schoolmates were white female seniors, one an Italian-Irish American girl and the other an Irish Catholic, who perceived themselves as "minorities" in this predominantly black, Asian, and Latino school. One of them, Natalia, discussed her own cultural flexibility: "I was the only Italian-Irish girl, and everybody thought I was some type of Latina, so they were like, 'Oh, what are you?' and they thought I was Cuban and white. Like, 'No. I'm Italian.' I hang out with a lot more Latino people just because, I don't know, so I, like, learn how to speak Spanish and stuff."

The Coleman Report pointed to the positive effects on achievement of interracial contact between students in schools. But how does that contact facilitate achievement in diverse schools where homophily (friendship preferences for one's own group) prevails? Further, how might the social organization of schools and classrooms undermine the goals of integration? As the sociologist James Moody (2001) found with a nationally representative data set, there is still a strong and generally positive relationship between heterogeneity (diversity) and friendship segregation in schools. Thus, simple exposure to one another does not promote integration. In addition, Moody found that friendship integration only occurs in spaces where students are encouraged to mix through extracurricular activities and classes in which status equality is permitted.

In some instances, the morality and merits of school diversity are clear (Allen 2004; powell 2005). In other instances, we still seek to understand why other research has not shown this increased contact to yield the strongest academic effects. As the legal scholar john powell has argued, "true integration" has not occurred in most U.S. schools. That is, desegregation (or spatial proximity) is not the same as integration—the transformation of a school's cultural, social, and political environment to incorporate all. (For a more theoretical discussion on this, see Fine, Weis, and Powell 1997; powell 2005.) The findings of my study suggest that researchers must deal with the racial, ethnic, and class "stuff"—the residual baggage and emotions fomented by historical and fraught relations—before they disavow the argument that school integration does not yield strong academic effects or fulfill the promise of the *Brown v. Board of Education* decision. At the same time, we have to question any assumptions created by the Coleman Report that sending students of diverse racial and ethnic backgrounds to school together will actually pay off academically for all groups. The school's sociocultural context matters. In actuality, South County Prep and North Village Prep had some of the finest educational resources in their communities, and students' families knew this. Paradoxically, these schools' resource contexts did not appear to be strongly associated with either students' propensity to cross social boundaries or educators' ability to facilitate that navigation so that all groups of students would have equal educational opportunity within these wealthier learning environments.

The Paradoxes of "Good Schools"
When it comes to the academic incorporation of historically disadvantaged groups of students, often traditional, high-performing majority-minority schools face significantly greater material (resource) challenges to lifting the attainment of all their students (Darling-Hammond 2010). High-performing majority-white schools, in comparison, tend to face significant social and cultural challenges (Carter 2012; Lewis and Diamond 2015; Tyson 2011). Meanwhile, some majority-minority schools, such as South City Honors and North City Tech, produce excellence with fewer resources, while some affluent majority-white schools produce mediocre outcomes, on average, among their African American and Latino stu-

dents. Like most urban schools in the United States, South City Honors and North City Tech faced the pressure to produce high test-score results. South City Honors prided itself on its multiyear history as a highly regarded high school in the state—and even in the nation, according to national ranking polls. Some students lamented the school's being "very obsessed with being a level five school." Darlene, an African American sophomore, declared to me: "They ain't worried about our future; they ain't worried about us. All they want is to look good [on the tests]." One of Darlene's peers, Danielle, sitting next to her in the in-school suspension room (the school auditorium), where I spoke to them, agreed: "They [the educators] worried about the school's future, not the students." Despite the school's reputation, some of its most academically vulnerable students still recognized the relative material disadvantages of South City Honors compared to a school like South County Prep down the road. Darlene continued: "I mean, for us to be such a good school and they always saying that South City Honors is so good, why can't we get some of the stuff that, like, South County Prep and all them get?" Although average test scores were excellent at South City Honors, Darlene and some of her peers did not perceive that they had access to the best learning environments. Certainly, high test-score performance masked the differential resource levels between South City Honors and South County Prep, but whether Darlene and Danielle were correct demands deeper levels of inquiry.

Much farther north, the families of students in the Voluntary Desegregation Program in Northern Capital City schools actively chose to send their children across municipal boundaries so that they would have access to better schools. "I don't like the schools in Northern Capital City! They're bad, [and] the kids don't like to learn anything!" exclaimed tenth-grader Briana when asked why she chose to go to North Village Prep High School. Briana's explanation was echoed by other VDP students when we interviewed them. Most of the youth in the VDP were relatively high-achieving students in their local communities; they were the kids who might have attended North City Tech, one of a very few competitive high schools in the central city. Once they entered North Village Prep, however, the standards and characterizations of "good" students changed drastically for them. VDP students encountered a more rigorous academic climate than they had yet encountered. They were reasonably aware of these academic differences, and students like tenth-grader Judah (introduced earlier) grappled with the greater difficulty of the classes. One afternoon Judah debated with some other classmates and fellow participants in the VDP about whether the achievement gap was the "fault" of the individual student or the school administration:

I think I have kind of a [*long pause*] theory. I don't know if you guys feel this way, but I think it's more of kind of feeling intimidated by the North Village kids just because there's just some of them that are so much smarter than you. Like, it's hard to compete with them in how they do and so you get discouraged. Like, am I going to do better? Like basically, like say you're in a class and you want to know . . . like the worst kid is really smart . . . and you want to know, am I going to do better than that worst kid? So you're trying to strive; you get nervous and you want to do better than him and you end up doing bad. It's kind of like, really . . . it's like a big weight falling on your chest and therefore you have to carry that weight around the whole year. Whole year! Thinking you want to do better than that worse kid and that's only the worse kid. Like saying, and I don't know if you guys feel that way, but sometimes it feels like . . . like I'm basically the dumb one in the class. Like I have to compete with all the smart kids, and it's really hard to do that when, like, all the kids are really smart, so therefore I think it hurts me on my test because I'm going into a test thinking that I'm going to do bad when I could probably do better.

Not only did Judah recognize how his North Village Prep peers differed from him in their academic preparation, but he also hinted at what the psychologist Claude Steele and his colleagues (Steele and Aronson 1995) have discovered about the concept of "stereotype threat." The pressure of competing with peers from better-resourced backgrounds produces an anxiety that may stifle performance. An analysis of the mean academic self-esteem of North Village Prep students by race and ethnicity confirmed this: black students possessed significantly lower academic self-esteem, on average, than their white ($p < 0.01$) and marginally lower than their Asian peers ($p < 0.10$), while the Latino students possessed marginally lower academic self-esteem than their white and Asian peers. (No significant differences like these were found at the other three schools.) Academic self-esteem, or what some social psychologists refer to it as "academic self-concept," is known to have a reciprocal relationship with academic performance. That is, academic self-concept is found to influence academic performance, and conversely, academic performance influences academic self-concept (see, for example, Marsh and O'Mara 2008).

When we examined the state test results for the students surveyed, we found various between- and within-school differences (see table 3).[11] In keeping with the main comparative focus of the study, first we analyzed student test scores within race between majority-minority and majority-white schools. Our analyses show that African American and Latino students performed better in math at the majority-minority high school than their African American peers at the majority-white school in Northern Capital City; no between-school differences were found on English test scores among African Americans and Latinos in either city. The converse is true for Asian and white students at North Village Prep *only:* these students scored significantly higher on the state English exam than their racial or ethnic counterparts at North City Tech, but no differences were found in students' math scores between the schools in Northern Capital City. As for regional comparisons, we found no significant within-race differences among students on test scores between Northern Capital City and Southern Capital City.

In contrast, within each school some significant racial and ethnic differences were found. At the most affluent school, North Village Prep, African American and Latino students scored significantly lower than their Asian and white peers on both the English and math state exams. Farther away at South County Prep, attended by only African American and white students, the same significant pattern held in both English and math. At the majority-minority North City Tech, the African American students surveyed scored significantly higher on their English exam than the other ethnic and racial groups, but African American students scored significantly lower on their math exams than their white schoolmates at South City Honors. In sum, across the board we found significantly higher outcomes for African American students at the schools where they were incorporated more deeply into various facets of school life.

These test-score findings and others converge with what other studies have found about the strong positive relationship between students' sense of belonging and their school performance. In experimental intervention studies, results show that when racial and ethnic minority students feel that they belong in a school, they perform better (Walton and Cohen 2007). As I explored other dimensions of the schools' sociocultural contexts, I examined students' sense of attachment or belonging to their schools. A survey question—using Likert-type response categories, with 1 being "strongly agree" and 4 being "strongly disagree"—asked a random-stratified sample of 647 students attending the four high schools to respond to the following statement: "I feel like I am a part of this school." As table 2 shows, African American students in the majority-minority schools (North City Tech and South City Honors) reported significantly higher levels of attachment to their schools than their African American peers in the majority-white schools (South County Prep and North Village Prep). At South City Honors, white and African American students felt a part of their school to nearly equal degrees—76 and 72 percent, respectively. At the other majority-minority high school, North City Tech, 83, 62, 69, and 66 percent of the African American, Asian American, Latino, and

---

11. Because the test results come from two different states, the range of scores varies among the four schools but are the same for the two schools in each state.

Table 3. Mean student test scores (Z-scores +50) of Sampled Students

	English Test Scores					Math Test Scores				
	Northern Capital City		Southern Capital City			Northern Capital City		Southern Capital City		
Student Race-Ethnicity	North Village Prep (Majority-White) [N=]	North City Tech (Majority-Minority) [N=]	South County Prep (Majority-White) [N=]	South City Honors (Majority-Minority) [N=]		North Village Prep (Majority-White) [N=]	North City Tech (Majority-Minority) [N=]	South County Prep (Majority-White) [N=]	South City Honors (Majority-Minority) [N=]	
African American	49.79 [26]	50.04*b [58]	49.68 [81]	49.89 [46]		48.58 [27]	50.16***a [58]	49.74 [73]	49.79 [31]	
Asian	50.75***ab [21]	49.48 [48]	—	—		50.36***b [21]	50.32 [48]	—	—	
Latino (any race)	49.98 [24]	49.77 [63]	—	—		48.91 [24]	50.14***a [63]	—	—	
White	50.79***ab [56]	49.79 [37]	50.46***b [67]	50.39 [19]		50.25***b [56]	50.28 [37]	50.33***b [63]	50.82*b [11]	

Source: Author's calculations.

Note: Since the available student test scores varied by state and by grade, all scores were standardized into z-scores and then added to a constant of 50 to bolster the readability of the comparisons.

[a] z-score difference within-race, between-schools are significant
[b] z-score difference between-race, within-schools are significant

* $p < .05$; ** $p < .01$

white students, respectively, felt a part of their school. Noticeably, white students felt less a part of North City Tech (the most racially and ethnically diverse of the four schools), where they were a numerical minority, than the African American students did, although white students' level of attachment was similar to that felt by Asian American and Latino students.

In comparison, at majority-white and high-income North Village Prep, the overwhelming majority of the three groups surveyed— 90, 84, and 74 percent of white, Asian, and Latino students, respectively—said that they felt they were a part of their school, while only 38 percent of the African American students agreed with this statement. Latino students felt more a part of North Village Prep than African Americans did, but to a still significantly lesser extent than their white peers. At the other majority-white school, South County Prep, the difference was not as wide between blacks and whites as at North Village Prep, but it was noticeable and significant nonetheless: 67 percent of South County Prep's white students agreed that they felt a part of their school, compared to 59 percent of African American students.

Students' sense of belonging can also be marked by a sense of group inclusion on a larger level. At both North Village Prep and South County Prep, faculty and students were unaccustomed to viewing people of color, even teachers of color, as models of high achievement or intelligence. One morning while engaging with students in a class, I offered some clarification on sociological terms like "inequality," "race," "socioeconomic status," and "ethnicity," ideas that they conflated. One of the few African American males in the class subsequently expressed his incredulity at how "smart" I was and noted that I was "his color." The comment was meant to be a compliment, but for me it was disheartening because it signaled that the students—Asian, black, Latino, white, and multiracial alike—clearly had not had the opportunity to interact with many highly educated persons of color. They were not getting the message in school that "black" or "brown" could be synonymous with intelligence. I asked Diane Newsome, the director of the VDP, why North Village Prep had so few African American (and no Latino) faculty or staff members—only two, including Diane—and she quipped, "Why is it that Harvard [my place of employment at the time] has so few tenured black faculty?" Good question. Diane and I began a long conversation after her pointed question about racism, discrimination, exclusion, and the idea that the impact of representation and incorporation on student performance and success at both South County and North Village High Prep (or even elite universities) cannot be underestimated. Teacher representation, like student belonging, is likely to interact with some social-psychological processes known to influence student achievement (Dee 2005; Gershensona, Holta, and Papageorgec 2016; Irvine 1990).

DISCUSSION

The Coleman Report is quite explicit about the benefits of schooling black and white youth together. But is spatial proximity alone sufficient for improving the educational experiences of students of color? Even within resource-rich schools such as North Village Prep and South County Prep, educational inequality occurs daily through unequal access to classrooms and programs. School practices such as tracking shape not only students' everyday engagement in school and the rigor of their academic experience (Carter 2012; Lewis and Diamond 2005; Tyson 2011) but also their preparation for higher education (Lucas, this issue). In turn, the separation of students in classrooms and extracurricular activities inhibits the development of interracial peer and friendship networks (Granovetter 1985; Moody 2001), which are potential forms of social capital.

Moreover, the resegregation of students within schools influences their attitudes toward one another, their classes, and their teachers, and it also influences how their teachers perceive them. A string of studies over the last five decades has found that teachers' attitudes and expectations are associated with student performance (Bates 1990, 11; see also Alexander, Entwisle, and Thompson 1987; Dee 2005; Gershensona, Holta, and Papageorgec 2016; Rosenthal and Jacobson 1968). At North Village High, we found no evidence on the surface that teachers did not care about their VDP students. In fact, several volunteered for extra tutorial work with these students and even spent weekends on "cultural tours" of their students' neighborhoods (see Carter 2013). They did not expect, however, that these students would ultimately fare as well as the majority of their students in terms of grades and further educational attainment. In contrast, my field notes from South Country Prep are filled with observations of more lackadaisical treatment of students by educators. Stunningly, of the teachers and students I casually queried, few perceived any of the African American students as either "bright" or "smart" or worthy of being pushed into the more academically rigorous classes. Those beliefs were mirrored in the actual course-taking patterns of the African American students at South County Prep (see table 2).

The observational and survey data from these four school case studies provide conceptual insights into how the schools' sociocultural contexts both directly and indirectly shape the educational experiences and well-being of historically marginalized groups of students. Other papers in this issue make strong, plausible arguments that the Coleman Report suffered from some significant measurement errors, which precluded the finding that schools' resource contexts are not significantly related to differences in student achievement by race.

My research team and I witnessed radically different resources among the four schools in this study. The two majority-minority schools, with nearly two-thirds of its students on free or reduced-price lunch, did not have nearly as many resources as the two more affluent, white-dominant schools. Still, the students of color attending the poorer, majority-minority schools covered the entire spectrum of school involvement and engagement: from those at one end who were taking college preparatory AP and honors courses and participating in orchestra, chorus, and Model UN to those at the other end who had disciplinary problems and tended to drop out of school. In contrast, their coethnic peers at the more resource-rich schools found themselves more heavily represented at the lower end of the educational and extracurricular status hierarchies. These findings offer a cautionary tale about what happens *within* schools even when students of diverse socioeconomic and racial-ethnic backgrounds share a school building.

These findings also help us distinguish between the "material" and "sociocultural" contexts of schooling. The following debate among a group of African American boys attending affluent North Village Prep High School sharply captured that distinction:

JUDAH: The system doesn't encourage us to interact. Think about it.

JARVIS: Why should we interact?

JONATHAN: Yeah, why?

MARCUS: Why do you need to be encouraged?

JUDAH: Because the VDP is not just about coming out to suburban schools, doing the homework and going back to our own homes. The VDP program is about teaching suburban schools, suburban students, what it's like to live in the inner city, what it feels like to be a person of color. It's about . . .

Jarvis: I thought that the [purpose of] VDP was to come out and get a good education.

MARCUS: Yeah.

JONATHAN: Yeah.

JUDAH: No, it's not. . . . That's its main purpose, but the other purpose is to teach each other what we have to offer.

In this debate about the academic and social purposes of the Voluntary Desegregation Program and going to school with more affluent white youth, most of the boys took the conventional, instrumental perspective: students of color should attend a "high-quality" school with good teachers, high scores, and strong financial resources if they want to do well. However, Judah, who was in the minority, challenged them to think beyond the material context because of their experiences and his observations at North Village Prep. To assume that social contact with one another will lead to better outcomes in educational engagement and attainment is to assume that status equality exists in schools, but that is often not the case (Carter 2012; Fine, Weis, and Powell 1997; Lewis and Diamond 2015; Moody 2001; Tyson 2011).

In conclusion, both observed and reported educational experiences from my study highlight a central tension in the American educational sphere. Policymakers and educators—informed, at times, by social science research—focus on the provision of "high-quality" schools for all groups without considering what that actually looks like in daily practice. Here is where various qualitative research studies are useful, although the findings of qualitative researchers are rarely featured in the debates about the roles and causes of "school effects." Such studies, however, frequently illuminate conceptual areas that large-scale research studies either miss or ignore in their analyses.

To fully understand the impact of school context on student outcomes, we must consider how schools maintain environments that compel students and educators to behave in ways that send strong signals about in- and out-groups. That is, the research must be vigilant about the social and symbolic boundaries embedded in school contexts that can privilege certain groups and marginalize others. Therefore, if researchers want to truly understand the persistence of educational disparities, then they must examine more deeply how inequality penetrates social relationships in school environments—from the lunchroom to the orchestra room to the classroom. They must also commit to understanding the relationship between the school's organizational and cultural context and educational opportunity gaps that stubbornly persist both within and across communities.

REFERENCES

Alexander, Karl L., Doris R. Entwisle, and Maxine S. Thompson. 1987. "School Performance, Status Relations, and the Structure of Sentiment: Bringing the Teacher Back In." *American Sociological Review* 52(5): 665–82.

Allen, Danielle S. 2004. *Talking to Strangers: Anxieties of Citizenship Since Brown v. Board of Education*. Chicago: University of Chicago Press.

Allen, Walter R. 1988. "The Education of Black Students on White College Campuses: What Quality Are the Experiences?" In *Towards Black Undergraduate Student Equality in American Higher Education*, edited by Michael Nettles. Albany: State University of New York Press.

———. 1992. "The Color of Success: African-American College Student Outcomes at Predominantly White and Historically Black Public Colleges and Universities." *Harvard Educational Review* 62(1): 26–44.

Anderson, James. 1988. *The Education of Blacks in the South, 1860–1935*. Chapel Hill: University of North Carolina Press.

Baker, Bruce D., David G. Sciarra, and Danielle Farrie. 2010. "Is School Funding Fair? A National Report Card." Newark, N.J.: Education Law Center. Available at: http://files.eric.ed.gov/fulltext/ED520522.pdf (accessed June 28, 2016).

Bates, Percy. 1990. "Can We Get There from Here?" *Phi Delta Kappan* 72(1): 8–17.

Bennett, Christine. 1984. "Interracial Contact Experience and Attrition Among Black Undergraduates at a Predominantly White University." *Theory and Research in Social Education* 12(2): 19–47.

Borman, Geoffrey D., and Jaymes Pyne. 2016. "What If Coleman Had Known About Stereotype Threat? How Social-Psychological Theory Can Help Mitigate Educational Inequality." *RSF: The Russell Sage Foundation Journal of the Social Sciences* 2(5). doi: 10.7758/RSF.2016.2.5.08.

Bourdieu, Pierre. 1977. "Cultural Reproduction and Social Reproduction." In *Power and Ideology in Education*, edited by Jerome Karabel and A. H. Halsey. New York: Oxford University Press.

Bowles, Samuel, and Herbert Gintis. 1976. *Schooling in Capitalist America: Educational Reform and the Contradictions of Economic Life*. New York: Basic Books.

Braddock, Jomills, Robert L. Crain, James M. McPartland, and Russell L. Dawkins. 1986. "Applicant Race and Job Placement Decisions: A National Survey Experiment." *International Journal of Sociology and Social Policy* 6(1): 3–24.

Card, David, and Jesse Rothstein. 2007. "Racial Segregation and the Black-White Test Score Gap." *Journal of Public Economics* 91(11–12): 2158–84.

Carter, Prudence L. 2012. *Stubborn Roots: Race, Culture, and Inequality in U.S. and South African Schools*. New York: Oxford University Press.

———. 2013. "(Im)permeable Boundaries: Why Integration into Affluent White-Majority Schools for Low-Income Minority Students Is Elusive." In *Children in Crisis: Ethnographic Studies in International Contexts*, edited by Manata Hashemi and Martín Sánchez-Jankowski. New York: Routledge Press.

Chavous, Tabbye M., Deborah Rivas, Laurette Green, and Lumas Helaire. 2002. "Role of Student Background, Perceptions of Ethnic Fit, and Racial Identification in the Academic Adjustment of African American Students at Predominantly White Universities." *Journal of Black Psychology* 28(3): 234–60.

Coleman, James S., Ernest Q. Campbell, Carol J. Hobson, James McPartland, Alexander M. Mood, Frederick D. Weinfeld, and Robert L. York. 1966. *Equality of Educational Opportunity*. Washington: U.S. Department of Health, Education, and Welfare, Office of Education.

Crain, Robert L. 1970. "School Integration and Occupational Achievement of Negroes." *American Journal of Sociology* 75(4, part 2): 593–606.

Crain, Robert L., and Rita E. Mahard. 1983. "The Effect of Research Methodology on Desegregation-Achievement Studies: A Meta-analysis." *American Journal of Sociology* 88(5): 839–54.

Cureton, Steven R. 2003. "Race-Specific College Student Experiences on a Predominantly White Campus." *Journal of Black Studies* 33(3): 295–311.

Dalbey, Matthew, and William E. Harris. 2001. "Urban Spatial Segregation in Jackson, MS: Planning for Equity." Paper presented at Lincoln Institute of Land Policy conference. Cambridge, Mass. (July 26–28).

Darling-Hammond, Linda. 2010. *The Flat World and Education: How America's Commitment to Equity Will Determine Our Future*. New York: Teachers College Press.

Dee, Thomas S. 2005. "A Teacher Like Me: Does Race, Ethnicity, or Gender Matter?" *American Economic Review* 95(2): 158–65.

Delpit, Lisa. 1997. "The Silenced Dialogue: Power and Pedagogy in Educating Other People's Children." In *Education: Culture, Economy, and Society*, edited by A. H. Halsey, Hugh Lauder, Phillip Brown, and Amy Stuart Wells. New York: Oxford University Press.

Du Bois, W. E. B. 1935. "Does the Negro Need Separate Schools?" *Journal of Negro Education* 4(3): 328–35.

Duncan, Greg J., and Richard J. Murnane, eds. 2011. *Whither Opportunity?: Rising Inequality, Schools, and Children's Life Chances*. New York: Russell Sage Foundation.

Eaton, Susan E. 2001. *The Other Boston Busing Story: What's Won and Lost Across the Boundary Line*. New Haven, Conn.: Yale University Press.

Farley, Reynolds, and William Frey. 1994. "Changes in the Segregation of Whites from Blacks During the 1980s: Small Steps Toward a More Integrated Society." *American Sociological Review* 59(1): 23–45.

Fine, Michelle, Lois Weis, and Linda Powell. 1997. "Communities of Difference: A Critical Look at Desegregated Spaces Created for and by Youth." *Harvard Educational Review* 67(2): 247–84.

Gamoran, Adam. 1987. "The Stratification of High School Learning Opportunities." *Sociology of Education* 60(3): 135–55. doi:10.2307/2112271.

Gershensona, Seth, Stephen B. Holta, and Nicholas W. Papageorgec. 2016. "Who Believes in Me? The Effect of Student-Teacher Demographic Match on Teacher Expectations." *Economics of Education Review* 52 (June): 209–24.

Granovetter, Mark. 1985. "The Micro-structure of School Desegregation." In *School Desegregation Research: New Directions in Situational Analysis*, edited by Jeffrey Prager, Douglas Longshore, and Melvin Seeman. New York: Plenum.

Guryan, Jonathan. 2004. "Desegregation and Black Dropout Rates." *American Economic Review* 94(4): 919–43.

Hanushek, Eric, John F. Kain, and Steven Rivkin. 2009. "New Evidence About *Brown v. Board of Education*: The Complex Effects of School Racial Composition on Achievement." *Journal of Labor Economics* 27(3): 349–83.

Hurtado, Sylvia. 1998. "Enhancing Campus Climates for Racial/Ethnic Diversity: Educational Policy and Practice." *Review of Higher Education* 21(2): 279–302.

Irvine, Jacqueline. 1990. *Black Students and School Failure: Policies, Practices, and Prescriptions*. New York: Praeger Publications.

Johnson, Monica K., Robert Crosnoe, and Glen H. Elder Jr. 2001. "Students' Attachment and Academic Engagement: The Role of Race and Ethnicity." *Sociology of Education* 74(1): 318–40.

Kena, Grace, Lauren Musu-Gillette, Jennifer Robinson, Xiaolei Wang, Amy Rathbun, Jijun Zhang,

Sidney Wilkinson-Flicker, Amy Barmer, and Erin Dunlop Velez. 2015. "The Condition of Education 2015." NCES 2015-144. Washington: U.S. Department of Education, National Center for Education Statistics. Available at: http://nces.ed.gov/pubsearch (accessed September 8, 2015).

Kluger, Richard. 1976. *Simple Justice: The History of* Brown v. Board of Education *and Black America's Struggle for Equality.* New York: Knopf.

Kraft, Christine L. 1991. "What Makes a Successful Black Student on a Predominantly White Campus?" *American Educational Research Journal* 28(2): 423–43.

Lamont, Michèle, and Virág Molnár. 2002. "The Study of Boundaries in the Social Sciences." *Annual Review of Sociology* 28: 167–95.

Lareau, Annette, and Erin McNamara Horvat. 1999. "Moments of Social Inclusion and Exclusion: Race, Class, and Cultural Capital in Family-School Relationships." *Sociology of Education* 72(1): 37–53.

Lewis, Amanda, and John Diamond. 2015. *Despite the Best Intentions: How Racial Inequality Thrives in Good Schools.* New York: Oxford University Press.

Lucas, Samuel R. 2016. "First- and Second-Order Methodological Developments from the Coleman Report." *RSF: The Russell Sage Foundation Journal of the Social Sciences* 2(5). doi: 10.7758/RSF.2016.2.5.06.

Marsh, Herbert W., and Alison O'Mara. 2008. "Reciprocal Effects Between Academic Self-Concept, Self-Esteem, Achievement, and Attainment Over Seven Adolescent Years: Unidimensional and Multidimensional Perspectives of Self-Concept." *Personality and Social Psychology Bulletin* 34(4): 542–52.

McIntire, Ronald G., Larry W. Hughes, and Michael W. Say. 1982. "Houston's Successful Desegregation Plan." *Phi Delta Kappan* 63(8): 536–38.

Mickelson, Roslyn Arlin. 2001. "Subverting Swann: First- and Second-Generation Segregation in the Charlotte-Mecklenburg Schools." *American Educational Research Journal* 38(2): 215–52.

Moody, James. 2001. "Race, School Integration, and Friendship in America." *American Journal of Sociology* 107(3): 679–701.

Neckerman, Kathryn M. 2007. *Schools Betrayed: Roots of Failure in Inner-City Education.* Chicago: University of Chicago Press.

Oakes, Jeannie. 2005. *Keeping Track: How Schools Structure Inequality.* New Haven, Conn.: Yale University Press.

Orfield, Gary. 2001. *Schools More Separate: Consequences of a Decade of Resegregation.* Cambridge, Mass.: Harvard University, Civil Rights Project.

Orfield, Gary, and Erica Frankenberg, with Jongyeoun Ye and John Kuscera. 2014. "*Brown* at 60: Great Progress, a Long Retreat, and an Uncertain Future." Los Angeles: University of California Civil Rights Project.

Pettigrew, Thomas F. 1998. "Intergroup Group Contact Theory." *Annual Review of Psychology* 49: 65–85.

powell, john a. 2005. "A New Theory of Integrated Education: *True* Integration." In *School Resegregation: Must the South Turn Back?* edited by John C. Boger and Gary Orfield. Chapel Hill: University of North Carolina Press.

Rosenthal, Robert, and Lenore Jacobson. 1968. *Pygmalion in the Classroom: Teacher Expectations and Pupils' Intellectual Development.* New York: Holt, Rinehart, and Winston.

Soudien, Crain. 2001. "Certainty and Ambiguity in Youth Identities in South Africa: Discourses in Transition." *Discourse: Studies in the Cultural Politics of Education* 22(3): 311–27.

Steele, Claude M., and Joshua A. Aronson. 1995. "Stereotype Threat and the Intellectual Test Performance of African Americans." *Journal of Personality and Social Psychology* 69(5): 797–811.

Tatum, Beverly Daniel. 1997. *"Why Are All the Black Kids Sitting at the Cafeteria Table?" and Other Conversations About Race.* New York: Basic Books.

Thompson, Charles H. 1968. "Race and Equality of Educational Opportunity: Defining the Problem." *Journal of Negro Education* 37(3): 191–203.

Tilly, Charles. 1999. *Durable Inequality.* Berkeley: University of California Press.

Tyack, David. 1974. *One Best System: The History of American Urban Education.* Cambridge, Mass.: Harvard University Press.

Tyson, Karolyn. 2011. *Integration Interrupted: Tracking, Black Students, and Acting White After* Brown. New York: Oxford University Press.

Vigdor, Jacob. 2011. "School Desegregation and the Black-White Test Score Gap." In *Whither Opportunity? Rising Inequality, Schools, and Children's*

Life Chances, edited by Greg J. Duncan and Richard J. Murnane. New York: Russell Sage Foundation.

Walton, Gregory M., and Geoffrey L. Cohen. 2007. "A Question of Belonging: Race, Social Fit, and Achievement." *Journal of Personality and Social Psychology* 92(1): 82–96. doi:10.1037/0022-3514.92.1.82.

Wells, Amy Stuart. 2000. "The 'Consequences' of School Desegregation: The Mismatch Between the Research and the Rationale." *Hastings Constitutional Law Quarterly* 28(4): 771–97.

Willie, Sarah Susannah. 2003. *Acting Black: College, Identity, and the Performance of Race.* New York: Routledge.

What If Coleman Had Known About Stereotype Threat? How Social-Psychological Theory Can Help Mitigate Educational Inequality

GEOFFREY D. BORMAN AND JAYMES PYNE

The Coleman Report has inspired various lines of inquiry offering new understandings of inequality of educational opportunity and the persistent achievement gaps in American schools. Of the various models and theories, stereotype threat, which focuses on social-psychological dimensions of inequality, has received considerable attention over the past twenty years. But what if stereotype threat theory, and associated interventions to combat it, had existed fifty years ago? Using data from the original Equality of Educational Opportunity Study, we find, consistent with the stereotype threat literature, that African American students confronted with more threatening educational contexts are burdened by a less favorable self-image; this finding partially explains how students' internalization of racial stereotypes depresses their test scores. Based on these findings and on results from numerous laboratory and field experiments documenting the impact of stereotype threat and how to mitigate it, we explore its usefulness for studying educational inequality in the years to come.

Keywords: stereotype threat, black-white achievement gap, educational inequality

Over the past fifty years, the Coleman Report and its findings have inspired continued scholarship on inequality of educational opportunity and the achievement gaps separating racial-ethnic minority students from their white counterparts. In some cases, new lines of inquiry and new analytical methods have offered different perspectives on the report's core finding that "schools bring little influence to bear on a child's achievement that is independent of his background and general social context" (Coleman et al. 1966, 325). For instance, research on seasonal learning differences, which decomposes students' achievement gains over the school year relative to their gains over the summer months, suggests that schools are important "equalizers" as gaps tend to grow much faster during the summer than during the school year (Alexander, Entwisle, and Olson 2001, 2007; Downey, von Hippel, and Broh 2004; Heyns 1978). In addition, by applying more recent and appropriate multilevel modeling methods to the analysis of the original Equality of Educational Opportunity Study (EEOS) data, Geoffrey Borman and Maritza Dowling (2010) have found that as much

Geoffrey D. Borman is Vilas Distinguished Achievement Professor of Education Policy and Sociology and director of the Interdisciplinary Training Program (ITP) at the University of Wisconsin–Madison. **Jaymes Pyne** is an advanced doctoral student in the Sociology Department and fellow of the ITP at the University of Wisconsin–Madison.

Research on this paper was supported by grants from the Institute of Education Sciences, U.S. Department of Education (R305A110136 and R305C050055) and the Spencer Foundation (201500044). Findings and conclusions are those of the authors and do not necessarily reflect the views of the supporting agencies. Direct correspondence to: Geoffrey D. Borman at geoffrey.borman@wisc.edu, School of Education, 348 Education Building, 1000 Bascom Mall, Madison, WI 53706-1326; and Jaymes Pyne at jpyne@wisc.edu.

as 40 percent of the variation in students' test scores is attributable to between-school differences, while within-school social inequalities are explained in part by teachers' biases favoring middle-class students and by schools' greater reliance on curriculum differentiation through the use of academic and non-academic tracking. These recent theories and analyses have offered important new perspectives on the Coleman Report and the conventional wisdom of our time. However, often missing from this discussion is how social stereotypes and harmful expectations about minority students' underperformance in school can undermine their social-psychological well-being and their ability to achieve their true potential in school.

As Clark McKown and Rhona Weinstein (2003) suggest, a critical component of ethnic and racial minority children's development is their growing awareness of their status as a member of a stigmatized group. The vast majority of ethnic and racial minority children report knowing that others—family or peers—have been the target of discrimination (Brown 2008; Quintana 1999). In addition to witnessing overt forms of discrimination, more subtle stereotypes within the academic domain may depress the performance of women in mathematics and related fields and African Americans and other non-Asian racial-ethnic groups in all academic areas. Claude Steele and Joshua Aronson, who coined the term in 1995, have referred to *stereotype threat* as the apprehension that individuals experience when confronted with a personally relevant stereotype that threatens their social identity or self-esteem. Steele and Aronson propose that the phenomenon could help explain group differences in performance on standardized tests and other academic outcomes. According to the theory, when individuals are aware that they belong to a group that is thought to perform poorly on a particular task, they often fear that they might perform in a way that confirms stereotypes about that group and thus be labeled as implicitly inferior to individuals for whom the stereotype does not apply. This largely unconscious fear elicits anxiety, lowered self-esteem, and other psychological responses that interfere with performance on evaluative activities in the classroom. In this way, individuals' psychological processes in response to socially constructed stereotypes and prejudices may contribute to persistent social inequalities (Steele and Aronson 2004).

Though stereotype threat can undermine the academic performance of minority students, a number of recent research programs suggest that interventions aimed at *reducing* stereotype threat can attenuate its effects in school-based contexts (for example, Borman, Grigg, and Hanselman 2015; Cohen et al. 2006; Cohen et al. 2009; Good, Aronson, and Inzlicht 2003; Walton and Cohen 2007), yielding significant gains on test scores and other academic outcomes (for reviews, see Aronson and McGlone 2009; Yeager and Walton 2011). A growing number of experimental studies have shown that relatively simple, brief, but well-conceptualized social-psychological interventions that focus on individual and socially constructed beliefs that affect school outcomes can have important impacts on secondary and postsecondary students' short- and longer-term educational outcomes (Cohen et al. 2006; Cohen et al. 2009; Sherman 2013; Yeager and Walton 2011). Typically, the interventions target student beliefs that may depress academic performance—such as stereotype threat, which overwhelmingly affects minority students.

These social-psychological theories and interventions, which did not exist during the development of the Coleman Report, emphasize the power that differing attitudes, mind-sets, and perceptions have on how people view themselves and how they succeed in education and beyond. But what if these theories and interventions *had* existed in 1966? At the time, the EEOS provided some correlational evidence suggesting that black students have higher achievement scores in majority-white schools relative to scores for their counterparts in schools comprising predominantly nonwhite students. This contextual feature was the most important malleable school characteristic that Coleman and his colleagues noted as a possible remedy to address inequality, and the policies that ensued, such as busing, were targeted at improving the racial integration of schools across the country.

Nevertheless, a vast literature on compositional, contextual, or peer effects (for example,

Erbring and Young 1979; Firebaugh 1978; Mayer and Jencks 1989) has led to varying interpretations for their causes. Stephen Raudenbush and Anthony Bryk (2002) suggest that such effects—which occur when the group-level aggregate of the person-level characteristic (for example, percentage minority, school mean socioeconomic status, or school-level average achievement) is related to the achievement outcome even after controlling for the effect of the student-level characteristic—may be due to normative effects associated with a school, other unmeasured school resources or characteristics for which the aggregate school-level characteristic acts as a proxy, or statistical artifacts whereby the school-level mean explains part of the effect of a poorly measured student-level characteristic.

Research on the composition of schools and groups is often atheoretical, offering only "black box" correlational data showing relationships between school compositional features and student achievement. However, some notable theories have been implicated, including the *contact hypothesis,* which is generally attributed to Gordon Allport (1954). Allport suggested that interpersonal contact can be a highly effective means to reduce prejudice between majority- and minority-group members, in that prejudice may be reduced as one learns more about a category of people. However, for optimal intergroup contact to occur, it must take place under appropriate conditions, which include: equal group status within the context, common goals, intergroup cooperation, and authority support. Robert Slavin (1985) has shown how *cooperative learning* methods can enact Allport's contact theory in a supportive context characterized by ethnically mixed learning groups of students who study material presented by the teacher and are rewarded based on the learning of the group as a whole. In most schools, however, minority students do not experience such a supportive environment. Black students—who tend to be tracked and effectively resegregated within lower-level courses (Mickelson 2001; Oakes 1995) and who often receive disproportionate (Losen 2011) and unusually harsh discipline from authority figures (Fisher, Wallace, and Fenton 2000)—are more often marginalized than considered of equal status with their white peers, and they often perceive limited authority support within their school.

Though the Coleman Report suggested that attending majority-white schools benefits the academic outcomes of black students—presumably through their access to potentially better resources, more challenging curricula, or higher-achieving white peers—these benefits may be offset by de facto segregation through academic tracking and by various social and psychological challenges that black students face in less-supportive school contexts. Indeed, some evidence suggests that black and Latino adolescents report more perceived discrimination as school racial-ethnic diversity increases and the relative size of their own ethnic group declines (Benner and Graham 2011; Hagan, Shedd, and Payne 2005; Seaton and Yip 2009). Aprile Benner and Sandra Graham (2009) further report that when the representation of black and Latino students' racial-ethnic groups decreases significantly across the transition from middle school to high school, these students experience declines in both feelings of belonging and academic achievement. If racial-ethnic minority students are poorly represented, evidence suggests, their small numbers may give rise to feelings of isolation or marginalization. In response, Robert Linn and Kevin Welner (2007), among others, have recently suggested that any racial-ethnic group should be at least 15 percent of the school population to mitigate both isolation and vulnerability to out-group hostility.

In this paper, we suggest that stereotype threat and other social-psychological factors can contribute to the achievement gap in significant ways and that the representation of black students in schools and classrooms appears to moderate social identity threats. We begin by describing the theories and evidence supporting the existence of stereotype threat and present evidence from several randomized field experiments attempting to alleviate stereotype threat among minority students. We then summarize how brief social-psychological interventions can work to reduce achievement gaps at low cost and with minimal time commitment. After these considerations, we highlight our findings from the Madison Writing and Achievement Project (MWAP). Being the first districtwide randomized field trial of stereotype threat interventions to date, MWAP provides empirical evidence of the particular school contexts in which stereotype threat is most likely to occur and in which the interventions are most likely to close academic performance gaps.

In the second part of the paper, drawing on stereotype threat theory and prior empirical evidence, we explore the following question: given our current knowledge of stereotype threat, the expansive data available from the original 1966 EEOS, and modern statistical techniques and computational power, would Coleman and his colleagues have been able to find evidence of stereotype threat in their data? We use the original EEOS data and apply stereotype threat theory to determine how the concept helps us better understand black-white achievement differences between students. In doing so, we find evidence that ninth-grade African American students of the 1960s probably experienced stereotype threat, particularly in learning environments where the majority of their classmates were white. It is likely that subtle psychological and social forces undermined the academic performance of these African American students. While much of the effect of race on academic performance can be explained by structural and institutional constraints on African American students, social-psychological forces also play a role through lowered positive self-image, partially explaining the effects of majority-white environments on black students' test scores. Ultimately, we argue that when considering integration as a solution to racial inequalities, an important piece of the puzzle is addressing the ways in which minority students internalize and process the subtle and overt forms of prejudice they experience at school. Following these findings, we close with some final thoughts on the connections between the legacy of EEOS and the expanding work on social-psychological "mind-set" interventions in schools.

STEREOTYPE THREAT AND EDUCATIONAL INEQUALITY

Though national data reveal achievement gaps at every age and grade level (Vanneman et al. 2009), considerable evidence suggests growing gaps in performance during the critical secondary school years. Grade point average, motivation, academic engagement, and achievement goals appear to decline during middle and high school for all students, but African American and Latino students suffer steeper declines in school performance than their Asian and white peers (Anderman 2003; Cook et al. 2012; Sherman 2013; Shim, Ryan, and Anderson 2008). Student achievement mirrors this trend. Although there are exceptions (see Reardon and Galindo 2009), most empirical evidence suggests that achievement gaps between white and nonwhite students persist and even grow as they progress through school (Benson and Borman 2010; Downey, von Hippel, and Broh 2004; Fryer and Levitt 2004; Jencks and Phillips 1998, 2011). Data from the National Assessment of Educational Progress (NAEP) show that achievement gaps persist between black and white students (Vanneman et al. 2009) and between Hispanic and white students (Hemphill, Vanneman, and Rahman 2011), with differences in mathematics achievement growing between ages nine and thirteen.

Work in social psychology suggests that stereotype threat contributes to these patterns of disengagement and growing inequality. As Steele and Aronson (1995, 797) originally explained:

Whenever African American students perform an explicitly scholastic or intellectual task, they face the threat of confirming or being judged by a negative societal stereotype—a suspicion—about their group's intellectual ability and competence.... And the self-threat it causes—through a variety of mechanisms—may interfere with the intellectual functioning of these students, particularly during standardized tests.

Steele and Aronson tested this hypothesis in a series of laboratory experiments. In the prototypical study in this series, they gave African

Figure 1. A Model of Stereotype Threat

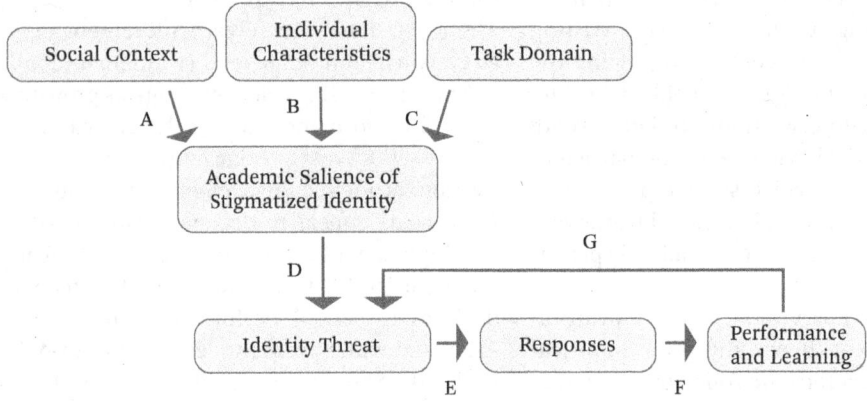

Source: Hanselman et al. 2014.

American and white college students a difficult section of a verbal Graduate Record Examination (GRE). The researchers led half of the participants to believe that the purpose of the test was to measure their intellectual ability, thereby activating the fear among African American students of confirming stereotypes about their race by performing poorly on a cognitive assessment. The others were told that the test was merely a non-evaluative laboratory exercise. Everything else about the situation was identical for the two groups, including the items on the test, the room in which they took the test, the experimenter, and so on. The results were striking: African American students who believed that the test was being used to diagnose their abilities performed significantly worse than African American students in the nondiagnostic group. The difference in the description of the test had no statistically significant effect on the white test-takers: they performed equally well in both conditions.

In the two decades since Steele and Aronson's (1995) identification of stereotype threat, more than 300 independent laboratory studies and a growing number of field studies have replicated their results, testing the phenomenon with, for instance, African American students in numerous academic settings, women and mathematics, and Latinos during verbal problem-solving. More recent research has provided clear evidence that stereotype threat effects can and do occur in real-world environments, including classrooms and schools (Good, Aronson, and Harder 2008; Good, Aronson, and Inzlicht 2003; Good, Rattan, and Dweck 2007; Huguet and Regner 2007; Keller 2002; Keller and Dauenheimer 2003; Kellow and Jones 2005; Roberson et al. 2003). Meta-analyses of this literature suggest that standard measures of ability underestimate the true abilities of black and Latino students by about one-quarter of a standard deviation (Nguyen and Ryan 2008; Walton and Cohen 2003). A meta-analysis of field experiments suggests that the psychological threats that African American and Hispanic students suffer while taking standardized tests cause them to underperform by one-fifth of a standard deviation (Walton and Spencer 2009).

Scholars believe that stereotype threat functions through psychological and contextual factors, both situationally and over time. Figure 1 (reproduced from Hanselman et al. 2014), explains how social context (A), individual characteristics (B), and task domain (C) act as exogenous influences, raising the salience of a student's stigmatized identity in school (D) under particular conditions suggested by A, B, and C. Under those conditions that promote the salience of stigmatized identity, the student feels threats to his or her identity. The physiological and psychological stress responses (E) resulting from identity threat subsequently work to the detriment of the threatened students' academic performance and learning (F). Poor performances on academic tasks or struggles with learning new material may then cause a recursive process (G) whereby these academic adversities further confirm students' worries about their stigmatized identity, which then reinforce their beliefs about the stigma, thus increasing identity threat.

Though evidence continues to accumulate regarding the specific mechanisms through which stereotype threat depresses academic performance, most researchers agree that physiological and psychological mechanisms such as stress responses, self-monitoring, and self-regulation are at play (Schmader, Johns, and Forbes 2008). In turn, these mechanisms manifest in counterproductive test-taking behaviors, such as selecting incorrect options on exams or changing answers more frequently than nonthreatened students do (Scherbaum et al. 2011). In addition, perceptions of negative stereotypes lead many individuals to engage in activities such as self-handicapping (Smith 2004), challenge avoidance (Good, Aronson, and Inzlicht 2003), and self-suppression (Pronin, Steele, and Ross 2004; Steele 1997).

Although many of the mechanisms of stereotype threat are psychological, contextual factors moderate whether stereotypes will threaten an individual's identity. This suggests that stereotype threat changes as context changes: identity as a person of African American background may hurt one's performance in one context, such as school, but be benign or advantageous in another context, such as a basketball game (Stone, Perry, and Darley 1997). If an organization has an ideology that is not inclusive of stigmatized groups or that gives them negative cues, or if a stereotype related to one's group membership is relevant to an important aspect of an organization, the potential for threat increases (Kray and Shirako 2011; Murphy, Steele, and Gross 2007; Murphy and Taylor 2011; Steele, Spencer, and Aronson 2002). One simple yet key contextual factor that can increase the threat to one's identity is the demographic makeup of an organization, which functions simply by raising the salience of an individual's identity in a threatening environment (Steele, Spencer, and Aronson 2002). Many researchers have found that the effects of stereotype threat are stronger when individuals identifying with stigmatized groups are underrepresented and thought to perform poorly at the tasks of the organization (Inzlicht and Ben-Zeev 2000; Murphy, Steele, and Gross 2007; Purdie-Vaughns et al. 2008; Sekaquaptewa and Thompson 2003).

Recent work has addressed the impact of stereotype threat on ongoing learning as a form of "double jeopardy" that interferes with both short-term performance and long-term knowledge acquisition (Taylor and Walton 2011). Kathryn Boucher and her colleagues (2012) find that the mathematics learning of women is compromised by negative stereotypes about women's math ability. Valerie Jones Taylor and Gregory Walton (2011) find that African American students—but not white students—who study under threatening conditions fare worse on a follow-up assessment conducted under nonthreatening conditions. The implication of these findings is that removing threats during evaluative situations alone is not a sufficient long-term solution when negative stereotypes are pervasive. Short-term underperformance due to stereotype threat might lead students to alter their career or professional aspirations and their sense of belonging in academic domains and contexts (Steele, James, and Barnett 2002). It might also lead students to "protectively disidentify" from academics (Aronson, Fried, and Good 2002; Major et al. 1998; Steele 1997), which in turn could lead to increased learning deficits (Appel and Kronberger 2012). Disengagement from the task or the context in which the task is to be performed can lead to growing disadvantages among negatively stereotyped students and might play a prominent role in the patterns of disengagement and widening achievement gaps found during the secondary school years.

Intervening to Combat Stereotype Threat

As mentioned earlier, several high-profile but small-scale experimental studies have demonstrated the important impacts of brief, well-conceptualized social-psychological interventions on educational outcomes for secondary and postsecondary students (Cohen et al. 2006; Cohen et al. 2009; Sherman 2013). Typically, these interventions target minority students' academic beliefs that might depress their academic performance. In an article published in

Science and reviewed by the What Works Clearinghouse (2010), Geoffrey Cohen and his colleagues (2009) report that brief self-affirmation tasks aimed at affirming students' personal values can reduce the black-white grade point average (GPA) gap by as much as 40 percent, improving African American students' performance over a three-month period and over a two-year follow-up.

Self-affirmation, or values affirmation, interventions administered in schools and classrooms typically consist of written prompts directing students to write about non-academic aspects of their lives that they value. Theory and recent empirical evidence suggest that when students who have doubts about their school abilities reflect on personally important domains beyond academics, they can buffer themselves against negative thoughts, stress responses, self-monitoring, and self-regulation —all of which undermine school performance (Schmader, Johns, and Forbes 2008). Students think broadly about the interests and attributes most important to them, such as friendships, family, athletics, religion, and creativity. Researchers tend to implement interventions just prior to high-stress evaluative school events—like high-stakes tests or other important exams—in order to reduce the effects of stereotype threat on academic outcomes. Ultimately, the interventions help improve students' overall self-image, and it is this enhanced self-image that allows them to demonstrate their full academic potential, unencumbered by threats to their performance.

Self-affirmation writing is a replicable and cost-effective strategy for reducing achievement gaps compared to other far costlier and more intensive school-based interventions. Indeed, the intervention typically consists of only several pieces of paper and can be administered to students in a regular classroom setting, taking approximately fifteen minutes of class time. Though self-affirmation and other similar psychological interventions are rooted in decades of research and theory, their power can be difficult to understand. That "magical" properties are often ascribed to these interventions underscores the misunderstood connections between students' psychological mindsets and their school performance (Yeager and Walton 2011). Coleman, along with many contemporary educational researchers, might not have considered brief social-psychological interventions a conventional school resource, since most educational treatments involve comprehensive, resource-intensive reforms to curriculum, instruction, and school and classroom organization. However, as few as two fifteen-minute exercises, Cohen and his colleagues (2009) report, have a sustained two-year impact on black students' GPAs of $d = 0.40$. In comparison, a recent review by Mark Lipsey and his colleagues (2012) of the effects of more complex and costlier elementary and middle school interventions reveals typical impacts on achievement test scores ranging from $d = 0.08$ to $d = 0.15$. Though GPAs and test scores are clearly different measures of student performance, recent work suggests that grades and attendance—not test scores—are the middle grade factors most strongly connected with both high school and college success (Allensworth et al. 2014).

How do relatively brief and inexpensive interventions lead to such substantial changes in academic performance? As proximal, relatively "quick wins" accumulate, researchers note that *recursive processes act like chain reactions* to carry forward the initial effects of the intervention (Cohen et al. 2009). As Valerie Purdie-Vaughns and her colleagues (2009) argue, a small improvement early in the year due to the intervention might, for example, give students a little extra confidence, and this confidence might lead to further gains in performance leading to more confidence, in a continuously repeating cycle. Teachers might also play a role by amplifying the effects of the invention via teacher expectancy effects. Prior field-based studies have been conducted using double-blind experiments in which neither teachers nor students knew the experimental condition to which students were randomized; under similar experimental conditions, small early improvements might lead teachers to see students as abler and more worthy of attention and mentoring (Purdie-Vaughns et al. 2009).

Cohen and his colleagues (2009) find that the greatest impacts of self-affirmation come in the later terms of the school year, providing evidence of a beneficial recursive process for students randomized to the self-affirmation treatment. By enhancing students' feelings of personal worth, the authors argue, the exercises change students' perceptions of bias at school and shift how they interpret their academic successes and failures. These steps particularly protected the study's struggling African American students; instead of feeling discouraged and falling into a pattern of disengagement, it was as though black students received an inoculation against the threat presented by negative stereotypes.

The Madison Writing and Achievement Project

Building on findings from small field-based interventions to alleviate stereotype threat, the Madison (Wisconsin) Writing and Achievement Project dealt with this source of inequality at scale for all beginning seventh-grade students across an entire urban school district. We conducted a student-level randomized trial in which we tested a self-affirmation intervention involving over 1,000 middle school students in all eleven Madison Metropolitan School District (MMSD) middle schools (grades 6–8). The intervention consisted of a sequence of writing exercises that students completed in school over the course of the academic year. Each teacher-administered exercise was designed to be similar to other classroom activities that students might experience. Following Cohen and his colleagues (2006, 2009; Sherman et al. 2013), we randomly assigned one-half of the participating students within each school to complete a self-affirmation writing exercise up to four times over the course of their seventh-grade school year. The exercises were intended to take place prior to two assessments: the Wisconsin Knowledge and Concepts Exam (WKCE) in November and the Measures of Academic Progress (MAP) tests in February and May.

The first-year MWAP outcomes revealed immediate impacts of these brief, cost-effective expressive writing exercises on Latino and African American seventh-graders' test scores and grades (Borman, Grigg, and Hanselman 2015). Howard Bloom and his colleagues (2008) report that the typical student gains 0.23 to 0.30 standard deviations on nationally normed standardized reading and math achievement tests between the spring of sixth grade and the spring of seventh grade. Understood in this context, the overall impacts of self-affirmation —which were typically between d = 0.13 and d = 0.25 in our MWAP work—actually exceed the effect sizes typically observed for other far more intensive and expensive educational interventions. Given how easily self-affirmation writing can be integrated into everyday classroom practice, self-affirmation through expressive writing appears to be a viable strategy for narrowing achievement gaps between minority students who may suffer from stereotype threat and their white and Asian peers.

Our MWAP evidence from across the eleven schools suggests that these results can be achieved at scale, but only in particular theoretically and practically relevant school contexts. Most pertinent to this paper, the project revealed that school context greatly affects the efficacy of the self-affirmation intervention (Hanselman et al. 2014). By classifying middle schools participating in the experiment as either "high-threat" (majority-white, large black-white achievement gaps) schools or "low-threat" (not majority-white, smaller black-white achievement gaps) schools, our results indicate that the effect of the intervention was large and of considerable consequence when we compared students in the high-threat schools relative to students in the low-threat schools.

STEREOTYPE THREAT IN THE EQUALITY OF EDUCATIONAL OPPORTUNITY STUDY DATA

Given what we now know about stereotype threat and educational inequality, we proceed to the empirical portion of our thought experiment: can we detect evidence of stereotype threat in the Coleman Report data? The original report looked at how racially-ethnically segregated schools might disadvantage minority students, but it did not give as much attention to how academic environments might *harm* minority students by activating social-psychological processes resulting from the salience of race, as stereotype threat theory and evidence predict. There are, however, some exceptions. For instance, Coleman and his colleagues (1966) did note that black students who were surveyed tended to report a higher externalized locus of control relative to white students. Also, relatedly, the Coleman Report mentions in a footnote a study in which black and white adults were offered an alternative between a risky situation in which the outcome depended on chance and one in which the outcome, though not necessarily more favorable, was contingent on their own response. "The [black] adults less often chose the alternative contingent on their own behavior, and more often chose the chance alternative, as compared to whites" (Coleman et al. 1966, 320). These findings and their mention in the report may suggest some awareness by Coleman of the possibility that black students attribute their educational and social outcomes to external, racially motivated discrimination and biases over which they have little internal control, and that these experiences can influence the psychological construct of locus of control. However, these brief thoughts, possibly hinting at what would come later in the stereotype threat literature, were at the time not mentioned as much more than asides to be considered. Coleman and his colleagues did not specifically hypothesize about the social or psychological mechanisms through which environment might be affecting black students in mostly white classes.

Today, with a vast literature to draw from, we may be able to take Coleman's aside a bit further. Since the concept and language of stereotype threat did not exist in 1966, there were no items on the EEO questionnaire explicitly tapping this concept. While we cannot detect the phenomenon directly, we can use items from the EEOS surveys to find evidence that is suggestive of stereotype threat. In the literature on stereotype threat summarized earlier (for example, Steele et al. 2002), the theory and evidence suggest that: (1) the phenomenon is stronger for potentially threatened students in contexts where the stereotype is salient for the student (for example, in schools where a student's group identity is noticeably underrepresented, such as a black student in a majority-white classroom); and (2) the phenomenon is stronger when the stereotype is important to the activity of interest (for example, "African American students do not do well in school"). When these two criteria are met, we would expect potentially threatened individuals to experience stereotype threat.

Based on this prior knowledge, we can create constructs from EEOS survey items that serve as proxies for the relative strength of identity threats by measuring the extent to which each black student senses that he or she is the racial-ethnic minority in his or her classes. As the prior review of the literature suggested, this perception of limited representation of one's group within an academic environment in which the individual is stereotyped to perform poorly tends to induce greater salience of race-ethnicity and its associated identity threats (Inzlicht and Ben-Zeev 2000; Murphy, Steele, and Gross 2007; Purdie-Vaughns et al. 2008; Sekaquaptewa and Thompson 2003) and a stronger perception of organizational discrimination among members of the stigmatized group (Benner and Graham 2011; Hagan, Shedd, and Payne 2005; Seaton and Yip 2009).

Following the work of Paul Hanselman and his colleagues (2014) in constructing what they term "high-threat" and "low-threat" schools, we similarly model the effects of the salience of race in school for black students' cognitive skills and psychic well-being in the EEOS data. High-threat schools can be characterized both by the potential discrimination felt by stereotyped students and by the extent to which stereotyped students report that they attend majority-white schools and classrooms. We observe measures of both sources of threat in the EEOS data, focusing primarily on whether a student's report of being in a majority-white learning environment increases black-white gaps. Psychic losses from stereotype threat would be logical recursive elements related to diminished academic performance. Since stereotype threat researchers theorize that a personally relevant stereotype threatens a student's social identity or self-esteem, we consider whether high-threat environments increase black-white achievement gaps by reducing positive self-image. In the following sections, we describe the variables we construct to accomplish this, as well as our methods and findings.

Data

Equality of Educational Opportunity Study data are maintained by both the National Archives and the Inter-university Consortium for Political and Social Research (ICPSR). The EEOS used a stratified, two-stage probability sample of U.S. public schools, including over 570,000 students from grades 1, 3, 6, 9, and 12, 4,000 principals, and 40,000 teachers. We retrieved ASCII files from the National Archives, which contained U.S. Office of Education school codes, and converted the ASCII files to statistical analysis system (SAS) data sets using code provided by ICPSR.

For this study, we used the ninth-grade student cohort records and the principal and teacher records that corresponded to those students' schools. These records contained 134,030 students within 930 schools. After accounting for students clustered in schools with complete principal and teacher data relevant to this study, as well as complete student data relevant to this study, the final analytic sample consisted of 46,078 students within 218 schools. Although there are considerable data missing in these data files, prior studies have produced final samples of similar size and composition that showed no statistically significant differences on observables compared to the full sample of ninth-grade students (Borman and Dowling 2010; Bowles and Levin 1968). We created both student-level and school-level variables, which replicated many of those created by Borman and Dowling (2010). However, since we are most interested in within-school black-white gaps, we have omitted some variables and added others. Summary statistics for our set of analytic variables are presented in table 1.

Main Variables

To measure *cognitive ability*, our main dependent variable, we used each student's overall score across the four EEOS academic achievement tests: total verbal, nonverbal, reading, and math. Final results did not vary substantively or statistically whether we simply added the subscale scores or averaged across the nonmissing subscale scores, so we chose the additive score for better descriptive interpretability. To not only test whether a high-threat context might influence black students psychologically but also include a potential mechanism through which stereotype threat affected student test scores, we created a *positive self-image* variable that measured whether students thought of themselves in a positive light. Student positive self-image was created using a reversed composite score of three variables found in the ninth-grade student questionnaire: (1) If I could change, I would be someone different from myself; (2) I sometimes feel that I just can't learn; (3) People like me don't have much chance to be successful in life. Each item was scored "disagree" = 2, "not sure" = 1, or "agree" = 0. The main test for the presence of an environment that might induce stereotype threat was the interaction between two variables in the EEOS data: (1) identification as black, and (2) a student's perception that he or she was learning in an environment with *majority-white classroom peers*. In the ninth-grade student survey, students were asked, "In your classes last year, how many students were white?" If the student responded with "more than half" or "all," we coded the student as having the perception of being in majority-white-peer classrooms at school. The interaction between these two variables is theoretically similar to the conditions we would expect to see for stereotype threat to be present.

Covariates

We used nine student-level covariates to obtain the *conditional* black-white test score gap: parental education; urbanicity; number of reading materials in the house; number of siblings; two-parent household; number of family resources; student's age; student's gender; and student self-reported prior-year math GPA. Additionally, we used other student-level covariates that might be relevant to black students in majority-white environments: the student's perception of teachers' expectations for his or her academic performance; the student's perception of high social standing of self and friends; the student's report of being in a high, or advanced, English track; and student-reported external locus of control. Rather than the largely unconscious weight of social-psychologically constructed stereotypes, these student covariates may help us account for

Table 1. Descriptive Statistics for Student- and School-Level Variables in the Final Sample

	N	Mean	Standard Deviation
Student-level variables			
Race-ethnicity			
White	31,403	0.65	
Black	13,165	0.27	
Hispanic	2,810	0.06	
Asian	214	0.00	
Native American	665	0.01	
Other	268	0.01	
Parent education			
Less than high school	15,501	0.32	
High school	17,679	0.36	
Some college	7,391	0.15	
BA degree or higher	7,954	0.16	
Urbanicity	16,191	0.33	
Reading materials	48,525	0.97	0.16
Number of siblings	48,525	3.71	2.22
Two-parent household	35,576	0.73	
Family resources	48,252	7.87	1.60
Age	50,821		
Female	24,701	0.51	
Total test score	48,525	95.80	28.44
Positive self-image	48,525	3.75	1.79
Majority white classroom	31,743	0.65	
Black subset threat context			
Majority white classroom	1,604	0.12	
School-level variables			
Percent parents some college	218	0.27	0.40
School type			
Rural	81	0.37	
Suburban	99	0.45	
Urban	38	0.17	
Teacher racial bias	218	13.49	1.93
Majority white school	134	61.19	

Source: EEOS data from the National Archives and the ICPSR.

other more *overt* social (for example, perception of social standing), psychological (such as locus of control), and structural (such as academic tracking) explanations of within-school black-white performance gaps.

The school-level covariates we used that might affect African American students in majority-white environments included average teacher racial bias, majority-white student school population, the percentage of parents at a school who had at least some college-level education, the school setting (rural, suburban, or urban), and the degree of track mobility. At the school level, these covariates account for potentially overt racial-ethnic biases held by school staff (for example, average teacher racial bias), structural challenges to equal opportunity (such as lack of track mobility), and the common contextual features of schools that Coleman and others have theorized may influence minority students' outcomes (such as the percentage of white students at the school or the educational background of the school's parents).

Analytical Approach

We begin our analyses by investigating black students' perceptions of their academic contexts, which, theoretically, might have made them susceptible to experiencing stereotype threat. We do so using several multilevel models with random intercepts, regressing students' positive self-image on the interaction between a student's identification as black and reporting that he or she had classrooms with peers who were majority-white. Student positive self-image is z-scored in these analyses. In model 1, we estimate the raw racial gap of student positive self-image. In model 2, we add the commonly used student-level controls described earlier. Model 3 adds the black-by-majority-white-classroom interaction that serves as our proxy measure for stereotype threat. Model 4 adds the student- and school-level variables that may explain the effect of the interaction.

Next, we look at the relationship between stereotype threat and students' academic achievement outcomes, as measured by the EEOS standardized test. Again, we use multilevel models with random intercepts, and the test score variable is z-scored. We employ five models for this outcome: Model 1 is the naive model predicting the black-white test score gap. Model 2 estimates the gap net of commonly used student- and school-level controls. Model 3 adds the black-by-majority-white-classroom interaction. Model 4 adds student-reported positive self-image as a mediator of the effect of stereotype threat on achievement scores, and model 5 adds other student- and school-level variables that might explain the effect of the black-by-majority-white-classroom interaction.

RESULTS

Table 1 displays the descriptive statistics for the final analytic sample. About 65 percent of students in the sample identified as white, 27 percent identified as black, and 8 percent identified with other race or ethnicity categories. Turning to the variables of interest, we see that 65 percent of ninth-graders reported being in classrooms that were majority-white. However, only 12 percent of black students reported having majority-white classrooms. These lower numbers could be attributed to either between- or within-school segregation, but we are not able to descriptively distinguish those differences with the available data. The average student in the sample scored a 3.75 out of 6.00 for the positive self-image scale (standard deviation = 1.79). The tabulated covariates are consistent in proportion and size with previous studies employing the same items in the EEOS data.

In our first set of analyses, the student-level stereotype threat indicators are modeled as predictors of students' reported self-image (table 2). Model 1 shows that black students on average had unconditional positive self-image scores about a 0.21 standard deviation lower than their white peers. After controlling for student-level covariates (model 2), their reports were only a 0.02 standard deviation lower than white students' reports. Turning to our primary variable of interest, model 3 includes the black-student-by-majority-white-classroom interaction. There is a statistically significant and negative relationship for black students in majority-white classrooms (standard deviation = −0.14), suggesting that, net of controls, when black students indicated that the majority of their classmates were white, their reported belief in themselves and their potential for success in life was depressed. School-level covariates that measure the racial and sociodemographic characteristics of schools and student-level explanatory covariates that measure student perceptions of school context do not account for the negative interaction effect (model 4).

Our second set of analyses examines how stereotype threat relates to black-white differences in test scores (table 3). Model 1 identifies the raw black-white test score gap for ninth-grade students, which is one full standard deviation in size to the detriment of black students. Net of common student-level covariates (model 2), that gap was approximately a −0.43 standard deviation. When adding the black-by-majority-white-classroom interaction (model

Table 2. Multilevel Model Predicting Positive Self-Image (Z-Scored)

	Model 1		Model 2		Model 3		Model 4	
	Estimate	Standard Error	Estimate	Standard Error	Estimate	Standard Error	Estimate	Standard Error
Student-level variables								
Race-ethnicity (reference = white)								
Black	-0.21	(0.01)	-0.02	(0.01)	0.03	(0.02)	0.04	(0.02)
Hispanic	-0.40	(0.02)	-0.21	(0.02)	-0.20	(0.02)	-0.15	(0.02)
Asian	-0.07	(0.06)	-0.06	(0.06)	-0.05	(0.06)	-0.01	(0.06)
Native American	-0.44	(0.04)	-0.20	(0.04)	-0.18	(0.04)	-0.15	(0.04)
Other	-0.32	(0.06)	-0.21	(0.05)	-0.19	(0.05)	-0.17	(0.05)
Majority white classrooms			0.09	(0.01)	0.13	(0.01)	0.09	(0.01)
Black-student-by-majority-white-classroom					-0.14	(0.03)	-0.14	(0.03)
Teacher high expectations							0.06	(0.01)
High social standing							0.11	(0.01)
High English track							0.12	(0.01)
External locus of control							-0.23	(0.00)
Student-level covariates								
Parent education (reference = high school)								
Less than high school			-0.09	(0.01)	-0.09	(0.01)	-0.07	(0.01)
Some college			0.08	(0.01)	0.08	(0.01)	0.03	(0.01)
BA degree or higher			0.11	(0.01)	0.11	(0.01)	0.04	(0.01)
Urbanicity			0.04	(0.01)	0.04	(0.01)	0.02	(0.01)
Reading materials			0.12	(0.03)	0.12	(0.03)	0.11	(0.03)

	(1)		(2)		(3)		(4)	
Number of siblings	-0.01	(0.00)	-0.01	(0.00)	-0.01	(0.00)	-0.00	(0.00)
Two-parent household	0.08	(0.01)	0.07	(0.01)	0.07	(0.01)	0.06	(0.01)
Family resources	0.03	(0.00)	0.04	(0.00)	0.04	(0.00)	0.02	(0.00)
Age	-0.05	(0.00)	-0.05	(0.00)	-0.05	(0.00)	-0.04	(0.00)
Female	0.00	(0.01)	0.00	(0.01)	0.00	(0.01)	0.00	(0.01)
Prior-year math grade (reference = A)								
B	-0.17	(0.01)	-0.16	(0.01)	-0.16	(0.01)	-0.11	(0.01)
C	-0.36	(0.01)	-0.36	(0.01)	-0.36	(0.01)	-0.24	(0.01)
D	-0.53	(0.02)	-0.53	(0.02)	-0.53	(0.02)	-0.37	(0.02)
F	-0.61	(0.03)	-0.60	(0.03)	-0.60	(0.03)	-0.44	(0.03)
School-level covariates								
Teacher racial bias							-0.02	(0.02)
Majority white school							-0.02	(0.02)
Percent parents with some college							0.01	(0.01)
School type (reference = suburban)								
Rural							-0.01	(0.02)
Urban							0.03	(0.02)
Track mobility							0.00	(0.01)
Student-level intercept	0.64	(0.07)	0.60	(0.07)	0.60	(0.07)	0.41	(0.07)
School-level variation								
Intercept	-2.49	(0.10)	-2.50	(0.10)	-2.50	(0.10)	-2.61	(0.10)
Observations	46,078		46,078		46,078		46,078	
Number of groups	218		218		218		218	

Source: EEOS data from the National Archives and the ICPSR.

Table 3. Multilevel Model Predicting Cognitive Ability (Z-Scored)

	Model 1		Model 2		Model 3		Model 4		Model 5	
	Estimate	Standard Error	Estimate	Standard Error	Estimate	Standard Error	Estimate	Standard Error	Estimate	Standard Error
Student-level variables										
Race-ethnicity (reference = white)										
Black	-1.01	(0.01)	-0.43	(0.01)	-0.40	(0.01)	-0.41	(0.01)	-0.39	(0.01)
Hispanic	-0.95	(0.02)	-0.48	(0.02)	-0.47	(0.02)	-0.43	(0.02)	-0.40	(0.01)
Asian	-0.28	(0.06)	-0.16	(0.05)	-0.15	(0.05)	-0.14	(0.05)	-0.12	(0.05)
Native American	-0.71	(0.03)	-0.37	(0.03)	-0.36	(0.03)	-0.33	(0.03)	-0.31	(0.03)
Other	-0.50	(0.05)	-0.29	(0.04)	-0.28	(0.04)	-0.24	(0.04)	-0.23	(0.04)
Majority white classrooms			0.33	(0.01)	0.35	(0.01)	0.33	(0.01)	0.33	(0.01)
Black-student-by-majority-white-classroom					-0.08	(0.02)	-0.05	(0.02)	-0.06	(0.02)
Positive self-image							0.20	(0.00)	0.14	(0.00)
Teacher high expectations									0.07	(0.01)
High social standing									-0.04	(0.01)
High English track									0.23	(0.01)
External locus of control									-0.19	(0.00)
Student-level covariates										
Parent education (reference = high school)										
Less than high school			-0.12	(0.01)	-0.12	(0.01)	-0.10	(0.01)	-0.09	(0.01)
Some college			0.21	(0.01)	0.21	(0.01)	0.19	(0.01)	0.16	(0.01)
BA degree or higher			0.29	(0.01)	0.29	(0.01)	0.27	(0.01)	0.22	(0.01)
Urbanicity			0.10	(0.01)	0.10	(0.01)	0.09	(0.01)	0.08	(0.01)
Reading materials			0.04	(0.02)	0.04	(0.02)	0.02	(0.02)	0.02	(0.02)

	(1)		(2)		(3)		(4)	
Number of siblings	-0.01	(0.00)	-0.01	(0.00)	-0.01	(0.00)	-0.01	(0.00)
Two-parent household	0.07	(0.01)	0.07	(0.01)	0.05	(0.01)	0.05	(0.01)
Family resources	0.06	(0.00)	0.06	(0.00)	0.05	(0.00)	0.04	(0.00)
Age	-0.09	(0.00)	-0.09	(0.00)	-0.08	(0.00)	-0.07	(0.00)
Female	0.07	(0.01)	0.07	(0.01)	0.07	(0.01)	0.06	(0.01)
Prior-year math grade (reference = A)								
B	-0.28	(0.01)	-0.28	(0.01)	-0.24	(0.01)	-0.19	(0.01)
C	-0.54	(0.01)	-0.54	(0.01)	-0.46	(0.01)	-0.37	(0.01)
D	-0.72	(0.01)	-0.72	(0.01)	-0.61	(0.01)	-0.50	(0.01)
F	-0.72	(0.02)	-0.72	(0.02)	-0.59	(0.02)	-0.49	(0.02)
School-level covariates								
Teacher racial bias							0.00	(0.05)
Majority white school							0.14	(0.03)
Percent parents with some college							-0.04	(0.02)
School type (reference = suburban)								
Rural							0.05	(0.03)
Urban							0.08	(0.04)
Track mobility							-0.01	(0.01)
Student-level intercept	1.09	(0.06)	1.06	(0.06)	0.94	(0.06)	0.07	(0.01)
School-level variation								
Intercept	-1.30	(0.06)	-1.29	(0.06)	-1.28	(0.06)	-1.47	(0.06)
Observations	46,078		46,078		46,078		46,078	
Number of groups	218		218		218		218	

Source: EEOS data from the National Archives and the ICPSR.

3), we see that although black students in majority-white classrooms performed better overall than their counterparts in other environments, black-white test score gaps were a 0.08 standard deviation larger in majority-white classrooms than in non-majority-white classrooms. Model 4 demonstrates that student-reported positive self-image explains about 31 percent of the effect of the interaction on test scores. Additional student- and school-level explanatory covariates do not further account for the statistically significant negative interaction effect (model 5).

DISCUSSION

The conclusions about social inequality furnished by the Coleman Report fifty years ago were largely overshadowed by the confounding implications of racial integration in the report. Those results suggested that black students would benefit from attending more integrated schools. However, after the desegregation policies implemented by the Nixon administration resulted in "white flight," Coleman responded by insisting that integration would work only if African American students attended schools that were majority-white. Many studies replicated Coleman's finding that black students do improve their test scores in majority-white schools. But what if Coleman had known about stereotype threat in 1966? After all, in the 1960s majority-white schools would probably have been hostile environments for black students. Stereotype threat theory and empirical evidence predict that African American students will underperform in majority-white academic environments because they are more likely to face discrimination and marginalization, to be more anxious about confirming racial stereotypes, and to think more about racial identity because their race is more salient in those environments. This interpretation of the EEOS results casts the improved performance of black students in majority-white schools in another light—would those same black students have done *even better* on the EEOS test had they not taken the test under the weight of others' perceptions of their ability based on 1960s stereotypes about race?

In our study of the EEOS data, we find that the test score gaps between white and black students were larger and statistically significant when black students reported being in majority-white classrooms, even after accounting for relevant student- and school-level covariates. This interaction effect, serving as a proxy measure for stereotype threat, supports the idea that this form of identity threat could be partly responsible for black students' lower performance, and that race might be more salient at the classroom level than at the school level. Consistent with theory, part of the effect of stereotype threat on test score gaps is explained by black students' reduced positive self-image, as reflected by their agreement with statements suggesting that they were not good learners, that people like them would not succeed in life, and that they would be someone different from themselves if they could change. This lower positive self-identity among black students explains approximately one-third of the effect of the salience of race on black students' test scores when black students were in majority-white classrooms. Other school-level covariates, such as teacher racial bias, majority-white school, the percentage of parents with some college, and school type, and other student-level contextual covariates, including students' reports of their teachers' expectations for their academic performance, their appraisals of their social standing within the school, and their reports of an externalized locus of control, do not further explain the interaction that serves as our proxy measure of stereotype threat. Of course, our results are only suggestive and neither definitively identify stereotype threat as the source of the decreased performance of black students in majority-white environments nor rule out all possible sources of increased test score gaps.

CONCLUSION

Would knowledge of stereotype threat have changed the design, results, or recommendations of the Coleman Report? Possibly, but the politics of desegregation and the more tangible policies it implied would most likely have overshadowed the significance of these social-psychological theories. Surely the prospect that black students would make great gains in majority-white schools would have outweighed the concern that these students might continue to perform below their ability in majority-white environments owing to the increased salience of racial-ethnic identity and associated stereotypes. As Christopher Jencks and his colleagues noted in 1972, and as Jencks and Meredith Phillips restated in 1998, the small differences in the long-run economic returns of education for black students in the 1960s—due to racism in the labor market—suggest that black students' improved performance on cognitive ability measures would not have substantially improved their adult incomes and occupational attainments compared to their lower-scoring black peers. Still, given the historical accounts of the threatening nature of integrated schools prior to desegregation policies, a knowledge of stereotype threat and the interventions we now know of that could have combated its effects might at the very least have helped create less stressful school experiences and higher-quality academic climates for black students. Improvements in black students' well-being alone would have been reason to implement the brief, low-cost social-psychological interventions of today.

Presently, as in the 1960s, discrimination and segregation pervade the U.S. public school system (Fiel 2013; Orfield and Lee 2007). Although we might not expect schools in 2016 to exhibit as many of the overtly prejudicial characteristics of schools in 1966, stigmatized groups of students are still threatened by discrimination, resulting in inhibited performance in school. Much remains to be learned about how, why, where, under what conditions, and for whom interventions addressing stereotype threat close academic achievement gaps. In school contexts that theoretically and empirically activate the threat—those with a small number of minority students and with large achievement gaps—we have found far greater evidence of impact (Hanselman et al. 2014). From other self-affirmation replications, it is becoming clear that the interventions are likely to have limited success when implemented in high-percentage-minority schools, such as those studied by Thomas Dee (2015) in Philadelphia. These social-psychological theories and interventions highlight important implications for the study of educational inequality in the schools of both the 1960s and today. What school resources, climate, and demographic makeup can effectively combine to reduce inequality? Social-psychological interventions can change students' mind-sets and unlock minority students' potential to perform in school unencumbered by the stereotypes that might hold them back. But without improved school climates, quality resources, and supportive and inclusive teachers, it is still unlikely that stigmatized minority students will realize their full potential (Purdie-Vaughns et al. 2009).

Researchers are still developing comprehensive understandings of how students' mind-sets and school environments interact and shape learning outcomes, but our work and the work of others clearly demonstrate that stereotype threat explains as much as one-quarter of the black-white achievement gap, and that interventions to buffer students from the harm of stereotype threat can help close that fraction of the gap. That we find empirical evidence of stereotype threat operating in the 1960s suggests that these social-psychological theories and interventions, if known at the time, might have been of interest to Coleman and could have provided some insights into the debates regarding the racial compositions of schools in the years of desegregation that were to follow.

REFERENCES

Alexander, Karl L., Doris R. Entwisle, and Linda Steffel Olson. 2001. "Schools, Achievement, and Inequality: A Seasonal Perspective." *Educational Evaluation and Policy Analysis* 23(2): 171–91.

———. 2007. "Lasting Consequences of the Summer Learning Gap." *American Sociological Review* 72(2): 167–80.

Allensworth, Elaine, Julia Gwynne, Paul Moore, and Marisa de la Torre. 2014. "Looking Forward to High School and College: Middle Grade Indicators of Readiness in Chicago Public Schools." Chicago: University of Chicago Consortium on Chicago School Research.

Allport, Gordon W. 1954. *The Nature of Prejudice.* Cambridge, Mass.: Addison-Wesley.

Anderman, Lynley H. 2003. "Academic and Social Perceptions as Predictors of Change in Middle

School Students' Sense of School Belonging." *Journal of Experimental Education* 72(1): 5–22.

Appel, Markus, and Nicole Kronberger. 2012. "Stereotypes and the Achievement Gap: Stereotype Threat Prior to Test Taking." *Educational Psychology Review* 24(4): 609–35.

Aronson, Joshua, Carrie B. Fried, and Catherine Good. 2002. "Reducing the Effects of Stereotype Threat on African American College Students by Shaping Theories of Intelligence." *Journal of Experimental Social Psychology* 38(2): 113–25.

Aronson, Joshua, and Matthew S. McGlone. 2009. "Stereotype and Social Identity Threat." *Handbook of Prejudice, Stereotyping, and Discrimination*, edited by Todd D. Nelson. New York: Psychology Press.

Benner, Aprile D., and Sandra Graham. 2009. "The Transition to High School as a Developmental Process Among Multiethnic Urban Youth." *Child Development* 80(2): 356–76.

———. 2011. "Latino Adolescents' Experiences of Discrimination Across the First 2 Years of High School: Correlates and Influences on Educational Outcomes." *Child Development* 82(2): 508–19.

Benson, James, and Geoffrey Borman. 2010. "Family, Neighborhood, and School Settings Across Seasons: When Do Socioeconomic Context and Racial Composition Matter for the Reading Achievement Growth of Young Children?" *Teachers College Record* 112(5): 1338–90.

Bloom, Howard S., Carolyn J. Hill, Alison Rebeck Black, and Mark W. Lipsey. 2008. "Performance Trajectories and Performance Gaps as Achievement Effect-Size Benchmarks for Educational Interventions." *Journal of Research on Educational Effectiveness* 1(4): 289–328.

Borman, Geoffrey D., and Maritza Dowling. 2010. "Schools and Inequality: A Multilevel Analysis of Coleman's Equality of Educational Opportunity Data." *Teachers College Record* 112(5): 1–2.

Borman, Geoffrey D., Jeffrey Grigg, and Paul Hanselman. 2015. "An Effort to Close Achievement Gaps at Scale Through Self-affirmation." *Educational Evaluation and Policy Analysis* 38(1): 21–42. doi: 10.3102/0162373715581709.

Boucher, Kathryn L., Robert J. Rydell, Katie J. Van Loo, and Michael T. Rydell. 2012. "Reducing Stereotype Threat in Order to Facilitate Learning." *European Journal of Social Psychology* 42(2): 174–79.

Bowles, Samuel, and Henry M. Levin. 1968. "The Determinants of Scholastic Achievement: An Appraisal of Some Recent Evidence." *Journal of Human Resources* 3(1): 3–24.

Brown, Christia Spears. 2008. "Children's Perceptions of Racial and Ethnic Discrimination: Differences Across Children and Contexts." In *Handbook of Race, Racism, and the Developing Child*, edited by Stephen M. Quintana and Clark McKown. New York: Wiley.

Cohen, Geoffrey L., Julio Garcia, Nancy Apfel, and Allison Master. 2006. "Reducing the Racial Achievement Gap: A Social-Psychological Intervention." *Science* 313(5791): 1307–10. doi: 10.1126/science.1128317.

Cohen, Geoffrey L., Julio Garcia, Valerie Purdie-Vaughns, Nancy Apfel, and Patricia Brzustoski. 2009. "Recursive Processes in Self-affirmation: Intervening to Close the Minority Achievement Gap." *Science* 324(5925): 400–403. doi: 10.1126/science.1170769.

Coleman, James S., Ernest Q. Campbell, Carol J. Hobson, James McPartland, Alexander M. Mood, Frederick D. Weinfeld, and Robert L. York. 1966. *Equality of Educational Opportunity*. Washington: U.S. Department of Health, Education, and Welfare, Office of Education.

Cook, Jonathan E., Valerie Purdie-Vaughns, Julio Garcia, and Geoffrey L. Cohen. 2012. "Chronic Threat and Contingent Belonging: Protective Benefits of Values Affirmation on Identity Development." *Journal of Personality and Social Psychology* 102(3): 479.

Dee, Thomas S. 2015. "Social Identity and Achievement Gaps: Evidence from an Affirmation Intervention." *Journal of Research on Educational Effectiveness* 8(2): 149–68.

Downey, Douglas B., Paul T. von Hippel, and Beckett Broh. 2004. "Are Schools the Great Equalizer? School and Non-school Sources of Inequality in Cognitive Skills." *American Sociological Review* 69(5): 613–35.

Erbring, Lutz, and Alice A. Young. 1979. "Individuals and Social Structure Contextual Effects as Endogenous Feedback." *Sociological Methods and Research* 7(4): 396–430.

Fiel, Jeremy E. 2013. "Decomposing School Resegregation: Social Closure, Racial Imbalance, and Racial Isolation." *American Sociological Review* 78(5): 828–48. doi: 10.1177/0003122413496252.

Firebaugh, Glenn. 1978. "A Rule for Inferring Individual-Level Relationships from Aggregate

Data." *American Sociological Review* 43(4): 557–72.

Fisher, Celia B., Scyatta A. Wallace, and Rose E. Fenton. 2000. "Discrimination Distress During Adolescence." *Journal of Youth and Adolescence* 29(6): 679–95.

Fryer, Roland G., Jr., and Steven D. Levitt. 2004. "Understanding the Black-White Test Score Gap in the First Two Years of School." *Review of Economics and Statistics* 86(2): 447–64.

Good, Catherine, Joshua Aronson, and Jayne Ann Harder. 2008. "Problems in the Pipeline: Stereotype Threat and Women's Achievement in High-Level Math Courses." *Journal of Applied Developmental Psychology* 29(1): 17–28. doi: http://dx.doi.org/10.1016/j.appdev.2007.10.004.

Good, Catherine, Joshua Aronson, and Michael Inzlicht. 2003. "Improving Adolescents' Standardized Test Performance: An Intervention to Reduce the Effects of Stereotype Threat." *Journal of Applied Developmental Psychology* 24(6): 645–62.

Good, Catherine, Aneeta Rattan, and Carol S. Dweck. 2007. "Why Do Women Opt Out? Sense of Belonging and Women's Representation in Mathematics." *Journal of Personality and Social Psychology* 102(4): 700–17.

Hagan, John, Carla Shedd, and Monique R. Payne. 2005. "Race, Ethnicity, and Youth Perceptions of Criminal Injustice." *American Sociological Review* 70(3): 381–407.

Hanselman, Paul, Sarah K. Bruch, Adam Gamoran, and Geoffrey D. Borman. 2014. "Threat in Context: School Moderation of the Impact of Social Identity Threat on Racial/Ethnic Achievement Gaps." *Sociology of Education* 87(2): 106–24. doi: 10.1177/0038040714525970.

Hemphill, F. Cadelle, Alan Vanneman, and Taslima Rahman. 2011. "How Hispanic and White Students in Public Schools Perform in Mathematics and Reading on the National Assessment of Educational Progress." Washington: U.S. Department of Education, National Center for Education Statistics.

Heyns, Barbara. 1978. *Summer Learning and the Effects of Schooling.* New York: Basic Books.

Huguet, Pascal, and Isabelle Regner. 2007. "Stereotype Threat Among Schoolgirls in Quasi-Ordinary Classroom Circumstances." *Journal of Educational Psychology* 99(3): 545.

Inzlicht, Michael, and Talia Ben-Zeev. 2000. "A Threatening Intellectual Environment: Why Females Are Susceptible to Experiencing Problem-Solving Deficits in the Presence of Males." *Psychological Science* 11(5): 365–71.

Jencks, Christopher, and Meredith Phillips. 1998. "America's Next Achievement Test: Closing the Black-White Test Score Gap." *The American Prospect* (September–October): 44–53.

———. 2011. "The Black-White Test Score Gap: An Introduction." In *The Black-White Test Score Gap,* edited by Christopher Jencks and Meredith Phillips. Washington, D.C.: Brookings Institution.

Jencks, Christopher, Marshall Smith, Henry Acland, Mary Jo Bane, David Cohen, Herbert Gintis, Barbara Heyns, and Stephan Michelson. 1972. *Inequality: A Reassessment of the Effect of Family and Schooling in America.* New York: Basic Books.

Keller, Johannes. 2002. "Blatant Stereotype Threat and Women's Math Performance: Self-handicapping as a Strategic Means to Cope with Obtrusive Negative Performance Expectations." *Sex Roles* 47(3-4): 193–98.

Keller, Johannes, and Dirk Dauenheimer. 2003. "Stereotype Threat in the Classroom: Dejection Mediates the Disrupting Threat Effect on Women's Math Performance." *Personality and Social Psychology Bulletin* 29(3): 371–81.

Kellow, J. Thomas, and Brett D. Jones. 2005. "Children's Stereotype Threat in African-American High School Students: An Initial Investigation." *Current Issues in Education* 8(20, July).

Kray, Laura J. J., and Aiwa Shirako. 2011. "Stereotype Threat in Organizations." In *Stereotype Threat: Theory, Process, and Application,* edited by Michael Inzlicht and Toni Schmader. New York: Oxford University Press.

Linn, Robert L., and Kevin G. Welner, eds. 2007. "Race-Conscious Policies for Assigning Students to Schools: Social Science Research and the Supreme Court Cases." Washington, D.C.: National Academy of Education, Committee on Social Science Research Evidence on Racial Diversity in Schools.

Lipsey, Mark W., Kelly Puzio, Cathy Yun, Michael A. Hebert, Kasia Steinka-Fry, Mikel W. Cole, Megan Roberts, Karen S. Anthony, and Matthew D. Busick. 2012. "Translating the Statistical Representation of the Effects of Education Interventions into More Readily Interpretable Forms." NCSER 2013-3000. Washington: U.S. Department of Education, National Center for Special Education Research (November).

Losen, Daniel. 2011. "Discipline Policies, Successful Schools, and Racial Justice." Policy brief. Boulder, Colo.: National Education Policy Center (October).

Major, Brenda, Steven Spencer, Toni Schmader, Connie Wolfe, and Jennifer Crocker. 1998. "Coping with Negative Stereotypes About Intellectual Performance: The Role of Psychological Disengagement." *Personality and Social Psychology Bulletin* 24(1): 34–50.

Mayer, Susan E., and Christopher Jencks. 1989. "Growing Up in Poor Neighborhoods: How Much Does It Matter?" *Science* 243(4897): 1441–45.

McKown, Clark, and Rhona S. Weinstein. 2003. "The Development and Consequences of Stereotype Consciousness in Middle Childhood." *Child Development* 74(2): 498–515.

Mickelson, Roslyn Arlin. 2001. "Subverting Swann: First- and Second-Generation Segregation in the Charlotte-Mecklenburg Schools." *American Educational Research Journal* 38(2): 215–52.

Murphy, Mary C., Claude M. Steele, and James J. Gross. 2007. "Signaling Threat: How Situational Cues Affect Women in Math, Science, and Engineering Settings." *Psychological Science* 18(10): 879–85.

Murphy, Mary C., and Valerie Jones Taylor. 2011. "The Role of Situational Cues in Signaling and Maintaining Stereotype Threat." In *Stereotype Threat: Theory, Process, and Application,* edited by Michael Inzlicht and Toni Schmader. New York: Oxford University Press.

Nguyen, Hannah-Hanh D., and Ann Marie Ryan. 2008. "Does Stereotype Threat Affect Test Performance of Minorities and Women? A Meta-analysis of Experimental Evidence." *Journal of Applied Psychology* 93(6): 1314–34.

Oakes, Jeannie. 1995. "Two Cities' Tracking and Within-School Segregation." *Teachers College Record* 96(4): 681–90.

Orfield, Gary, and Chungmei Lee. 2007. "Historic Reversals, Accelerating Resegregation, and the Need for New Integration Strategies." Los Angeles: UCLA, Civil Rights Project/Proyecto Derechos Civiles.

Pronin, Emily, Claude M. Steele, and Lee Ross. 2004. "Identity Bifurcation in Response to Stereotype Threat: Women and Mathematics." *Journal of Experimental Social Psychology* 40(2): 152–68.

Purdie-Vaughns, Valerie, Geoffery L. Cohen, Julio Garcia, Rachel Sumner, Jonathan C. Cook, and Nancy Apfel. 2009. "Improving Minority Academic Performance: How a Values-Affirmation Intervention Works." *Teachers College Record* (September 23).

Purdie-Vaughns, Valerie, Claude M. Steele, Paul G. Davies, Ruth Ditlmann, and Jennifer Randall Crosby. 2008. "Social Identity Contingencies: How Diversity Cues Signal Threat or Safety for African Americans in Mainstream Institutions." *Journal of Personality and Social Psychology* 94(4): 615–30. doi: 10.1037/0022-3514.94.4.615.

Quintana, Stephen M. 1999. "Children's Developmental Understanding of Ethnicity and Race." *Applied and Preventive Psychology* 7(1): 27–45.

Raudenbush, Stephen W., and Anthony S. Bryk. 2002. *Hierarchical Linear Models: Applications and Data Analysis Methods.* Thousand Oaks, Calif.: Sage Publications.

Reardon, Sean F., and Claudia Galindo. 2009. "The Hispanic-White Achievement Gap in Math and Reading in the Elementary Grades." *American Educational Research Journal* 46(3): 853–91. doi: 10.3102/0002831209333184.

Roberson, Loriann, Elizabeth A. Deitch, Arthur P. Brief, and Caryn J. Block. 2003. "Stereotype Threat and Feedback Seeking in the Workplace." *Journal of Vocational Behavior* 62(1): 176–88.

Scherbaum, Charles A., Victoria Blanshetyn, Elizabeth Marshall-Wolp, Elizabeth McCue, and Ross Strauss. 2011. "Examining the Effects of Stereotype Threat on Test-Taking Behaviors." *Social Psychology of Education* 14(3): 361–75.

Schmader, Toni, Michael Johns, and Chad Forbes. 2008. "An Integrated Process Model of Stereotype Threat Effects on Performance." *Psychological Review* 115(2): 336–56.

Seaton, Eleanor K., and Tiffany Yip. 2009. "School and Neighborhood Contexts, Perceptions of Racial Discrimination, and Psychological Well-being Among African American Adolescents." *Journal of Youth and Adolescence* 38(2): 153–63.

Sekaquaptewa, Denise, and Mischa Thompson. 2003. "Solo Status, Stereotype Threat, and Performance Expectancies: Their Effects on Women's Performance." *Journal of Experimental Social Psychology* 39(1): 68–74.

Sherman, David K. 2013. "Self-affirmation: Understanding the Effects." *Social and Personality Psychology Compass* 7(11): 834–45.

Sherman, David K., Kimberly A. Hartson, Kevin R. Binning, Valerie Purdie-Vaughns, Julio Garcia, Suzanne Taborsky-Barba, Sarah Tomassetti, A. David Nussbaum, and Geoffrey L. Cohen. 2013. "Deflecting the Trajectory and Changing the Narrative: How Self-Affirmation Affects Academic Performance and Motivation Under Identity Threat." *Journal of Personality and Social Psychology* 104(4): 591–618.

Shim, S. Serena, Allison M. Ryan, and Carolyn J. Anderson. 2008. "Achievement Goals and Achievement During Early Adolescence: Examining Time-Varying Predictor and Outcome Variables in Growth-Curve Analysis." *Journal of Educational Psychology* 100(3): 655.

Slavin, Robert E. 1985. "Cooperative Learning: Applying Contact Theory in Desegregated Schools." *Journal of Social Issues* 41(3): 45–62.

Smith, Jessi L. 2004. "Understanding the Process of Stereotype Threat: A Review of Mediational Variables and New Performance Goal Directions." *Educational Psychology Review* 16(3): 177–206.

Steele, Claude M. 1997. "A Threat in the Air: How Stereotypes Shape Intellectual Identity and Performance." *American Psychologist* 52(6): 613–29.

Steele, Claude M., and Joshua A. Aronson. 1995. "Stereotype Threat and the Intellectual Test Performance of African Americans." *Journal of Personality and Social Psychology* 69(5): 797–811.

———. 2004. "Stereotype Threat Does Not Live by Steele and Aronson (1995) Alone." *American Psychologist* 59(1): 47–48.

Steele, Jennifer, Jacquelyn B. James, and Rosalind Chait Barnett. 2002. "Learning in a Man's World: Examining the Perceptions of Undergraduate Women in Male-Dominated Academic Areas." *Psychology of Women Quarterly* 26(1): 46–50.

Steele, Claude M., Steven J. Spencer, and Joshua Aronson. 2002. "Contending with Group Image: The Psychology of Stereotype and Social Identity Threat." *Advances in Experimental Social Psychology* 34: 379–440.

Stone, Jeff, W. Perry, and John M Darley. 1997. "'White Men Can't Jump': Evidence for the Perceptual Confirmation of Racial Stereotypes Following a Basketball Game." *Basic and Applied Social Psychology* 19(3): 291–306.

Taylor, Valerie Jones, and Gregory M. Walton. 2011. "Stereotype Threat Undermines Academic Learning." *Personality and Social Psychology Bulletin* 37(8): 1055–67.

Vanneman, Alan, Linda Hamilton, Janet Baldwin Anderson, and Taslima Rahman. 2009. "Achievement Gaps: How Black and White Students in Public Schools Perform in Mathematics and Reading on the National Assessment of Educational Progress: Statistical Analysis Report." NCES 2009-455. Washington: U.S. Department of Education, National Center for Education Statistics.

Walton, Gregory M., and Geoffrey L. Cohen. 2003. "Stereotype Lift." *Journal of Experimental Social Psychology* 39(5): 456–67.

———. 2007. "A Question of Belonging: Race, Social Fit, and Achievement." *Journal of Personality and Social Psychology* 92(1): 82–96.

Walton, Gregory M., and Steven J. Spencer. 2009. "Latent Ability: Grades and Test Scores Systematically Underestimate the Intellectual Ability of Negatively Stereotyped Students." *Psychological Science* 20(9): 1132–39.

What Works Clearinghouse. 2010. "WWC Quick Review of the Article 'Recursive Processes in Self-Affirmation: Intervening to Close the Minority Achievement Gap.'" Available at: http://ies.ed.gov/ncee/wwc/pdf/quick_reviews/selfaffirm_020910.pdf (accessed June 27, 2016).

Yeager, David S., and Gregory M. Walton. 2011. "Social-Psychological Interventions in Education: They're Not Magic." *Review of Educational Research* 81(2): 267–301. doi: 10.3102/0034654311405999.

A New Framework for Understanding Parental Involvement: Setting the Stage for Academic Success

ANGEL L. HARRIS AND KEITH ROBINSON

The Coleman Report posited that the inequality of educational opportunity appears to stem from the home itself and the cultural influences immediately surrounding the home. However, this line of inquiry assumes that school and home processes operate in isolation, which is often not the case. An example of how families and schools can reinforce one another is through parental involvement. Whereas some studies suggest that children have better achievement outcomes when their parents are involved in their education, other studies challenge the link between parental involvement and academic outcomes. One major reason for this lack of consensus among scholars is that parents' involvement has been measured differently across studies. Thus, scholars' disagreements about how parents should be involved and about which aspects of parental involvement are associated with improvements in children's academic outcomes have contributed to inconsistent findings. We argue that the mixed results observed in previous studies indicate that parental involvement does not operate through the typical channels posited by researchers, educators, and policymakers and that traditional measures of parental involvement fail to capture the fundamental ways in which parents help their children academically. We propose a framework of parental involvement that might provide some clarity on how parental involvement operates.

Keywords: parental involvement, academic achievement

The Coleman Report states that "the sources of inequality of educational opportunity appear to lie first in the home itself and the cultural influences immediately surrounding the home" (Coleman et al. 1966, 73–74). The findings of James Coleman and his colleagues suggest that nonschool factors such as family and neighborhood characteristics are more consequential for student outcomes than school factors. However, proceeding with this line of inquiry assumes that school and home processes operate in isolation. As Karl Alexander notes elsewhere in this issue, this "school versus family framing" does not account for the ways in which families, schools, and neighborhoods matter for youth outcomes, both separately

Angel L. Harris is professor of sociology and director of the Program for Research on Education and Development of Youth at Duke University. **Keith Robinson** is a researcher (most recently with the University of Texas) now unaffiliated.

We want to thank Danielle Allen, Paul Attewell, Rob Crosnoe, Janeria Dunlap, Linsey Edwards, Tod Hamilton, Mark Hayward, Bob Hummer, Sara McLanahan, Seth Moglen, Chandra Muller, Kelly Raley, and Marcelo and Carola Suarez-Orozco. We would not have been able to complete this project without the generosity of the Institute for Advanced Study or without "STEM in the New Millennium: Preparation, Pathways, and Diversity," a grant funded by the National Science Foundation (DUE-0757018) to Chandra Muller and Catherine Riegle-Crumb. Direct correspondence to: Angel Harris at angel.harris@duke.edu, Duke University, Department of Sociology, Soc/Psych Building, 417 Chapel Dr., Durham, NC 27708; and Keith Robinson at keithdion@gmail.com.

and together. One such example of how families and schools can reinforce one another is through parental involvement.

The notion that parents play a key role in children's educational success has become conventional wisdom, and parental involvement in children's schooling has been a major component of school reform efforts and federal education policies over the last two decades (Comer 1992; Epstein 1985). For example, the Improving America's Schools Act of 1994 proposed to afford "parents meaningful opportunities to participate in the education of their children at home and at school," and one of the six aims of the No Child Left Behind Act of 2001 was to increase parental involvement (section 1118).

Decades of research generally support the conclusion that children have better achievement outcomes when parents are involved in their education (Domina 2005; Muller 1995, 1998; Sui-Chu and Willms 1996). However, not all studies confirm a link between parental involvement and academic outcomes (Izzo et al. 1999; Pomerantz, Moorman, and Litwack 2007), and others suggest that parents sometimes initiate involvement as a response to their children's academic difficulties (Catsambis 2001; Desimone 2001). Furthermore, though numerous researchers have focused on variation in parental involvement in children's education (Domina 2005; Jeynes 2003; Stein and Thorkildsen 1999; Zellman and Waterman 1998), scholars disagree about how parents should be involved and which aspects of parental involvement are associated with improvements in children's academic outcomes.

In a recent study that contains nearly every measure of parental involvement used in previous studies—sixty-three in total, across four data sets—and conducted by social class and across six racial groups, we find that there is no clear positive connection between parental involvement and academic outcomes (Robinson and Harris 2014). Specifically, parental involvement was *not* related to achievement in more than half (53 percent) of the 1,556 associations between parental involvement and achievement examined in our study. In fact, there were more negative associations (27 percent) between parental involvement and achievement than positive associations (20 percent). The benefits associated with parental involvement appear to be strongest for younger children (grades 1 to 5), though there are an equal number of positive and negative associations between parental involvement and achievement for children in this group. Furthermore, parental involvement is insufficient for reducing racial differences in achievement. Although a critique can be raised about each measure of involvement and outcome contained in our study, the extensiveness of our approach provides a compelling portrait of the role of parental involvement in children's schooling based on the sheer preponderance of evidence.

It is important to note that there is a lack of consensus among scholars on what constitutes parental involvement in schooling. For example, Dean Hoge, Edna Smit, and John Crist's (1997) conception of involvement entails four components: parental expectations, parental interest, involvement in school, and family and community. Wei-Cheng Mau (1997) claims that the most important involvement measure is parental supervision of homework. Darcy Hango (2007) emphasizes the relational aspect of parents' time with children, primarily because it provides children with the social capital to mediate harmful effects of financial deprivation. Joyce Epstein (2010) summarizes the ranges of family involvement within a classification system that includes school-home communications, parent involvement within the school and community, home learning activities, and parents serving as decision-makers. Moreover, traditional measures of parental involvement often do not capture some very important features of parent behavior that impact youth outcomes, such as vocabulary usage (Hart and Risley 1995). Such conceptual differences contribute to inconsistent findings. Additionally, some studies examine the parental involvement–student achievement link for elementary school children (Dearing and Taylor 2007; Schulting, Malone, and Dodge 2005), whereas others focus on adolescents (McNeal 1999).

We argue that traditional measures of parental involvement fail to capture the fundamental ways in which parents actually help their children academically. We propose a framework of parental involvement that might provide some clarity on how parental involvement operates. We argue that the mixed results observed in previous studies indicate that parental involvement does not operate through the typical channels posited by researchers, educators, and policymakers. We provide a brief introduction to the framework followed by a discussion of what served as the impetus for the theory. We then elaborate further on the theory and discuss how it might apply to social class and race. We conclude with a discussion of whether the claim in the Coleman Report that inequality of educational opportunity stems primarily from the home and culture is consistent with empirical evidence fifty years later.

TOWARD A NEW FRAMEWORK OF PARENTAL INVOLVEMENT

Several years ago, during a personal conversation, a colleague mentioned that her sibling was enrolled in a prestigious law school. When asked what her parents did to attain such success from their children, she recalled that her parents rarely talked to them about school, did not help with homework, and did not read to them. Despite their lack of involvement, however, her parents had high expectations of them and they knew from an early age that doing well in school was important. Although she was discussing the role her parents played in helping her attain academic success, she could not recall a set of home- or school-based practices her parents employed. This conversation motivated us to explore the types of things parents do that might not be reflected in studies on parental involvement.

We employ the metaphor of "stage-setting" to convey the theory. In theater, stage-setters are responsible for creating a context that allows the cast to successfully enact the performance. Stage-setters create a life space—the parameters within which the actor's performance occurs—that corresponds with the intended action. Poor stage-setting can compromise an actor's ability to successfully play a role, thereby leading to a poor performance because it does not draw the audience into the world intended by the playwright. The stage-setter reinforces the performance at critical transition points, such as between acts. Thus, a good performance can be characterized as a partnership between two critical components: (1) the actor embodying his or her role, and (2) the stage-setter creating and maintaining an environment that reinforces (or does not compromise) the actor's embodiment of the role. Likewise, many parents construct and manage the social environment around their children in a manner that creates the conditions in which academic success is possible. In our view, this analogy captures what many parents do to position their children for academic success.

This concept stems from focus groups we conducted with students enrolled at a major public university in the Southwest. Students were asked to identify the involvement activities that their parents employed specifically to help them succeed academically (see Robinson and Harris 2014). The focus groups yielded four themes that are helpful for explaining stage-setting. First, students reported that their parents were *supportive,* not just in their schooling but in their extracurricular activities. They interpreted this support as instrumental for their academic success because it effectively communicated that their parents cared about their overall success in life and were not simply imposing pressure on them to perform well academically. They described a type of support that did not involve micromanagement of their academic lives (which can be intrusive or overbearing). Second, students credited their parents with *skillfully navigating school choices* through the K–12 school system. Their parents enrolled them in expensive private schools or made vigorous efforts to enroll them in high-quality public schools. Third, parents *effectively conveyed the importance of school,* often in a manner we thought might lead their children to make academic success central to their purpose in life; for example, if parents had immigrated to the United States seeking better opportunities, their children had come to understand that academic success was the key to such advancement. Their parents also provided clear examples of the undesirable outcomes of not taking school seriously. Finally, many students recalled being told, "You're the smart one," at various points throughout their childhood and adolescence. They regarded this *label of being smart* as particularly important because it motivated them to succeed academically owing primarily to a sense of responsibility to their parents and siblings. This labeling defined an academic identity for them distinct from the identities of their siblings.[1]

Despite not being mutually exclusive, cumulative, or completely related, the four themes provide important context for understanding the role of parents in children's schooling. Students in the focus groups struggled to identify their parents' most important involvement *activity* (or activities) that had contributed to their academic success. Many students noted that their parents could not help much with schoolwork beyond fifth grade. Although their expectations for success were high, it bears repeating that these parents conveyed their expectations in ways that would not be considered intrusive or resembling micromanagement. Their children's difficulty in identifying their involvement activities is a telling point we discuss in the next section.

STAGE-SETTING

Stage-setting reflects parents' messages about the importance of schooling and the overall quality of life they create for their children. Although we certainly conceptualize these factors as parental involvement, they are fundamentally distinct from the traditional conception of parental involvement in children's schooling, such as reading to the child, helping with homework, and meeting with teachers. If parental involvement is conceived of in the traditional manner, then previous research on whether parental involvement "works" is mixed. However, stage-setting is closer to the intangible type of parenting, described by Annette Lareau (2003), that is more about cultivating or enriching the child than effecting a particular academic outcome. For example, activities such as trips to museums and involvement in extracurricular endeavors (such as ballet or piano lessons) are only tangentially about increasing achievement; the benefits of such activities are related to "broadening horizons" rather than earning an A in math.

Stage-setting is a conception of parental involvement with two components: (1) conveying the importance of education to a child, and (2) creating and maintaining an environment or life space in which learning can be maximized (or not compromised). Parents vary in the extent to which they can successfully convey this message and create this life space. For instance, *most* parents express that education is important, yet some parents are able to make this message more central to their children's frame of reference. Parents' level of success in conveying the importance of education can be measured by gauging a student's academic identification: the degree to which academic pursuits and outcomes form the basis for his or her overall self-evaluation, or global self-esteem (Osborne 1997). To sustain school success, a child usually must identify school achievement as a part of his or her self-definition (Steele 1997). It is important to note that the relationship between academic self-concept and academic achievement is weaker for black youths, perhaps because they believe that performance evaluations do not reflect their academic abilities and therefore discount them more than do their white peers (Morgan and Mehta 2004). Thus, some groups experience obstacles in maintaining an academic identity, which we discuss later.

In terms of creating a life space conducive to academic success, parents who engage in successful stage-setting are likely to consider the impact of both home and school. At home an ideal learning environment is one in which a child's basic and essential needs (such as food and shelter) are met. As a result, he or she need not worry about the family's ability to survive. Whereas the needs of both economically disadvantaged youth and affluent youth might be adequately met, the former are likely to be much more aware of the tenuous nature

---

1. We would not necessarily suggest motivating children by defining one child's "smartness" relative to his or her siblings. What seems important is that motivation to do well academically was fostered through the positive labeling and reinforcement given at various points in children's lives rather than on a daily basis.

of their parents' efforts to meet their needs. At the neighborhood level, an environment conducive to learning is one in which children feel safe and residents enjoy a good quality of life. We elaborate further on each of these stage-setting components in the next sections.

MESSAGES ABOUT THE VALUE OF SCHOOLING

Although most parents want the best for their children—which in most cases includes some level of academic success—they vary in the degree to which they succeed in conveying the importance of school to their children. Within the context of stage-setting, the difference between conveying that message and *successfully* conveying that message lies in how well the message "sticks": in the latter case, it becomes a major basis for how children define themselves. Thus, success is entirely measured by how deeply the message about the importance of education is engrained within the child's identity.

Ideally, students' global self-esteem (their overall view of the self) is entirely determined by their academic self-concept: they are completely identified with academic success. It is important to note that an individual's self-concept in a particular domain (such as academic ability) is both conceptually and empirically distinct from that person's global self-esteem (Marsh 1986; Rosenberg 1979; Rosenberg et al. 1995). A student may evaluate himself negatively in terms of academic ability yet still have positive self-esteem, while another may evaluate herself positively in terms of academic ability and have negative self-esteem (Crocker and Major 1989). In both cases, academic ability is not central to the student's identity and thus not crucial for his or her overall evaluation of self. Osborne (1997, 728) notes that "students who are more identified with academics should be more motivated to succeed because their self-esteem is directly linked to academic performance. For these students, good performance should be rewarding and poor performance should be punishing." By contrast, for a student with a low academic identity, there is no contingency between academic outcomes and self-esteem: good performance is not rewarding, and poor performance is not punishing. As such, students who do not identify with academics have little incentive to expend effort in academic endeavors and may focus their efforts elsewhere (that is, on whatever is most consequential for their self-esteem).[2]

Some parents experience external challenges in their efforts to link their children's academic success to their global self-esteem. Claude Steele (1997, 613) notes that identification with a particular domain requires that one perceives "good prospects in the domain, that is, that one has the interests, skills, resources, and opportunities to prosper there, as well as that one belongs there, in the sense of being accepted and valued in the domain." He further argues that societal pressures against certain groups "can frustrate this identification; and that in school domains where these groups are negatively stereotyped, those who have become domain identified face the further barrier of stereotype threat, the threat that others' judgments or their own actions will negatively stereotype them in the domain." Numerous studies demonstrate that school practices such as differential disciplinary enforcement in school, the privileging of white and middle-class norms (Lareau 2003), and tracking (Bowles and Gintis 1976; Lucas 1999; Tyson 2011) perpetuate group differences and make blacks

---

2. Academic disidentification is not synonymous with a resistance to schooling. Although students who resist academic success as described by the oppositional culture theory may not identify with schooling, some students may disidentify from academics simply to avoid further feelings of inadequacy or to protect their global self-esteem (Crocker and Major 1989). However, one can disidentify from a particular domain without engaging in active or purposeful resistance within the domain, and while understanding the value associated with success in the domain. For example, an inability to regularly exercise and maintain a healthy diet can lead one to disidentify from both endeavors despite having a strong understanding of the value associated with each of them. For those who disidentify from regular exercise and a healthy diet, their performance in both areas has no bearing on how they feel about themselves in general. Stephen Morgan and Jai Mehta (2004) posit that some mild rejection of performance evaluations can be protective of the sense of self, thereby forestalling a descent into full-blown disidentification.

and Hispanics more susceptible to stereotype threat. In fact, Geoffrey Borman and Jaymes Pyne present findings in this issue suggesting that youth from racial minority groups have been susceptible to stereotype threat since the publication of the Coleman Report.

We argue that whereas most parents convey the importance of education to their children, socioeconomic status partially determines the extent to which the message becomes a central feature of youths' self-definition. Relative to working-class and poor parents, middle-class parents are better able to place their children within contexts that can reinforce the connection between their academic self-esteem and their global self-esteem and minimize those factors that can challenge the centrality of academic success to their self-definition.

A LIFE SPACE CONDUCIVE TO LEARNING

The degree to which messages about the importance of education are successfully transmitted also depends on the life space that parents create for their children at home and in the neighborhood. The very space itself may transmit messages that impact children's approach to schooling. Sometimes messages from within the home and the neighborhood conflict with each other. For example, a parent may attempt to link her child's self-esteem with his academic success, but if the family is surrounded by a neighborhood that does not transmit the same message, these efforts at home can be compromised. Thus, identical academic messages from two different sets of parents can result in different levels of academic identity if they live in different types of neighborhoods (say, Beverly Hills versus inner-city Detroit). Not only does the neighborhood context facilitate or hinder parental efforts to convey the importance of academics, but it also serves as an important frame of reference in which to identify the connection between school and children's future self in these spaces.

Parents have greater control of their children's life space inside their home. They can control the physical space in ways that reinforce or convey messages about the relative importance of school. For example, each decision as to whether to have a television in a child's bedroom, whether to put a desk in the child's bedroom or in a more common area, or whether to have bookshelves in the living room or a home office communicates nonverbally something about the importance of learning. Outside the home, parental control of the life space is limited, mainly to the "selection" of where to live. Once that decision is made, the neighborhood has its own influence independent of parents. In neighborhoods characterized as unsafe, the most parents can do is limit their children's movement within the neighborhood in hopes of minimizing the effect of factors that may compromise their academic success. Parents' ability to secure spaces conducive to learning is not entirely driven by personal choice; social class is a major determinant of the extent to which parents can influence their children's life space.

Stage-setting deems the context of children's lived experiences to be just as important as the educational messages they receive from their parents. Consider a fictional middle-class parent named Tom and his child. Tom's home is located in a neighborhood inhabited by professionals and their families. Nearby is a well-funded high school, a thriving business section, coffee shops and restaurants, a major university, and several large parks where youth sporting events occur. On weekends, parents from the neighborhood attend their children's games and often arrange postgame trips to a local restaurant. Such activities provide opportunities for parents and children to interact about their children's current school experiences, academic progress, and college plans.

Tom's child is in a fortuitous position because the pro-academic messages he receives from his father are reinforced by his interactions with the community. Tom values education and has set the stage for his child to succeed. As a middle-class parent, Tom is likely to be quite involved in his child's schooling. His home may contain many books, he attends school functions, he knows his child's teachers, and he is well aware of the literature touting the benefits of involved parents. When we as researchers view Tom in the data set, he will be a parent who is high on involvement (home and school) with a child who is high-achieving.

Others in the data like Tom and his child will lead us toward the connection that highly involved parents tend to produce academically successful children. This conclusion would not recognize that Tom set the stage for his child to do well in school. Once the stage was set, his child was on course to being academically successful. Tom might proceed to be highly involved, but his involvement is not what is driving his child's school success. It is the fact that Tom has created a space that sets this child up for success. This stage-setting process is what is not adequately captured in quantitative data sets.

Effective stage-setting becomes easier to conceptualize when one considers the strong connection between the educational attainment of parents and their children. For example, most academicians have academically successful children, and certain aspects of their lifestyle reinforce the importance they attribute to education or living a "life of the mind": having a home office, regularly reading national media sources like the *New York Times, Los Angeles Times,* or *Washington Post,* hosting occasional dinner parties, effortlessly (and even obliviously) engaging in (or enacting) critical thinking in common everyday discussions, and living among peers with levels of education above the national norm. This lifestyle would describe many academics regardless of whether they have children. In most cases, children growing up under these conditions cannot help but be academically successful; they certainly are not at risk of becoming high school dropouts. Whereas for most people a high school diploma is a major marker or transition point, college professors often consider K–16 compulsory. For academicians, high educational expectations are built into their lifestyle and the lifestyle they create for their child. They are able to (1) convey the importance of education to their children—indeed, the very concept of education is woven into the fabric of their identity—and (2) create a life space for their children that constantly reinforces the message. Thus, their children are likely to be academically successful regardless of how involved they are in their children's schooling.

This aspect of stage-setting is consistent with the conclusion from the Coleman Report that nonschool factors are a major determinant of group differences in academic outcomes. We argue that parents' influence does not stem from their involvement in their children's schooling in the traditional sense, but rather from their location within a larger socioeconomic structure. However, the Coleman Report underestimates the extent to which schools contribute to group differences in academic outcomes. Schools are also a component of the life space that youth navigate. They are not fixed autonomous structures, but rather dynamic social systems, consisting of teachers and students, that have implications for youths' academic experiences. Parents can intervene in this space on behalf of their children. Also, a positive life space at home can create a buffer against negative experiences at school. But similar to neighborhoods, schools can affect academic achievement independent from the life space parents create in the home. As Prudence Carter notes elsewhere in this issue, school officials can perpetuate unequal educational experiences inside and outside of classrooms because their actions are informed by intensely embedded racial and class meanings that reinforce the strength and rigidity of social boundaries.

STAGE-SETTING VERSUS TRADITIONAL PARENTAL INVOLVEMENT

The difference between stage-setting and the traditional conception of parental involvement examined in previous studies becomes apparent when we consider how each might be employed by parents. Whereas traditional forms of involvement comprise any number of parental activities, stage-setting requires that parents focus on only two factors: messages and life space. Certainly, parents can be traditionally involved in their children's schooling in some ways to accomplish each of these factors. However, stage-setting aims can also be achieved without employing any traditional forms of involvement. Thus, a busy parent with a demanding career can be a successful stage-setter with minimal direct involvement in his or her child's schooling.

Analysis of traditional forms of parental involvement does not capture the life space within which children operate, which is independent of parents' actual activities. Students in our focus groups struggled when asked to name their parents' most important involvement activities that contributed to their academic success. They described their parents in ways such as: "They were supportive in life"; "They attended my band concerts"; "They left schooling up to me"; or "They did not talk much at all about school." At one point students were asked, "Did any of your parents read books to you when you were a child, attend PTA meetings, regularly converse with your teachers, or discuss college plans with you?" Many students shook their heads, and a male student recalled, "My parents didn't do any of those things with me. I have two older siblings that my parents gave attention to, so by the time I came along they were too tired to do anything academically with me."

These students' struggle in answering our questions highlights the challenge of trying to conceptualize how their parents assisted academically. It should be fairly easy to recall your parents being PTA members, reading books to you when you were young, having rules about homework, or having discussions with you about college or school courses. However, if your parents were in the background, so to speak, affecting your academic performance in abstract ways such as gradually changing your perspective on life, giving you the feeling that they supported your efforts in school and extracurricular activities, or instilling an academic motivation in you when you first began formal schooling, it is probably more difficult to quantify the behavioral contributions they made to your academic life. After reviewing the discussion with students in both focus groups, we had the impression that most of them had never thought about the specific activities their parents employed to enhance their school performance or whether these activities contributed to their academic success.

The themes that emerged from the focus groups describe the importance that parents placed on children's academic success in ways that differ from the conventional involvement activities that schools and policymakers currently advocate. Parents' primary contributions, according to students, stemmed from setting high academic expectations and creating a comfortable space in which they could develop their own academic motivations. These are core principles that advocates for parental involvement understand as important. In fact, they are the very same principles the educational community is attempting to capture in proscribing conventional involvement activities. Yet the ways in which the parents of the students we spoke with acted upon these principles were different from conventional involvement activities.

STAGE-SETTING PROFILES

For further clarity, we provide a cross-tabulation for stage-setting in figure 1 that yields four distinct profiles. Children's *quality or conduciveness-to-learning environment* (QCLE) is listed along the y-axis, and the degree of successful *internalization of the message that schooling is important* is listed along the x-axis. Although cross-tabs convey that the factors along the x- and y-axes are dichotomized, they are useful in this case because they highlight four general profiles associated with stage-setting. However, both QCLE and the degree of internalization of messages about education for youth fall along a continuum, which label *low, moderate,* and *high*. It is more accurate to imagine the figure superimposed on a scatterplot of the relationship between measures that capture children's QCLE and the degree to which they identify with success in academic domains.

Each quadrant in figure 1 provides a general description of the children who fall under that profile. Children whose values on each factor place them in the top left quadrant typically live in environments that can be characterized as very conducive to (and reinforcing of) learning, but they have low levels of academic identification (thus the label "high-low"). Despite not feeling strongly defined by academics, these children will perform well enough in school to graduate from high school and even to attend college. This quadrant represents the typical children in a middle-class or affluent community whose academic performance places them in the middle or at the lower end of the achievement distribution in their schools. Although they are not among the high achievers, their achievement levels do not raise red

Figure 1. The Learning Environment and Parents' Message About the Value of Schooling: Stage-Setting

		I. High-Low	II. High-High
Quality or Conducive-to-Learning Environment	High	Parents unable to adequately convey importance of education, but have resources to create "good" environment and counteract negative and counterproductive environments	Parents convey importance of education well and have resources to create "good" environment and counteract negative and counterproductive environments
		Outcome: Average Achievers	Outcome: Solid High Achievers
		III. Low-Low	IV. Low-High
	Moderate	Parents unable to adequately convey importance of education and lack resources to create "good" environment or counteract negative or counterproductive environments	Parents convey importance well, but lack resources to create "good" environment or counteract negative or counterproductive environments
	Low	Outcome: Low Achievers	Outcome: Mediocre or Average Achievers
		Low Moderate High	

Quality (Internalization) of the Message
About the Importance of Schooling

Source: Authors' calculations.

flags; their likelihood of dropping out of school is low.

Children in the top right quadrant (high-high) live in a similar environment (high on QCLE) but have internalized the positive messages about the value of schooling they receive in a manner that embeds academics within their self-definition. These children will be high achievers, and maybe even overachievers, who graduate from high school toward the top of their class and gain admission into selective colleges and universities.

The bottom left quadrant (low-low) represents children whose life space is not conducive to learning and who are not strongly identified with academics. These children would be low achievers *regardless* of their parents' level of involvement in their schooling. The message about the importance of schooling is not conveyed in a manner that anchors academics to these children's self-definition, and the environment they navigate compromises this process even further. This quadrant captures the typical low-achieving child living in a disadvantaged community.

Finally, children in the low-high group (bottom right quadrant) are those who strongly identify with academics but live in an environment that does not reinforce their academic identity. These children are typically the average to high achievers in disadvantaged communities.

Figure 1 provides some direction for how the concept of stage-setting can be tested. We argue that children's location within this framework strongly determines their achievement independent of their parents' level of *direct* involvement. This framework is also helpful for understanding why achievement varies between students who appear to be similar in many ways, such as in the schools they attend, the communities in which they live, and even the families from which they come. Although children in the top quadrants could be similar along numerous dimensions, their achievements will be determined by how strongly they identify with academics. Students with high QCLE levels are virtually assured of never being at any serious risk of dropping out of high school. Even when compared to children in the bottom left quadrant, children in the top left quadrant will perform better academically; being able to ride the wave of their high QCLE allows them to overcome their lack of academic identity. In fact, the identity they establish in the other domains made available to them by their middle-class status (for example, lacrosse, gymnastics, soccer) might enable them to gain admission into good colleges despite their average levels of academic achievement. Similarly, the variations in levels of academic identification among children who are situated within low-QCLE contexts (the bottom quadrants) might account for the variation in achievement observed among children who appear to be similarly disadvantaged.

STAGE-SETTING, SOCIAL CLASS, AND RACE

As noted earlier, we did not attach students' family SES to their parents' involvement activities when describing the themes that emerged from our focus groups. We would suggest, however, that the ease with which parents can set the stage for academic achievement is related to their socioeconomic resources, primarily because the resources commonly found in affluent communities are more reinforcing of parents' attempts to instill in their children the value of schooling. In fact, the spatial concentration of advantage within neighborhoods has an independent effect on youths' academic outcomes. James Ainsworth (2002) finds that as the percentage of adults with a college education and a professional or managerial occupation within a community increases, so do youths' educational aspirations and achievement. Furthermore, Ainsworth shows that the benefit of having high-status residents in a neighborhood overshadows the effects of negative neighborhood characteristics. He finds that more than half of the detrimental effect of living in economically deprived neighborhoods is attributable to a lack of high-status residents in such neighborhoods.

Conversely, living in areas with high concentrations of poverty can compromise the extent to which parents' messages about the value of schooling are ingrained in their children. Classic sociological studies note that disadvantaged communities lack the resources to sustain neighborhood institutions and public services and are characterized by persistent joblessness, which contributes to making these areas breeding places for the factors, such as crime, violence, and substance abuse, that can disconnect academic self-esteem from global self-esteem (Massey and Denton 1993; Wilson 1987, 1996). These conditions inhibit the development of educational skills, depress school achievement, and discourage teachers. William Julius Wilson (1987, 57) argues that "a vicious cycle is perpetuated through family, through the community, and through the schools"—all three being aspects of youths' life space.

Race can also have implications for parents' ability to effectively set the stage for their children's academic success. Parents from historically subordinate racial groups—such as black Americans—face challenges within their environments that are beyond their control and directly affect their children's life space. Elsewhere (Robinson and Harris 2014), we have found that levels of parental involvement in children's schooling *at home* are relatively similar across racial groups (whites, Asian Americans, Hispanics, and blacks), but that parental involvement *with schools* differs by race and some of these differences may result from schools reaching out to minority parents—particularly Hispanics—less than they do to white parents. Thus, black parents must raise children to identify with a domain in which evidence suggests they are rejected. For example, Eric Hanushek, John Kain, and Steven Rivkin (2004) provide strong evidence that a higher rate of minority enrollment increases the probability that white teachers will exit a school, even more than a lower rate of wages. They find that a 10 percent increase in black enrollment would require about a 10 percent increase in salaries to neutralize the elevated probability that white teachers will leave a school. Furthermore, they find that the racial composition of schools is an important determinant of the probability that white teachers—particularly newer teachers—will leave public schools entirely or switch school districts. Catherine Freeman, Benjamin Scafidi, and David Sjoquist (2005) also find that white teachers are much more likely to leave schools that serve higher proportions of black students in favor of schools that serve lower proportions of black and low-income students and have students who score higher on achievement exams.

The reality that black parents must cultivate an academic identity in their children in contexts where some educators are attempting to avoid doing so is particularly disconcerting given that this avoidance appears to adversely affect the quality of the instruction these children receive. In a study of the implications of school racial composition for teacher quality, Kirabo Jackson (2009) finds that in schools in which the share of black student enrollment increased following the repeal of a busing program to maintain racial balance across schools within a school district, there was a decrease in the proportion of experienced teachers, teachers with high licensure exam scores, and teachers who had demonstrated an ability to improve student test scores. Jackson's study design supports the conclusion that the absence of high-quality teachers in schools with high proportions of black students is caused by the racial composition of the schools rather than by neighborhood characteristics. Further, the change in school quality immediately following the repeal of the busing program indicated that teachers exited in anticipation of the arrival of more black students. Given the negative implications of attending a predominantly black school—which is the case for many black youth in the United States—black parents have a particularly unique challenge in effectively setting the stage for their children's academic success.

The findings from Sean Reardon's study reported in this issue identify a potential explanation for why segregated schools present challenges that minority parents must overcome: higher school poverty rates. Reardon finds very clear evidence that disparity in average school poverty rates between whites and blacks is consistently the single most powerful correlate of racial disparities in achievement. This implies that high-poverty schools—which blacks are more likely to attend than whites—are less effective than lower-poverty schools. The strategy of reducing children's exposure to poor classmates, which may lead to meaningful reductions in racial disparities in academic achievement, is less viable for black and Hispanic parents.

Racial differences also exist in parents' ability to influence the school environment, even in affluent schools. In a study conducted in a well-funded school in an affluent community, Amanda Lewis and John Diamond (2015) find that white parents display a sense of entitlement to challenge their children's track placement. They push their children into honors and Advanced Placement (AP) courses—where instruction is superior, the curriculum is more challenging, and teachers are more experienced—against the advice of teachers and regardless of whether the courses are above their children's academic ability. White parents are able to do this with little to no resistance from school personnel. In fact, the process is smooth and requires minimal interaction with school officials. Furthermore, Lewis and Diamond show that school personnel often respond to the pressure to placate white middle-class parents by making decisions that go against their instincts and provide benefits to some students (mostly white and middle-class) but not others (mostly black and Hispanic).

Although stage-setting may be easier for families with more socioeconomic resources compared to families with fewer socioeconomic resources, stage-setting should not be conflated with social class. In theory, socioeconomically disadvantaged parents can effectively set the stage for their child to experience academic success, and in fact there are socioeconomically disadvantaged high achievers. However, their exceptionality suggests that disadvantaged parents are less likely to be successful stage-setters because they face greater challenges in doing so than more affluent parents. Thus, stage-setting is not a proxy for social class but a mechanism that explains the link between social class and achievement. For example, scholars have been able to observe a strong negative association between poverty and achievement because poverty can be disruptive to children's everyday lives (Duncan and Rodgers 1988). Karen Seccombe (2000) highlights several studies that show that over the course of a year a majority of the poorest families experience at least one of the following deprivations: eviction, crowded housing, disconnection of utilities, no stove, no refrigerator, or housing with upkeep problems. All these aspects of the life space impact stage-setting; they are the mechanisms that explain why lower socioeconomic circumstances are related to poor achievement.

Figure 2. Conceptual and Empirical Model for Parental Involvement as a Mechanism for Explaining the Social Class and Race–Achievement Link

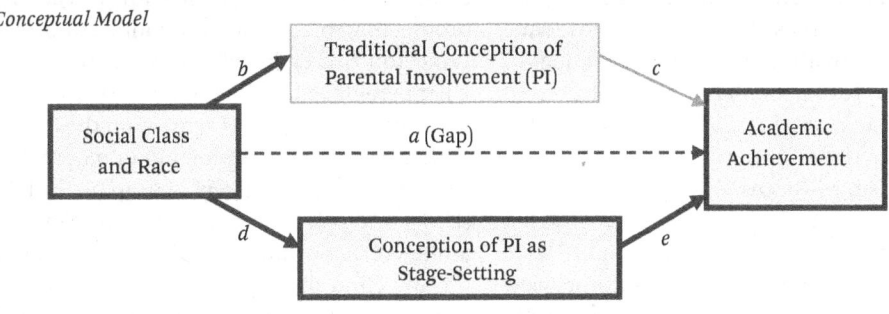

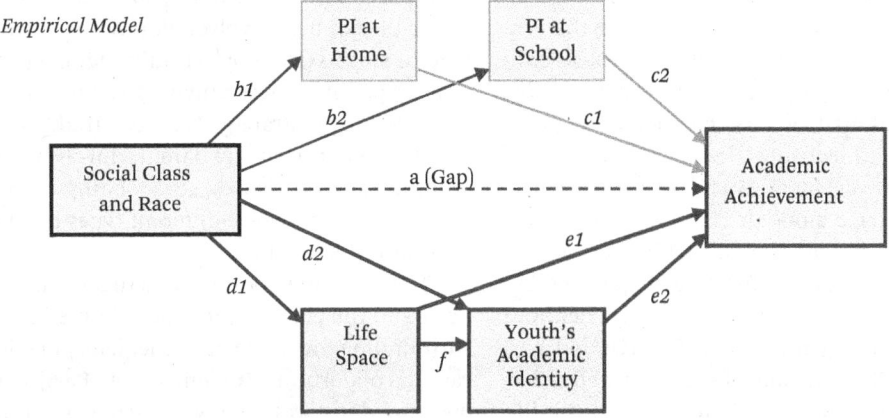

Source: Authors' calculations.

We posit that stage-setting explains a greater share of the link between social class and achievement than traditional forms of parental involvement. We illustrate this link in figure 2, which shows the conceptual and empirical models we are describing. The models depict the role of parental involvement in children's achievement relative to social class and race. The conceptual model suggests that class and race differences exist in traditional forms of parental involvement (path b). However, we portray path c in gray to convey that the connection between traditional forms of parental involvement and achievement is tenuous. Instead, it is *stage-setting* that accounts for class and race differences in academic achievement; groups vary in their ability to successfully set the stage (path d), and stage-setting strongly determines academic achievement (path e).

The empirical model provides some clarity on the overall process of our perspective. Because the traditional conception of parental involvement contains two components, home and school, we decompose path b into paths $b1$ and $b2$. Similarly, the "effects" for parental involvement are decomposed into paths $c1$ (home) and $c2$ (school). The empirical model depicts the variation along class and racial lines in the forms of parental involvement at home and at school and shows that these forms of involvement are only modestly related to children's achievement (represented by the gray paths). Instead, the factors associated with stage-setting, illustrated in the bottom portion of the empirical model, are the driving forces behind the impact of parents on their children's academic lives. Specifically, class and race are major factors in determining the quality or conduciveness to learning of children's life space (path *d1*) and the extent to which children identify with academics (path *d2*), and each of these factors affects academic achievement (paths *e1* and *e2*) independent of traditional forms of parental involvement. Path *f* denotes that the quality of children's life space influences—either by reinforcing or by compromising—youths' academic identity.

Affluent parents tend to be more involved in their children's academic lives and to have high-achieving children. Many educators view the success of these children as resulting in large part from their parents' involvement. We suspect that affluent parents are being credited with superior parental involvement when in fact it is stage-setting that is driving the academic success of their children. These children are likely to attend well-funded schools with excellent teachers, characteristics of a conducive-to-learning life space more than of parental involvement. We recognize that a positive life space alone does not guarantee academic success and that school finance reform has greatly reduced funding disparities between high-performing suburban districts and low-performing urban districts (Odden and Picus 2007). What contributes to the effectiveness of these positive factors within the life space, however, is that messages about the importance of schooling have a more lasting effect on the children of affluent parents because there are fewer threats in their lives that could disconnect their academic self-esteem from their global self-esteem. To be clear, we acknowledge that affluent parents are more involved than their less advantaged counterparts. It is also true, however, that many educators find the anecdotally observed relationship between parental involvement and high achievement too appealing to ignore and thus promote parental involvement as the answer to most of the problems within K–12. We propose instead that affluent parents have created a space that sets their children up for success largely independent from their involvement.

CONCLUSION

In sum, effective stage-setting is more rooted in lifestyle than in parental involvement activities. Once the stage is set for academic success, children are on course toward being academically successful. A child with an academic profile that places her on course to attend Princeton University will not suddenly "tank" if her parents reduce their level of involvement. Although she might not remain on the Princeton trajectory after a reduction of parental involvement, she is unlikely to drop out of high school and will probably gain admission into a fine college or university. Our point is that for any child to remain on a positive trajectory—toward Princeton or elsewhere—the parents might simply need to maintain a positive space conducive to academic success, and that this space may or may not include traditional forms of parental involvement. A key advantage of stage-setting over traditional conceptions of parental involvement is that it is not a one-size-fits-all strategy. Whereas traditional conceptions advocate for parents' involvement in all the same activities, stage-setting is contextual and can involve different types of support for different children.

The Coleman Report posited that the home itself and the cultural influences immediately surrounding the home drive inequality of educational opportunity (Coleman et al. 1966). Our own previous work, however, suggests that black and Hispanic parents value education either the same as or more than their white counterparts (Harris 2011; Robinson and Harris 2014), and that achievement inequality in outcomes by race and class persist even net of forms of parental involvement within parents' control (Robinson and Harris 2014). Additionally, the configuration and resources of cities, neighborhoods, and schools play a significant role in educational inequality (Alexander, Entwisle, and Olson 2014). In fact, analysis of national data shows that inequality in academic outcomes is smallest upon school entry and widens (rather than remaining constant) as children matriculate through the early grades (Fryer and Levitt 2006). Schools also operate and respond differently for parents based on race and class, with white parents being advantaged at the expense of black and Hispanic parents and children (Lareau 2003; Lewis and Diamond 2015). Thus, not all parents have the same ability to influence their children's academic outcomes or opportunities. In our view, suggesting that inequality of educational opportunity stems primarily from the home itself and the culture does not square well with recent empirical evidence. The conception of school and family as being in competition ignores the reality that these factors both jointly and independently influence how the stage is set in the first place.

The stage-setting framework suggests that the concept of parental involvement needs to be conceptualized differently in policy and in practice. Several states and districts have recently called for increases in parental involvement both in and out of school. However, given the differences that parents experience in setting the stage, educators and school personnel should take more active roles in providing parents with effective strategies to help their children academically. Furthermore, educators should work to assist parents with setting the stage by addressing the inequality in how students experience the school setting. More specifically, addressing the issues discussed by Prudence Carter in this issue, by Lewis and Diamond (2015), and by Tyson (2011) would minimize the extent to which school personnel perpetuate racial inequality by responding to youth based on racialized and class-based assumptions and tracking racial minorities into lower academic tracks.

REFERENCES

Ainsworth, James W. 2002. "Why Does It Take a Village? The Mediation of Neighborhood Effects on Educational Achievement." *Social Forces* 81(1): 117–52.

Alexander, Karl. 2016. "Is It Family or School? Getting the Question Right." *RSF: The Russell Sage Foundation Journal of the Social Sciences* 2(5). doi: 10.7758/RSF.2016.2.5.02.

Alexander, Karl, Doris Entwisle, and Linda Olson. 2014. *The Long Shadow: Family Background, Disadvantaged Urban Youth, and the Transition to Adulthood*. New York: Russell Sage Foundation.

Borman, Geoffrey D., and Jaymes Pyne. 2016. "What If Coleman Had Known About Stereotype Threat? How Social-Psychological Theory Can Help Mitigate Educational Inequality." *RSF: The Russell Sage Foundation Journal of the Social Sciences* 2(5). doi: 10.7758/RSF.2016.2.5.08.

Bowles, Samuel, and Herbert Gintis. 1976. *Schooling in Capitalist America: Educational Reform and the Contradictions of Economic Life*. New York: Basic Books.

Carter, Prudence. 2016. "Educational Equality Is a Multifaceted Issue: Why We Must Understand the School's Sociocultural Context for Student Achievement." *RSF: The Russell Sage Foundation Journal of the Social Sciences* 2(5). doi: 10.7758/RSF.2016.2.5.07.

Catsambis, Sophia. 2001. "Expanding Knowledge of Parental Involvement in Children's Secondary Education: Connections with High School Seniors' Academic Success." *Social Psychology of Education* 5(2): 149–77.

Coleman, James S., Ernest Q. Campbell, Carol J. Hobson, James McPartland, Alexander M. Mood, Frederick D. Weinfeld, and Robert L. York. 1966. *Equality of Educational Opportunity*. Washington: U.S. Department of Health, Education, and Welfare, Office of Education.

Comer, James P. 1992. "Educational Accountability: A Shared Responsibility Between Parents and Schools." *Stanford Law and Policy Review* 4(1): 113–22.

Crocker, Jennifer, and Brenda Major. 1989. "Social Stigma and Self-esteem: The Self-Protective Properties of Stigma." *Psychological Review* 96(4): 608–30.

Dearing, Eric, and Beck A. Taylor. 2007. "Home Improvements: Within-Family Associations Between Income and the Quality of Children's Home Environments." *Journal of Applied Developmental Psychology* 28(5–6): 427–44.

Desimone, Laura. 2001. "Linking Parent Involvement with Student Achievement: Do Race and Income Matter?" *Journal of Educational Research* 93(1): 11–30.

Domina, Thurston. 2005. "Leveling the Home Advantage: Assessing the Effectiveness of Parental Involvement in Elementary School." *Sociology of Education* 78(3): 233–49.

Duncan, Greg J., and Willard L. Rodgers. 1988. "Longitudinal Aspects of Childhood Poverty." *Journal of Marriage and the Family* 50(4): 1007–21.

Epstein, Joyce L. 1985. "Home and School Connections in Schools of the Future: Implications of Research on Parental Involvement." *Peabody Journal of Education* 62(2): 18–41.

———. 2010. "School/Family/Community Partnerships: Caring for the Children We Share." *Phi Delta Kappan* 92(3): 81–96.

Freeman, Catherine, Benjamin Scafidi, and David L. Sjoquist. 2005. "Racial Segregation in Georgia Public Schools, 1994–2001: Trends, Causes, and Impact on Teacher Quality." In *School Segregation: Must the South Turn Back?* edited by John Charles Boger and Gary Orfield. Chapel Hill: University of North Carolina Press.

Fryer, Roland G., and Steven D. Levitt. 2006. "The Black-White Test Score Gap Through Third Grade." *American Law and Economics Review* 8(2): 249–81.

Hango, Darcy. 2007. "Parental Investment in Childhood and Educational Qualifications: Can Greater Parental Involvement Mediate the Effects of Socioeconomic Disadvantage?" *Social Science Research* 36(4): 1371–90.

Hanushek, Eric A., John F. Kain, and Steven G. Rivkin. 2004. "Why Public Schools Lose Teachers." *Journal of Human Resources* 39(2): 326–54.

Harris, Angel L. 2011. *Kids Don't Want to Fail: Oppositional Culture and the Black-White Achievement Gap.* Cambridge, Mass.: Harvard University Press.

Hart, Betty, and Todd R. Risley. 1995. *Meaningful Differences in the Everyday Experience of Young American Children.* Baltimore: Paul H. Brooks Publishing.

Hoge, Dean R., Edna K. Smit, and John T. Crist. 1997. "Four Family Process Factors Predicting Academic Achievement in Sixth and Seventh Grade." *Educational Research Quarterly* 21(2): 27–42.

Izzo, Charles V., Roger P. Weissberg, Wesley J. Kasprow, and Michael Fendrich. 1999. "A Longitudinal Assessment of Teacher Perceptions of Parent Involvement in Children's Education and School Performance." *American Journal of Community Psychology* 27(6): 817–39.

Jackson, C. Kirabo. 2009. "Student Demographics, Teacher Sorting, and Teacher Quality: Evidence from the End of School Desegregation." *Journal of Labor Economics* 27(2): 213–56.

Jeynes, William. 2003. "A Meta-analysis: The Effects of Parental Involvement on Minority Children's Achievement." *Education and Urban Society* 35(2): 202–23.

Lareau, Annette. 2003. *Unequal Childhoods: Class, Race, and Family Life.* Berkeley: University of California Press.

Lewis, Amanda E., and John B. Diamond. 2015. *Despite the Best Intentions: How Racial Inequality Thrives in Good Schools.* New York: Oxford University Press.

Lucas, Samuel Roundfield. 1999. *Tracking Inequality: Stratification and Mobility in American High Schools.* New York: Teachers College Press.

Marsh, Herbert W. 1986. "Global Self-Esteem: Its Relation to Specific Facets of Self-Concept and Their Importance." *Journal of Personality and Social Psychology* 51(6): 1224–36.

Massey, Douglas, and Nancy Denton. 1993. *American Apartheid.* Cambridge, Mass.: Harvard University Press.

Mau, Wei-Cheng. 1997. "Parental Influences on the High School Students' Academic Achievement: A Comparison of Asian Immigrants, Asian Americans, and White Americans." *Psychology in the Schools* 34(3): 267–77.

McNeal, Ralph B., Jr. 1999. "Parental Involvement as Social Capital: Differential Effectiveness on Science Achievement, Truancy, and Dropping Out." *Social Forces* 78(1): 117–44.

Morgan, Stephen L., and Jai Mehta. 2004. "Beyond the Laboratory: Evaluating the Survey Evidence for the Disidentification Explanation of Black-White Differences in Achievement." *Sociology of Education* 77(1): 82–101.

Muller, Chandra. 1995. "Maternal Employment, Parental Involvement, and Mathematics Achievement Among Adolescents." *Journal of Marriage and the Family* 57(1): 85–100.

———. 1998. "Gender Differences in Parental Involvement and Adolescents' Mathematics Achievement." *Sociology of Education* 71(4): 336–56.

Odden, Allen R., and Lawrence O. Picus. 2007. *School Finance: A Policy Perspective.* New York: McGraw-Hill.

Osborne, Jason W. 1997. "Race and Academic Disidentification." *Journal of Educational Psychology* 89(4): 728–35.

Pomerantz, Eva, Elizabeth Moorman, and Scott D. Litwack. 2007. "The How, Whom, and Why of Parents' Involvement in Children's Academic Lives: More Is Not Always Better." *Review of Educational Research* 77(3): 373–410.

Reardon, Sean. 2016. "School Segregation and Racial Academic Achievement Gaps." *RSF: The Russell Sage Foundation Journal of the Social Sciences* 2(5). doi: 10.7758/RSF.2016.2.5.03.

Robinson, Keith, and Angel L. Harris. 2014. *The Broken Compass: Parental Involvement with Chil-*

dren's Education. Cambridge, Mass.: Harvard University Press.

Rosenberg, Morris. 1979. *Conceiving the Self.* New York: Basic Books.

Rosenberg, Morris, Carmi Schooler, Carrie Shoenbach, and Florence Rosenberg. 1995. "Global Self-Esteem and Specific Self-Esteem: Different Concepts, Different Outcomes." *American Sociological Review* 60(1): 141–56.

Schulting, Amy B., Patrick S. Malone, and Kenneth A. Dodge. 2005. "The Effect of School-Based Kindergarten Transition Policies and Practices on Child Academic Outcomes." *Developmental Psychology* 41(6): 860–71.

Seccombe, Karen. 2000. "Families in Poverty in the 1990s: Trends, Causes, Consequences, and Lessons Learned." *Journal of Marriage and the Family* 62(4): 1094–113.

Steele, Claude M. 1997. "A Threat in the Air: How Stereotypes Shape Intellectual Identity and Performance." *American Psychologist* 52(6): 613–29.

Stein, Melanie R., and Ron J. Thorkildsen. 1999. *Parental Involvement in Education: Insights and Applications from the Research.* Research Practitioner Series. Bloomington, Ind.: Phi Delta Kappa International.

Sui-Chu, Esther Ho, and J. Douglas Willms. 1996. "Effects of Parental Involvement on Eighth-Grade Achievement." *Sociology of Education* 69(2): 126–41.

Tyson, Karolyn. 2011. *Integration Interrupted: Tracking, Black Students, and Acting White After Brown.* New York: Oxford University Press.

Wilson, William Julius. 1987. *The Truly Disadvantaged: The Inner City, the Underclass, and Public Policy.* Chicago: University of Chicago Press.

———. 1996. *When Work Disappears: The World of the New Urban Poor.* New York: Knopf.

Zellman, Gail L., and Jill M. Waterman. 1998. "Understanding the Impact of Parent School Involvement on Children's Educational Outcomes." *Journal of Educational Research* 91(6): 370–80.

Necessary but Not Sufficient: The Role of Policy for Advancing Programs of School, Family, and Community Partnerships

JOYCE L. EPSTEIN AND STEVEN B. SHELDON

Since the release of Equality of Educational Opportunity, *researchers have emphasized the importance of applying the results of research to policies for school improvement. Policies tell educators* to do something, *but not* how *to enact specific laws. This study analyzes data from 347 schools in 21 districts to identify variables that support the enactment of policies for parental engagement. We address research questions on how school and district practices affect the quality of school-based partnership programs. Our results indicate that a policy on parental involvement may be a good first step, but other factors—principals' support for family and community engagement and active facilitation of research-based structures and processes by district leaders—are important for establishing a basic partnership program. These factors promote programs that engage all students' families. Schools that take these steps have higher percentages of engaged families and report higher rates of average daily attendance among their students.*

Keywords: district leadership, school leadership, family and community involvement, partnership program development

There are interesting questions to ask about the role of federal, state, and local policies in improving programs of school, family, and community partnerships. For instance, though policies are important for promoting school improvement, how much do policies affect school change? This study explores the responses of schools and districts to policy recommendations for partnership programs and the connections between these programs and family engagement and student attendance.

THE HISTORICAL CONTEXT
The *Equality of Educational Opportunity* (*EEO*) report (Coleman et al. 1966) focused attention on the importance of families in children's education, based mainly on analyses of measures of family socioeconomic status. Its findings about the strong connections of family background and weak contributions of school resources to student achievement sparked a decade-long argument among social scientists on the question: which is more important for student learning—the school or the family? The debate spurred the field of education research into action that has continued to this day. To study influences on student learning, researchers began collecting new and better data on school and classroom environments, students' opportunities and motivation to learn, family factors, and the connections between home, school, and community.

Joyce L. Epstein is research professor of education and sociology at Johns Hopkins University and director of the Center on School, Family, and Community Partnerships. **Steven B. Sheldon** is associate professor of education at Johns Hopkins University and associate director of the Center on School, Family, and Community Partnerships.

Direct correspondence to: Joyce Epstein at jepstein@jhu.edu, 2701 N. Charles St., Suite 300, Baltimore, MD 21218; and Steven Sheldon at ssheldon@jhu.edu, 2701 N. Charles St., Suite 300, Baltimore, MD 21218.

We and our colleagues were inspired by the controversy to change our research question away from the "contest" of family versus school and away from the seemingly fixed inequities in family involvement linked to parents' socioeconomic status (SES). We posed a new question: *if* families are so important for student success in school, how can all schools engage all families so that more students benefit from their parents' support and encouragement to do their best in school? This new, more difficult question required research on school policies, school organization, leadership, and the alterable variables that might produce more equitable programs in family and community engagement for the success of more students.

Historically, family engagement has been treated as about the parents, that is, as external to schools. Our new question asked whether and how teachers and administrators could work with all students' parents and with community partners from the earliest years on to ensure students' readiness for school, grade-level learning, progress and promotion to the next grade, and on-time graduation from high school. This approach, in making school, family, and community partnerships a component of school organization—one that is central to other school improvements—ultimately was about the students.

THE PRESENT POLICY CONTEXT

The Elementary and Secondary Education Act (ESEA) lists requirements for parent and family engagement at the school, district, and state levels, building on guidelines in ESEA reauthorizations since 1988.[1] Schools are required to engage all families in ways that support student achievement. Districts are told to assist all schools in developing partnership programs. States are expected to collect and review district policies on parental involvement, and the requirements are monitored for compliance to justify the continuation of Title I funds (Cowan 2003). The policy tells educators to engage families, but does not specify how to meet these requirements or how to improve the quality of their partnership programs. There is, then, a critical gap between the intent and enactment of the law.

THEORETICAL PERSPECTIVES ON LEADERSHIP DEVELOPMENT

We have drawn on three theoretical perspectives to guide our research questions and analyses. Sociocultural and organizational learning theories posit that districts and schools learn from each other when they share leadership and responsibilities for school improvement, including family and community engagement (Honig 2006, 2008; Huber 1991; Spillane and Diamond 2007; Stein and Coburn 2008). *Sociocultural learning theory* asserts that good communication between and among colleagues who gain knowledge, exchange ideas, and take actions to develop a "culture of collaboration" affects the organization as a whole (Knapp 2008; Wenger 1998).

Organizational learning theory states that organizations improve when leaders share knowledge, plan actions, conduct evaluations, gather evidence, make sense of data, and identify best practices (Elmore 2004; Senge 1990; Supovitz 2006; Weick 1995). In combination, the two theories reinforce each other with expectations that organizations and individuals will learn and advance. That is, the interpersonal exchanges at the heart of sociocultural learning theory are informed by attention to useful data, which is central to organizational learning theory (Honig 2008; Leithwood and Prestine 2002; Louis 2008; Mayrowetz 2008).

A third theory calls attention to the *content* of leadership for developing programs for school, family, and community partnerships. The *theory of overlapping spheres of influence* asserts that children learn and grow at school, at home, and in the community, and that they benefit when parents, teachers, and others in

---

1. Section 1010 on "parent and family engagement" specifies that districts ([local education agencies] LEAs) must have a policy and must "(B) provide the coordination, *technical assistance, and other support necessary to assist and build the capacity of all participating schools* in planning and implementing effective parent and family involvement activities to improve student academic achievement and school performance" (U.S. Department of Education 2015, emphasis added).

the community collaborate in ways that encourage learning and development (Epstein 1987, 2011). Goal-linked involvement activities implemented by educators, parents, students, and community members should reduce the distance and potential discord between home, school, and community and increase the quality of school-based partnership programs. Outreach and information from schools should increase the number of involved families and improve goal-linked results for students.

This interdisciplinary theory of overlapping spheres of influence specifies an external model that represents the degree of the shared interests and actions of home, school, and community concerning student learning and school success. An internal model recognizes that the student is the central actor in learning and specifies the complex relationships and interactions of parents, teachers, and community partners.

In research on the practices that occur in the overlapping contexts of home, school, and community, we identified a *framework of six types of involvement* that helps categorize separable practices of partnership that pose unique challenges to engaging all families and that produces different results for student achievement and behavior. The six types of involvement—*parenting, communicating, volunteering, learning at home, decision-making,* and *collaborating with the community*—can be activated to engage families with children on specific school improvement goals (such as improving students' reading skills and attitudes, attendance, or health) (Epstein et al. 2009).

Programs based on this theory change family involvement from an external factor unrelated to schools to an essential component of school and classroom organization (Bryk et al. 2010; Epstein and Sheldon 2006). Partnership programs require leaders to set policy, select or customize and conduct practices, and evaluate progress in engaging all families. In each school, an Action Team for Partnerships (ATP) provides the structure for planning, implementing, and evaluating a site-based program of family and community engagement linked to goals for student learning and development (Epstein et al. 2009).

The three theories support the *process* of side-by-side leadership (Epstein, forthcoming). In contrast to top-down directives from districts to schools or bottom-up reports of good practice, side-by-side leadership recognizes the importance of multidirectional learning that is enriched—not restricted—by the dissimilar roles of participants in diverse learning communities. Rather than focusing only on prescribed procedures or narrow monitoring for compliance (as in top-down vertical networks), or only on atheoretical trial-and-error approaches (as in bottom-up networks), side-by-side leaders customize communications, develop tools, collect and analyze data, and take action to continually improve school programs (as in Continuous Progress Learning Communities; see Bryk et al. 2015). Researchers, district leaders, principals, teachers, parents, and others work side by side to exchange information and ideas and raise questions to improve research and practice.

We draw from these theories to test whether and how school-based actions, district assistance, and the simultaneous and joint work of school team members with district leaders improve the nature and extent of family and community engagement and results for parents and students.

BRIDGING THE GAP BETWEEN POLICY STATEMENTS AND ENACTMENTS

The National Network of Partnership Schools (NNPS) at Johns Hopkins University was established in 1995 to close the gap between written policies with directives for family and community engagement and actions taken at the school, district, and state levels to engage all families in ways that contribute to student success in school. In NNPS, results of research on the structures and processes for organizing effective and equitable programs of partnership are translated into training, tools, and publications for educators and parents. Leaders who join NNPS are guided to use the research-based approaches to enact policy and improve practices so that all families are involved in their children's education in age- and grade-appropriate ways from preschool through high school.

In NNPS, each district must identify a leader for partnerships who facilitates and encourages school-based ATPs to build their capacities to plan, implement, and continually improve their programs to create a welcoming school climate and support site-specific goals for student success. At the end of each academic year, district leaders and schools in NNPS complete *UPDATE* surveys to evaluate their work and progress. NNPS developed reliable scales and measures on these surveys to assess district and school progress on essential elements that affect the quality of partnership programs from one year to the next. The data are collected and analyzed for annual reports for NNPS members and for the public (Epstein and Ames 2016; Sheldon and Ames 2016).

PRIOR RESEARCH ON PARTNERSHIP PROGRAM DEVELOPMENT

Prior studies based on data collected separately from districts and from schools in NNPS explored factors that affected the quality of school-based and district-level partnership programs and practices. Research on schools found that those with well-functioning ATPs, strong support from principals, and positive ratings of the assistance received from district leaders were more likely than other schools to have higher-quality programs of family and community involvement (Hutchins and Sheldon 2013; Sanders and Sheldon 2009; Sheldon 2005, 2008; Van Voorhis and Sheldon 2004). Research on districts found that leaders who directly and actively facilitated school ATPs were more likely than other district leaders to report that their schools were making more progress in developing and improving programs of family and community involvement (Epstein 2008; Sanders 2008, 2009).

One study went further, studying schools nested within districts to understand the simultaneous efforts of district leaders and school teams to work together to improve school-based partnership programs (Epstein, Galindo, and Sheldon 2011). In that study, which combined independently collected school and district data, schools with at least three years of assistance from district leaders developed more advanced family engagement activities and engaged more families than did schools without consistent district support.

RESEARCH QUESTIONS

This study builds on the prior work with extended analyses of schools nested within districts to learn whether and how district assistance to school-based teams affects partnership program development and results for parents and students. We set four research questions:

1. How do *school factors* affect the implementation of:
   a. Basic structures and processes to implement school-based programs of family and community involvement?
   b. Advanced outreach activities to involve families who are typically uninvolved or "hard to reach"?
2. How do *district factors* affect schools' basic and advanced partnership programs?
3. How do basic and advanced partnership programs affect the percentage of parents who are good partners with the school in their children's education?
4. How do basic and advanced programs and the percentage of parents who are good partners with their schools affect school reports of students' average daily attendance?

Figure 1 presents the research model and hypothesized paths of influence to address the research questions. Analyses were conducted to learn whether and how school and district practices affected the quality of schools' basic partnership program implementation and advanced outreach to involve more families, and whether the quality of these programs measurably predicted the percentage of involved parents and students' average daily attendance.

SAMPLE

Survey data were collected in 2014 from 347 schools in 21 districts that were members of NNPS at Johns Hopkins University. The schools were located in large urban (20.9 percent), small urban (32.2 percent), suburban (26.6 percent), and rural (20.3 percent) areas across the country. The majority of schools (67.7 percent) served elementary and K–8 students; the rest were middle and junior high schools (18.4 percent) and high schools (13.9 percent). A few schools with mixed-grade organizations were

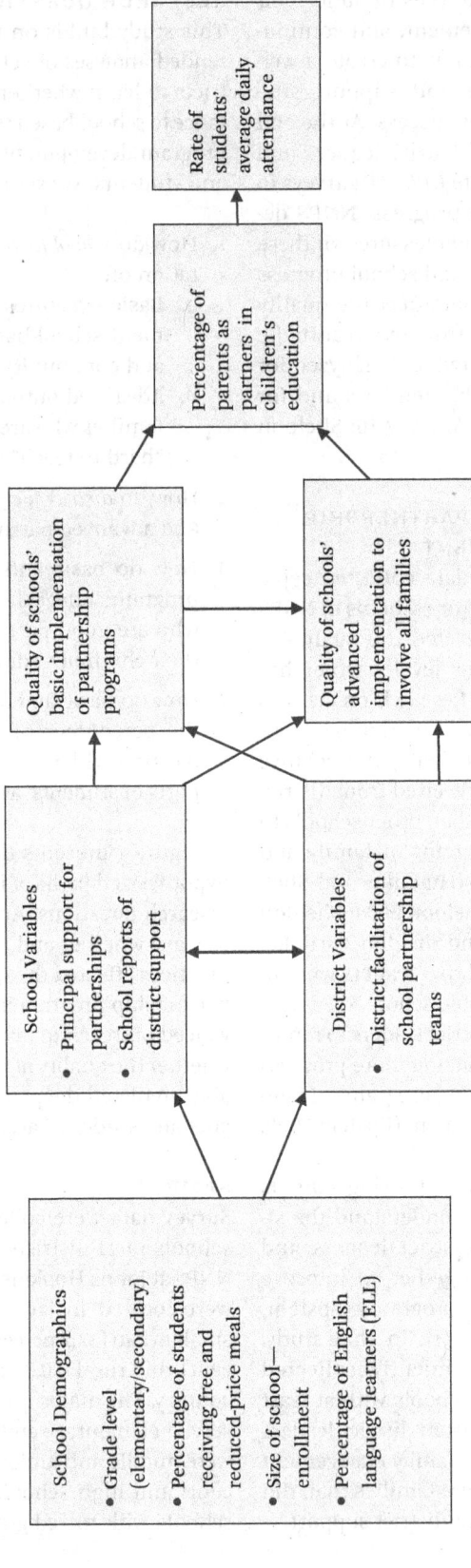

Figure 1. Theoretical Effects Model: Connections Between School and District Leadership on the Quality of School-Based Partnership Programs, Parent Participation, and Rates of Student Attendance

Source: Authors' compilation.

excluded from the analyses. The sample closely matches the proportion of elementary and secondary schools in the nation as a whole (National Center for Education Statistics 2015).

Most schools (69.9 percent) received Title I funds. Within schools, on average, 67.8 percent of students were eligible for free or reduced-price lunches. About 39.9 percent of students were African American, 41.1 percent white, 14.9 percent Latino/Hispanic, and 2.6 percent Asian American, and a small percentage of students had other backgrounds. Across schools, an average of 5.1 languages other than English were spoken at home by students' families, ranging from only English to over 38 languages. The schools enrolled an average of 628 students, with school size ranging from under 50 to over 3,000 students. The variation in the demographics of this sample generally reflects the diversity in the nation's schools.

In addition to diverse demographics, districts and schools in NNPS varied in how long they had worked on research-based approaches to partnership program development, ranging from one to nineteen years. Some had joined recently, whereas others had become expert leaders on partnerships.[2]

Because all districts and schools join NNPS to obtain guidance and support to implement the structures and processes that enable them to organize effective partnership programs, the sample eliminates one kind of selection bias. However, each site enters the network with a unique history and works to improve its program at its own pace. In this way, the variations among sites make it possible to study whether and how district and school leaders' actions affect the quality of partnership programs.

MEASURES

Dependent Variables

Two measures of the quality of partnership program implementation at the school level are of interest in this study: basic program implementation and advanced program outreach. Two measures of the results of partnership programs extend prior studies: the percentage of involved parents and students' average daily attendance.

The Quality of Basic Program Implementation
This twelve-item scale ($\alpha = 0.92$) measured whether and how well schools organized the basic components of a partnership program. The items were scored from 1 (did not do) to 4 (did very well) to reflect low-to-high implementation of structures and processes such as whether the school established an action team; wrote an action plan; implemented activities for six types of involvement; implemented involvement activities linked to school improvement goals for student success; evaluated the activities that were implemented; and conducted other basic organizational activities. Schools averaged 3.22 on this scale (standard deviation = 0.59), indicating that most teams viewed their work on the basics as "okay," with clear variation among the schools in the sample.

Advanced Implementation
This nine-item scale ($\alpha = 0.85$) measured whether and how well a school implemented activities to solve challenges to engage all families, including those who are typically hard to reach, and to improve the implementation of activities for six types of involvement. The items were scored from 1 (not yet working on this challenge) to 4 (solved this challenge) and averaged to reflect low-to-high attention to engaging all students' families. For example, teams reported on whether they worked to get information from workshops to families who could not attend; communicated with families who did not speak English at home; involved major demographic groups of families in school decisions; recruited and trained volunteers; and addressed other challenges that might limit family and community involvement. Schools averaged 2.76 on this scale (standard deviation = 0.56), indicating that most were making fair-to-good progress in addressing challenges, whereas others were not yet focused on advanced implementations to engage uninvolved families.

Percentage of Involved Parents
This five-item scale ($\alpha = 0.82$) measured school reports on the percentage of parents who at-

---

2. See the award-winning sites in the section on "Success Stories" at www.partnershipschools.org.

tended back-to-school nights, attended parent-teacher conferences, volunteered at school, monitored children's homework, and were considered "good partners" in children's education. The items ranged in six increments from 0 percent (none) to 100 percent (all) and were averaged to reflect low-to-high parental participation.

Students' Average Daily Attendance

This single item reported students' average daily attendance (ADA), which ranged from as 31 to 100 percent across schools.

Independent Variables

School Variables (Level 1):
Principal's Support

This ten-item scale ($\alpha = 0.92$) measured how strongly the principal supported the work of the ATP. Items were scored from 1 to 4 to indicate whether a principal never, seldom, often, or always provided time for team meetings; encouraged families to participate in involvement activities; encouraged teachers to work on partnerships; allocated funds for involvement activities; and offered other support for the school's program of family and community involvement. The average sum for this scale was 3.5 (standard deviation = 0.54), indicating that most principals were positive about teamwork for partnerships, but varied in the kind and extent of their support.

School Variables (Level 1): School Reports of District Support

This seven-item scale ($\alpha = 0.90$) measured ATP reports on the extent and helpfulness of assistance from district Leaders for Partnership in program development. The items, which were scored 1 (no district support provided), 2 (not helpful), 3 (helpful), or 4 (very helpful), focused on district leaders' training teams for partnerships, funding, recognition, help with evaluations, ideas for best practices, and other assistance. The average school report on district assistance was 3.12 (standard deviation = 0.75), indicating that most teams acknowledged some support from district leaders, but varied in which facilitative actions they experienced and how helpful they rated these actions to have been.

District Variables (Level 2):
District Facilitation

This seven-item scale ($\alpha = 0.89$) measured the reports of district Leaders for Partnerships on whether and how well they facilitated school-based Action Teams for Partnerships to organize and improve their partnership programs. The items, which were scored 1 (not conducted), 2 (need to improve), 3 (okay), or 4 (conducted very well), focused on assistance to schools on basic actions to establish their partnership programs. This included help forming an Action Team for Partnerships, understanding and using the framework of six types of involvement, writing a One-Year Action Plan for Partnerships, collecting the schools' plans to follow work and progress, helping to develop a budget, meeting with the principal about teamwork and partnerships, and helping to evaluate work and progress. The average facilitation score was 3.05 (standard deviation = 0.80), indicating that most district leaders provided some direct assistance to schools in ways they deemed "okay," but varied in how well facilitation was progressing.

Background Measures

Analyses statistically controlled school demographic variables, including grade level (elementary = 0, secondary = 1), size of school enrollment, percentage of students receiving free or reduced-price lunch, and percentage of English language learners (ELL). In prior studies, grade level was a significant variable, whereas the poverty level of the school and students' language services were less consistently important for the development or quality of a partnership program (Epstein 2008; Epstein, Galindo, and Sheldon 2011; Sheldon 2008). The background variables remain of interest in studies of parental involvement and were included in all major analyses in this study.

ANALYSIS

Using Stata, we analyzed two-level hierarchical linear models (HLM) that permitted attention to the independent and simultaneous relationships of key explanatory variables at the district and school levels.[3] HLM accounts for the fact that schools within a district are guided by the same policies and leaders and are likely to be more similar to one another in many ways than schools selected at random. HLM techniques, which adjust for the impact of clustered errors (Raudenbush and Bryk 2002), produce less-biased and more accurate estimates than do less rigorous methods for studying school (level 1) and district (level 2) effects on the quality of partnership program implementation and outreach.

To address this study's first two research questions, we analyzed a series of HLM models focused on two dependent variables—the quality of *basic program implementation* and the extent of *advanced outreach* to all families. First, we estimated a fully unconditional model with no predictors to identify within- and between-district variance for each outcome. Then we analyzed conditional models that tested the relationships of school-level variables and the district-level variable with each outcome.

In all models, the intercept was defined as random, slopes were fixed, and continuous measures were grand-mean-centered so that each level 1 coefficient represented the average effect across schools. Significant coefficients for level 1 variables indicate that school-based actions and experiences affected the quality of basic program implementation and advanced outreach to involve all families. Significant coefficients for the level 2 variables indicate that district leaders' assistance to ATPs independently affected the quality of schools' basic organization and the advanced outreach of their partnership programs.

To address the third and fourth research questions, we conducted ordinary least squares (OLS) regression analyses in step-wise progression to examine whether the school variables in the HLM analyses (principal and school reports of district support for partnerships) were associated with parents' participation in their children's education and students' average daily attendance. We also explored a constellation of district variables to see whether the duration (years) of districts' membership in NNPS was associated with leadership qualities and with district leaders' reports about their schools' progress on partnership program development.

RESULTS

The initial HLM unconditional analyses showed that 12.1 percent of the variance in basic program implementation and 11.4 percent of the variance in advanced outreach to involve all families were between districts. There was, then, enough between-district variance to explore the relationships between district characteristics and the two program outcome variables at the school level.

Basic Program Implementation

In table 1, school-level data in model 1 show that schools with a greater percentage of students receiving free or reduced-price meals reported lower levels of basic program implementation ($B = 0.003$, $p \leq 0.006$). Model 1 also shows that, with demographic characteristics statistically controlled, schools were more likely to implement a partnership program at a basic level when there was strong principal support for partnerships and when schools' ATPs reported receiving helpful support from their district leaders ($B = 0.466$, $p \leq 0.000$, and $B = 0.201$, $p \leq 0.000$, respectively). With poverty level, principal support, and schools' reports of district support taken into account, elementary and secondary schools in NNPS, large and small schools, and those with more or fewer ELLs did not differ significantly on the nature and extent of their basic program implementation.

Model 2 shows the two-level model for basic partnership program implementation that adds district leaders' reports of the extent and quality of their facilitation of schools' ATPs to the equation in place of the schools' reports of district support. The analysis confirms the results reported for model 1 indicating that schools had stronger basic partnership pro-

---

3. The authors thank Sol Bee Jung, graduate student at Johns Hopkins University's School of Education, for her assistance with these analyses.

Table 1. Multilevel Models Predicting Basic and Advanced Partnership Program Implementation

	Basic Implementation		Advanced Implementation	
	Model 1	Model 2	Model 3	Model 4
School-level predictors				
School level (elementary/secondary)	-0.075	-0.090	-0.078	-0.080
Total enrollment	0.050	-0.059	0.004	-0.007
Percent free or reduced-price meals	-0.003*	0.002	0.000	0.000
Percent English language learners (ELL)	0.002	0.002	0.002	0.001
Principal support	0.466***	0.550***	0.361***	0.465***
School reports of district support	0.201***	—	0.177***	—
District-level predictors				
Active facilitation of schools	—	0.108**	—	-0.017

Source: 2014 NNPS School UPDATE Survey and 2014 District UPDATE Surveys.
Notes: N = 290 schools in 21 districts. Unstandardized coefficients are reported.
*$p < .05$; **$p < .01$; ***$p < .001$

gram implementation when there was greater principal support for family and community engagement ($B = 0.550, p \leq 0.000$). Model 2 extends knowledge by showing that district leaders' reports of the nature and quality of their active facilitation of schools' partnerships programs were associated with schools' stronger implementation of basic partnership program elements ($B = 0.108, p \leq 0.003$). These findings spotlight the independent important impact of both school leadership and district leadership on the extent to which schools organize, plan, and implement efforts to engage families in their children's education.

Advanced Program Implementation

In table 1, models 3 and 4 report results of HLM analyses predicting advanced implementation of partnership programs that aimed to engage all students' families, especially those who were previously uninvolved or "hard to reach." In these models, the demographic characteristics of school populations are not significant explanatory variables. In model 3, principal support and schools' reports of district support are significantly and positively associated with more active outreach to engage all families ($B = 0.361, p \leq 0.000$, and $B = 0.177, p \leq .001$, respectively). In model 4, only principal support remains an important variable for meeting challenges to engage all families ($B = 0.465$, $p \leq 0.000$).

Results for Parents and Students

Table 2 uses OLS regression to extend the results of the HLM analyses by exploring the temporal nature of schools' partnership program development. Column 1 reproduces the school-level HLM analyses indicating that low-poverty schools reported stronger basic partnership program implementations. With demographic variables accounted for, schools with strong principal support for partnerships and school teams' reports of helpful district support were significantly associated with strong partnership programs.

In column 2, analyses indicate that in addition to principal support ($\beta = 0.140, p \leq 0.016$), the nature and quality of schools' basic program implementation was positively and significantly linked to advanced implementation to engage all students' families in productive ways ($\beta = 0.471, p \leq 0.000$).

Following potential influence paths, column 3 shows that elementary schools and low-poverty schools had greater percentages of parents engaged than did secondary schools ($\beta = -0.351, p \leq 0.000$, and $\beta = -0.463, p \leq 0.000$, respectively). Additionally, with all background variables statistically controlled, schools with more advanced program implementations had more parents engaged in their children's education ($\beta = 0.286, p \leq 0.000$).

Column 4 indicates that when more families were engaged, students attended school on

Table 2. OLS Regression Analyses of School-Level Predictors of Partnership Program Implementation, Parent Participation, and Student Average Daily Attendance

Variables	Basic Implementation	Advanced Implementation	Parent Participation	Average Daily Attendance
School level (elementary/secondary)	−0.067	−0.067	−0.351***	−0.043
Total enrollment	0.014	−0.077	0.024	0.076
Percent free or reduced-price meals	−0.162***	0.060	−0.463***	−0.083
Percent ELLs	0.073	0.017	0.069	−0.004
Principal support	0.443***	0.140*	0.049	−0.031
School report of district support	0.265***	0.084	−0.036	−0.033
Basic implementation		0.471***	−0.014	−0.037
Advanced implementation			0.286***	0.052
Parent participation				0.172*

Source: 2014 NNPS School *UPDATE* Survey.
Notes: N = 303 schools. Standardized coefficients are reported.
*p < .05; **p < .01; ***p < .001

a more regular basis, as reported in rates of average daily attendance ($\beta = 0.172$, $p \leq 0.023$). Table 2 suggests the stage-wise development of partnership programs. Plans and actions to implement a basic partnership program to address challenges to engage all families were likely to have taken place before advanced work and to have contributed to it. More parents in these schools became engaged and more engaged parents contributed to better student attendance.

The results reported in tables 1 and 2 suggest that programs of partnership can be strengthened and improved over time. Some schools do more than others to organize the structures and processes of a basic partnership program. The stronger the basic program, the more likely a school is to address challenges to engage parents who typically are under- or uninvolved, including fathers and parents who speak languages other than English.

Qualities of District Leadership

To delve deeper into the finding that district leadership matters for schools' programs and progress on partnerships, we used an independent measure from NNPS records that was separate from the survey data. District leaders had been members of NNPS for one to nineteen years, with an average of 6.8 years. Using this indicator for all districts that reported *UPDATE* data in 2014 (N = 39, including the twenty-one districts with four or more schools in the HLM sample), we explored whether the number of years in NNPS affected the nature and extent of district leadership and reports of whether schools were making good progress versus no or little progress in their programs of family and community engagement.[4]

Table 3 reports a constellation of informative correlates. Years in NNPS was not significantly related to general leadership qualities (for example, for establishing a district office for partnership program development, planning a budget, and writing work plans, $r = 0.127$ NS). This reflects the fact that districts joined NNPS with a common goal to get some assistance in improving their partnership programs. By contrast, years in NNPS was significantly correlated with major measures of how

---

4. In addition to the district facilitation scale explained in the section on measures and used in the HLM analyses in table 1, measures explored in table 3 include a fourteen-item *leadership* scale ($\alpha = 0.66$) on efforts to establish an office for partnerships; a seven-item *emphasis on evaluation* scale ($\alpha = 0.66$) on whether district leaders evaluated their own and schools' partnership programs; and a thirteen-item *collegial support* scale ($\alpha = 0.84$) on cooperation for partnership program development from district, school, family, and community members (Epstein and Ames 2016).

Table 3. Constellation of Correlates of Years of Membership in NNPS with District Leadership, Facilitation, Evaluation, Support, and Schools' Progress on Partnerships

	Leadership	Facilitation	Emphasis on Evaluation	Collegial Support	Percent Schools Making Good Progress
Duration of district effort on partnerships (years in NNPS)	0.127 (NS)	0.482**	0.373*	0.395*	0.384*

Source: 2014 NNPS District *UPDATE* Survey.
Notes: N = 39 districts. Zero-order correlation coefficients are reported.
$*p < .05; **p < .01$

well district leaders facilitated school teams ($r = 0.483, p < 0.01$), emphasized the evaluation of progress on partnerships ($r = 0.373, p < 0.05$), and worked with colleagues on the partnership agenda ($r = 0.395, p < 0.05$). The duration variable also was related to district leaders' reports of the percentage of schools making good progress on partnership program development ($r = 0.384, p < 0.01$). The consistent pattern of correlates in table 3 suggests that NNPS plays a role in guiding district leaders to increasingly take action to assist their schools in implementing research-based approaches to program development with the goal of increasing the number and diversity of families who become engaged in their children's education.

SUMMARY AND DISCUSSION

We drew from organizational learning and leadership theories to study the development of school-based programs of family and community engagement. The study extended prior research with new evidence that school and district attention to partnership program development is associated with outreach to families, responses from parents, and results for students.

Independent reports from school-based ATPs and from district leaders identified a likely progression in program development. Results suggest that strong principal support and active guidance from district leaders—for example, in forming teams and writing plans—helped school teams establish their basic partnership programs. School teams with strong principal support and helpful district leaders progressed to more advanced implementation activities to engage families who often are hard to reach (for example, multicultural families, fathers, volunteers). Stronger school programs increased the prevalence of parents who were partners in education, and schools with more engaged families reported higher rates of students' average daily attendance. These well-organized, goal-linked partnership programs that increased the involvement of more and different parents helped improve student attendance as well as other academic and behavioral outcomes.

The interactions of school principals, partnership teams, and district Leaders for Partnerships reflected the assumptions of sociocultural and organizational learning theories and activated the content of the theory of overlapping spheres of influence for school, family, and community partnerships. The nonsurvey measure of district leaders' years of NNPS membership suggested that these leaders benefited over time from participating in the research-based network. Longer experience was linked to various leadership qualities—active facilitation of school teams, strong collegial support, attention to evaluation—and to reports that more schools were making good progress in developing programs of family and community engagement.

It should be noted that all schools in NNPS are guided by handbooks, tools, evaluation requirements, professional development workshops and webinars, and frequent communications to help them establish, implement, and continually improve their programs of family and community engagement. District leaders are guided to prepare and motivate school-based teams to organize and improve their school-based programs to engage students' families and community partners.

The variable "years in NNPS" reminds us that districts and schools join NNPS with different histories and experiences conducting family and community engagement activities. No school—whether an NNPS member or not—is at "ground zero" in connecting with families. All schools conduct at least a few traditional activities (for example, sending home report cards, having some parent-teacher conferences, distributing a school newsletter, conducting a favorite activity such as a spring fair or a family reading night). Most schools, however, do not plan, evaluate, and improve their programs and practices of partnerships in systematic ways. Districts and schools join NNPS to learn to work systematically to organize partnership programs as a component of good school organization and to engage all students' families—not just a few—as partners in children's education. Good plans, evaluations, and continuous improvements are needed by district leaders and school teams to change what may be haphazard or random family and community engagement activities (Weiss, Lopez, and Rosenberg 2010) into more effective and equitable partnership programs (Epstein et al. 2009).

This study supports and extends other studies that have linked family engagement with improved student attendance (Sheldon 2007; Sheldon and Jung, 2015). Student attendance is a leading indicator of student learning, achievement test scores, and graduation from high school (Balfanz et al. 2007; Mac Iver and Messel 2013). This study suggests that systematic efforts by district leaders and school teams to engage families in their children's education can help, albeit indirectly, to improve attendance.

Countless other studies, reviews, and meta-analyses have shown that goal-linked family engagement significantly improves student learning in specific academic subjects across the grades (Catsambis 2001; Fan and Chen 2001; Galindo and Sheldon 2012; Jeynes 2003, 2012; Sénéchal and LeFevre 2002; Van Voorhis 2011; Van Voorhis et al. 2013). This study extends knowledge by identifying a sequence of program development actions that help schools strengthen their programs to engage more and different families and contribute to results for students.

Tables 1 and 2 raise an interesting question about whether schools face challenges in engaging subgroups of families. Results show that the percentage of students who are English language learners is not significantly associated with schools' basic or advanced program implementations. Results also show that the measure of poverty—the percentage of students eligible for free or reduced-price meals—is a more serious challenge for programs of family engagement. There are typically fewer ELL students in schools—under 10 percent, except in a few states—than students in poverty, who make up about 48 percent of the student body in the average school in the United States (National Center for Education Statistics 2015) and over 65 percent, on average, in this sample.

Federal law (U.S. Department of Education 2015) requires educators to communicate with all families in languages they understand. Most districts and schools in NNPS are taking this regulation seriously and report that immigrant and refugee families are responsive to outreach activities (Epstein and Ames 2016; Sheldon and Ames 2016). Having relatively few ELL students and specific goals to communicate with families who speak languages other than English at home may help to explain why the ELL variable is not a significant determinant of schools' partnership programs.

By contrast, schools with a large number of students in families with low income often face many challenges and are themselves underresourced. Educators may be challenged to give attention to family and community engagement at the same time that they are working to improve academic, behavioral, and health-related programs for children in poverty. This is understood, but the most important coefficients in table 1 show that with all other variables statistically controlled, schools that serve diverse students in any community can organize basic and advanced partnership programs if they have strong principal support for family engagement and helpful assistance from district leaders.

The results of this study are of interest because, across the country, districts and schools are becoming more diverse economically, racially, culturally, and linguistically (Fortuny and Hernandez 2010). Most educators still struggle to communicate with and engage all students' families at all grade levels (Markow and Pieters 2012). At the same time, most parents still struggle with remaining engaged in their children's education at each grade level to help them do their best in school (Harris and Robinson, this issue). Schools in this study served diverse populations of students and families, with the majority in high-poverty communities. It is important to note that the schools that did more to apply research-based structures and processes to their work on partnerships were more likely to conduct basic and advanced activities that engaged more families in their children's education, regardless of the families' demographics.[5]

LIMITATIONS

Although this study extends knowledge on partnership programs with new analyses of nested data from schools and their district leaders, it has limitations that need attention in future research. The limited number of districts in the sample seriously restricted the HLM analyses at the district level in table 1 to one key variable—district facilitation of schools. Future studies with larger samples of districts will be able to more fully explore the dynamics of district leaders' influence on schools' partnership programs. Table 3 introduced other measures of district leadership that may affect the quality of schools' programs of family and community engagement.

The data in this study were cross-sectional. It was possible to frame analyses with measures that represented early and later time periods to explore potential paths of influence from initial basic organization of programs to advanced outreach, to parents' responses, and to rates of student attendance. However, these were proxies for measures taken over time. The suggested step-wise progress in program development must be tested in future studies with longitudinal school, district, parent, and student data to confirm or correct the reported results. Future longitudinal studies of districts and their schools will permit more complex and better-specified multilevel models to understand the temporal order of actions in the development of district leadership and school programs of family and community engagement.

This study relied on survey data, which, like all research methods, have strengths and weaknesses. One strength, which permitted our HLM analyses, was having data from multiple reporters at the district and school levels. Another strength was having data at the school level on the percentage of engaged parents and rates of average daily student attendance, which extended our ability to focus on the results of partnership programs beyond prior studies. We also introduced an independent measure, years in NNPS, to explore how the duration of their efforts affected district leaders' support for and guidance of schools' partnership programs. Still, the reported results would be strengthened by nonsurvey data, such as site visits for independent observations of district leaders' work with schools and action team meetings, or in-depth interviews with purposeful samples of district leaders, school principals, teachers, parents, and students to confirm or refute the survey results.[6] Similarly, the survey data on students' average daily attendance would be stronger if official records on attendance were collected, and the scope of the study could also be enlarged with data on student achievement, behavior, and other indicators of students' success in school.

The study worked to minimize shared reporter bias and mono-source bias (Spector

---

5. See evidence of how these processes work in economically advantaged and disadvantaged districts and schools that serve families with diverse socioeconomic, cultural, racial, and linguistic backgrounds in Thomas et al. (2015) and in "Success Stories" at the NNPS website, www.partnershipschool.org.

6. See Sanders (2008, 2009) for prior qualitative studies on how district leaders' facilitative actions helped ATPs improve the quality of their partnership programs and engagement of families.

2014) with independent reports from multiple reporters—namely, district leaders and school-based ATPs. This permitted us to check whether school reports about district leaders' assistance matched the reports from the district leaders themselves. These features of the multilevel sample strengthened the credibility of results indicating the importance of district leadership for schools' progress on partnerships. However, although districts and schools in this study varied in their demographics and the duration of their work on partnerships, they all were active members of NNPS. Thus, they could carry a shared bias to emphasize their positive work on partnerships.

Future studies should guard against shared reporter bias by collecting multiple sources of information (for example, school records of parent participation in parent-teacher conferences, workshops, or other events) to double-check school and district reports on the extent of parents' participation. Comparisons of the patterns of program development in NNPS-member schools with non-NNPS sites will clarify whether research-based approaches result in more effective and more equitable partnership programs. Multiple reporters, multiple records, case and control situations, and useful artifacts will minimize the biases that are inherent in survey data and help to validate or refute the findings of this study.

CONCLUSION

At the time of the EEO report, family involvement was reported for and expected from those with high income and more formal education. This study suggests that family involvement is not a prescribed or "fixed" behavior, but a matter of school and district organization to promote equitable connections between the home, the school, and the community that benefit more—or all—students. Our results show that when schools and districts successfully plan and implement programs of partnerships, they can change old patterns that limit involvement to some parents and engage more and different families in children's education.

We started research on the design, development, and implementation of partnership programs in the early 1980s by recognizing the social fact repeated in EEO and other studies in the 1960s and1970s that children whose parents are involved in their education tend to do better in school. If families are so important in children's education, we asked, how can all schools engage all families in ways that increase student success in school? How can all schools engage those families with fewer educational and economic advantages in their children's education across the grades? And in schools that succeed in engaging these families, do the families respond and are there improvements in their children's attendance, achievement, and other indicators of success in school?

Although there is value in ongoing research on what parents do on their own to increase their children's learning and development, such studies are likely to continue to report that some parents are engaged and others are confused or waiting for guidance on how to be productively engaged in their children's education. We believe that it is critical to extend research on whether and how district and school leadership and programs of partnership increase the number and diversity of involved parents and whether and how their engagement affects student success in school. This study suggests that when effective and equitable school organizational practices are in place, more parents become involved and students benefit.

The results of this study have implications for policy and practice. Education policy is not an end in itself. In complex, multilevel systems, an official policy cannot be enacted without establishing a leadership structure, professional development, a budget, evaluations, incentives, and consequences. This study suggests that even though it may be necessary to have a policy on the books to encourage attention to parental involvement, it is not enough to tell schools or districts just to do something to engage families. Rather, it is critical to have knowledgeable leaders, research-based structures and processes, and strong content in place at the school and district levels to establish and improve plans and practices that promote more equitable and meaningful partnerships with all students' families. When policy is accompanied by factors that support enactment, more schools do more to engage all families in goal-linked practices that may contribute to improved attendance and student success in school.

Since the time of the EEO report—and indeed, spurred by it—sociologists, psychologists, and education researchers have built a field of study that goes well beyond the "contest mentality" of the 1960s and 1970s. The question once phrased as a competition—which is more important, the family or the school?—is no longer useful and instead has become one about an ongoing research agenda: what are the contributions of collaborative relationships among schools, families, and the community to student learning and development?

There are some in research and in education who still hold the old view that family engagement is about the parents and that it is up to parents to get involved—or not—in their children's education. This view omits the concept of *partnership* and ignores the benefits of a strong agreement among educators, parents, and policy leaders that education is a shared responsibility of home, school, and community. NNPS aims to help districts and schools understand that partnerships are a means to help more students succeed and as such should be part of school organization—not external to the school. With this view, it is possible for districts and schools to fulfill the intent of written policies for parental involvement with effective actions that promote more equal educational opportunities for more students.

It is a social fact that families are important in children's lives. The new question that we pose for research, policy, and practice focuses on whether it is possible to change the distribution of involved families from a few economically advantaged families to all families, so that more students benefit from family support, encouragement, and participation in their education. This study suggests that this challenge is being met, incrementally, by districts and schools that apply research-based approaches to organize and continually improve programs and practices of family and community engagement as an essential component of school organization.

REFERENCES

Balfanz, Robert, Liza Herzog, and Douglas J. Mac Iver. 2007. "Preventing Student Disengagement and Keeping Students on the Graduation Path in Urban Middle-Grades Schools: Early Identification and Effective Interventions." *Educational Psychologist* 42(4): 223–35.

Bryk, Anthony S., Louis M. Gomez, Alicia Grunow, and Paul G. LeMahieu. 2015. *Learning to Improve: How America's Schools Can Get Better at Getting Better*. Cambridge, Mass.: Harvard Education Press.

Bryk, Anthony S., Penny B. Sebring, Elaine Allensworth, Stuart Luppescu, and John Q. Easton. 2010. *Organizing Schools for Improvement: Lessons from Chicago*. Chicago: University of Chicago Press.

Catsambis, Sophia. 2001. "Expanding Knowledge of Parental Involvement in Children's Secondary Education: Connections with High School Seniors' Academic Success." *Social Psychology of Education* 5(2): 149–77.

Coleman, James S., Ernest Q. Campbell, Carol J. Hobson, James M. McPartland, Alexander M. Mood, Frederick D. Weinfeld, and Robert L. York. 1966. *Equality of Educational Opportunity*. Washington: U.S. Department of Health, Education, and Welfare, Office of Education.

Cowan, Kristen Tosh. 2003. "Parental Involvement." In *The New Title I: The Changing Landscape of Accountability* by Kristen Tosh Cowan. Washington, D.C.: Thompson Publishing.

Elmore, Richard F. 2004. *School Reform from the Inside Out: Policy, Practice, and Performance*. Cambridge, Mass.: Harvard Education Publishing Group.

Epstein, Joyce L. 1987. "Toward a Theory of Family-School Connections: Teacher Practices and Parent Involvement." In *Social Intervention: Potential and Constraints*, edited by Klaus Hurrelmann, Franz-Xaver Kaufmann, and Friedrich L. Lösel. New York: DeGruyter.

———. 2008. "Research Meets Policy and Practice: How Are School Districts Addressing NCLB Requirements for Parental Involvement?" In *No Child Left Behind and the Reduction of the Achievement Gap: Sociological Perspectives on Federal Educational Policy*, edited by Alan R. Sadovnik, Jennifer O' Day, George Bohrnstedt, and Kathryn Borman. New York: Routledge.

———. 2011. *School, Family, and Community Partnerships: Preparing Educators and Improving Schools.* 2nd ed. Boulder, Colo.: Westview Press.

———. Forthcoming. "Creating a National Network on School, Family, and Community Partnerships: Multi-level Goals, Challenges, and Successes." In *Proceedings of the Projecto ESCXEL—Rede de Escolas de Excelência.* First International Conference, New University of Lisbon, Portugal (November 2014).

Epstein, Joyce L., and R. Tyler Ames. 2016. *Annual NNPS Report: 2015 District Data.* Baltimore: Johns Hopkins University, Center on School, Family, and Community Partnerships.

Epstein, Joyce L., Claudia Galindo, and Steven B. Sheldon. 2011. "Levels of Leadership: Effects of District and School Leaders on the Quality of School Programs of Family and Community Involvement." *Educational Administration Quarterly* 47(3): 462–95.

Epstein, Joyce L., and Steven B. Sheldon. 2006. "Moving Forward: Ideas for Research on School, Family, and Community Partnerships. In *SAGE Handbook for Research in Education: Engaging Ideas and Enriching Inquiry*, edited by Clifton F. Conrad and Ronald C. Serlin. Thousand Oaks, Calif.: Sage Publications.

Epstein, Joyce L., et al. 2009. *School, Family, and Community Partnerships: Your Handbook for Action.* 3rd ed. Thousand Oaks, Calif.: Corwin.

Fan, Xitao, and Michael Chen. 2001. "Parental Involvement and Students' Academic Achievement: A Meta-analysis." *Educational Psychology Review* 13(1): 1–22.

Fortuny, Karina, and Donald J. Hernandez. 2010. "Characteristics of Children of Immigrants." Paper presented to the conference "Young Children in Immigrant Families and the Path to Educational Success." Urban Institute, Washington, D.C. (June 28).

Galindo, Claudia, and Steven B. Sheldon. 2012. "School and Home Connections and Children's Kindergarten Achievement Gains: The Mediating Role of Family Involvement." *Early Childhood Research Quarterly* 27(1): 90–103.

Harris, Angel L., and Keith Robinson. 2016. "A New Framework for Understanding Parental Involvement: Setting the Stage for Academic Success." *RSF: The Russell Sage Foundation Journal of the Social Sciences* 2(5). doi: 10.7758/RSF.2016.2.5.09.

Honig, Meredith I. 2006. "Street-Level Bureaucracy Revisited: Frontline District Central Office Administrators as Boundary Spanners in Education Policy Implementation." *Educational Evaluation and Policy Analysis* 28(4): 357–83.

———. 2008. "District Central Offices as Learning Organizations: How Sociocultural and Organizational Learning Theories Elaborate District Central Office Administrators' Participation in Teaching and Learning Improvement Efforts." *American Journal of Education* 114(4): 627–64.

Huber, George P. 1991. "Organizational Learning: The Contributing Processes and the Literatures." *Organizational Science* 2(1): 88–115.

Hutchins, Darcy J., and Steven B. Sheldon. 2013. *Annual Report: 2012 School Update Data.* Baltimore: Johns Hopkins University. Center on School, Family, and Community Partnerships.

Jeynes, William H. 2003. "A Meta-analysis: The Effects of Parental Involvement on Minority Children's Academic Achievement." *Education and Urban Society* 35(2): 202–18.

———. 2012. "A Meta-analysis of the Efficacy of Different Types of Parental Involvement Programs for Urban Students." *Urban Education* 47(4): 706–42.

Knapp, Michael S. 2008. "How Can Organizational and Sociocultural Learning Theories Shed Light on District Instructional Reform?" *American Journal of Education* 114(4): 521–39.

Leithwood, Kenneth, and Nona A. Prestine. 2002. "Unpacking the Challenges of Leadership at the School and District Level." In *The Educational Leadership Challenge: Redefining Leadership for the 21st Century*, edited by Joseph Murphy. Chicago: University of Chicago Press.

Louis, Karen Seashore. 2008. "Learning to Support Improvement: Next Steps for Research on District Practice." *American Journal of Education* 114(4): 681–89.

Mac Iver, Martha A., and Matthew Messel. 2013. "The ABCs of Keeping on Track to Graduation: Research Findings from Baltimore." *Journal of Education for Students Placed at Risk* 18(1): 50–67.

Markow, Dana, and Andrea Pieters. 2012. *The MetLife Survey of the American Teacher: Teachers, Parents, and the Economy.* New York: MetLife, Inc.

Mayrowetz, David. 2008. "Making Sense of Distributed Leadership: Exploring the Multiple Usages of the Concept in the Field." *Educational Administration Quarterly* 44(3): 424–35.

National Center for Education Statistics (NCES). 2015. "Fast Facts: Educational Institutions." *Digest of Educational Statistics 2013* (NCES 2015-011). Available at: https://nces.ed.gov/fastfacts/display.asp?id=84 (accessed October 12, 2015).

Raudenbush, Steven, and Anthony Bryk. 2002. *Hierarchical Linear Models: Applications and Data Analysis Methods*. Thousand Oaks, Calif.: Sage Publications.

Sanders, Mavis G. 2008. "Using Diverse Data to Develop and Sustain School, Family, and Community Partnerships: A District Case Study." *Education Management, Administration, and Leadership* 36(4): 530–45.

———. 2009. "Collaborating for Change: How an Urban School District and Community-Based Organization Supports and Sustains School, Family, and Community Partnerships." *Teachers College Record* 111(7): 1693–1712.

Sanders, Mavis G., and Steven B. Sheldon. 2009. *Principals Matter: A Guide to School, Family, and Community Partnerships*. Thousand Oaks, Calif.: Corwin Press.

Sénéchal, Monique, and Jo-Anne LeFevre. 2002. "Parental Involvement in the Development of Children's Reading Skill: A Five-Year Longitudinal Study." *Child Development* 73(2): 455–60.

Senge, Peter. 1990. *The Fifth Discipline: The Art and Practice of the Learning Organization*. New York: Doubleday.

Sheldon, Steven B. 2005. "Testing a Structural Equations Model of Partnership Program Implementation and Parent Involvement." *The Elementary School Journal* 106(5): 171–87.

———. 2007. "Improving Student Attendance with a School-Wide Approach to School-Family-Community Partnerships." *Journal of Educational Research* 100(5): 267–75.

———. 2008. "Getting Families Involved with NCLB: Factors Affecting Schools' Enactment of Federal Policy." In *No Child Left Behind and the Reduction of the Achievement Gap: Sociological Perspectives on Federal Educational Policy*, edited by Alan R. Sadovnik, Jennifer O' Day, George Bohrnstedt, and Kathryn Borman. New York: Routledge.

Sheldon, Steven B., and R. Tyler Ames. 2016. *Annual NNPS Report: 2014 School Data*. Baltimore: Johns Hopkins University, Center on School, Family, and Community Partnerships.

Sheldon, Steven B., and Sol Bee Jung. 2015. "Exploring How School-Family Partnerships Improve Attendance: Principals, Teachers, and Program Organization." Paper presented to the annual conference of the American Educational Researchers Association. Chicago (April).

Spector, Paul E. 2014. "Survey Design and Measure Development." In *Oxford Handbook of Quantitative Methods in Psychology*, edited by Todd D. Little. Oxford: Oxford University Press.

Spillane, James P., and John B. Diamond. 2007. *Distributed Leadership in Practice*. New York: Teachers College Press.

Stein, Mary Kay, and Cynthia E. Coburn. 2008. "Architectures for Learning: A Comparative Analysis of Two Urban School Districts." *American Journal of Education* 114(4): 583–626.

Supovitz, Jonathan A. 2006. *The Case for District-Based Reform*. Cambridge, Mass.: Harvard University Press.

Thomas, Brenda G., Marsha D. Greenfeld, Courtney R. Sender, and Joyce L. Epstein. 2015. *Promising Partnership Practices 2015*. Baltimore: Johns Hopkins University, National Network of Partnership Schools.

U.S. Department of Education. 2015. Elementary and Secondary Education Act (ESEA), also known as Every Student Succeeds Act (ESSA). Public Law 114-95. Washington: U.S. Government Printing Office.

Van Voorhis, Frances L. 2011. "Costs and Benefits of Family Involvement in Homework." *Journal of Advanced Academics* 22(2): 220–49.

Van Voorhis, Frances L., Michele Maier, Joyce L. Epstein, and Chrishana M. Lloyd. 2013. *The Impact of Family Involvement on the Education of Children Ages 3–8*. New York: MDRC.

Van Voorhis, Frances L., and Steven B. Sheldon. 2004. "Principals' Roles in the Development of U.S. Programs of School, Family, and Community Partnerships." *International Journal of Educational Research* 41(1): 55–70.

Weick, Karl E. 1995. *Sensemaking in Organizations*. Thousand Oaks, Calif.: Sage Publications.

Weiss, Heather, M. Elena Lopez, and Heidi Rosenberg. 2010. *Beyond Random Acts: Family, School, and Community Engagement as an Integral Part of Education Reform.* Cambridge, Mass.: Harvard Family Research Program. Information available at: http://www.hfrp.org/publications-resources/browse-our-publications/beyond-random-acts-family-school-and-community-engagement-as-an-integral-part-of-education-reform (accessed October 6, 2015).

Wenger, Etienne. 1998. *Communities of Practice: Learning, Meaning, and Identity.* Cambridge: Cambridge University Press.

Accountability, Inequality, and Achievement: The Effects of the No Child Left Behind Act on Multiple Measures of Student Learning

JENNIFER L. JENNINGS AND DOUGLAS LEE LAUEN

Scholars continue to debate whether gains on the state tests used for accountability generalize to other measures of student achievement. Using panel data on students from a large urban school district, we estimate the impact of accountability pressure related to the No Child Left Behind Act on two measures of academic achievement: the state test and an "audit" test that is not tied to the accountability system. Overall, we find that accountability pressure is associated with increased state test scores in math and lower audit math and reading test scores. However, the sources of state and audit test score divergence varied by students' race. Black students in schools facing the most accountability pressure made no gains on state tests, and their losses on audit math tests were twice as large as those of Hispanic students. These findings highlight the importance of better understanding the mechanisms that produce heterogeneous effects of accountability pressure across achievement measures and subgroups.

Keywords: inequality, accountability, testing

How do we know whether students are learning? At the time of the 1964 Civil Rights Act, the prevailing view on assessing educational opportunity was to measure the inputs of schooling, such as teacher qualifications and the presence of science laboratories in predominantly minority schools. Coleman's *Equality of Educational Opportunity* report, required by section 402 of the Civil Rights Act, examined differences in inputs, but in a first for a national evaluation, it also examined differences in performance on standardized achievement tests. By shifting the discussion about equity from inputs to outputs, the EEO report transformed policy debates about the meaning of educational opportunity. For better or worse, in the years following the publication of the EEO Report scholars and policymakers came to define school quality in terms of standardized test scores. Culminating in the passage of the No Child Left Behind Act (NCLB), federal accountability relied heavily on standardized test scores, and teacher evaluations were increasingly tied to these scores as well.

With the newest reauthorization of the Elementary and Secondary Education Act—termed the Every Student Succeeds Act (ESSA) —authority over school-based accountability and teacher evaluation has devolved to the states, but the heavy reliance on standardized tests remains. Researchers have used state test scores to evaluate a wide range of policies, including high-stakes school accountability, charter schools' effectiveness, and teacher merit

Jennifer L. Jennings is associate professor of sociology at New York University. **Douglas Lee Lauen** is associate professor of public policy at the University of North Carolina at Chapel Hill.

We thank Peter Crosta, Kari Kozlowski, Casey Megan, and Heeju Sohn for their research assistance and Karl Alexander and Steve Morgan for their helpful comments. Direct correspondence to: Jennifer L. Jennings at jj73@nyu.edu, 295 Lafayette St., 4th Floor, New York, NY 10003; and Douglas Lee Lauen at dlauen@unc.edu, Department of Public Policy, UNC-Chapel Hill, Abernethy Hall, CB#3435, Room 121A, Chapel Hill, NC 27599.

pay. Policymakers also have called on these scores to make claims about changes in American students' achievement over time, as well as changes in achievement gaps between historically advantaged and disadvantaged groups. Because state test score gains have not always been reflected in gains on other tests, such as the National Assessment of Educational Progress (NAEP) or international assessments, others have suggested that state test score gains in the NCLB era may be illusory (Koretz 2008).

Given substantial increases in accountability pressure in the last decade, there is renewed scholarly (Koretz 2013; Neal 2013) and media interest in understanding why state test score gains may not generalize to other assessments. At least three reasons that do not reflect changes in teachers' instructional practice have been offered for the divergence between state test scores and audit test (those that are not directly tied to accountability) scores. The first is measurement error. In any given year, if a dog is barking outside of the classroom during a test, students may not perform up to their "true ability" on the test. However, we would not expect a measurement error–based mechanism such as this one to consistently favor state test performance, since random errors of measurement are equally likely to affect both types of test. Second, the timing of tests may differ, and that difference alone could lead to disparities in performance across tests. For example, if student growth curves on two tests are not parallel, or if test gains from one test depreciate over the summer more quickly than test gains from another, we might expect students to perform differently on tests given at the beginning of the school year compared to those given at the end of the school year. In addition, if differential rates of growth and depreciation vary by test *and* by student group (for example, lower- versus higher-income students), test timing may matter more for some groups than others. Third, students may not exert equal effort across all tests. For example, if a school holds a pep rally for the state test, students may try harder on that test than on other assessments.

The next three reasons for divergence may reflect accountability-induced changes in educational practice that are important in assessing the meaning of state test gains. The first of these is alignment between the domains to which the two tests intend to generalize. If these domains differ, we would not expect gains on state tests to generalize, and students in schools more "aligned" with state tests are likely to perform better on those tests. There is a fine line between alignment, however, and the second mechanism, which we describe as "teaching to the test."

For our purposes, "teaching to the test" refers to activities intended to increase test scores more than students' learning of the material has increased. This practice can raise scores because tests are based on a sampling principle, so that only a fraction of the domain is tested in any given year. Coaching students on material that predictably appears on the state test or presenting content in formats that mirror the state test are two of the most common forms of teaching to the test. State tests do not randomly sample from the state standards each year, so alignment to the state standards ("teaching to the standards") may produce different instructional practices than alignment to the specific frequency with which standards predictably appear on state tests ("teaching to the test").

Multiple factors have facilitated this type of teaching to the test. Test preparation firms have analyzed item maps from state tests to create benchmark tests and other materials that focus on predictably assessed standards. Teachers themselves can also access item maps linked to standards on many state education department websites. Recent studies provide suggestive evidence that teachers are responsive to test predictability: in a study of three states during the NCLB era (Jennings and Bearak 2014), students made larger gains on items testing predictable standards than on novel items. This finding could result from teaching to the test as opposed to teaching to the standards. If standards heavily sampled on the state test are not sampled at the same rate on an audit test, we would expect students to make larger gains on the state test.

Whether focusing on predictable content is a desirable practice depends on the relevance of each standard to the inference one wants to make from state test scores. State policymakers may believe that some standards are more important than others and explicitly build such guidance into their instructions to test designers. However, we are aware of no states that provided guidance to test firms at the individual standard level during the NCLB era; ultimately, testing contractors have made these decisions. If state tests are not designed with specific inference weights in mind for each standard, state test results may overstate learning and diverge from other test results when a small fraction of state standards are predictably tested over time and teachers focus their instruction on these standards.

Finally, heightened incentives to cheat on the state test may lead educators to alter student responses on the state test and not on other tests. One study that estimated the prevalance of cheating in the pre-NCLB era found that a minimum of 4 to 5 percent of Chicago Public Schools elementary teachers had cheated (Jacob and Levitt 2003). The prevalance of cheating in the NCLB era is unknown, but multiple cities have experienced cheating scandals in recent years. Some, like the scandal in Atlanta, have involved a significant number of administrators and teachers (Aviv 2014).

Despite the ongoing public debate about the meaning of state test score gains, no study has examined the impact of accountability pressure from NCLB on multiple tests taken by the same students. Our study addresses two research questions and, in doing so, informs policy debates about the effects of schools' responses to external pressures on achievement and inequality and the possible heterogeneous effects of accountability policy across schools and student groups. First, we investigate the average effects of accountability pressure from failing to meet NCLB's adequate yearly progress (AYP) targets for performance on both state tests and a second test, the Stanford Achievement Test, which we refer to as an "audit test." We are interested in the direction and magnitude of these effects on both tests, as well as in whether accountability pressure is associated with an increased performance gap between the two tests. Second, we establish whether the effects of accountability pressure on the two tests differ across schools facing varying risks for failing to reach AYP targets. In both cases, we also ask whether accountability pressure increases the performance gap between the two tests for some types of students and schools more than others.

LITERATURE REVIEW

In what follows, we review the literature in two areas: the effects of accountability pressure on multiple measures of student learning and subgroups, and heterogeneity in responses to accountability pressure across schools.

The Effects of Accountability Pressure on Multiple Measures of Student Learning

A number of studies have found that accountability systems improve average student outcomes on both state and national tests (Carnoy and Loeb 2002; Dee and Jacob 2009; Hanushek and Raymond 2004; Jacob 2005, 2007; Rouse et al. 2007; Lauen and Gaddis 2012). We would not expect state test gains and state NAEP gains to perfectly track each other, but state test gains typically outpace state NAEP gains, and the magnitudes of these differences are large. Most recently, Brian Jacob (2007) has found that state scores grew twice as much as NAEP scores in Texas, North Carolina, Arkansas, and Connecticut. Studies conducted in the pre-NCLB era established similar patterns. For example, Daniel Koretz and Sheila Barron (1998) found gains in math scores on Kentucky's state test three to four times as large as on the NAEP. Steven Klein and his colleagues (2000) found not only a similar pattern in Texas but also greater score inflation for black students than for white students. This research raises important questions about whether accountability pressure increases student learning more generally.

On the other hand, three national studies have found positive effects of No Child Left Behind on measures of student achievement beyond state test scores. These studies are distinctive from those just reviewed in that they use econometric approaches to establish NCLB effects; previous studies have looked at differential trends on two tests. The magnitude of these effects, however, is substantially smaller than the gains found on state tests. Thomas Dee and Brian Jacob's (2009) study of the effects of NCLB on NAEP scores relies on a comparison of states that implemented accountability systems prior to NCLB with those that did not. They find that NCLB increased state NAEP scores in fourth- and eighth-grade math, but not in fourth- or eighth-grade reading. A strategy similar to Dee and Jacob's is used in a related study by Manyee Wong, Thomas Cook, and Peter Steiner (2009), but they add to the analysis the level of difficulty of proficiency in each state; their results largely confirm Dee and Jacob's. Wong and her colleagues find positive effects on fourth- and eighth-grade math scores and evidence of positive effects on fourth-grade reading scores when states also had high standards for proficiency. Randall Reback, Jonah Rockoff, and Heather Schwartz's (2011) national study of schools in the Early Childhood Longitudinal Study: Kindergarten (ECLS-K) cohort finds small positive effects of NCLB accountability pressure on ECLS-K reading and science assessment scores, but no significant effects on ECLS-K math scores.

Our assessment of the importance of the generalizability of state test score gains to other measures of student achievement may also be affected if generalizability varied across student groups. For example, if gains for white students generalized from the state test to other exams but those for black students did not, we would want to assess further the instructional practices producing these results and consider whether differential exposure to particular instructional practices raises equity concerns.

Three previous studies of NAEP performance have examined the heterogeneous treatment effects of accountability systems but have focused only on their effects on one test—the NAEP. While Martin Carnoy and Susanna Loeb (2002) argue that strong accountability systems could narrow achievement gaps, Eric Hanushek and Margaret Raymond (2004) find that, relative to whites, Hispanics gained more in accountability states and black students gained less, though both of these point estimates fell short of statistical significance. Thus, the black-white achievement gap has actually increased as a result of accountability. More recently, as noted earlier, Dee and Jacob (2009) have estimated the impact of the No Child Left Behind Act by race and found decidedly mixed results across grades and subjects. For example, they identify larger positive effects for black and Hispanic students than for white students in fourth-grade math, but in fourth-grade reading white students gained while black and Hispanic students did not.

Taken together, these studies paint a mixed picture of the ability of accountability systems to narrow racial achievement gaps. Largely consistent across studies is the larger benefit for Hispanic students relative to black and white students, and the null effects of accountability on black students with the exception of fourth-grade math. Still, little is known about the effects of accountability pressure across demographic groups on multiple measures of student learning; addressing this gap is one goal of our study.

In sum, all of the studies described here establish positive average effects of NCLB beyond state tests but do not assess the generalizability of state test gains to other measures of achievement. Our study contributes to a small but growing literature examining the relationship between school-based responses to accountability pressure and student performance on multiple measures of learning, which requires student-level data and test scores from multiple exams. Only one study has examined the effect of accountability pressure on multiple tests, but this study is from the pre-NCLB era. Jacob (2005) used item-level data to better understand the mechanisms underlying differential gains across tests. Analyzing data from the Chicago Public Schools Iowa Test of Basic Skills (ITBS)—which at that time was high-stakes and used for student promotion decisions as well as school accountability—and a second measure of achievement, the Illinois Goals Assessment Program (IGAP), he found large gains on the high-stakes ITBS following the introduction of accountability, but no similar effects of the accountability system on the IGAP. Our study builds on those reviewed here by examining the effects of NCLB accountability pressure on schools in a district with multiple exams.

In the next section, we examine not only the average effects of accountability but the heterogeneous effects of accountability pressure across schools facing varying risks of failing AYP targets.

Heterogeneity in Responses to Accountability Pressure Across Schools

While the studies reviewed here have established the effects of accountability systems on outcomes, they have devoted less attention to studying heterogeneity in how educators perceive external pressures and react to them. Because the lever for change in accountability systems is educational improvement in response to external pressure, this is an important oversight.

The dominant view of educators' responses to accountability incentives predicts that in the absence of accountability systems, "schools choose an allocation [of resources] based on preferences about the relative importance of helping students improve different types of skills and the relative importance of helping different types of students make improvements" (Reback et al. 2011, 3). NCLB, in this view, introduces costs and benefits that are a function of the fraction of students passing state tests. High-performing schools gain no benefit from resource reallocation if they are almost certain to make AYP targets with current practices. Low-performing schools, on the other hand, reap the benefit of meeting the AYP target, assuming resource reallocation is successful, but such reallocation may be excessively costly for schools that face little chance of making that target. The cost-benefit ratio is therefore likely to be largest for schools near, but below, passing thresholds, and smaller for schools well below or well above passing thresholds.

From this perspective, educators calculate how close they are to making AYP targets and are most likely to respond if their calculations place their school on the margin of making those targets. This is the extant view on schools' responses to incentives in most of the economic and policy literature, which has documented a wide range of ways in which educators respond to accountability pressure by gaming the system (Figlio and Getzler 2002; Jacob 2005; Jacob and Levitt 2003; Neal and Schanzenbach 2010; Reback 2008). To be sure, work in this tradition acknowledges that schools with a low probability of making their AYP targets also face pressure to improve over a longer time frame. But these scholars generally contend that marginal schools will be the most responsive in the short term.

Other empirical evidence, however, is not consistent with this perspective. Combining school-level data on test performance and survey data from the RAND study of the implementation of NCLB in three states (Pennsylvania, Georgia, and California), Reback, Rockoff, and Schwartz (2011) find that the schools furthest from AYP targets were more likely to focus on students close to proficiency relative to those close to making AYP targets (53 percent of teachers versus 41 percent), to focus on topics emphasized on the state test (84 percent versus 81 percent), and to "look for particular styles and formats of problems in the state test and emphasize them in [their] instruction" (100 percent versus 80 percent). Another study reports larger effects of accountability pressure for the lowest-achieving schools than for schools near the margin of meeting proficiency targets (Jennings and Sohn 2014). Ethnographic and qualitative studies also suggest that schools with little chance of making the required targets nonetheless make substantial changes to their practice (Booher-Jennings 2005).

Our paper helps to adjudicate between these perspectives by contrasting modeling strategies that reflect these two theories of action. Determining whether schools on the margin of passing AYP targets are more responsive than those further away from doing so is important because it helps inform a theoretical understanding of schools' responses to external pressure, as well as to shape the design of accountability systems.

DATA AND METHODS

We analyze a longitudinal administrative data set of sixth- through eighth-grade students tested in the Houston Independent School District (HISD) between 2003 and 2007. HISD is the seventh-largest school district in the country and the largest in the state of Texas. Our sample is 58 percent Hispanic, 29 percent black, 9.5 percent white, and 3 percent Asian. About 80 percent of students in our sample are considered by the state to be economically disadvantaged, which is defined based on free and reduced-price lunch and welfare eligibility.

A unique feature of this study is the availability of multiple test scores for each student—both the Texas Assessment of Knowledge and Skills (TAKS) and the Stanford Achievement Test battery. The TAKS is administered to students in grades 3 to 11 in reading and English language arts, mathematics, writing, science, and social studies; reading and math are the only subjects tested every year between grades 3 and 8. The Stanford Achievement Test is administered to all students in grades 1 to 11 in reading, math, language, science, and social science. In 1996, HISD added the Stanford Achievement Test under pressure from a business task force that sought a nationally normed benchmark test (McAdams 2000). In this respect, the Stanford was intended to serve as an additional audit on state tests scores. Since that time, all students except for those with severe disabilities have been required to take the Stanford. The TAKS and the Stanford have similar test administration features: both have flexible time limits, and all of these tests are given in the spring, from early March (Stanford) to mid to late April (TAKS).

For several reasons, the TAKS represents the district's "high-stakes" test. First, and most important for our study, TAKS test scores are used to compute AYP under NCLB. Second, passing rates on these tests have been an integral part of Texas's accountability system since 1994 (Reback 2008). Under this system—which served as the model for No Child Left Behind—schools and districts are labeled "exemplary," "recognized," "acceptable," or "low-performing" based on their proficiency rates in each subject area. In most years, monetary rewards have been available for high-performing or improving schools, while low-performers are subject to sanctions, including school closure or reconstitution. Second, HISD has operated a performance pay plan since 2000 that provides monetary rewards to schools and teachers for state test results. Historically, the district based these rewards on campus accountability ratings, but in recent years it has rewarded individual teachers and schools based on their value-added on state tests. Third, during our study period, Texas required third-grade students to pass the TAKS reading test for grade promotion beginning in 2003. From 2005, fifth-grade students have been required to pass both the math and reading TAKS to be promoted.

The Stanford can be considered HISD's "audit" test in that it is not tied to the state accountability system. However, this test plays several important roles in the district. For example, it is used as one criterion for grade promotion in grades 1 through 8. HISD students are expected to perform above a minimum standard on the Stanford (for example, one grade level below average or above) as well as on the TAKS. While the Stanford is not a binding standard, as it is in districts and states with strict promotion policies, HISD's policy does provide an incentive for students to exert effort on the Stanford. In addition, the Stanford is used to place students in gifted, special education, and other programs. Finally, value-added measures from the Stanford tests have been a component of HISD's teacher performance pay plan since 2007, the final year of our study. In sum, the Stanford is lower stakes for adults relative to the TAKS, but not so for students. For our purposes, it is ideal that students have good reason to exert effort on both tests, but that the significance of the state and audit tests for educators varies.

It is worth noting other similarities and differences between these tests beyond their uses in the school district. Both tests are untimed and multiple-choice. The TAKS is intended to be a test of the Texas state standards, which enumerate what students should know and be able to do. For example, the eighth-grade math test asks students to master thirty-eight standards in five areas of mathematics (algebra, geometry, measurement, numbers and operations, and statistics and probability). Our analyses of item-level data from Texas that link each item to a state standard show that just half of these standards make up 65 percent of the test points—more than enough to pass the test.

The Stanford, on the other hand, is intended to provide a broader portrait of students' mastery in mathematics. Because the test is proprietary, we could not examine each

Table 1. Counts and Percentages of Students and Schools Failing to Meet AYP Targets, by Year

	Students			Middle Schools		
	No	Yes	Total	No	Yes	Total
2004	29,097	2,254	31,351	45	4	49
	92.81%	7.19%	100%	91.84%	8.16%	100%
2005	32,999	2,322	35,321	48	5	53
	93.43%	6.57%	100%	90.57%	9.43%	100%
2006	22,171	13,137	35,308	34	18	52
	62.79%	37.21%	100%	65.38%	34.62%	100%
2007	23,061	10,996	34,057	38	15	53
	67.71%	32.29%	100%	71.70%	28.30%	100%
Total	107,328	28,709	136,037	165	42	207
	78.90%	21.10%	100%	79.71%	20.29%	100%

Source: Authors' calculations from Houston Independent School District data.

item to assess content and complexity, but the test is aligned with National Council of Teachers of Mathematics standards. We have only been able to identify one analysis (Hoey, Campbell, and Perlman 2001) that maps the standards on the Texas Assessment of Academic Skills (TAAS) math test (in grade 4 only) to those covered on the Stanford; it finds considerable overlap, with 83 percent of the Texas standards represented on the Stanford. The Stanford is a bit more inclusive, with 74 percent of Stanford standards represented on the TAAS. Though we cannot quantify the breadth of the Stanford relative to the TAKS test, our analyses of item-level data from the TAKS suggest that predictable recurrences of certain standards may produce opportunities for teachers to focus more narrowly on tested content. The TAKS and Stanford tests are intended to test similar grade-level domains, but we do not argue that these domains are identical.

In sum, we believe that the Stanford is the best available instrument for assessing TAKS gains, but we recognize its limitations as well. Neither test has been validated against long-term outcomes. It is possible that gains on the TAKS do not transfer to the Stanford but nonetheless have important impacts on students' long-term outcomes (Deming et al. 2013).

Our study focuses on the effects of accountability pressure, defined as failing to meet AYP targets, on the gap between the two tests for middle school students in HISD. We note that this is a conservative estimate of accountability pressure, as even schools with little risk of missing state accountability targets probably feel pressure to perform since test results are made public. We limit our analysis to middle school students because by 2005 sufficient numbers of middle schools had failed to meet AYP targets to permit variation on our independent variable of interest. (Such was not the case for elementary schools.) Relatively few middle schools failed to reach AYP targets in 2003 or 2004, so only 6 to 7 percent of middle school students were exposed to NCLB accountability pressure in the early years of our study (see table 1).[1]

However, two changes in Texas education policy led to a large increase in schools failing to meet AYP targets over the period we study, and our analysis takes advantage of these policy changes. The cut scores for state tests were raised one standard error of measurement between 2003 and 2004 and again between 2005 and 2006. The percentage of students required to pass tests to make AYP standards also increased over this time: a nine- and six-

---

1. We have "forward-lagged" school accountability status, so schools failing to meet AYP targets in 2003 appear in table 1 as failing in 2004. Accountability ratings appear over the summer following spring testing. Therefore, the following year's AYP status could affect school practices and student test scores only in the following year.

percentage-point increase for math and reading, respectively, between 2004 and 2005, and another eight- and seven-percentage-point increase between 2006 and 2007. As a result of both the increase in cut scores and the level of performance required to make AYP targets, in 2006 and 2007 about one-third of students attended schools that faced pressure from NCLB to raise test scores, while very few students had faced such pressure in 2003.[2] These policy changes allow us to provide a cleaner estimate of the effects of accountability pressure than would be the case in a setting in which standards for proficiency are constant. In that case, variation in exposure to accountability pressure would be driven more by year-to-year shocks in performance and related processes, such as mean reversion. In contrast, we can observe changes in test score performance both before and after schools are exposed to pressure to meet AYP targets.

One important additional feature of the TAKS tests that allows for analytical leverage is that the proficiency standard for reading is much less difficult relative to the distribution of student performance than the standard for math. In 2003, the base year of our study, 64.7 percent of sixth- to eighth-grade students were deemed proficient on the math test, while 84.1 percent were deemed proficient on the reading test. As a result, about 65.9 percent of school AYP failures between 2003 and 2007 were a function only of math performance, while approximately 19.5 percent were a function of both reading and math performance and another 14.6 percent were because of reading performance only. Although we lack the power in this study to formally test for the effects of these different types of failure, we predict that we will see more divergence between the math tests than between the reading tests when schools face accountability pressure.

There is also variation on failing to meet AYP targets among HISD high schools—given that some estimates place the high school dropout rate in HISD at about 50 percent (Swanson 2006)—but a high school estimation sample would be censored and greatly reduced in size. In 2005, for example, we had 13,991 ninth-graders; by 2007, we had only 8,569 eleventh-graders, a shortfall of about 39 percent. There appears to be some attrition from middle schools, but it is much lower than among high school students. In 2005, we had 11,854 sixth-graders; by 2007, we had 11,202 eighth-graders, a shortfall of about 6 percent.

We have also taken care to rule out the influence of other non-accountability shocks to the district during our study period. In the 2005–2006 school year, Houston schools enrolled more than 5,200 students (3 percent of that year's student population) displaced by hurricanes Katrina and Rita. Two middle schools, Fondren and Revere, enrolled large numbers of displaced students. These schools failed to meet AYP targets owing to the performance of the special education subgroup, not that of the displaced students who had been exempted by the U.S. Department of Education from 2005–2006 AYP performance calculations.[3] Nevertheless, the addition of hundreds of traumatized students to the already struggling middle schools in Houston probably had spillover effects that made it much harder for middle schools serving these students to meet AYP targets. That situation does not, however, affect our results, which, because we are examining the incentive effects of accountability

---

2. An ideal analysis would not only examine the effects of overall AYP status but estimate the effects of subgroup-specific failure. In our study, only half of the schools that failed to reach AYP targets did not also miss the "all students" AYP target, so we lack the power to estimate these impacts on individual subgroups. By estimating the effect of AYP failure on all students, our analysis may miss responses at the subgroup level. This makes it more likely that the AYP effects reported here are *lower bounds of the true effect* (that is, that they are conservative estimates).

3. Statistics and background related to students displaced by hurricanes Katrina and Rita come from letters from the Texas Education Agency and the U.S. Department of Education dated August 1, 2006, and August 8, 2006, respectively (available from authors upon request). The results presented here include Revere, while sample restrictions exclude Fondren from our analysis sample. Excluding Revere from our analysis sample does not affect our findings (results from authors upon request).

threats on state and audit tests taken by the same students, are not sensitive to the exclusion of these schools from our sample.

We include all students enrolled in sixth through eighth grade between the years 2004 and 2007. We exclude students who took their TAKS test on a different campus than their Stanford test because of school mobility in the month between the two tests. Also excluded are those whose schools were exempted from AYP rating by NCLB (in 2003, four of forty-nine middle schools were exempted; in 2004 and 2005, two of fifty middle schools were exempted; and in 2006, two of forty-nine schools were exempted), schools with fewer than thirty students in any year, and schools with fewer than four panels. (In other words, we keep only schools with sufficient data on each year between 2004 and 2007, inclusive.) Our final repeated measures analysis sample includes about 74,000 unique students. Descriptive statistics on the sample of about 136,000 student-year observations are shown in table 2.

The primary dependent variable in our study is the gap between the state test (TAKS) and audit test (Stanford) scores, which have been standardized by grade level and year. However, beyond estimating the size of the gap, we are interested in how the gap arises. For example, a gap of 0.1 standard deviations could arise if students made progress on both tests, if they made progress on the state tests and not the audit tests, or if they fell back on both tests. We thus present models of the gap along with models separately predicting state test and audit test performance. The focal independent variable in our study is an indicator, coded [1,0], recording whether a school failed NCLB's AYP target in the previous year. We posit that schools failing to reach the AYP target would be under pressure to increase test score achievement the following year.[4] Whether teacher and principal actions focus on raising general academic skills or test-specific skills is the primary question of this study. Therefore, we hypothesize that students attending schools under accountability pressure from failing to reach AYP targets in the previous year will have larger test score gaps between the two tests than the same students had in years in which their schools met AYP targets in the previous year. In our view, this is because accountability pressure alters the relative costs and benefits of teaching state test–specific versus general academic skills content. As we discuss in detail later, whether teaching state test–specific skills is a positive or negative outcome is the subject of substantial debate.

Our primary specification is a regression with student fixed effects:

$$Gap_{ti} = \lambda_i + \beta_1 FailAYP_{t-1i} + \beta_2 X_{ti} + \beta_3 S_{ti} + \beta_4 Y_t + \beta_5 G_{ti} + \beta_6 Y_t G_{ti} + \varepsilon_{ti} \qquad (1)$$

In brief, equation 1 predicts the state test–audit test score gap for student i at time t as a function of whether the student's current school failed to meet AYP targets the previous year, controlling for student fixed effects, λ_i, student time-varying controls, X_{ti}, school time varying controls, S_{ti}, and year, grade, and year-by-grade fixed effects, Y_t, G_{ti}, and $Y_t G_{ti}$, respectively. We hypothesize that net of controls, β_1 will be positive because failure to meet accountability targets will cause teachers to focus more time and effort on state test–specific skills rather than on more general skills. We use a student fixed-effects model to control for students sorting into schools based on fixed unobservable student and family background characteristics. This approach eliminates all time-invariant between-student confounding and produces consistent parameter estimates when there is no within-student confounding of the accountability effect (that is, the accountability effect is uncorrelated with time-varying unmeasured student characteristics). The student fixed-effects approach requires within-student variation on accountability status to identify parameters. We identify the accountability effect

---

4. As noted previously, schools may fail to meet AYP targets because they miss targets for one or more subgroups. In a large enough sample, we could model the impact of subgroup-specific failure on students' academic progress. In our sample, however, approximately half of schools fail on the "all students" indicator as well as for subgroups; this limited sample does not allow us to investigate the role of subgroup failure. We note that our estimates should thus provide a conservative estimate of the impact of failing AYP on all students.

Table 2. Descriptive Statistics

Variable	Observations	Mean	Standard Deviation	Minimum	Maximum
Failed AYP	136,037	0.2110	0.4080	0	1
Risk of failing AYP					
Low	136,037	0.7998	0.4002	0	1
Medium	136,037	0.1005	0.3007	0	1
High	136,037	0.0997	0.2997	0	1
Math					
State test (math)	138,395	−0.0048	0.9961	−5.3568	4.5219
Audit test (math)	138,395	−0.0046	0.9982	−4.0058	5.2242
Math gap	138,395	−0.0002	0.6289	−7.3477	3.6538
Reading					
State test (reading)	133,416	−0.0021	1.0004	−6.3744	3.0515
Audit test (reading)	133,416	−0.0001	1.0020	−6.6144	5.1820
Reading gap	133,416	−0.0021	0.6719	−7.9530	5.4714
Student grades					
6	139,143	0.3349	0.4719	0	1
7	139,143	0.3403	0.4738	0	1
8	139,143	0.3248	0.4683	0	1
Observation years					
2004	139,143	0.2476	0.4316	0	1
2005	139,143	0.2538	0.4352	0	1
2006	139,143	0.2538	0.4352	0	1
2007	139,143	0.2448	0.4299	0	1
Student characteristics					
Female	139,140	0.5074	0.4999	0	1
Limited English proficiency	139,140	0.1217	0.3270	0	1
Special education	139,140	0.0622	0.2415	0	1
Economically disadvantaged	139,140	0.7971	0.4022	0	1
Student race					
Black	139,140	0.2932	0.4552	0	1
Hispanic	139,140	0.5780	0.4939	0	1
Asian	139,140	0.0330	0.1787	0	1
White	139,140	0.0950	0.2932	0	1
School characteristics					
Percent black	139,143	29.3240	24.9079	0	98.9691
Percent special education	139,143	6.2255	3.2788	0	25.1724

Source: Authors' calculations from Houston Independent School District data.

from year-to-year variation in the accountability status of students' schools. This status changes due to (a) students switching to schools that differ on accountability status, and (b) variations in the classification of students' schools as they progress through grade levels in the same middle school. Following standard practice in longitudinal data analysis, our student fixed-effects models have cluster-correct standard errors to adjust for non-independence within students. (We have repeated observations within students over time.)

As robustness checks, we present alternative specifications with school fixed effects and both student and school fixed effects. We also present random effects specifications. These alternative specifications, reported in tables 6 and 7, produce almost identical results. The school fixed-effects models in these tables have cluster-corrected standard errors to adjust for the non-independence of student observations within schools. Models including both student and school fixed effects have cluster-corrected standard errors to adjust for non-independence within student-school "spells."[5] In addition, in response to potential concerns that our findings could be driven by mean reversion, we replace the dependent variable with a gain measure that explicitly adjusts for the student's position in the previous year's test score distribution (Reback 2008). Results with this dependent variable (tables 6 and 7) are consistent with those with test score level as the dependent variable.

The student fixed-effects model shown in equation 1 assumes a homogeneous treatment effect of failing to meet the target, that is, that all schools *below* the metric's threshold will experience the same incentives for improvement, and that all schools *above* the metric's threshold will experience the same incentives for improvement. To relax this assumption, we also test a model that defines accountability pressure in terms of risk of failing AYP targets. As we discussed in the literature review, there are two competing perspectives about schools' responses to accountability pressure. It could be that schools at the margin of passing AYP targets have the largest incentive to boost state test scores, while schools well above or well below that margin have weaker incentives to do so. On the other hand, qualitative work suggests that schools at high risk of missing targets are very responsive to accountability pressure (Hallett 2010) even when their odds of making targets are extremely low.

To test for heterogeneous effects by school risk of failing AYP targets, we first compute the year- and school-specific probability of failing as a function of school average and subgroup average test scores and compositional characteristics:

$$Log\ Odds[FailAYP]_{tj} = \beta_0 + \beta_1 T_{tj} + \beta_2 C_{tj} + \beta_3 SGT_{tj} + \beta_4 Y_t \quad (2)$$

where T is a vector of school-level average state and audit math and reading test scores along with squared and cubed terms of each, C is a vector of compositional characteristics (percentage black and percentage economically disadvantaged and squared and cubed terms of each), SGT is a vector of subgroup-specific average test scores (school-level subgroup test score averages for black, Hispanic, and economically disadvantaged students), and Y is a vector of year fixed effects. Using the predictions from equation 2, which correctly classifies 91 percent of the school-year observations, we define the following risk categories: low risk (0 to 0.35 probability of failing to meet AYP targets), medium risk (0.35 to 0.65), and high risk (0.65 to 1). Across all years, most schools fall into the low-risk category (81 percent), and about 9 to 10 percent fall into the medium- or high-risk categories (table 3).

The probability of failing to meet AYP targets, however, increases over time. For example, between 2004 and 2007, the percentage of middle schools in the low-risk category fell from 96 to 70 percent, and the percentage of schools in the high-risk category increased from 0 to 21 percent. We thus define indicator variables for high and low risk of failing to meet AYP targets and estimate that:

$$Gap_{ti} = \lambda_i + \beta_1 High\ Risk_{ti}\ \beta_2 Low\ Risk_{ti} + \beta_3 X_{ti} + \beta_4 S_{ti} + \beta_5 Y_t + \beta_6 G_{ti} + \beta_7 Y_t G_{ti} + \varepsilon_{ti} \quad (3)$$

Negative coefficients on the *High Risk* and *Low Risk* variables would indicate that students in schools at the margin of passing AYP targets have larger gaps between the two tests than students in schools either well below or well above the margin. Because previous research suggests that the effects of accountability pres-

---

5. Spells are student panels that lie within the same school. A student who spends all three years in the same middle school has only one spell. A student who switches schools once has two spells in two different schools.

Table 3. Schools' Risk of Failing to Meet AYP Targets, 2004–2007

Year	Low Risk	Medium Risk	High Risk	Total
2004	47	2	0	49
	95.92%	4.08%	0.00%	100%
2005	52	0	1	53
	98.11%	0.00%	1.89%	100%
2006	31	12	9	52
	59.62%	23.08%	17.31%	100%
2007	37	5	11	53
	69.81%	9.43%	20.75%	100%
Total	167	19	21	207
	80.68%	9.18%	10.14%	100%

Source: Authors' calculations from Houston Independent School District data.

sure differ for Hispanic and black students (Hanushek and Raymond 2004), we estimate models 1 and 3 separately for black, Hispanic, and economically disadvantaged students.

RESULTS

The results of student fixed-effects models based on equation 1 estimated on the state test–audit test gaps in each subject are shown in models 3 and 6 of table 4. Also shown in the table are models with the state and audit test scores as dependent variables. The first row displays estimates from all students in our analytic sample. The next three provide separate estimates for black, Hispanic, and economically disadvantaged students, respectively; we do not separately estimate regressions for white and Asian students because only a small fraction of these students were in schools facing accountability pressure. The all-student coefficient on the *Failed AYP* variable from model 1, 0.0374, indicates that students in schools in the year immediately following an accountability threat from NCLB have state math test scores that are about 4 percent of a standard deviation higher than students in schools that face no accountability threat from NCLB. The coefficient from model 2, −0.0232, from a regression with the audit math test as the outcome, indicates a significant negative test score difference between students in schools facing accountability threats relative to those in schools not facing such threats. The math gap, shown in model 3, is essentially the difference between columns 1 and 2. The coefficient, 0.0607, is positive and statistically distinguishable from zero, which suggests that the NCLB accountability threat has a larger effect on math state test scores than on audit math scores. Increases in the state test–audit test gap in math suggest that schools are responding to the incentives in NCLB to raise test scores on the assessment linked to the state standards and AYP calculations. In this case, these effects do not generalize to performance on the audit test; in fact, they produce a small decline in these scores.

In reading, the small and negative effects we find on both reading scores produce a null reading gap. This could have occurred for at least two reasons. First, many of the studies cited earlier have found larger effects of accountability pressure on math compared to reading. Second, the fraction of students in Houston failing mathematics tests was significantly higher than for reading, such that schools facing accountability pressure were more likely to have missed AYP targets because of their math scores and thus to have had an incentive to focus more heavily on math.

The conclusion that schools facing accountability threats tend to produce larger state test–audit test math gaps holds across black, Hispanic, and economically disadvantaged subgroups, which all have positive math gap effects. That is, we find that accountability pressure increases the gap in performance on the two tests. The point estimate for blacks is somewhat larger than for other groups, and the patterns across the state and audit tests

Table 4. Student Fixed-Effects Models Predicting the Effect of Failing to Meet AYP Targets on Standardized Achievement Levels and Gaps in Levels

	(1) Math State Test	(2) Math Audit Test	(3) Math Audit Test–State Test Gap	(4) Reading State Test	(5) Reading Audit Test	(6) Reading Audit Test–State Test Gap
Failed AYP						
All	0.0374***	−0.0232***	0.0607***	−0.0033	−0.0131*	0.0098
	(0.0056)	(0.0050)	(0.0065)	(0.0065)	(0.0052)	(0.0077)
N		135,303			130,355	
Black	−0.0041	−0.0599***	0.0558***	−0.0003	−0.0279**	0.0281*
	(0.0101)	(0.0090)	(0.0120)	(0.0117)	(0.0094)	(0.0138)
N		39,744			38,389	
Hispanic	0.0266***	−0.0102+	0.0369***	−0.0187*	−0.0022	−0.0165+
	(0.0068)	(0.0062)	(0.0080)	(0.0081)	(0.0064)	(0.0096)
N		78,858			75,544	
Economically disadvantaged	0.0122*	−0.0258***	0.0380***	−0.0176*	−0.0157**	−0.0020
	(0.0059)	(0.0054)	(0.0070)	(0.0070)	(0.0055)	(0.0082)
N		108,662			104,103	

Source: Authors' calculations from Houston Independent School District data.

Notes: All models control for Limited English Proficient, free and reduced-priced lunch, special education, percent special education[2], percent economically disadvantaged, percent economically disadvantaged[2], percent economically disadvantaged[3], grade, year, and grade-by-year. Standard errors are in parentheses.

+$p < .10$; *$p < .05$; **$p < .01$; ***$p < .001$

differ. While the Hispanic gap between the two tests emerges because of gains on the state test and small losses on the audit test, black students experience no gains on the state test and a loss of 0.06 standard deviations on the audit test. We see this pattern emerge again for reading tests, where the effects on reading gaps between the state test and audit test are small, positive, and statistically significant for black students. This gap is produced by black students making no gains on the state test and experiencing losses on the audit test.

These effects may be conservative because they do not distinguish among the types of schools most at risk under NCLB. As noted earlier, we have defined "risk sets" of schools based on their probability of failing to meet AYP targets. Incentives-based perspectives predict that the effects of incentives to increase state test scores rather than audit test scores will be the strongest for schools at the margin of failing to meet AYP targets. This hypothesis predicts that (1) schools at very low risk of failing to meet AYP targets will have null or negative accountability-induced gaps (that is, their gains on the audit test will be larger than those on the state test) as these schools focus more on skills that are not test-specific, and (2) schools at the margin of failing to meet AYP targets will have large accountability-induced gaps and schools virtually certain of failing to meet AYP targets will have somewhat smaller accountability-induced gaps than schools at the margin of failing. On the other hand, schools well below the AYP threshold face the most severe sanctions in the medium to long term. This perspective predicts that schools virtually certain to fail to meet AYP targets will have the largest accountability-induced gaps, schools at the margin will have somewhat smaller gaps, and schools at low risk of failure will have no gap or negative gaps overall.

Table 5 presents the effects of accountability pressure defined as high and low risk of failing to meet AYP targets for all students and separate estimates for black, Hispanic, and economically disadvantaged students. If schools are only focused on short-term incentives, we would expect to see the greatest response by schools at medium risk of failing to meet AYP targets. The first coefficient in column 1 of table 5, 0.0418, indicates that for all students the high-risk–medium-risk difference in math state test scores is about 4 percent of a standard deviation. In other words, students in schools at high risk of failing to meet AYP targets have higher math state test scores in the subsequent year than students in schools at the margin of passing AYP targets. By contrast, students in schools at high risk have lower math audit test scores (−0.0585) in the subsequent year than students in schools at the margin. The accountability-induced state test–audit test gap is therefore 0.100 of a standard deviation, which indicates that relative to students in schools at the margin of passing AYP targets, students in schools at high risk of doing so have larger gaps. The high-risk–medium-risk differential in the reading gap is also positive, but smaller, at 0.0413. Turning to the low-risk–medium-risk differential, we find *negative* gap scores in math and no gap in reading. Students in low-risk schools gained on audit tests even as their state tests declined. We note that these results are not due to ceiling effects on the state tests.

Overall, the pattern of coefficients in table 5 suggests that when schools face additional pressure, they either become more aligned to state standards or "teach to the test." We make this inference because high-risk schools see increases in state test scores and decreases in audit test scores in both subjects, while low-risk schools are more likely to make progress on the audit test. Our results alone cannot differentiate between these two mechanisms, but we believe that it is important to note that greater accountability pressure appears to produce specific versus general gains. We return to the normative questions raised by this finding in the discussion.

Moving to the subgroup results, the bottom panels of table 5 show that black, Hispanic, and economically disadvantaged students experience approximately the same accountability-induced state test–audit test gap in high- and low-risk schools in both subjects. However, the sources of the gap vary across subgroups, for the math test in particular. Based on our point estimates, black students in high-risk schools experience audit test losses approximately twice as large as those experienced by Hispanic

Table 5. Student Fixed-Effects Models Predicting the Effect of Schools' Risk of Failing to Meet AYP Targets on Standardized Achievement Levels and Gaps in Levels

	(1) Math State Test	(2) Math Audit Test	(3) Math Audit Test–State Test Gap	(4) Reading State Test	(5) Reading Audit Test	(6) Reading Audit Test–State Test Gap
All						
High risk	0.0418***	−0.0585***	0.1000***	0.0168+	−0.0245**	0.0413**
	(0.0085)	(0.0078)	(0.0100)	(0.0098)	(0.0082)	(0.0118)
Low risk	−0.0456***	0.0174**	−0.0630***	0.0040	0.0043	−0.0003
	(0.0072)	(0.0065)	(0.0083)	(0.0082)	(0.0067)	(0.0099)
N	135,303	135,303			130,335	
Black						
High risk	−0.0088	−0.108***	0.0989***	0.0143	−0.0391**	0.0534*
	(0.0156)	(0.0136)	(0.0186)	(0.0176)	(0.0147)	(0.0212)
Low risk	−0.0383*	−0.0029	−0.0355*	0.0137	−0.0074	0.0211
	(0.0142)	(0.0122)	(0.0169)	(0.0161)	(0.0131)	(0.0195)
N	39,744				38,389	

Hispanic						
High risk	0.0570***	−0.0428***	0.0998***	0.0104	−0.0224*	0.0329*
	(0.0104)	(0.0099)	(0.0122)	(0.0123)	(0.0103)	(0.0148)
Low risk	−0.0062	0.0346***	−0.0407***	0.0190*	0.0050	0.0140
	(0.0086)	(0.0079)	(0.0098)	(0.0097)	(0.0080)	(0.0118)
N	78,858			75,544		
Economically disadvantaged						
High risk	0.0439***	−0.0544***	0.0982***	0.0178+	−0.0265**	0.0443**
	(0.0090)	(0.0083)	(0.0105)	(0.0104)	(0.0086)	(0.0125)
Low risk	−0.0089	0.0234***	−0.0322***	0.0238**	0.0081	0.0158
	(0.0077)	(0.0070)	(0.0088)	(0.0088)	(0.0072)	(0.0106)
N	108,662			104,103		

Source: Authors' calculations from Houston Independent School District data.

Notes: Table 5 includes the same controls as table 4. Standard errors are in parentheses.

+$p < .10$; *$p < .05$; **$p < .01$; ***$p < .001$

Table 6. Comparison of Alternative Specifications of the Effect of Failing to Meet AYP Targets

	(1) Student Fixed Effects	(2) School Fixed Effects	(3) Student and School Fixed Effects	(4) Student Random Effects
Standardized math gap in levels				
Failed AYP	0.0607***	0.0644*	0.0582***	0.0694***
	(0.0065)	(0.0313)	(0.0067)	(0.00482)
N	135,303	135,303	135,303	135,303
Standardized math gap—adjusted gain				
Failed AYP	0.0911***	0.0554	0.0894***	0.0564***
	(0.0181)	(0.0459)	(0.0187)	(0.0093)
N	116,685	116,685	116,685	116,685
Standardized reading gap in levels				
Failed AYP	0.0098	0.0010	0.0117	0.0155**
	(0.0077)	(0.0139)	(0.0079)	(0.0051)
N	130,335	130,335	130,335	130,335
Standardized reading gap—adjusted gain				
Failed AYP	-0.0053	-0.0270	-0.00301	-0.0391***
	(0.0197)	(0.0277)	(0.0204)	(0.0101)
N	113,662	113,662	113,662	113,662

Source: Authors' calculations from Houston Independent School District data.
Notes: Standard errors are in parentheses. All models control for Limited English Proficient, free and reduced-priced lunch, special education, percent special education^2, percent special education^3, percent economically disadvantaged, percent economically disadvantaged^2, percent economically disadvantaged^3, grade, year, and grade-by-year.
⁺$p < .10$; *$p < .05$; **$p < .01$; ***$p < .001$

students (0.108 standard deviations versus 0.043 standard deviations for Hispanics) and do not benefit on the state test. In contrast, Hispanic students gain 0.057 standard deviations on the state test. Although our data cannot explain why black students lose more than Hispanic students on the audit math tests, we note that the pattern of Hispanic students benefiting more from accountability pressure has been documented in other studies (Hanushek and Raymond 2004; Lauen and Gaddis 2012).

Sensitivity Analysis

Alternative Fixed- and Random-Effects Specifications
A student fixed-effects model removes observable and unobservable within-student confounding. We estimate two alternative specifications to determine whether our results are vulnerable to different kinds of confounding threats. Including school fixed effects removes between-school confounding. This model identifies the effect of failing to meet AYP targets on state test–audit test gaps on across-cohort variation within the same school over time. This model, presented in model 2 of table 6, produces almost identical effects on math and reading gaps as the student fixed-effects model. (Included in this table are results from all students in the analytic sample.) Including both student and school fixed effects in the same model identifies the effect of failing to meet AYP targets on gaps in within-school variation across time only for groups of students who remain in the same school (the "stayers"). This

Table 7. Comparison of Alternative Specifications of the AYP Risk Effect

	(1) Student Fixed Effects	(2) School Fixed Effects	(3) Student and School Fixed Effects	(4) Student Random Effects
Standardized math gap in levels (N = 135,303)				
High risk	0.1010***	0.0667⁺	0.0971***	0.107***
	(0.0100)	(0.0383)	(0.0102)	(0.0081)
Low risk	−0.0630***	−0.0626⁺	−0.0615***	−0.0677***
	(0.0083)	(0.0332)	(0.0085)	(0.0065)
Standardized math gap—adjusted gain (N = 116,685)				
High risk	0.145***	0.0910	0.144***	0.127***
	(0.0280)	(0.0744)	(0.0287)	(0.0161)
Low risk	−0.0735**	−0.0588	−0.0776***	−0.0494***
	(0.0229)	(0.0635)	(0.0236)	(0.0134)
Standardized reading gap in levels (N = 130,335)				
High risk	0.0413***	0.0192	0.0397**	0.0441***
	(0.0118)	(0.0173)	(0.0121)	(0.0081)
Low risk	−0.0003	0.0003	−0.0020	−0.0115⁺
	(0.0099)	(0.0175)	(0.0101)	(0.0068)
Standardized reading gap—adjusted gain (N = 113,662)				
High risk	0.0502	0.0238	0.0484	0.0120
	(0.0309)	(0.0386)	(0.0316)	(0.0173)
Low risk	0.0444⁺	0.0369	0.0446⁺	0.0293*
	(0.0253)	(0.0402)	(0.0259)	(0.0145)

Source: Authors' calculations from Houston Independent School District data.
Notes: Standard errors are in parentheses. All models control for Limited English Proficient, free and reduced-price lunch, special education, percent special education^2, percent special education^3, percent economically disadvantaged, percent economically disadvantaged^2, percent economically disadvantaged^3, grade, year, and grade-by-year.
⁺$p < .10$; *$p < .05$; **$p < .01$; ***$p < .001$

specification also produces very similar effects (model 3 of table 6). These alternative specifications do not alter our conclusions about the differences between high- and medium-risk schools (see table 7). The school fixed-effects models provide somewhat weaker evidence on differentials among the three risk categories, but the models with both student and school fixed effects, which adjust for both between-student and between-school confounding, reproduce the student fixed-effects results. In addition, when we estimate our models with random rather than fixed effects, the results (reported in column 4 of table 6) are similar.

Testing for Mean Reversion

Another concern is that our results could be driven by mean reversion. We have performed two additional analyses to address this threat. First, we have added additional test score lags to our model to help control for the possibility that students in schools failing to meet AYP targets had a one-year deflection from their "true" score and led the school to fail. Second, we have estimated additional models with an "adjusted gain" measure as the dependent variable to account for the possibility that one-year differences signify larger or smaller gains at different points in the prior-year achievement distribution. Following Reback (2008), for each subject we define a standardized adjusted gain score as the difference between the actual test score of a student (i in equation 4) in year t and the expected score for students in the same grade (g) who had the exact same score as in the previous year, normalized by the standard deviation of the scores in year t for that group of students (that is, the same grade and score in the previous year):

$$AdjGainScore = \frac{Score_{igt} - E[Score_{igt} \mid Score_{i,g-1,t-1}]}{\sqrt{E[Score^2_{i,g,t} \mid Score_{i,g-1,t-1}] - E[Score^2_{i,g,t} \mid Score_{i,g-1,t-1}]^2}} \quad (4)$$

Our results are robust to both of these alternative specifications. For example, the all-student estimate in math shown in table 4 is 0.0607 (0.0065), $p < 0.001$. The same estimate with one- and two-year lags in both reading and math (four total) is 0.0506 (0.0088), $p < 0.001$. As shown in table 6, the estimate from a model with adjusted gain in math as the dependent variable is 0.0911 (0.0181), $p < 0.001$.

DISCUSSION

To summarize our results, we find that accountability pressure from the No Child Left Behind Act is associated with increased scores on math state tests, but lower math and reading scores on audit tests. The state test–audit test gap is largest for math, and the fact that two-thirds of schools in our study missed AYP targets because of the math test helps to contextualize this finding; we would expect to see more divergence on the math test than on the reading test.

We believe that our study provides the best available evidence about the effects of accountability pressure on multiple tests in the NCLB era, since we are able to measure the performance of the *same* students on two different tests and compare their own performances in years when their schools faced different levels of accountability pressure. For students in schools most at risk of failing to meet AYP targets, the gap between the gains in math state test scores and losses in math audit test scores is a nontrivial 0.10 standard deviations; the gap for reading is 0.04 standard deviations. To benchmark the size of these effects, the math effects are approximately the same size as the estimated effects of accountability in a recent National Research Council (NRC) report, which estimates the effects at 0.08 standard deviations (Elliott and Hout 2011). We also find that the sources of state test–audit test gaps vary across student groups. Most importantly, black students in higher-risk schools do not experience gains on the state reading and math tests, but experience losses twice as large as Hispanics do on the audit math test.

In addition to identifying these average effects, our findings on heterogeneous responses across schools help to revise the current "rational choice," incentives-based approach to understanding educators' responses to external pressures. Our results demonstrating that schools well below AYP targets have larger state test increases than schools at the margin of those targets raise doubts that educators are driven primarily by short-term, "rational" responses to incentives and show that the lowest-performing schools are indeed responsive to pressure, even when they have little chance of making the target. That increases on state tests do not generalize to audit tests, however, indicates that educators are also driven by short-term incentives to raise test scores on the state test. This mix of findings suggests that educators in this era of accountability are best understood as driven by both short- and longer-term imperatives.

In this discussion, we evaluate our findings in light of the most likely mechanisms for divergence across tests that we outlined at the outset of the paper. Understanding these mechanisms is important for evaluating their implications for equality of educational opportunity. One possibility is that effort alone explains differences between state test and audit test performance in schools failing to meet AYP targets. It is useful to make clear the conditions that are necessary for differential effort to explain these effects. Recall that any time-invariant component of lower motivation on the audit test (the possibility that students *always* try harder on the state test and less hard on the audit test) is removed in our specifications because of our use of student fixed effects. For student effort to explain our results, students would have to exert less effort on the audit test in years when their schools face pressure relative to *their own effort* when their schools do not face pressure. This could occur, for example, if teachers in these schools explicitly or implicitly tell students, or students conclude on their own, that the audit test is not worthy of the same effort in years when their schools face pressure and that the state test deserves additional effort. To explain our math findings, both of these conditions must be met. Second, we note that the audit tests are given in each year approximately a month *before* the state tests, which makes "test fatigue" less likely as an explanation for worse audit test performance. We do not believe that the pattern of results presented in this paper provides strong support for the effort explanation, but we note that our study cannot definitively rule out this possibility.

A second possibility is that when schools face accountability pressure, educators increase their alignment with state standards. If state tests are aligned with state standards, better instructional alignment alone should produce an increase in state test scores. Increased alignment may also reduce the coverage of topics that are tested on the audit test. If the skills represented in the state test are sufficiently narrow, alignment would tend either to leave audit scores unchanged or to decrease those scores if other material has been supplanted.

Whether increases in state scores at the expense of audit scores is a positive outcome depends on one's understanding of alignment. In the current testing debate, one person's "alignment" is another person's "teaching to the test." One perspective on alignment holds that if standards represent skills that we want students to learn and tests are aligned with these standards, alignment-based increases in scores are a positive outcome and declines in performance on tests less aligned with these standards are of little importance.

Another perspective suggests that alignment-based increases should be evaluated more critically. According to Koretz (2005, 112), because of the sampling principle of testing, "alignment of instruction with the test is likely to produce incomplete alignment of instruction with the standards, even if the test is aligned with the standards. . . . Despite its benefits, alignment is not a guarantee of validity under high-stakes conditions." In theory, the issues raised by Koretz could be addressed if we are willing to fully articulate the domain of skills that we care about and to devote unlimited testing time and resources toward fully sampling the domain and a variety of representations of these skills. The experience of testing under No Child Left Behind, however, has been that tests have not been aligned with state standards, and state tests have often predictably sampled a small number of standards that are not a priori the "most important" (Holcombe, Jennings, and Koretz 2013).

As with any quantitative analysis using only administrative data, we cannot determine the mechanisms that produce state test gains that do not generalize to the audit tests, but we believe that we have presented compelling evidence here to encourage future scholars to investigate how instruction changes when schools face accountability pressure, why gains vary across different measures of achievement, and why gains vary across different subgroups of students.

REFERENCES

Aviv, Rachel. 2014. "Wrong Answer." *The New Yorker*, July 13.

Booher-Jennings, Jennifer. 2005. "Below the Bubble: 'Educational Triage' and the Texas Accountability System." *American Educational Research Journal* 42(2): 231–68.

Carnoy, Martin, and Susanna Loeb. 2002. "Does External Accountability Affect Student Outcomes? A Cross-State Analysis." *Educational Evaluation and Policy Analysis* 24(4): 305–31.

Dee, Thomas, and Brian Jacob. 2009. "The Impact of No Child Left Behind on Student Achievement." Working Paper 15531. Cambridge, Mass.: National Bureau of Economic Research.

Deming, David, Sarah Cohodes, Jennifer L. Jennings, and Christopher Jencks. 2013. "High-Stakes

Testing, Post-Secondary Attainment, and Earnings." Working Paper 19444. Cambridge, Mass.: National Bureau of Economic Research (September).

Elliott, Stuart W., and Michael Hout, eds. 2011. *Incentives and Test-Based Accountability in Education.* Washington, D.C.: National Academies Press.

Figlio, David N., and Lawrence Getzler. 2002. "Accountability, Ability, and Disability: Gaming the System." Working Paper 9307. Cambridge, Mass.: National Bureau of Economic Research.

Hallett, Tim. 2010. "The Myth Incarnate: Recoupling Processes, Turmoil, and Inhabited Institutions in an Urban Elementary School." *American Sociological Review* 75(1): 52–74.

Hanushek, Eric A., and Margaret E. Raymond. 2004. "Does School Accountability Lead to Improved Student Performance?" Working Paper 10591. Cambridge, Mass.: National Bureau of Economic Research.

Hoey, Lesli, Patricia B. Campbell, and Lesley Perlman. 2001. "Where's the Overlap? Mapping the SAT-9 and TAAS 4th Grade Test Objectives." Unpublished manuscript, Campbell-Kibler Associates.

Holcombe, Rebecca, Jennifer L. Jennings, and Daniel Koretz. 2013. "Predictable Patterns That Facilitate Score Inflation: A Comparison of the New York and Massachusetts State Tests." In *Charting Reform, Achieving Equity in a Diverse Nation*, edited by Gail L. Sunderman. Charlotte, N.C.: Information Age Publishing.

Jacob, Brian A. 2005. "Accountability, Incentives, and Behavior: Evidence from School Reform in Chicago." *Journal of Public Economics* 895–96: 761–96.

———. 2007. "Test-Based Accountability and Student Achievement: An Investigation of Differential Performance on NAEP and State Assessments." Working Paper 12817. Cambridge, Mass.: National Bureau of Economic Research.

Jacob, Brian A., and Steven Levitt. 2003. "Rotten Apples: An Investigation of the Prevalence of Teacher Cheating." *Quarterly Journal of Economics* 118(3): 843–77.

Jennings, Jennifer L., and Jonathan M. Bearak. 2014. "'Teaching to the Test' in the NCLB Era: How Test Predictability Affects Our Understanding of Student Performance." *Educational Researcher* 43(8): 381–89.

Jennings, Jennifer L., and Heeju Sohn. 2014. "Measure for Measure: How Proficiency-Based Accountability Systems Affect Inequality in Academic Achievement." *Sociology of Education* 87(2): 125–41.

Klein, Steven, Laura Hamilton, Daniel McCaffrey, and Brian Stecher. 2000. *What Do Test Scores in Texas Tell Us?* Santa Monica, Calif.: RAND.

Koretz, Daniel M. 2005. "Alignment, High Stakes, and the Inflation of Test Scores." *Yearbook of the National Society for the Study of Education* 1042(1): 99–118.

———. 2008. *Measuring Up: What Educational Testing Really Tells Us.* Cambridge, Mass.: Harvard University Press.

———. 2013. "Adapting the Practice of Measurement to the Demands of Test-Based Accountability." Working Paper. Cambridge, Mass.: Harvard University.

Koretz, Daniel M., and Sheila I. Barron. 1998. *The Validity of Gains on the Kentucky Instructional Results Information System KIRIS.* Santa Monica, Calif.: RAND.

Lauen, Douglas Lee, and Michael Gaddis. 2012. "Shining a Light or Fumbling in the Dark? The Effects of NCLB's Subgroup-Specific Accountability Pressure on Student Performance." *Educational Evaluation and Policy Analysis* 34(2): 185–208.

McAdams, Douglas R. 2000. *Fighting to Save Our Urban Schools . . . and Winning!* New York: Teachers College Press.

Neal, Derek. 2013. "The Consequences of Using One Assessment System to Pursue Two Objectives." Working Paper 19214. Cambridge, Mass.: National Bureau of Economic Research.

Neal, Derek, and Diane Whitmore Schanzenbach. 2010. "Left Behind by Design: Proficiency Counts and Test-Based Accountability." *Review of Economics and Statistics* 92(2): 263–83.

Reback, Randall. 2008. "Teaching to the Rating: School Accountability and the Distribution of Student Achievement." *Journal of Public Economics* 92(5): 1394–1415.

Reback, Randall, Jonah Rockoff, and Heather Schwartz. 2011. "Under Pressure: Job Security, Resource Allocation, and Productivity in Schools Under NCLB." Working Paper. New York: Barnard College.

Rouse, Cecilia, Jane Hannaway, Daniel Goldhaber, and David Figlio. 2007. "Feeling the Florida

Heat? How Low-Performing Schools Respond to Voucher and Accountability Pressure." NBER Working Paper 13681. Cambridge, Mass.: National Bureau of Economic Research.

Swanson, Chris. 2006. "High School Graduation Rates in Texas: Independent Research to Understand and Combat the Graduation Crisis" (research report). Bethesda, MD: Editorial Projects in Education, Education Week Research Center (October).

Wong, Manyee, Thomas D. Cook, and Peter M. Steiner. 2009. "No Child Left Behind: An Interim Evaluation of Its Effects on Learning Using Two Interrupted Time Series Each with Its Own Nonequivalent Comparison Series." Working paper. Evanston, Ill.: Northwestern University.

Can Technology Help Promote Equality of Educational Opportunities?

BRIAN JACOB, DAN BERGER, CASSANDRA HART, AND SUSANNA LOEB

This chapter assesses the potential for several prominent technological innovations to promote equality of educational opportunities. We review the history of technological innovations in education and describe several prominent innovations, including intelligent tutoring, blended learning, and virtual schooling.

Keywords: education technology, online learning, virtual schooling

The 1966 release of the Coleman Report (Coleman et al. 1966) is widely recognized as a pivotal moment in the history of education in the United States. The report documented vast inequities in academic achievement between white and nonwhite children. Coleman and his colleagues found a great deal of racial segregation across schools along with important differences in the family resources (including factors such as parental education and household composition) available to white and nonwhite children. On the other hand, they uncovered substantially fewer differences in school resources (for example, pupil-teacher ratio and school facilities) by race. The analysis conducted by the researchers suggested that the variation in student performance was driven primarily by socioeconomic conditions in families and neighborhoods. Schools—and thus any differential resources across schools—explained relatively little of the achievement differences.

The report spurred new research and policy action aimed at improving school productivity and attempting to close the achievement gap. Although there has been progress on some fronts, many of the key findings of the Coleman Report remain true today, as is highlighted in other papers in this issue. Schools made rapid progress toward racial desegregation in the 1960s and 1970s, but that progress has either stalled or reversed since the 1980s, depending on how segregation is measured (Reardon and Owens 2014). While achievement gaps have narrowed, African American and Latino children still score roughly 13 percent lower than their Caucasian and Asian peers on standardized exams.[1] In an effort to overcome

Brian Jacob is professor at the University of Michigan. **Dan Berger** is a doctoral student at the University of Michigan. **Cassandra Hart** is associate professor at the University of California, Davis. **Susanna Loeb** is professor at Stanford University.

Thanks to our research partners at the Florida Virtual Schools, the Florida Department of Education, and Miami-Dade County Public Schools. Funding for this research was provided by the Walton Family Foundation, the Spencer Foundation, and the Institute of Education Sciences (grant R305A150163). Results, information, and opinions are the authors' and do not reflect the views or positions of any funding agency or research partner. Direct correspondence to: Brian Jacob at bajacob@umich.edu, University of Michigan, Weill Hall, 735 S. State St. #5124, Ann Arbor, MI 48109; Dan Berger at djberger@umich.edu; Cassandra Hart at cmdhart@ucdavis.edu; and Susanna Loeb at sloeb@stanford.edu.

1. Authors' calculations using National Assessment of Educational Progress (NAEP) Data Explorer.

continued inequalities, policies have cycled in and out of favor, much like a pendulum swinging. The emphasis on test-based accountability (for example, high school exit exams) in the early 1970s reappeared several decades later in the federal accountability policy No Child Left Behind, enacted in 2002. The focus on rigorous standards in the 1980s (such as the push for states to require high school students to complete at least three years of math and science) is reminiscent of the current focus in the Common Core. And today's push to explore new educational technologies recalls earlier efforts to introduce computers into schools (Christensen, Johnson, and Horn 2010).

New technologies are not new. Blackboards were new before they were replaced by whiteboards. Slates were new, then replaced by paper and now, to some extent, computers and tablets. Filmstrips were new, and then replaced by DVDs and now web-accessed videos. In each case, the new technology brought both costs and benefits. Often it brought little change in teaching or learning. In his influential book *Oversold and Underused: Computers in the Classroom,* Larry Cuban (2003) argues that teachers and students use computers in schools far less frequently than commonly assumed and that the presence of computers has not changed the traditional instructional paradigm of whole-class, teacher-centered instruction. When teachers use computers, it is primarily for mundane tasks. Students write essays using word processors, practice math problems using simplistic software, or use the Internet to do web-based research. Teachers use computers to record grades, prepare lessons, and read email (Cuban 2003; Gray et al. 2010).

However, recent technological innovations have expanded the capabilities of digital learning tools in ways that boosters argue offer new potential to "disrupt" the provision of education and reduce disparities in educational opportunities (Christensen, Johnson, and Horn 2010). First, the increasing speed and availability of Internet access can reduce many of the geographic constraints that have disadvantaged poor students. Students can now access online videos that provide instruction on a wide variety of topics at various skill levels and participate in real-time video conferences with teachers or tutors located a state (or even a continent) away.[2] This technology has even expanded opportunities for the long-distance professional development of teachers, enabling novice teachers to receive mentorship from master teachers regardless of distance (Dede 2006).

Second, these technologies scale easily so that innovations (or even good curriculum) can reach more students. Much like a well-written textbook, a well-designed educational software application or online lesson can reach students not just in a single classroom or school but across the state or country.

Third, advances in artificial intelligence technology now allow teachers to differentiate instruction, providing extra support and developmentally appropriate material to students whose knowledge and skill is far below grade-level norms. The latest "intelligent" tutoring systems are able to not only assess a student's current weaknesses but also diagnose *why* the student is making the specific errors (Graesser, Conley, and Olney 2012). Related to this development, the explosion of "big data," in theory, can allow researchers and program developers to utilize the experience of thousands or even millions of learners to determine more effective instructional approaches—again tailored for students with very particular needs.[3]

Although technologies such as virtual instruction and the suite of programs known collectively as intelligent tutoring offer great promise, they are not guaranteed to improve educational equality. Use of these technologies

---

2. Similarly, the Internet has enhanced the ability of non-experts, including classroom teachers, to create and upload their own videos.

3. The evolution of touch-screen technology on smart phones and tablets has enabled very young children to engage in technology-aided instruction. Prior to tablets, it was difficult for preschool, kindergarten, and even early primary grade students to work with educational software, which required the use of a mouse or keyboard. Now there are hundreds of applications that expose children to early literacy and numeracy skills without the need to manipulate a keyboard or mouse.

often reduces oversight of students, and that can be particularly detrimental for children who are less motivated or who receive less structured educational supports at home. These technologies may also be less effective in engaging reluctant learners in the way a dynamic and charismatic teacher can, suggesting that even if educational technology improves quality overall, any "peak" education experience it provides may fall short of a "peak" face-to-face experience. Perhaps more importantly, technologies such as intelligent tutoring and systems that blend online and face-to-face (FtF) instruction are notoriously difficult to implement well. There is a substantial risk that they could be ineffective or even harmful in places that lack the capacity to implement the technologies with fidelity.

In this paper, we assess the potential for these "next generation" technologies to promote equality of educational opportunities. To begin, we focus on virtual instruction, which is arguably the most visible and controversial of the new technologies. Utilizing detailed administrative data from Florida, we describe which types of students are most likely to take virtual courses, and how students who take virtual courses fare in comparison with their peers taking FtF courses. We then discuss the theory behind and evidence for intelligent tutoring systems. In the final section, we discuss the implications of the findings reported here for education policy in the future.

VIRTUAL INSTRUCTION

One of the most visible examples of technology-aided learning involves virtual course-taking. An estimated 1.5 million K–12 students participated in some online learning in 2010 (Wicks 2010), and online learning enrollments are projected to grow in future years (Picciano et al. 2012; Watson et al. 2012).[4] Although full-time virtual schools have grown in recent years, the vast majority of students participating in online instruction are part-time—that is, they are enrolled in a traditional brick-and-mortar school but take one or more classes online. Typically, these classes are *asynchronous:* students and teachers are not communicating with each other in real time through video conferencing technology. Students often take these courses outside of school (for example, at home or in a public library), although in recent years many schools have allowed students to take online courses at school during the day. Note that the online instruction we describe here is distinct from *blended learning* models, which combine online and FtF instruction (discussed later).

How Online Instruction Might Influence Student Outcomes

Online classes can affect students' outcomes either by affecting their *access* to courses, and thereby changing their choice of courses, or by affecting the *quality* of the educational environment they experience. Access to online courses may change the courses that students are able to take and thus their progress through school in terms of both their accumulation of credits and the types of classes they complete. Students may benefit from being able to take additional courses online during the school year or during the summer, either for catchup or for enrichment. With regard to enrichment, smaller and poorer high schools tend to have fewer Advanced Placement (AP) offerings, elective courses, and foreign language courses compared to larger schools with better resources (Barker 1985; Pufahl and Rhodes 2011). As discussed in other papers in this issue, this raises several concerns. First, the lack of advanced-level course availability has implications for students in low-income and minority schools when they transition to college (Schneider and Saw, this issue). Second, even when such courses are available, social boundaries may stymy nondominant groups' participation in them (Carter, this issue). Access to virtual courses could help alleviate both of these concerns. With regard to the first concern, students who fail a course during one school year may opt to take that course online in lieu of attending summer school or repeating the course the following school year (Cooper et al. 2000; Watson and Gemin 2008). Moreover, virtual schooling

---

4. The International Association for K–12 Online Learning (iNACOL) defines online learning as teacher-led education that takes place over the Internet with teacher and student separated by geography.

can provide some consistency of course access for highly mobile populations or students who must spend time away from their traditional brick-and-mortar school because of health, incarceration, or other personal situations.

The best evidence on whether simply improving access to different courses through virtual schools affects students' academic outcomes comes from a large-scale random assignment study carried out in Maine and Vermont (Heppen et al. 2012). Sixty-eight schools that had not historically offered Algebra I to eighth-graders were randomly assigned to either a treatment group, which was given access to an online Algebra I course, or a control group, which did not receive access. Algebra-ready students in treated schools showed improvements on test scores and took more advanced courses in high school (Heppen et al. 2012). Although these results are encouraging, this efficacy study took place under idealized conditions—selected students were particularly advanced, and virtual classes were held during the school day with an on-site proctor who, in 80 percent of the schools, was a math teacher.

As described earlier, online instruction may also influence the quality of the educational environment in several ways. Individuals teaching online courses may be more or less effective than their counterparts teaching FtF courses. One's peers in an online course may be different than in a FtF course, and perhaps more importantly, it seems likely that peer effects would be less pronounced in an online setting. Finally, it is likely that curricular and instructional approaches differ, given both the constraints and opportunities of online courses relative to those in traditional classrooms. The online platform may allow for course characteristics that are simply not possible in the FtF environment. For instance, students can work at their own pace (Anderson 2008), and if they do not understand key concepts in lectures or become distracted, they can replay the lectures to bolster their understanding. Moreover, the setup of online courses may allow the same material to be presented in multiple ways to best match a student's learning style.

The online platform may also provide opportunities for planning, oversight, and uniformity that are far more difficult in FtF classrooms. Curriculum specialists can plan the course, including quite detailed scripts for teachers. Teachers can implement these specified curricula, focusing their time and skills on responding to students' questions and needs. For this reason, the quality of courses may be much more homogeneous in virtual settings than in brick-and-mortar classes, though course quality may depend on the quality of the curriculum planning team. Insofar as we are concerned about the potential for the "teaching to the test" behaviors discussed by Jennifer Jennings and Douglas Lauen (this issue), this homogeneity of virtual courses makes them less likely to be impacted by local accountability pressures. On the other hand, FtF courses provide opportunities for interaction with peers and teachers that are not available in the online environment. The proximity of teachers and students in FtF settings may also make it easier for teachers to monitor students' work, keep them on task, or read facial clues to determine whether students are confused about course concepts (Anderson 2008). Classes in one environment may meet the same needs met in the other environment, but the process may be more difficult.

The extent to which a student benefits from a virtual class is likely to depend on the characteristics of the individual student. For instance, the benefits of being able to repeat material at a slower pace might be more pronounced for low-achieving students. Non-native English speakers might benefit from online instruction that allows them to pause and look up unfamiliar words. For each of these groups, plausible stories could be told in the opposite direction as well.

The utility of taking online courses is also likely to vary based on the counterfactual conditions that individual students would experience in the absence of the virtual option. For instance, we might expect that even if there were no differences across sectors in average teacher (or peer) quality, the option to take a virtual course with an average teacher (or an average-ability peer group) might be more advantageous to a student attending a brick-and-mortar school with very low-quality teachers (or very low-achieving peers). This would suggest that a potential benefit of the expansion of virtual courses could be to reduce the inequality in educational opportunities for more affluent versus poorer students, given that past research indicates that high-poverty schools tend to be staffed by teachers with less experience and lower value-added scores (Sass et al. 2012; Boyd et al. 2008) and that, within schools, classes with a higher share of low-achieving, poor, and minority students are most likely to receive novice teachers (Kalogrides and Loeb 2013).

Despite heated debate in the policy realm, there has been little rigorous research examining the effect on student achievement of online courses in comparison to FtF courses. The majority of research on the impacts of online course-taking comes from studies at postsecondary institutions. There have been several careful randomized control trials to compare learning for college students in FtF classes versus hybrid delivery models. These studies tend to find either null results (Bowen et al. 2014) or modest benefits to FtF instruction (Figlio, Rush, and Yin 2013; Joyce et al. 2015).[5] These studies, however, look only at a limited range of classes (for example, one section of statistics or economics) and tend to be based in selective institutions. Other studies use quasi-experimental methods to explore the impact of virtual course-taking at less elite, broad-access institutions. Studies of public community colleges in a variety of states (Xu and Jaggars 2011, 2013; Hart, Friedmann, and Hill 2014; Streich 2014) and of for-profit broad-access institutions operating nationally (Bettinger et al. 2015) consistently find poorer outcomes for students who take online courses. However, given the greater latitude that postsecondary instructors generally have to develop courses, online course-taking may have different effects for K–12 students.

Unfortunately, little evidence of the effects of online learning exists at the K–12 level. Indeed, a recent meta-analysis of online learning has found only five studies that compare students in K–12 online courses to an FtF alternative that features an experimental or quasi-experimental design and includes sufficient information to be included in a meta-analysis (Means et al. 2010). Of these studies, all use blended rather than fully online instruction. The authors find no significant differences between blended and FtF alternatives in K–12 settings, a finding echoed in other meta-analyses with slightly less stringent inclusion criteria (Cavanaugh et al. 2004).

The best test of whether online coursework boosts student learning for K–12 students comes from a randomized controlled trial for students taking Algebra I. Cavalluzzo et al. (2012) compare a hybrid Algebra I curriculum implemented in thirteen high schools in Kentucky to an FtF curriculum and find no evidence of a difference in learning. Although the Kentucky study provides compelling evidence with regard to this particular course and context, the results from this context may not generalize. We return to the evidence on blended learning models in the following section.[6]

Online Instruction in Florida

To shed light on some of these unanswered questions, we examine virtual course-taking in Florida. Florida is a sensible location for studying online learning because it is one of only a few states that require students to take at least one online course in order to receive a high school diploma (Watson et al. 2012). This requirement can be met through an online course offered by the Florida Virtual School (FLVS, a virtual education provider approved by the State Board of Education and the largest virtual course provider in Florida), a high school, or an online dual-enrollment course. Florida's virtual schools are subject to many of the same regulations that FtF schools face. In order for the state to pay for classes, curricula in virtual schools must be aligned to the state's standards and teachers must be fully credentialed in Florida. Also, like brick-and-mortar schools,

---

5. Lectures in Figlio, Rush, and Yin (2013) were delivered fully online, but those students had access to FtF time with instructors during traditional office hours as well.

6. Several recent studies that focus on full-time virtual schools serving K–12 students find mixed results (see Center for Research on Educational Outcomes 2011; Molnar et al. 2013; Ritter and Lueken 2013).

virtual schools that provide state-funded full-time education for students receive grades through Florida's accountability system.[7]

The vast majority of students taking online courses in Florida do so through FLVS, a public school founded in 1997 that provides courses for both full-time and part-time online students. Most commonly, students access online courses at home or another location with broadband access such as a public library. FLVS fills courses on a first-come, first-served basis. Each course in FLVS has a maximum enrollment size, and FLVS fills courses sequentially—that is, students are assigned a particular teacher until that teacher reaches his or her enrollment cap, at which point FLVS opens another "section" of the course (Teresa King, FLVS, personal communication, July 2013). Students are accepted on a rolling basis, and they can work at their own pace. Given the flexibility of course pacing, FLVS instructors tend to be "on call" from 8:00 AM to 8:00 PM, Monday through Sunday (Bakia et al. 2011). Indeed, FLVS teachers are required to respond to any student query within twenty-four hours and to return completed assignments with feedback within forty-eight hours (Teresa King, FLVS, personal communication, July 2013).

FLVS teachers are not unionized, but they are paid on the basis of a traditional salary schedule comparable to other public districts, with salary increases for experience and additional education. FLVS teachers complete a one-week in-person training session upon induction and receive thirty hours of additional training (delivered virtually) each year.

FLVS maintains tight control over the curriculum presented to students (Teresa King, personal communication, August 9, 2013). The school's Curriculum Services Department designs the curriculum and student assignments, and teachers have little latitude to alter the assignments. All courses include discussion-based assignments in which students talk with teachers (by phone) about the material so that the instructor can assess student understanding and clarify questions in real time.[8] All students in the same course take centrally designed exams in which questions drawn from a test bank are randomly presented to students. Final exams are proctored only if teachers raise concerns about academic integrity.

In recent years, many public schools have begun offering virtual courses during the school day within the school building (for example, in a computer lab or school library). In such cases, the course is described as a virtual learning lab (VLL).

Data and Sample

We draw on data from two main sources for our examination of virtual course-taking in Florida. To characterize growth across all sectors, we draw on student enrollment data from the Florida Virtual School. All other tables rely on data from the Florida Department of Education (FDOE). Using FDOE data, we assembled a student-level longitudinal data set for all public school students in Florida from 2005–2006 through 2013–2014. Because our data are drawn from high school transcripts, we limit our sample to students in grades 9 to 12 who attend traditional, charter, or magnet public schools.[9] Because a subset of the variables we construct rely on next-year outcomes, many of our results will focus on the 2012–2013 school year. In that year, we observe 6,501,111 course enrollments taken by 801,480 students.

The FDOE high school transcript data provide information on the institutions that provide instruction for each class, allowing us to identify courses provided by virtual schools. In addition, the FDOE data include demographic background characteristics (student sex, race-ethnicity, subsidized lunch use); classification in special programs (limited English proficiency, special education, gifted programs);

---

7. 2013 Florida Statutes, Title XLVIII (K–20 Education Code), Chapter 1002.45 (virtual instruction programs).

8. These calls also help FLVS identify instances of student cheating—for example, if the level of student understanding revealed during a phone call does not match that student's performance on written assignments.

9. We drop a small number of observations (fewer than 5 percent) where students attended special education schools, alternative schools, career or vocational education schools, or schools run by the Department of Juvenile Justice.

and student outcomes (statewide standardized test scores and grades) for all students.

To obtain school characteristics, we merge data on students' home institutions (the brick-and-mortar institutions in which students are enrolled, also sometimes called their "enrollment institutions") from the Common Core of Data (CCD) files maintained by the National Center for Education Statistics (NCES). Specifically, NCES data are used to characterize schools' urbanicity, charter or magnet school status, total enrollment, and share of students using free or reduced-price (FRL) lunch. We describe several sources of data on specific measures of in-school and out-of-school access to technological resources later in the paper.

The Distribution of Resources Across Schools in Florida

Before analyzing virtual course–taking in Florida, it is useful to review how resources are distributed across schools in the state. The Coleman Report documented dramatic differences in the 1960s in resources such as spending and class size across schools attended by black and white children. But many things have changed since the time of the report.

Table 1 presents descriptive statistics on the distribution of various resources for students across quartiles based on the share of the student body using subsidized meals. For example, quartile 1 includes schools with the lowest fraction of students eligible for subsidized meals in the sample—namely, fewer than 36 percent of students. Conversely, quartile 4 includes schools with the highest fraction of students eligible for subsidized meals—at least 71 percent of low-income students. The fifth column in the table gives the F-statistic and p-value for regression-based tests of whether there are differences across quartiles in the extent to which schools offer each resource.

As measures of traditional resources, we focus on teacher advanced degree–holding, teacher experience, and school student-to-teacher ratios. There is considerable evidence that teacher experience, particularly in the first few years, is strongly correlated with student achievement (Nye, Konstantopoulos, and Hedges 2004; Rivkin, Hanushek, and Kain 2005). Although many studies fail to find a similar benefit to teacher advanced-degree receipt (Harris and Sass 2011; Rivkin, Hanushek, and Kain 2005; but see Clotfelter, Ladd, and Vigdor 2007), we view this as the best available proxy for unmeasured teacher quality. Student-to-teacher ratios proxy for school class sizes; evidence suggests that achievement is enhanced by smaller class sizes (Angrist and Lavy 1999; Jepsen and Rivkin 2009; Krueger 1999; but see Hoxby 2000).

High-poverty schools have significantly fewer teachers with advanced degrees and significantly more teachers with three or fewer years of experience. For example, roughly 45 percent of teachers in the most advantaged schools have advanced degrees compared with fewer than 40 percent of teachers in the highest-poverty schools. About 31 percent of teachers in quartile 1 schools are novices compared with nearly 37 percent in quartile 4 schools. However, low-SES schools have lower student-to-teacher ratios than do higher-SES schools, probably because of the supplemental funding provided to these schools.

The success of virtual instruction requires access to the appropriate technology. Given the inequitable distribution of traditional resources across schools, one should naturally be concerned about the distribution of technology access. We use two sources of data to establish the technological resources available at the school level. The first is the October 2014 report on connectivity capability in Florida, "Community Anchor Institutions," including K–12 schools, conducted by the Florida Department of Management Services (FLDMS) and provided to the National Telecommunications and Information Administration (NTIA) for its State Broadband Initiative (SBI) (Florida Department of Management Services 2014). The report provides maximum download speeds for the service to which each institution subscribes. We dichotomize this to capture whether schools report download speeds of 100 megabits per second or greater; this is the median download speed reported for schools, and it corresponds roughly with what experts view is the minimum acceptable speed for networking.

The second source of data comes from the fall 2014 "Technology Resources Inventory"

Table 1. Student Access to Resources by Quartile of School (Fraction of Students Using Free or Reduced-Price Lunch, 2012–2013)

	Source	(1) Quartile 1	(2) Quartile 2	(3) Quartile 3	(4) Quartile 4	(5) F-, p-Values from Joint Test of Equality Across Quartiles
Fraction students using subsidized lunch	FLDOE EDW	0.235 (0.099)	0.459 (0.052)	0.626 (0.049)	0.814 (0.073)	$F = 2618.59$, $p = 0.00$
Non-technological resources						
Fraction of teachers with advanced degrees	FLDOE EDW	0.449 (0.183)	0.425 (0.146)	0.396 (0.134)	0.395 (0.129)	$F = 7.24$, $p = 0.00$
Indicator: more than 45 percent of teachers with advanced degree	FLDOE EDW	0.401 (0.491)	0.385 (0.487)	0.282 (0.451)	0.328 (0.471)	$F = 3.64$, $p = 0.01$
Fraction of teachers with zero to three years of experience	FLDOE EDW	0.312 (0.274)	0.306 (0.240)	0.291 (0.209)	0.368 (0.239)	$F = 5.78$, $p = 0.00$
Indicator: more than 25 percent of teachers with zero to three years of experience	FLDOE EDW	0.400 (0.491)	0.460 (0.499)	0.476 (0.500)	0.639 (0.481)	$F = 12.03$, $p = 0.00$
Fraction of teachers with ten or more years of experience	FLDOE EDW	0.402 (0.236)	0.401 (0.198)	0.410 (0.172)	0.345 (0.183)	$F = 7.13$, $p = 0.00$
Indicator: more than 45 percent of teachers with ten or more years of experience	FLDOE EDW	0.487 (0.501)	0.441 (0.497)	0.429 (0.496)	0.281 (0.450)	$F = 9.95$, $p = 0.00$
Student-to-teacher ratio	NCES	18.281 (4.275)	18.443 (4.035)	17.876 (3.346)	17.155 (3.347)	$F = 6.50$, $p = 0.00$
Indicator: student-to-teacher ratio greater than 19:1	NCES	0.367 (0.483)	0.331 (0.471)	0.286 (0.453)	0.226 (0.419)	$F = 4.66$, $p = 0.00$

(continued)

Table 1. (continued)

	Source	(1) Quartile 1	(2) Quartile 2	(3) Quartile 3	(4) Quartile 4	(5) F-, p-Values from Joint Test of Equality Across Quartiles
In-school technological resources						
Indicator: school maximum download speed greater than 100 megabits per second	FLDMS CAI	0.718 (0.451)	0.700 (0.459)	0.690 (0.463)	0.647 (0.479)	$F = 0.98, p = 0.40$
Computers per student	FLDOE TRI	0.373 (0.152)	0.399 (0.191)	0.408 (0.165)	0.482 (0.197)	$F = 15.17, p = 0.00$
Indicator: more than 0.33 computers per student	FLDOE TRI	0.579 (0.495)	0.593 (0.492)	0.675 (0.469)	0.787 (0.410)	$F = 10.62, p = 0.00$
Number of IEEE 802.11n compliant wireless access points per classroom	FLDOE TRI	0.580 (0.424)	0.624 (0.465)	0.598 (0.373)	0.553 (0.412)	$F = 1.18, p = 0.32$
Indicator: more than 0.67 wireless access points per classroom	FLDOE TRI	0.390 (0.489)	0.424 (0.495)	0.445 (0.498)	0.463 (0.500)	$F = 0.89, p = 0.44$
Proxies for out-of-school internet access						
Fraction of students with nonschool internet	FLDOE TRI	0.852 (0.121)	0.746 (0.165)	0.659 (0.186)	0.582 (0.209)	$F = 122.01, p = 0.00$
Indicator: more than 75 percent of students have internet outside school	FLDOE TRI	0.776 (0.418)	0.498 (0.501)	0.321 (0.468)	0.188 (0.392)	$F = 84.81, p = 0.00$
Residential broadband providers per 1,000 people (ZIP code)	NTIA SBI	0.652 (0.397)	0.656 (0.384)	0.572 (0.399)	0.559 (0.382)	$F = 4.54, p = 0.00$
Indicator: one or more residential broadband provider per 2,700 people (ZIP code)	NTIA SBI	0.745 (0.437)	0.763 (0.426)	0.679 (0.468)	0.655 (0.476)	$F = 3.59, p = 0.01$
N		274	274	274	275	

Source: Authors' tabulations from Florida Department of Education Data Warehouse (FLDOE EDW); National Center for Education Statistics (NCES); National Telecommunications and Information Administration, State Broadband Initiative (NTIA SBI); Florida Department of Education School Technology Resources Inventory (FLDOE TRI); and Florida Department of Management Services report, "Community Anchor Institutions" (FLDMS CAI), made available through NTIA.

Notes: Units = unique schools. Quartiles defined to hold roughly equal numbers of schools. Poverty quartile cut-points at 36.07 percent, 54.50 percent, and 70.95 percent.

surveys collected by the Florida Department of Education (Florida Bureau of Educational Technology 2014).[10] These surveys ask schools to report on their technology environment, including the source and speed of Internet at the school. We create two measures of in-school technological resources from this survey. The first is a measure of computers per student. Schools report the number of desktop and mobile computers in the school that are used for student instruction and that meet certain minimum technical standards in terms of memory, processing speeds, and so on.[11] We standardize this measure by the school enrollment. The second is a measure of wireless service in the school. The Technology Resources Inventory surveys ask schools to report the number of IEEE 802.11n compliant wireless access points in the building. Wireless access points allow wireless devices to connect to wired networks using Wi-Fi. This measure is standardized by the number of classrooms in the building as a proxy for the physical space that the wireless access points are working to cover.

Table 1 suggests that there is less discrepancy across socioeconomic categories for technological resources than for nontechnological ones. Indeed, high-poverty schools have more computers per student than do lower-poverty schools. Few of the other resources have clear relationships to socioeconomic status.

Success in online courses is likely to depend, at least in part, on access to high-speed Internet outside of school. And here the so-called digital divide might be an important constraint on the ability of virtual instruction to reduce the achievement gap. Our supplemental calculations on home Internet access among households with school-age children (five to eighteen) using 2013 and 2014 American Community Survey (ACS) data (Ruggles et al. 2015) suggest that affluent children are more likely to have home access to high-speed Internet than their low-income peers. Among households with family income at or below the poverty line, 42.6 percent lack access to high-speed Internet options (including DSL, cable Internet service, satellite Internet service, fiber-optic Internet service, or mobile broadband plans). Over 20 percent of households above the poverty threshold but still below the threshold for subsidized lunch eligibility (185 percent of the federal poverty line) lack high-speed Internet access, while fewer than 10 percent of households not eligible for free or reduced-price lunch lack such access.

Because, unfortunately, we do not have data on each student's access to high-speed Internet at home, we rely on two school-level proxies. In the Technology Resources Inventory surveys, school administrators are asked to estimate the fraction of students in their school who have access to high-speed Internet at home. We supplement this information with information on the geographic distribution of broadband providers collected by the NTIA and the Federal Communications Commission (FCC) (U.S. Department of Commerce 2014). Following Lisa Dettling, Sarena Goodman, and Jonathan Smith (2015), we aggregate block-level information on residential broadband providers to create the population-weighted number of providers of residential broadband service in the school's ZIP code, which serves as our measure of at-home access to high-speed Internet at the school level.

Out-of-school technological resources show clearer relationships to socioeconomic status. Schools with higher-SES student bodies estimate that a larger percentage of their students have access to the Internet outside of school; the estimated rate of out-of-school Internet access is 85 percent in the lowest-poverty schools versus 58 percent in schools with the highest poverty rates. Schools in higher-poverty areas are also less likely to be located in ZIP codes with at least one broadband provider per 2,700 people. Nearly 75 percent of low-poverty schools

---

10. For an example of the survey layout and responses for a single school, see: http://www.flinnovates.org/survey/FlinnovatesInventory/Reports/SchoolsPublicRpt?schoolCode=05%203011&inventoryTypeId=2 (accessed June 28, 2016).

11. Standards include 1GHz or faster processor; 1GB RAM or greater memory; 1024-by-768 screen resolution; and 9.5-inch (10-inch class) or larger screen size measured diagonally. Windows computers must use Windows 7 or higher; Apple computers must use MAC OS X 10.7 or higher.

Figure 1. Change over Time in Florida Virtual School Enrollments

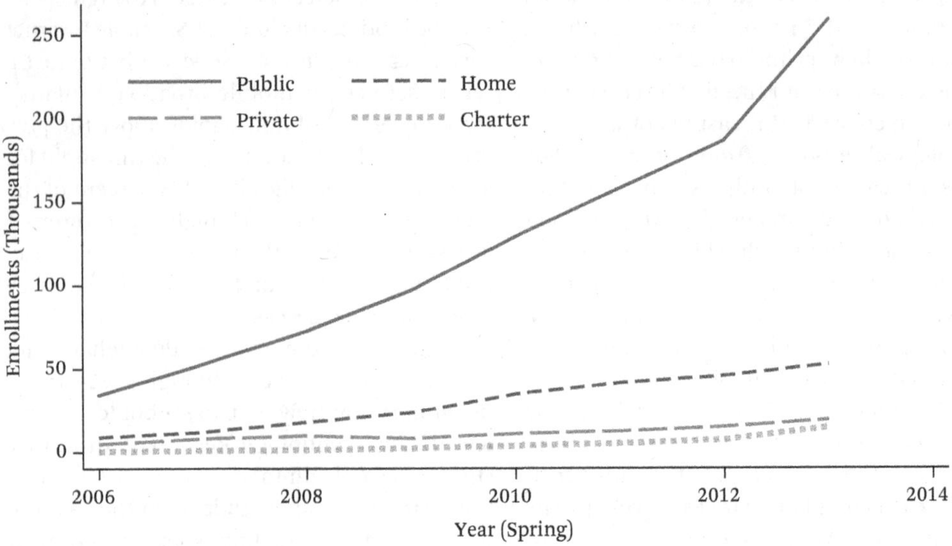

Source: Authors' calculations from FLVS data.

are located in broadband-rich communities versus about 65 percent of the highest-poverty schools.

Findings

Virtual course enrollments have expanded dramatically in the last decade. Figure 1 illustrates this using FLVS data from 2005–2006 through 2012–2013 for four different schooling sectors: public schools, private schools, charter schools, and home schools. We see dramatic enrollment growth over this period, particularly among public school students. For example, the number of total enrollments in virtual courses across all school types grew from just under 50,000 in 2006 to roughly 350,000 by 2013, with public school enrollments in virtual courses accounting for roughly three-quarters of all enrollments in the last year.

Virtual course–taking rates appear roughly constant across the core academic subject areas in 2012–2013, with math, social studies, English language arts, foreign language, and science each accounting for 9 to 15 percent of virtual course enrollments (table 2). Interestingly, physical education and driver's education are also among the most popular virtual courses, accounting for 4 and 14 percent of enrollments, respectively. Note that while each of the subjects listed has seen explosive growth in enrollments over time, the growth is especially marked in some areas; foreign languages, for instance, had more than a 1,000 percent increase in enrollments from 2005–2006 to 2012–2013.

During the 2012–2013 school year, nearly 21 percent of students took at least one virtual course. Virtual courses constituted about 4 percent of total course enrollments, suggesting that students who take any virtual courses take about one out of five of their courses online.[12] Table 3 presents virtual course–taking rates separately by student and school characteristics.

Students who were more advantaged, both academically and economically, appear to have been more likely to take virtual courses. For example, only 17.6 percent of students who were eligible for subsidized meals took a virtual course, and only 13.1 percent of students receiving special education services did so (column 1). By contrast, over 27 percent of gifted students took virtual courses. This finding is echoed by differences in virtual course–taking

12. This seemingly high rate is probably due to the requirement that, as mentioned earlier, all Florida high school students must take a virtual course as of the cohort that entered ninth grade in 2011–2012 (Watson et al. 2012).

Table 2. Florida Virtual School Course Enrollments in Different Subject Areas, 2006 and 2013

	2006	2013	Percent Change 2006 to 2013
Math	5,601 (14%)	45,577 (15%)	714%
Driver's education	0	44,261 (14%)	
Social studies	7,192 (18%)	43,381 (14%)	503
English language arts	5,654 (14%)	40,798 (13%)	622
Foreign languages	3,247 (8%)	38,852 (12%)	1,097
Science	4,233 (11%)	29,082 (9%)	587
Physical education	6,961 (17%)	13,674 (4%)	96
Business technology and computer science	1,931 (5%)	7,641 (2%)	296
Other	5,154 (13%)	51,122 (16%)	892
Total	39,973 100%	314,388 100%	

Source: Authors' calculations from Florida Department of Education Data.
Notes: Counts represent unique student-course combinations. Percentages represent the share of virtual student-course enrollments taken in each subject area, but may not sum to exactly 100 percent due to rounding used here. Courses that span multiple semesters in the same year count only once.

based on students' eighth-grade standardized test scores. Students are characterized according to the quartile into which their average standardized math and reading scores fall. Nearly 27 percent of students scoring in the top quartile of eighth-grade standardized tests (not shown) took a virtual course compared with only 14 percent of students in the bottom quartile, and the likelihood of taking any virtual class increased monotonically with prior achievement quartile. African American and Latino students were significantly less likely than average to take a virtual class in 2012–2013, and Asian students were significantly more likely than average to take one. The pattern of results is nearly identical using enrollment-weighted estimates (column 2): high-achieving students and higher-income students took a higher share of their courses virtually compared to their lower-achieving and less affluent peers.

Students in traditional public schools were the most likely to take at least one course online (22.62 percent); virtual course–taking was less prevalent in charter (20.68 percent) and magnet (18.65 percent) schools. Rural students had the lowest prevalence of virtual course–taking on both measures. Mirroring the student-level results, we see that the poorest schools had the lowest rates of virtual course–taking. Virtual course–taking was also somewhat more prevalent among students with access to higher-quality teachers, measured by on-paper credentials. In particular, virtual course–taking was more prevalent in schools with higher concentrations of novice teachers (18.5 percent) versus those with lower concentrations of novice teachers (22.38 percent).

Surprisingly, in-school technological resources had little relationship to online course-taking. Indeed, students in schools with more computers per student were actually some-

Table 3. Virtual Class–Taking Prevalence in Florida in 2012–2013

	Share of Students Taking At Least One Virtual Course (%)	Share of Classes Taken Virtually (%)
All students	20.82	4.10
By student characteristics		
Eligible for subsidized meals	17.63	3.31
Female	24.67	4.98
Black	19.12	3.31
Hispanic	16.48	3.14
Asian	26.39	5.09
Other race/race missing	23.48	5.04
Limited English proficiency	14.70	2.60
Gifted	27.16	5.11
Special education	13.09	2.54
Eighth-grade test score: first (lowest) quartile	13.95	2.64
Eighth-grade test score: second quartile	19.85	3.74
Eighth-grade test score: third quartile	22.94	4.38
Eighth-grade test score: fourth (highest) quartile	26.62	5.10
Grade 9	16.63	3.20
Grade 10	21.86	4.11
Grade 11	20.72	4.38
Grade 12	24.84	4.88
By school characteristics		
Charter	20.68	3.56
Magnet	18.65	3.29
Traditional public school	22.62	4.74
Urban	20.37	4.45
Suburban	21.22	3.88
Rural	19.95	3.68
By percentage of students eligible for subsidized meals		
First (lowest) quartile	25.33	5.09
Second quartile	23.06	4.92
Third quartile	19.02	3.36
Fourth (highest) quartile	15.89	2.70
In-school nontechnological resources		
Share of teachers with advanced degrees greater than 45 percent	21.06	4.42
Share of teachers with advanced degrees 45 percent or less	20.59	3.69
Share of teachers with zero to three years of experience greater than 25 percent	18.50	3.31
Share of teachers with zero to three years of experience 25 percent or less	22.38	4.47
Share of teachers with ten or more years of experience greater than 45 percent	22.10	4.08
Share of teachers with ten or more years of experience 45 percent or less	19.38	3.88
Pupil-teacher ratio of 19:1 or less	20.38	3.72
Pupil-teacher ratio greater than 19:1	20.76	3.74

Table 3. (continued)

	Share of Students Taking At Least One Virtual Course (%)	Share of Classes Taken Virtually (%)
In-school technological resources		
School maximum download speed of 100 megabits per second or higher	20.53	3.68
School maximum download speed of less than 100 megabits per second	20.01	3.48
More than 0.33 computers per student	19.08	3.35
0.33 computers per student or less	22.10	4.03
More than 0.67 wireless access points per classroom	19.88	3.52
0.67 wireless access points per classroom or less	20.45	3.66
Proxies for out-of-school internet resources		
More than 75 percent of students have internet access	22.38	4.05
75 percent or less of students have internet access	18.60	3.28
One or more residential broadband provider per 2,700 people (ZIP code)	21.54	4.21
Less than one residential broadband provider per 2,700 people (ZIP code)	18.89	3.51

Source: Authors' tabulations based on data from the FLDOE EDW, NCES, FLDMS CAI, NTIA SBI, and FLDOE TRI. (See table 1 source note.)
Note: FCAT quartiles are based on average of eighth-grade math and reading scores.

what less likely to take online courses. Our out-of-school proxy measures were more predictive of online course–taking. Students from schools where over 75 percent of students were estimated to have out-of-school access to the Internet were more likely (22.4 percent) to have taken at least one online course than were students in schools with less estimated home Internet access (18.6 percent). Likewise, students attending schools in ZIP codes with greater residential broadband provision (at least one provider per 2,700 people) had higher virtual course–taking rates (21.5 percent) than did students in more sparsely serviced areas (18.9 percent).

Although we see students from all different school and family backgrounds taking virtual courses, they may be differentially likely to do so based on their reasons for taking a particular class. To explore this possibility, table 4 breaks down the share of virtual class enrollments by the reason for attempting these classes. We distinguish four types of attempts, which we impute based on whether students had previously taken the same class and past performance in the class if it was previously taken. Classes are designated as "first attempts" if students had never taken the same course in any previous year. "Credit recovery" classes are flagged when students had taken the same course in a previous year and received a failing grade. "Grade improvement" is flagged if students had taken the same course in a previous year and received a D grade but never an F. "Other attempts" (not shown) are flagged when students had taken the same course across multiple years but there was no evidence that they had done so owing to poor prior performance.[13]

The top panel presents the prevalence of

---

13. "Other attempts" include both classes that could be taken multiple times for credit (like some special education courses) and cases where students took one term of a class in one year and a second term in a subsequent year.

Table 4. Florida Virtual Class Enrollments in 2012–2013 Conditional on Attempt Type

	(1)	(2)	(3)	(4)	(5)	(6)	(7)	(8)
		\multicolumn{7}{c}{By Student Type}						
	All	Free or Reduced-Price Lunch	Not Free or Reduced-Price Lunch	Black	Hispanic	White or Asian	FCAT Quartile 1	FCAT Quartile 4
All attempt types	4.1%	3.3%	5.1%	3.3%	3.1%	5.1%	2.6%	5.1%
First attempts	3.7	3.0	4.5	3.0	2.8	4.5	2.4	4.6
Credit recovery	13.5	10.2	21.0	10.6	11.3	17.5	8.0	31.4
Grade improvement	11.7	6.7	22.5	7.0	8.0	18.8	3.0	53.1

	(1)	(2)	(3)	(4)	(5)
	\multicolumn{5}{c}{By Class Type}				
	Core Subjects	Life Skills	Foreign Languages	Other Electives	AP/IB
All attempt types	3.6%	10.1%	8.5%	2.9%	0.9%
First attempts	2.9	10.4	7.1	2.8	0.8
Credit recovery	12.8	13.2	29.3	10.2	24.3
Grade improvement	11.4	5.8	44.8	3.2	38.1

Source: Authors' tabulations from FLDOE data.

Notes: FCAT = Florida Comprehensive Assessment Test, AP = Advanced Placement, and IB = International Baccalaureate. Core courses include math, English, language arts, science, and social studies and exclude AP/IB courses. "Life skills" includes physical education, driver's education, and health.

course-taking conditional on attempt type for all students (column 1) and by student characteristics of interest, including subsidized lunch use (free or reduced-price lunch versus full-price lunch); race (black, Hispanic, and white or Asian); and prior achievement (students in the highest and lowest Florida Comprehensive Assessment Test [FCAT] achievement quartiles). Among the full population of students, we see that students took the smallest share of their first attempts at a course virtually. Only 3.7 percent of first attempts at classes were taken virtually, compared to over 13 percent of attempts at credit recovery and nearly 12 percent of attempts at grade improvement.

Columns 2 to 7 give these breakdowns for different subtypes of students. Across all course types, students on subsidized lunch took a lower share of their courses virtually than did their more affluent peers. In some cases, the differences are quite sizable: more affluent children took over twice as many virtual courses in credit recovery attempts compared to lower-income children, and over three times more in grade improvement attempts. White and Asian children also took a higher share of virtual courses across all class types compared to their black and Hispanic peers. The gaps are most dramatic when comparing lower-achieving and higher-achieving children. Students in the highest quartile of FCAT performance were nearly four times more likely to make their credit recovery attempts virtually and were roughly eighteen times more likely to make their grade improvement attempts virtually.[14]

The bottom panel presents the share of virtual courses taken within each attempt type for five different types of courses. "Core subjects" includes math, science, social studies, and English language arts. "Foreign languages" covers foreign language offerings, and "life skills" includes health, physical education, and driver's education classes. "Other electives" includes all other subjects. We removed Advanced Placement (AP) and International Baccalaureate (IB) classes from these four types of courses; these accelerated options are presented separately as "AP/IB" classes.

Virtual course–taking is not equally prevalent in all course areas. Aggregating all attempt types (row 5), life skills and foreign language courses were most often taken virtually—roughly 8 to 10 percent. By contrast, only about 3.5 percent of core courses and 3 percent of other elective classes were taken virtually. Virtual course–taking was very uncommon for AP/IB classes: fewer than 1 percent of students took their AP and IB courses virtually.

There are a few surprising patterns when these results are broken down by course attempt types. For instance, though fewer than 1 percent of AP classes were taken virtually, a very high share of grade improvement (38 percent) and credit recovery (24 percent) attempts in AP/IB classes were made virtually.[15] Likewise, nearly one-third of credit recovery attempts and over 40 percent of grade improvement attempts in foreign language courses were made virtually. This suggests that virtual classes serve different purposes for students depending on the class type.

In an effort to distinguish the association between virtual course–taking and specific student and school characteristics, table 5 presents estimates from OLS regressions. The unit of observation in these regressions is a student-course, so in most cases there will be multiple observations for each student. We predict the likelihood that a course will be taken virtually given the characteristics of the student taking the class and the student's home institution. Standard errors are all clustered at the school (home institution) level, which subsumes all observations for each student.

Each column reflects the results from a separate regression, with the sample indicated in the top row. Columns 1 and 2 focus on all course types and all attempt types shown in

---

14. Although relatively few high-achieving students took classes for credit recovery or grade improvement purposes, each category still had several thousand enrollments: we observe about 2,250 grade improvement attempts and about 7,500 credit recovery attempts for the highest-achieving students. This suggests that the high numbers are not purely an artifact of unstable measures due to small sample sizes.

15. This is on a very small base of 200 to 450 enrollments each for AP credit recovery and grade improvement attempts.

Table 5. Predictors of Online Course-Taking, 2012–2013

	(1) Any Course Type, Any Attempt	(2) Any Course Type, Any Attempt	(3) Any Course Type, Any Attempt	(4) Core Classes, First Attempt	(5) All Classes, Credit Recovery	(6) AP Classes, Any Attempt
Student characteristics						
Free or reduced-price lunch	−0.006***	−0.006***	−0.006***	−0.003***	−0.055***	0.000
	(0.000)	(0.000)	(0.000)	(0.000)	(0.003)	(0.000)
Female	0.019***	0.019***	0.019***	0.010***	0.038***	−0.000
	(0.001)	(0.001)	(0.000)	(0.000)	(0.002)	(0.000)
Black	−0.004***	−0.004***	−0.005***	−0.005***	−0.020***	0.001
	(0.001)	(0.001)	(0.000)	(0.001)	(0.004)	(0.001)
Hispanic	−0.009***	−0.009***	−0.008***	−0.008***	−0.027***	−0.001*
	(0.001)	(0.001)	(0.000)	(0.001)	(0.004)	(0.001)
Asian	0.010***	0.009***	0.009***	0.006***	0.019	0.008***
	(0.001)	(0.001)	(0.001)	(0.002)	(0.013)	(0.002)
Limited English proficiency	−0.007***	−0.006***	−0.003***	−0.005***	−0.030***	−0.000
	(0.001)	(0.001)	(0.000)	(0.001)	(0.004)	(0.001)
Gifted	0.004**	0.004***	0.009***	0.004*	0.074***	−0.001
	(0.002)	(0.002)	(0.001)	(0.002)	(0.014)	(0.001)
Special education	−0.009***	−0.009***	−0.007***	−0.004***	−0.027***	0.002
	(0.001)	(0.001)	(0.000)	(0.001)	(0.003)	(0.001)
Composite eighth-grade FCAT (standard)	0.010***	0.010***	0.010***	0.006***	0.043***	0.005***
	(0.000)	(0.000)	(0.000)	(0.000)	(0.002)	(0.001)
School characteristics						
Charter	−0.046***	−0.035**		−0.042***	−0.050	−0.004
	(0.018)	(0.015)		(0.016)	(0.043)	(0.006)
Magnet	−0.010***	−0.010***		−0.010***	−0.036***	−0.003
	(0.004)	(0.004)		(0.003)	(0.010)	(0.002)
Urban	0.001	0.001		0.003	−0.013	0.002
	(0.004)	(0.004)		(0.004)	(0.010)	(0.002)
Rural	−0.008**	−0.001		−0.000	−0.017	−0.000
	(0.004)	(0.005)		(0.005)	(0.012)	(0.002)
Log enrollment	−0.007	0.006		0.005	−0.007	0.005
	(0.009)	(0.011)		(0.012)	(0.016)	(0.006)
Fraction of enrollment on free or reduced-price lunch	0.011	0.035		0.037	−0.099**	0.008
	(0.020)	(0.023)		(0.023)	(0.049)	(0.013)
Fraction of enrollment black/Hispanic	0.003	−0.002		−0.009	0.164***	−0.011*
	(0.011)	(0.010)		(0.010)	(0.031)	(0.007)
School mean: eighth-grade FCAT	0.035***	0.045***		0.039***	0.189***	0.002
	(0.012)	(0.013)		(0.012)	(0.036)	(0.007)
Grade: A	−0.007*	−0.007*		−0.008**	−0.016	−0.001
	(0.004)	(0.004)		(0.004)	(0.013)	(0.003)
Grade: B	−0.001	0.001		0.002	0.005	−0.001
	(0.004)	(0.004)		(0.004)	(0.012)	(0.003)
Grade: D	0.005	0.007		0.002	0.021	0.003
	(0.008)	(0.008)		(0.009)	(0.020)	(0.005)
Grade: F	0.020	0.019		0.025	0.011	−0.001
	(0.016)	(0.016)		(0.019)	(0.041)	(0.007)

Table 5. (continued)

	(1) Any Course Type, Any Attempt	(2) Any Course Type, Any Attempt	(3) Any Course Type, Any Attempt	(4) Core Classes, First Attempt	(5) All Classes, Credit Recovery	(6) AP Classes, Any Attempt
Nontechnological school resources						
Fraction of teachers with advanced degrees	0.047** (0.021)	0.041** (0.018)		0.054*** (0.019)	0.071 (0.047)	0.023* (0.013)
Fraction of teachers with zero to three years of experience	−0.004 (0.018)	−0.028* (0.016)		−0.027 (0.017)	−0.078** (0.037)	−0.018* (0.009)
Student-to-teacher ratio	−0.000 (0.001)	−0.001 (0.001)		−0.001 (0.001)	0.000 (0.002)	−0.001 (0.000)
In-school technological resources						
School maximum download speed 100 megabits per second or higher		0.005* (0.003)		0.002 (0.003)	−0.023** (0.011)	−0.001 (0.001)
Computers per student		−0.023*** (0.008)		−0.020** (0.008)	−0.095*** (0.028)	0.002 (0.005)
Proxies for out-of-school internet access						
Fraction of students with nonschool internet access		−0.020** (0.009)		−0.023*** (0.009)	−0.052* (0.030)	−0.008 (0.005)
Residential broadband providers per 1,000 people (ZIP code)		−0.003 (0.003)		−0.003 (0.003)	−0.001 (0.012)	−0.003** (0.001)
Sample mean	0.041	0.041	0.041	0.029	0.135	0.009
School fixed effects	No	No	Yes	No	No	No
Unique enrollments	6,186,426	6,186,426	6,186,426	3,124,889	133,285	430,516
Unique schools	1,234	1,234	1,234	1,099	648	645

Source: Authors' tabulations based on data from the FLDOE EDW, NCES, FLDMS CAI, NTIA SBI, and FLDOE TRI. (See table 1 source note.)

Notes: Missing variable dummies and grade-level dummies are included but not shown. Columns 1 to 3 include course-type by attempt-type fixed effects

***$p < .01$; **$p < .05$; *$p < .10$

table 3. Consistent with the group comparisons presented in table 3, we see that subsidized lunch use is negatively associated with virtual course-taking, as is black and Latino race-ethnicity and limited English proficiency. Gifted students were more likely than nongifted students, and special education students less likely than non-exceptional students, to take virtual courses. Prior achievement, measured by the average of the student's standardized eighth-grade math and English language arts FCAT scores, is positively associated with virtual course-taking. Courses were less likely to be taken virtually in charter and magnet schools than in traditional public schools, and less likely to be taken virtually in rural schools than in suburban schools. School size is negatively associated, and the average eighth-grade achievement of the school's student body is positively associated, with the likelihood that a course would be taken virtually. Results are substantively similar in terms of both the direction and significance of coefficients when we use school fixed effects to determine which student factors predict virtual course-taking, comparing students to their peers in the same school (column 2). Specifications that focus on characteristics that predict core academic classes being taken virtually on the first attempt (column 4) are also consistent with those in column 1, with low-income, male, lower-achieving, special education, and black and Hispanic students being less likely to take these courses virtually.

Given that virtual course–taking is especially common for credit recovery attempts, we wanted to explore which student characteristics most strongly predict the use of virtual courses for credit recovery holding other factors constant (column 5). Although the pattern of results is largely the same as the pattern in the first three columns, the magnitude of the coefficients is substantially larger. For instance, while subsidized lunch use is associated with only a 0.7-percentage-point reduction in the likelihood of taking a given course virtually across all classes and attempt types (column 1), it is associated with a nearly 6.0-percentage-point reduction in the likelihood of making credit recovery attempts virtually (column 4).

Two competing interpretations may emerge from these results. In one interpretation, the greater uptake of virtual courses for credit recovery by affluent and high-achieving students may be evidence that they are using virtual classes more strategically. To the extent that advantaged students are better poised to access the potential benefits of virtual courses for credit recovery, these differential patterns in uptake could worsen inequality. A second interpretation is that students have a good read on which course delivery formats are most likely to work for them: if lower-achieving and relatively disadvantaged students accurately perceive that they would benefit more from face-to-face instruction than from virtual instruction, the differential patterns in uptake would not be worrisome.

Column 6 focuses on AP/IB courses. Unlike in our other specifications, we find few characteristics that predict the likelihood that a student will take AP/IB courses virtually: Asian students and students with higher prior achievement were more likely—and charter students, students from larger schools, and rural students less likely—to take AP courses virtually, all else held constant. The latter result is especially surprising. Because rural schools are less likely to be able to offer a full suite of AP courses, we had anticipated that rural students might be especially likely to pursue advanced courses online.[16]

Although disadvantaged students are somewhat less likely to take virtual courses, online instruction might be more beneficial for these students for any of the reasons discussed in the prior section. A complete causal analysis of the relationship between virtual instruction and student achievement is beyond the scope of this paper, but we present several figures that illustrate how outcomes differ by mode of instruction for two popular core academic classes: Algebra I and World History. For this analysis, we limit our sample to students making their first attempt to take these courses in 2012–2013. We further exclude students who were taking these courses at an unusual point in their academic career, such as twelfth-graders taking Algebra I for the first time. Students are characterized according to whether they were observed in any term in a virtual section of the course under consideration. That is, if they were observed in a FtF Algebra I section in one term and a virtual Algebra I section the next, they appear only in the "ever-virtual" column. Students who took all face-to-face classes in the relevant course are considered "only-FtF."

We examine student performance in the next course in the sequence, which we identify by examining high school transcripts for all students in Florida. For Algebra I, the next course is Geometry. For World History, the next course could be any of the following: U.S. History, U.S. Government, or Economics. Grades are reported on a standardized four-point scale. We compare the cumulative perfect frequency distributions for virtual vs. FtF students; at each grade point, the figures depict the share of virtual (or FtF) students who received that grade or lower.

Figures 2, 3, 4, and 5 show the distribution of subsequent course grades for students taking Algebra I virtually versus face-to-face, separately by quartile of eighth-grade math and reading scores. Specifically, we group ninth-grade students who took Algebra I in 2012–2013 into quartiles based on the average of their

---

16. The coefficient on rural is negative even when we do not simultaneously control for enrollment.

Figure 2. Florida Students' Next-Course Grade, Algebra 1, 2012–2013, All Students

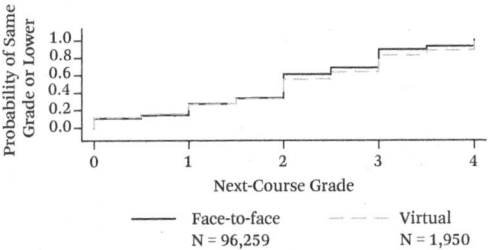

Face-to-face — — — Virtual
N = 96,259   N = 1,950

Source: Authors' calculations from FDOE data.
Notes: Grade = grade in next course on four-point scale. FCAT = Florida Comprehensive Achievement Test. Quartile based on averaged reading and math eighth-grade standardized scores. The next course is Geometry.

Figure 3. Florida Students' Next-Course Grade, Algebra 1, 2012–2013, Free or Reduced-Price Lunch Students

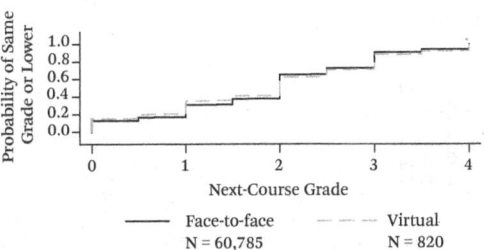

Face-to-face — — — Virtual
N = 60,785   N = 820

Source: Authors' calculations from FDOE data.
Notes: Grade = grade in next course on four-point scale. FCAT = Florida Comprehensive Achievement Test. Quartile based on averaged reading and math eighth-grade standardized scores. The next course is Geometry.

Figure 4. Florida Students' Next-Course Grade, Algebra 1, 2012–2013, Quartile 1 (Lowest) FCAT Students

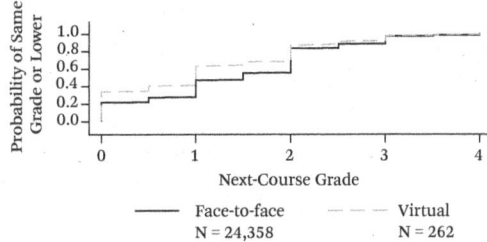

Face-to-face — — — Virtual
N = 24,358   N = 262

Source: Authors' calculations from FDOE data.
Notes: Grade = grade in next course on four-point scale. FCAT = Florida Comprehensive Achievement Test. Quartile based on averaged reading and math eighth-grade standardized scores. The next course is Geometry.

Figure 5. Florida Students' Next-Course Grade, Algebra 1, 2012–2013, Quartile 4 (Highest) FCAT Students

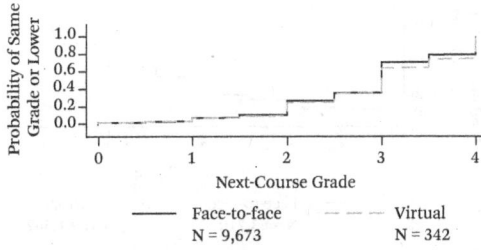

Face-to-face — — — Virtual
N = 9,673   N = 342

Source: Authors' calculations from FDOE data.
Notes: Grade = grade in next course on four-point scale. FCAT = Florida Comprehensive Achievement Test. Quartile based on averaged reading and math eighth-grade standardized scores. The next course is Geometry.

eighth-grade math and reading scores. Overall, it appears that students who took the course virtually did slightly better than students who took the course face-to-face. However, if we look separately by prior eighth-grade performance, we see that bottom-quartile students did worse in Geometry if they took the course virtually, while top-quartile students performed somewhat better if they took the course virtually. One complication in these results is that a lower share (64 percent) of virtual Algebra I students were observed taking Geometry compared to FtF students (72 percent), suggesting that virtual students who appear in Geometry may be a more positively selected group.

Results are more positive for virtual course-taking among World History students (figures 6, 7, 8, and 9). Although comparable shares of virtual and FtF students were observed in follow-on courses (roughly 68 percent in each sector), virtual students slightly outperformed their FtF peers in each of the samples studied. Moreover, the advantages were more pronounced—though still modest—for virtual students who qualified for free or reduced-

Figure 6. Florida Students' Next-Course Grade, World History, 2012–2013, All Students

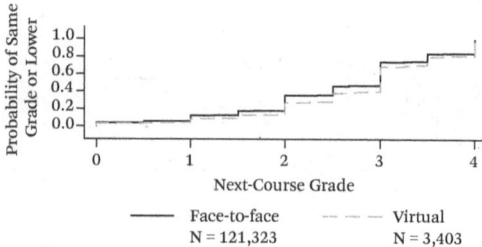

Source: Authors' calculations from FDOE data.
Notes: Grade = grade in next course on four-point scale. FCAT = Florida Comprehensive Achievement Test. Quartile based on averaged reading and math eighth-grade standardized scores. The next course includes U.S. History, U.S. Government, or Economics (regular or honors).

Figure 7. Florida Students' Next-Course Grade, World History, 2012–2013, Free or Reduced-Price Lunch Students

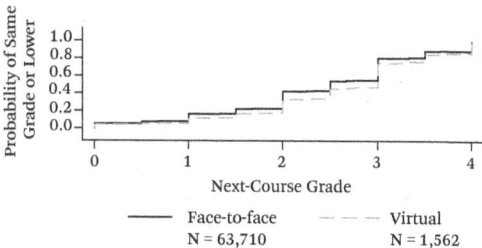

Source: Authors' calculations from FDOE data.
Notes: Grade = grade in next course on four-point scale. FCAT = Florida Comprehensive Achievement Test. Quartile based on averaged reading and math eighth-grade standardized scores. The next course includes U.S. History, U.S. Government, or Economics (regular or honors).

Figure 8. Florida Students' Next-Course Grade, World History, 2012–2013, Quartile 1 (Lowest) FCAT Students

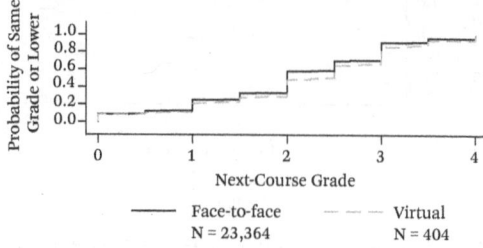

Source: Authors' calculations from FDOE data.
Notes: Grade = grade in next course on four-point scale. FCAT = Florida Comprehensive Achievement Test. Quartile based on averaged reading and math eighth-grade standardized scores. The next course includes U.S. History, U.S. Government, or Economics (regular or honors).

Figure 9. Florida Students' Next-Course Grade, World History, 2012–2013, Quartile 4 (Highest) FCAT Students

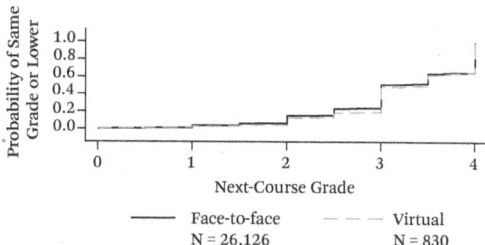

Source: Authors' calculations from FDOE data.
Notes: Grade = grade in next course on four-point scale. FCAT = Florida Comprehensive Achievement Test. Quartile based on averaged reading and math eighth-grade standardized scores. The next course includes U.S. History, U.S. Government, or Economics (regular or honors).

price lunch and for students with low eighth-grade FCAT scores than they were for their higher-achieving peers.

In interpreting these differences, it is important to keep in mind that students are rarely randomly sorted into a virtual course. In most cases, a student can decide whether or not to take a course virtually, and this decision is likely to be determined by many unobservable as well as observable factors. For this reason, we do not interpret these figures as reflecting the causal impact of the instructional mode. In future work, we plan to estimate more rigorously the causal impact of virtual instruction.

BEYOND VIRTUAL INSTRUCTION

Our analysis of virtual schooling in Florida suggests that virtual course-taking has the potential to be scaled up for broader use. While traditionally less advantaged student groups—lower-income, nonwhite, lower-achieving—are somewhat less likely to take virtual courses, the differences remain relatively modest. Moreover, a large and growing proportion of traditionally disadvantaged students do enroll in and complete online courses.

However, more equal access to online course–taking may not meaningfully affect achievement gaps if course quality is not superior in online courses. We find mixed (descriptive) evidence on the subsequent performance of virtual versus face-to-face students. While virtual course-taking in World History is positively associated with performance on subsequent social science classes, results are more ambiguous for Algebra: free and reduced-price lunch students did no better on average, and students with low prior achievement did worse, in Geometry after taking virtual courses. Although the evidence we have presented should certainly not be interpreted causally, it seems unlikely that the causal impact is large and positive considering that students taking virtual courses are positively selected (on observables) and thus, if anything, the unconditional comparisons we present may overstate the benefits of virtual instruction for disadvantaged students. Unless the benefits are large and positive, at current uptake levels it is unlikely that virtual schooling will do much to improve educational inequality.

We turn now to explore evidence on a distinct set of educational technologies that could be incorporated in either virtual or face-to-face courses to produce better opportunities for disadvantaged children. Known as computer-aided instruction (CAI) or intelligent tutoring systems (ITS), these technologies are designed to quickly diagnose and target student needs. In this section, we describe these systems, discuss how they might promote student learning, and then review the evidence on their effectiveness.

The Theory and Development of Computer-Aided Instruction

Broadly speaking, computer-aided instruction refers to any computerized learning environment in which computer software provides instruction, practice, and timely feedback to students. However, the earliest CAI was not much more than a computerized textbook that provided predeveloped content with very little interactivity. Gradually these programs became more flexible, providing relevant content in response to student inputs (Nwana 1990). As they began to leverage more sophisticated artificial intelligence technology, these programs became known as intelligent tutoring systems (ITS).

Intelligent tutoring systems rely on the interaction between its domain and pedagogical models and a dynamically updated student model (Conati 2009). As a student works through problems, completed steps, missteps, hint requests, and so on, are used to update the student model and estimate the student's understanding; after this estimate is compared against domain knowledge models to determine gaps, the pedagogical model can intelligently implement tutoring strategies to fill in these gaps (Graesser, Conley, and Olney 2012). A fundamental development in newer-generation ITS is the ability to diagnose student errors and build remediation from these diagnoses (Shute and Psotka 1994). Newer intelligent tutoring systems also focus on smaller "pieces" of the learning process, emphasizing individual steps that students must take to solve a problem (VanLehn et al. 2005).

ITS might be expected to influence student learning in several ways. Perhaps most importantly, the growing sophistication of ITS may provide teachers with an opportunity to tailor content and instructional techniques to each student's individual needs.[17] This type of "differentiated instruction" is often cited by researchers and practitioners as the key to effective teaching, particularly for disadvantaged students whose performance might be quite far below that of their peers and expected grade-level standards. Second, the different modes of instruction available through videos and online formats might be better able to engage students (Ma et al. 2014). One example is the emphasis on "game-based" learning. Third, the use of intelligent tutoring systems that are constantly collecting and analyzing data on student performance could encourage the use of data to guide instruction more broadly.

---

17. For a more detailed discussion, see Ma et al. (2014).

Fourth, these technologies might provide all students with access to high-quality content. Like virtual instruction, intelligent tutoring systems rely on centrally developed curricular content and instructional techniques. This type of specialization should, in theory, allow for more meticulous planning and development of material, including quite detailed scripts for teachers. As with virtual instruction, then, ITS could produce a high-quality classroom experience—and should produce a relatively uniform one—for students from a broad range of backgrounds.

New technologies offer the possibility of improving instruction in all these ways, but they also have important limits. Perhaps most importantly, approaches that completely forgo direct interpersonal interaction are unlikely to be able to teach certain skills. Learning is an inherently social activity. While an intelligent tutoring system might be able to help a student master specific math concepts, it may not be able to teach students to critically analyze a work of literature or debate the ethics of new legislation.

The recent experience of Rocketship, a well-known charter school network, illustrates this concern. Developed in the Bay Area of California in 2006, Rocketship's instructional model revolves around a blended learning approach in which students spend a considerable amount of time each day engaged with computer-aided learning technologies. The network received early praise for its innovative approach to learning and, most importantly, for the high achievement scores posted by its mostly poor, nonwhite student population (Schorr and McGriff 2011). In 2012, however, researchers and educators raised concerns about graduates from Rocketship elementary schools, noting that they had good basic skills but were struggling with the critical analysis required in middle schools (Herold 2014; Guha et al. 2015).

Does Computer-Aided Instruction Help Students Learn?

There have been hundreds of studies of CAI programs over the past twenty-five years, and the results are decidedly mixed. A number of early syntheses concluded that there are positive average effects of educational software for reading and mathematics (Fletcher-Flinn and Gravatt 1995; Kulik 1994), but others did not (Kirkpatrick and Cuban 1998). Mark Dynarski and his colleagues (2007) conducted experimental evaluations of ten educational technology products that had been judged by an expert review panel to have the greatest potential for success. They find that only one of the ten has a positive effect on student learning, calling into question many earlier positive findings.

While recent meta-analyses attempt to bring coherence to the large body of existing research, no clear consensus has emerged. A careful review of these studies and the associated meta-analyses reveals an interesting pattern. First, studies that use an experimental design yield much smaller effects than those using quasi-experimental methods (Cheung and Slavin 2011, 2013; Ma et al. 2014; Steenbergen-Hu and Cooper 2013). Second, studies using standardized outcome measures as opposed to locally development assessments tailored specifically to the technology being studied exhibit considerably smaller impacts (Koedinger et al. 1997; Kulik and Fletcher 2015; Steenbergen-Hu and Cooper 2013). Finally, studies with smaller samples generally exhibit larger effect sizes (Cheung and Slavin 2011, 2013; Kulik and Fletcher 2015; Steenbergen-Hu and Cooper 2013). Taken together, the most rigorous studies (those with large samples, standardized outcome measures, and an experimental design) yield effect sizes around 0.10, which aligns more closely with the findings of Dynarski and his colleagues (2007).

However, these evaluations do suggest important lessons for developers and practitioners. First, substantial evidence points to the importance of implementation barriers. For example, researchers who studied Thinking Reader found that students used the program far less frequently than recommended and that, when they did use it, they spent less time per book than indicated by program guidelines (Drummond et al. 2011). Similarly, in a study of the Cognitive Tutor Geometry program, John Pane and his colleagues (2010) find that teachers had trouble implementing the program's instructional practices. For example, teachers reported difficulties in implementing the collaborative work that required students to articulate mathematical thinking, making strong connections between computer-based activities and classroom instruction, and maintaining the expected learning pace with many students who lacked prior math and reading skills.

Moreover, even successful programs took more than one year to show positive effects. Pane and his colleagues (2014) conducted a large, experimental evaluation of Cognitive Tutor Algebra I in over 140 schools, with 25,000 students, across the country. Although there were no treatment effects in year one, by the second year students in the treatment classrooms were scoring 0.20 standard deviations higher than their peers in control classes. Following a subset of the original Dynarski et al. (2007) sample whose teachers continued using the programs for a second year, Larissa Campuzano and her colleagues (2009) find a statistically significant positive effect size of 0.15 on student achievement for these students.

Second, the benefit of ITS depends on the context in which it is implemented, including the counterfactual instruction that students would receive in the absence of the technology. In a reanalysis of the Dynarski et al. (2007) study, Eric Taylor (2015) finds important heterogeneity in the effects across classrooms. He shows that the CAI/ITS programs had a positive impact on students in classrooms with less effective teachers and a negative impact on students in classrooms with more effective teachers, consistent with the fact that the new technology was intended, in part, to be a substitute for the classroom teacher. Although the average effect was indistinguishable from zero, the effects for some students were not. This result highlights the importance of considering not only the quality of the new technology but also the quality of the education for which it is substituting. Consistent with this dynamic, evaluations of CAI in developing countries, in settings with fewer resources and arguably less skilled teachers, often find positive effects. For example, in a large randomized policy evaluation conducted in India, Abhijit Banerjee and his colleagues (2005) find strong positive effects of computer-assisted mathematics programs on math scores in high-poverty urban areas in Mumbai and Vadodara.

DISCUSSION AND CONCLUSIONS

The Coleman Report shone light on vast differences in achievement between poor and nonpoor children and provided evidence that public schooling systems were doing little to close these achievement gaps. Nonetheless, public schools are the primary lever by which governments seek to affect children's learning and create more equitable opportunities. Their lack of effect at the time of the report is not necessarily an indictment of their potential. Many forces work against schools' ability to close achievement gaps, particularly between highly resourced groups and those that are not highly resourced. Policy choices and technological innovations can exacerbate the inequalities that already exist between families, but alternatively, they may mitigate or even overcome those forces. In this paper, we have highlighted the potential mechanisms by which new technologies may reduce or add to the existing gaps. As with all prior technologies, this potential depends not only on their innovative features but also on their implementation.

The combination of residential segregation and, to some extent, local control of schools can disadvantage schools serving children from lower-income families, reducing or even reversing the potential in these cases for a public education system to reduce gaps. Even within schools, more powerful families can advocate for their children to receive greater resources, such as more effective teachers, or additional supports. When students attend different schools, this potential is far greater, as higher-income families can pool resources to benefit just their own school, either through the tax system or even independently. If the teaching jobs are more appealing in these schools serving higher-resourced families, as they often are, these schools can recruit better teachers and school leaders—perhaps the most important of all education resources—even without additional dollars.

Unlike teachers, technologies have no preferences for the schools in which they work. As such, technologies may reduce inequalities in resources across schools. The resources available on the Internet, for example, are equally available to all schools with the same Internet access, and Internet access costs the same for all schools in the same area, regardless of the student population served. Technologies can reduce differences in peer groups in other ways as well. Online courses, for example, can mix peers from schools across wide geographic areas. Even within schools, technologies can have equalizing effects across teachers, increasing the effectiveness of less effective teachers by substituting for their areas of weakness. Similarly, technologies that allow teachers to better differentiate instruction may help them reach students who are further from the average within their classroom, to the academic benefit of those students.

The effects of technologies on gaps, however, may not be all positive. If less capable teachers have difficulty making use of the benefits of new technologies—that is, if technologies and teaching skills are complementary—differences across classrooms could increase. These differences might add to gaps to the extent that less capable teachers are concentrated in schools with students from less-resourced families. Similarly, to be effective some technologies may require students to have either adult oversight or a set of prior skills that will help them make use of the opportunities the technologies offer. To the extent that students from less-resourced families have access to fewer supports or have lower prior skills, they may not be positioned to reap these benefits and inequalities could increase.

Given the potential for new technologies to both reduce and exacerbate inequalities, their actual effect is an empirical question. Based on the evidence presented here, new technologies such as virtual courses and ITS, as currently implemented, are making little headway in closing achievement gaps. With respect to virtual course–taking, uptake is somewhat lower among low-achieving and low-income students than among high-achieving and affluent students, and our new data provide mixed evidence on students' performance in virtual versus face-to-face classes. Most importantly, virtual courses are not a sufficiently superior option that we would expect them to measurably close the achievement gap even if uptake among disadvantaged students were higher. Current evidence on intelligent tutoring systems is more internally valid and more sanguine: high-quality research finds positive (but modest) effects, and results seem to be more pronounced for students in lower-quality classrooms. ITS may be reducing gaps, but only to a small degree, owing to both its limited scale and its only modest effect on gaps when implemented.

These results point not to the uselessness of new technologies for closing achievement gaps, but to the importance of understanding how technology interacts with the school and home contexts. We leave our analysis of new technologies and achievement gaps with four conclusions.

First, technologies have the potential to overcome some of the strong forces in U.S. public education that lead to inequalities in resources across schools. In particular, new technologies can bring high-quality curriculum, instruction, and peers to schools that have difficulty recruiting these resources owing to residential segregation, educator preference, and differential ability to raise funds.

Second, technologies can be either substitutes for or complements to resources already available in the school. To the extent that technologies are substitutes, they are inherently equalizing. When they are complements, however, such as when their successful implementation requires skilled teachers or students with strong prior skills, they must be accompanied by additional resources if traditionally underserved populations are to benefit.

Third, the range of mechanisms that underlie the potential for individual technologies to close achievement gaps includes quality, efficiency, differentiation, flexibility, and motivation. If technologies bring materials of both higher and more equal *quality* to schools, they might reduce achievement gaps by reducing the differences in access to quality instruction. If new technologies reduce extraneous work for either teachers or students—such as by reducing paperwork for teachers or enabling students to access the materials they need for their work more quickly—their *efficiency* can benefit students and, if these barriers were greater for some groups than others, reduce achievement gaps. If new technologies can better *differentiate* instruction to meet the needs of students whose performance is further from the mean, then they benefit those students who are not at the average. As far as closing achievement gaps, this differentiation may particularly help high-achieving students from low-income backgrounds who may not be the focus of instruction at schools serving differentially low-performing students. They may also benefit particularly low-achieving and high-achieving students across all schools.

New technologies allow for greater *flexibility* that could benefit students who are more likely to face shocks at home, such as from health or family issues. Technologies make it easier to access consistent material when children are ill and need to stay home or when families move and students need to switch schools. The flexibility afforded by new technologies may be particularly useful to families with resource constraints that affect their residential location or health, and this is another way in which they may help to reduce the achievement gap. Finally, new technologies can either *motivate* or demotivate students. If technologies can draw in otherwise disenfranchised students through the personalization of material to a student's interest or through gaming technology, they can benefit poor students and reduce achievement gaps. Alternatively, however, if the technologies increase reliance on students' internal motivation or require the oversight of adults, they may exacerbate achievement gaps.

Each of these mechanisms—quality, efficiency, differentiation, flexibility, and motivation—can play a role in the impact of new technologies on achievement gaps, though sometimes not always for the better.

Fourth, the benefit of new technologies in schools for closing achievement gaps may not rest primarily in the classroom. The infrastructure of schools depends on technologies. The process of recruiting and hiring educators has benefited from online applications and assessments. Predictive analytics that can identify students in need of further supports, in combination with greater communication and coordination technologies to link students in need with resources inside and outside of schools, have great potential to aid those students most in need. In considering the potential of new technologies to reduce achievement gaps, it would be a mistake to focus solely on computer-aided instruction, virtual courses, or other innovations that involved direct interaction with students.

The evidence to date suggests that technologies alone cannot eliminate the achievement gaps that the Coleman Report so clearly illuminated. Political pressures, uneven existing resources, and the dependence of even the most advanced new approaches on high-quality implementation point to the work needed to capitalize on the potential of these new technologies. However, their potential is growing, and with it their capacity to counter some of the forces that have led to unequal school quality across communities and kept public schools from being the lever that they could be to reduce achievement gaps and equalize opportunities.

REFERENCES

Anderson, Terry. 2008. *The Theory and Practice of Online Learning*. Edmonton, Calif.: Athabasca University Press.

Angrist, Joshua D., and Victor Lavy. 1999. "Using Maimonides' Rule to Estimate the Effect of Class Size on Scholastic Achievement." *Quarterly Journal of Economics* 114(2): 533–75.

Bakia, Marianne, K. Anderson, Eryn Heying, Kaeli Keating, and Jessica Mislevy. 2011. "Implementing Online Learning Labs in Schools and Districts: Lesson's from Miami-Dade's First Year." Menlo Park, Calif.: SRI International.

Banerjee, Abhijit, Shawn Cole, Esther Duflo, and Leigh Linden. 2005. "Remedying Education: Evidence from Two Randomized Experiments in India." Working Paper 11904. Cambridge, Mass.: National Bureau of Economic Research.

Barker, Bruce. 1985. "Curricular Offerings in Small and Large High Schools: How Broad Is the Disparity?" *Research in Rural Education* 3(1): 35–38.

Bettinger, Eric, Lindsay Fox, Susanna Loeb, and Eric Taylor. 2015. "Changing Distributions: How Online College Classes Alter Student and Professor Performance." Working Paper 15-10. Stanford, Calif.: Stanford University, Center for Education

Policy Analysis (October). Available at: http://cepa.stanford.edu/sites/default/files/WP15-10.pdf (accessed December 14, 2015).

Bowen, William G., Matthew M. Chingos, Kelly A. Lack, and Thomas I. Nygren. 2014. "Interactive Learning Online at Public Universities: Evidence from a Six-Campus Randomized Trial." *Journal of Policy Analysis and Management* 33(1): 94–111.

Boyd, Donald, Hamilton Lankford, Susanna Loeb, Jonah Rockoff, and James Wyckoff. 2008. "The Narrowing Gap in New York City Teacher Qualifications and Its Implications for Student Achievement in High-Poverty Schools." *Journal of Policy Analysis and Management* 27(4): 793–818.

Campuzano, Larissa, Mark Dynarski, Roberto Agodini, and Kristina Rall. 2009. "Effectiveness of Reading and Mathematics Software Products: Findings from Two Student Cohorts." NCEE 2009-4041. Washington: U.S. Department of Education, Institute of Education Sciences, National Center for Education Evaluation and Regional Assistance.

Carter, Prudence L. 2016. "Educational Equality Is a Multifaceted Issue: Why We Must Understand the School's Sociocultural Context for Student Achievement." *RSF: The Russell Sage Foundation Journal of the Social Sciences* 2(5). doi: 10.7758/RSF.2016.2.5.07.

Cavalluzzo, Linda, Deborah L. Lowther, Christine Mokher, and Xitao Fan. 2012. "Effects of the Kentucky Virtual Schools' Hybrid Program for Algebra I on Grade 9 Student Math Achievement: Final Report." NCEE 2012-4020. Washington: U.S. Department of Education, Institute of Education Sciences, National Center for Education Evaluation and Regional Assistance.

Cavanaugh, Cathy, Kathy Jo Gillan, Jeff Kromrey, Melinda Hess, and Robert Blomeyer. 2004. "The Effects of Distance Education on K–12 Student Outcomes: A Meta-analysis." Naperville, Ill.: Learning Point Associates/North Central Regional Educational Laboratory (NCREL).

Center for Research on Educational Outcomes (CREDO). 2011. *Charter Schools' Performance in Pennsylvania*. Stanford, Calif.: Stanford University, CREDO.

Cheung, Alan C. K., and Robert E. Slavin. 2011. "The Effectiveness of Education Technology for Enhancing Reading Achievement: A Meta-analysis." Baltimore: Center for Research and Reform in Education.

———. 2013. "The Effectiveness of Educational Technology Applications for Enhancing Mathematics Achievement in K–12 Classrooms: A Meta-analysis." *Educational Research Review* 9(1): 88–113.

Christensen, Clayton M., Curtis W. Johnson, and Michael B. Horn. 2010. *Disrupting Class: How Disruptive Innovation Will Change the Way the World Learns*. Expanded ed. New York: McGraw-Hill.

Clotfelter, Charles T., Helen F. Ladd, and Jacob L. Vigdor. 2007. "Teacher Credentials and Student Achievement: Longitudinal Analysis with Student Fixed Effects." *Economics of Education Review* 26(6): 673–82. doi: http://dx.doi.org/10.1016/j.econedurev.2007.10.002.

Coleman, James S., Ernest Q. Campbell, Carol J. Hobson, James McPartland, Alexander M. Mood, Frederick D. Weinfeld, and Robert L. York. 1966. *Equality of Educational Opportunity*. Washington: U.S. Department of Health, Education, and Welfare, Office of Education.

Conati, Cristina. 2009. "Intelligent Tutoring Systems: New Challenges and Directions." In *Twenty-First International Joint Conference on Artificial Intelligence* 9(1): 2–7.

Cooper, Harris, Kelly Charlton, Jeff C. Valentine, Laura Muhlenbruck, and Geoffrey D. Borman. 2000. "Making the Most of Summer School: A Meta-analytic and Narrative Review." *Monographs of the Society for Research in Child Development* 65(1): i–127.

Cuban, Larry. 2003. *Oversold and Underused: Reforming Schools Through Technology, 1980–2000*. Cambridge, Mass.: Harvard University Press.

Dede, Christopher. 2006. *Online Professional Development for Teachers: Emerging Models and Methods*. Cambridge, Mass.: Harvard Education Press.

Dettling, Lisa J., Sarena F. Goodman, and Jonathan Smith. 2015. "Every Little Bit Counts: The Impact of High-Speed Internet on the Transition to College." Finance and Economics Discussion Series 2015-108. Washington, D.C.: Board of Governors of the Federal Reserve System. doi: http://dx.doi.org/10.17016/FEDS.2015.108.

Drummond, Kathryn, Marjorie Chinen, Teresa Garcia Duncan, H. Ray Miller, Lindsay Fryer, Courtney Zmach, and Katherine Culp. 2011. "Impact of the Thinking Reader Software Program on Grade 6 Reading Vocabulary, Comprehension, Strategies, and Motivation." NCEE 2010-4035. Washington: U.S. Department of Education, Institute of Education Sciences, National Center for Education Evaluation and Regional Assistance.

Dynarski, Mark, Roberto Agodini, Sheila Heaviside, Timothy Novak, Nancy Carey, Larissa Campuzano, Barbara Means, Robert Murphy, William Penuel, Hal Javitz, Deborah Emery, and Willow Sussex. 2007. "Effectiveness of Reading and Mathematics Software Products: Findings from the First Student Cohort." NCEE 2007-4005. Washington: U.S. Department of Education, Institute of Education Sciences, National Center for Education Evaluation and Regional Assistance.

Figlio, David N., Mark Rush, and Lu Yin. 2013. "Is It Live or Is It Internet? Experimental Estimates of the Effects of Online Instruction on Student Learning." *Journal of Labor Economics* 31(4): 763–84.

Fletcher-Flinn, Claire M., and Breon Gravatt. 1995. "The Efficacy of Computer Assisted Instruction (CAI): A Meta-analysis." *Journal of Educational Computing Research* 12(3): 219–41.

Florida Bureau of Educational Technology. 2014. "Bureau of Educational Technology Archives: Fall 2014 Technology Resources Inventory." Available at: http://www.fldoe.org/about-us/division-of-technology-info-services/educational-technology/archives (accessed January 3, 2016).

Florida Department of Management Services (FLDMS). 2014. Official update submission to the National Telecommunications and Information Administration under the State Broadband Initiative Program for the State of Florida (October). Available at National Broadband Map, http://www.broadbandmap.gov/data-download (accessed June 28, 2016).

Graesser, Arthur C., Mark W. Conley, and Andrew Olney. 2012. "Intelligent Tutoring Systems." In *APA Educational Psychology Handbook*, vol. 3, *Application to Learning and Teaching*, edited by Karen R. Harris, Steve Graham, and Tim Urdan. Washington, D.C.: American Psychological Association.

Gray, Lucinda, Nina Thomas, Laurie Lewis, and Peter Tice. 2010. "Teachers' Use of Educational Technology in U.S. Public Schools: 2009." NCES 2010-040. Washington: U.S. Department of Education, National Center for Education Statistics.

Guha, Roneeta, Naomi Tyler, Samantha Astudillo, and Betsey Wolf. 2015. "Evaluation of Rocketship Students' Middle School Outcomes: First-Year Findings." Menlo Park, Calif.: SRI International.

Harris, Douglas N., and Tim R. Sass. 2011. "Teacher Training, Teacher Quality, and Student Achievement." *Journal of Public Economics* 95(7–8): 798–812. doi: http://dx.doi.org/10.1016/j.jpubeco.2010.11.009.

Hart, Cassandra, Elizabeth Friedmann, and Michael Hill. 2014. "Online Course-Taking and Student Outcomes in California Community Colleges." Unpublished paper, University of California, Davis.

Heppen, Jessica B., Kirk Walters, Margaret Clements, Ann-Marie Faria, Cheryl Tobey, Nicholas Sorensen, and Katherine Culp. 2012. "Access to Algebra I: The Effects of Online Mathematics for Grade 8 Students." NCEE 2012-4021. Washington: U.S. Department of Education, Institute of Education Sciences, National Center for Education Evaluation and Regional Assistance.

Herold, Benjamin. 2014. "New Model Underscores Rocketship's Growing Pains." *Education Week* 33(19): 26.

Hoxby, Caroline M. 2000. "The Effects of Class Size on Student Achievement: New Evidence from Population Variation." *Quarterly Journal of Economics* 115(4): 1239–85.

Jennings, Jennifer L., and Douglas Lee Lauen. 2016. "Accountability, Inequality, and Achievement: The Effects of the No Child Left Behind Act on Multiple Measures of Student Learning." *RSF: The Russell Sage Foundation Journal of the Social Sciences* 2(5). doi: 10.7758/RSF.2016.2.5.11.

Jepsen, Christopher, and Steven Rivkin. 2009. "Class Size Reduction and Student Achievement: The Potential Trade-off Between Teacher Quality and Class Size." *Journal of Human Resources* 44(1): 223–50.

Joyce, Ted J., Sean Crockett, David A. Jaeger, Onur Altindag, and Stephen D. O'Connell. 2015. "Does Classroom Time Matter?" *Economics of Education Review* 46: 64–77.

Kalogrides, Demetra, and Susanna Loeb. 2013. "Different Teachers, Different Peers: The Magnitude of Student Sorting Within Schools." *Educational Researcher* 42(6): 304–16.

Kirkpatrick, Heather, and Larry Cuban. 1998. "Computers Make Kids Smarter—Right?" *Technos* 7(2): 26–31.

Koedinger, Kenneth R., John R. Anderson, William H. Hadley, and Mary A. Mark. 1997. "Intelligent Tutoring Goes to School in the Big City." *International Journal of Artificial Intelligence in Education* 8(1): 30–43.

Krueger, Alan B. 1999. "Experimental Estimates of Education Production Functions." *Quarterly Journal of Economics* 114(2): 497–532.

Kulik, James A. 1994. "Meta-analytic Studies of Findings on Computer-Based Instruction." In *Technology Assessment in Education and Training,* edited by Eva L. Baker and Harold F. O'Neil Jr. Hillsdale, N.J.: Lawrence Erlbaum Associates.

Kulik, James A., and J. D. Fletcher. 2015. "Effectiveness of Intelligent Tutoring Systems: A Meta-analytic Review." *Review of Educational Research* (April 17). doi:10.3102/0034654315581420.

Ma, Wenting, Olusola O. Adesope, John C. Nesbit, and Qing Liu. 2014. "Intelligent Tutoring Systems and Learning Outcomes: A Meta-analysis." *Journal of Educational Psychology* 106(4): 901–18.

Means, Barbara, Yukie Toyama, Robert Murphy, Marianne Bakia, and Karla Jones. 2010. "Evaluation of Evidence-Based Practices in Online Learning: A Meta-analysis and Review of Online Learning Studies." Washington: U.S. Department of Education, Office of Planning, Evaluation, and Policy Development.

Molnar, Alex (ed.), Gary Miron, Luis Huerta, Jennifer King Rice, Larry Cuban, Brian Horvitz, Charisse Gulosino, and Sheryl Rankin Shafer. 2013. "Virtual Schools in the U.S. 2013: Politics, Performance, and Research Evidence." Boulder, Colo.: National Education Policy Center.

Nwana, Hyacinth S. 1990. "Intelligent Tutoring Systems: An Overview." *Artificial Intelligence Review* 4(4): 251–77.

Nye, Barbara, Spyros Konstantopoulos, and Larry Hedges. 2004. "The Effects of Small Classes on Academic Achievement: The Results of the Tennessee Class Size Experiment." *American Educational Research Journal* 37(1): 123–51.

Pane, John F., Beth Ann Griffin, Daniel F. McCaffrey, and Rita Karam. 2014. "Effectiveness of Cognitive Tutor Algebra I at Scale." *Educational Evaluation and Policy Analysis* 36(2): 127–44.

Pane, John F., Daniel F. McCaffrey, Mary Ellen Slaughter, Jennifer L. Steele, and Gina S. Ikemoto. 2010. "An Experiment to Evaluate the Efficacy of Cognitive Tutor Geometry." *Journal of Research on Educational Effectiveness* 3(3): 254–81.

Picciano, Anthony G., Jeff Seaman, Peter Shea, and Karen Swan. 2012. "Examining the Extent and Nature of Online Learning in American K-12 Education: The Research Initiatives of the Alfred P. Sloan Foundation." *The Internet and Higher Education* 15(2): 127–35.

Pufahl, Ingrid, and Nancy C. Rhodes. 2011. "Foreign Language Instruction in U.S. Schools: Results of a National Survey of Elementary and Secondary Schools." *Foreign Language Annals* 44(2): 258–88.

Reardon, Sean F., and Ann Owens. 2014. "60 Years After *Brown:* Trends and Consequences of School Segregation." *Annual Review of Sociology* 40: 199–218.

Ritter, Gary, and Martin F. Lueken. 2013."Value-Added in a Virtual Learning Environment: An Evaluation of the Arkansas Virtual Academy." Paper prepared for the Thirty-Eighth Annual Conference of the Association for Education Finance and Policy. New Orleans (March 14–16).

Rivkin, Steven, Eric Hanushek, and John F. Kain. 2005. "Teachers, Schools, and Academic Achievement." *Econometrica* 73(2): 417–58.

Ruggles, Steven, Katie Genadek, Ronald Goeken, Josiah Grover, and Matthew Sobek. 2015. "Integrated Public Use Microdata Series: Version 6.0" [machine-readable database]. Minneapolis: University of Minnesota.

Sass, Tim R., Jane Hannaway, Zeyu Xu, David Figlio, and Li Feng. 2012. "Value Added of Teachers in High-Poverty Schools and Lower-Poverty Schools." *Journal of Urban Economics* 72(2): 104–22.

Schneider, Barbara, and Guan Saw. 2016. "Racial and Ethnic Gaps in Postsecondary Aspirations and Enrollment." *RSF: The Russell Sage Foundation Journal of the Social Sciences* 2(5). doi: 10.7758/RSF.2016.2.5.04.

Schorr, Jonathan, and Deborah McGriff. 2011. "Future Schools: Blending Face-to-Face and Online Learning." *Education Next* 11(3). http://uconnhealth2020.uchc.edu/knowledgebase/pdfs/education/future_schools.pdf (accessed September 14, 2015).

Shute, Valerie J., and Joseph Psotka. 1994. "Intelligent Tutoring Systems: Past, Present, and Future." Report 94-17332. Brooks Air Force Base, TX: Armstrong Laboratory, Human Resources Directorate.

Steenbergen-Hu, Saiying, and Harris Cooper. 2013. "A Meta-analysis of the Effectiveness of Intelligent Tutoring Systems on K-12 Students' Mathematical Learning." *Journal of Educational Psychology* 105(4): 970–87.

Streich, Francine E. 2014. *Online Education in Community Colleges: Access, School Success, and Labor-Market Outcomes.* PhD diss., University of Michigan.

Taylor, Eric 2015. "New Technology and Teacher Productivity." Working paper. Cambridge, Mass.: Harvard Graduate School of Education.

U.S. Department of Commerce (USDOC). National Telecommunications and Information Administration (NTIA). 2014. "State Broadband Initiative." Washington: USDOC (June 30).

VanLehn, Kurt, Collin Lynch, Kay Schulze, Joel A. Shapiro, Robert Shelby, Linwood Taylor, Don Treacy, Anders Weinstein, and Mary Wintersgill. 2005. "The Andes Physics Tutoring System: Lessons Learned." *International Journal of Artificial Intelligence in Education* 15(3): 147–204.

Watson, John, and Butch Gemin. 2008. "Using Online Learning for At-Risk Students and Credit Recovery." Vienna, Va.: North American Council for Online Learning.

Watson, John, Amy Murin, Lauren Vashaw, Butch Gemin, and Chris Rapp. 2012. "Keeping Pace with K–12 Online Learning: An Annual Review of Policy and Practice 2011." Durango, Colo.: Evergreen Education Group.

Wicks, Matthew. 2010. "A National Primer on K–12 Online Learning: Version 2." Vienna, Va.: International Association for K–12 Online Learning.

Xu, Di, and Shanna Jaggars. 2011. "The Effectiveness of Distance Education Across Virginia's Community Colleges: Evidence from Introductory College-Level Math and English Courses." *Educational Evaluation and Policy Analysis* 33(3): 360–77.

———. 2013. "The Impact of Online Learning on Students' Course Outcomes: Evidence from a Large Community and Technical College System." *Economics of Education Review* 3: 46–57.

Connecting Research and Policy to Reduce Inequality

RUTH N. LÓPEZ TURLEY

Why did the Coleman Report and the decades of education research that it influenced not result in greater reductions in educational inequality? What can be done to ensure that future education research is more effective in this respect? This paper describes the significant disconnect between education researchers and policymakers, characterized by three problems: (1) researchers do not inform policymakers about the results of their research, (2) policymakers do not inform researchers about their policy goals, and (3) when policymakers and researchers do exchange information, they often do so in a highly political context in which many interests supersede the interests of students. However, important changes since the Coleman Report have created a context more conducive to effective collaboration, including a nationwide movement among researchers, policymakers, and funders to create more meaningful and effective partnerships. These changes present a unique opportunity for improving the connection between research and policy and reducing educational inequities over the next fifty years.

Keywords: educational inequality, research-practice partnerships, decision making

Commissioned by Congress in the Civil Rights Act of 1964, James Coleman's seminal work on educational inequality was the most ambitious national study on the condition of education to date, and not surprisingly, it had a tremendous influence on decades of education research that followed. However, as the papers in this issue have shown, educational inequities by race, ethnicity, and economic status stubbornly persist, despite countless research studies and the expenditure of many millions of research dollars. Significant victories ensued, but many researchers and policymakers would agree that educational inequalities and inequities have not been reduced sufficiently. Why did the Coleman Report and the decades of research that it influenced not result in more significant gap closures? More importantly, what can be done to ensure that current and future education research has a greater impact?

This paper focuses on the significant disconnect that persists between education research and policy, despite repeated efforts to bring the two together. First, I briefly describe the persistent gaps and the role of researchers and policymakers in maintaining them. Second, I describe the political context that impedes an effective connection between researchers and policymakers. Third, I describe some important changes that have created a better context for improving the connection between research and policy, including an emphasis on evidence-based decision-making with a local focus, funders' initiatives that support a movement away from the traditional

Ruth N. López Turley is professor of sociology at Rice University, director of the Houston Education Research Consortium, and associate director of the Kinder Institute for Urban Research.

Direct correspondence to: Ruth N. López Turley at turley@rice.edu, Rice University, 6100 Main St., MS28, Houston, TX 77005.

academic research model toward a partnership research model, and changing institutional incentives for academic researchers. These important changes are promoting a political context quite different from what existed fifty years ago—one that is primed for much better collaboration between researchers and decisionmakers. Finally, this paper ends with several recommended approaches to seizing this moment to improve the connection between research and policy and reduce educational inequities over the next fifty years.

PERSISTENT GAPS IN EDUCATIONAL ATTAINMENT

Although educational attainment has improved over time for all groups, progress in closing the gaps between groups has stalled, and even regressed, relative to when we began documenting gaps with national assessment data in the early 1970s. All racial groups have experienced improvements in high school and college completion, but gaps between these groups remain significant. For example, the black-white high school completion gap declined sharply during the 1970s and 1980s, but the decline since then has been much slower and the black-white gap in college completion has actually grown since 1970, and sharply so since 1995 (National Center for Education Statistics 2013). In terms of income, achievement gaps based on the National Assessment of Educational Progress (NAEP) have grown significantly over the last three decades. For example, the reading achievement gap between the top and bottom 10 percent of the income distribution has increased substantially, from 0.9 of a standard deviation among those born in the 1950s, 1960s, and early 1970s to 1.25 standard deviations among those born just twenty to twenty-five years later (Reardon 2013). Finally, combining income and race for all school districts in the United States, sixth-graders in the richest districts are about four grade levels ahead of children in the poorest districts, and within districts there are very large gaps between white, black, and Hispanic students in a majority of districts across the country (Reardon, Kalogrides, and Shores 2016).

These persistent gaps surprised some astute observers of educational inequality. Adam Gamoran (2001) had optimistically predicted that inequality in educational achievement and attainment would remain stable by socioeconomic status but diminish by race because successes in one generation, he predicted, would produce even greater successes in the next generation. I was equally hopeful about this "virtuous cycle," but it did not take hold as expected. More recently, Gamoran (2015) has explained that a primary reason for this disappointment is that educational and socioeconomic gains do not pay off as well for blacks as they do for whites. This was corroborated by a study from the Federal Reserve Bank of St. Louis, which reported that although African Americans and Hispanics with four-year college degrees had a higher income and a much higher net worth in 2013 than those without degrees, between 1992 and 2013 the median real net worth of college-educated African Americans and Hispanics dropped by 56 and 27 percent, respectively, while the median real net worth of college-educated whites and Asian Americans increased by 86 and 90 percent, respectively, during the same time period (Emmons and Noeth 2015). These disparities in asset gains and losses have a substantial impact on the resources transferred from one generation to the next.

There are multiple reasons for the impeded progress in reducing inequality, but an important one, I propose, stems from the underlying disconnect between education research and policy. This disconnect is characterized by three problems: (1) researchers do not inform policymakers about their results, (2) policymakers do not inform researchers about their policy goals, and (3) when policymakers and researchers do exchange information with each other, it is often done in a highly political context in which many interests supersede the interests of students. As a result, not all academic researchers and policymakers believe that research should be used for policymaking, given the many dangers associated with research manipulation and the possibility that studies that do not support a preexisting viewpoint will be excluded. Although these dangers are real, I assert that research should be used for policymaking and that steps can be taken to promote its proper use. Under the right conditions, research can be an extremely informative tool for policymaking, it can help to secure resources for implementing effective policy, and it can even help to generate political will.

THE DISCONNECT BETWEEN EDUCATION RESEARCH AND POLICY

Although education researchers and policymakers often work together—as with the Coleman Report, which was commissioned by Congress—they are not typically linked in a manner that is conducive for collective impact. Three conditions foster this disconnect between research and policy: (1) academic researchers generally focus on informing other researchers of their results rather than decision-makers; (2) decision-makers generally do not have easy access to timely, context-specific research to inform their decision-making; and (3) decision-makers generally do not inform researchers of their research needs and sometimes even make data access difficult for researchers interested in analyzing their data. Ie consider each of these conditions in turn.

First, academic researchers typically have few or no incentives to take measures to ensure that decision-makers use their work. Instead, they are largely rewarded for publishing their work with the most prestigious academic publishers or in the most cited academic journals, which are read primarily by other academics, not by decision-makers. Many institutions even frown upon applied work, deeming it not as worthy as the intellectual pursuit of interesting questions without regard for what is popular at the moment. Basic research is certainly important and should continue, and publishing in academic journals should also continue, especially because the blind review process pushes authors to improve and polish their work in ways that they would not do otherwise. However, research universities should recognize and reward efforts to apply research in settings that could really benefit from it, such as state and local education agencies, and academics should not make publishing in academic journals their end goal but instead take additional steps to ensure that their research actually informs decision-makers.

Second, decision-makers in state and local education agencies often do not have access to academic research publications, as access can be very expensive. Even if they do, they generally do not have time to read lengthy research articles to stay current on the research literature, and they are hesitant to use research conducted in other regions with different populations. Also, decision-makers in school districts and state agencies often do not have adequate staff and resources to conduct their own research. Even urban school districts large enough to have their own research departments are typically understaffed and have to focus on reporting requirements rather than large-scale studies that could be used for decision-making and tackling long-standing problems. Furthermore, decision-makers often need access to independently produced research, as in-house research that reports favorable results is sometimes dismissed or viewed with skepticism by the public.

Finally, state and local policymakers generally do not inform researchers of their research needs and sometimes even make data access difficult for researchers interested in analyzing their data. The sensitive nature of student and teacher data certainly requires that data access be restricted, and education agencies must take security measures to protect their constituents' identities. However, the dangers associated with not sharing data are much greater than the dangers associated with doing so. With protective measures in place, data sharing greatly increases research capacity and capitalizes on the expertise of external researchers. Furthermore, data owners can and should place expectations on researchers to produce research that is timely and useful for the education agency providing the data. They can inform researchers of their most urgent research needs, they can request research briefs and presentations designed to inform their decision-makers, and they can request meetings to discuss research results, limitations, and implications.

THE IMPEDIMENTS OF THE POLITICAL CONTEXT

Although education researchers and policymakers do work together sometimes, they are not typically linked in a manner that is conducive to collective impact. When policymakers and researchers do work together, they must often contend with a highly political context in which many interests compete for their attention besides the interests of students. Those interests, such as job security, career advancement, and access to funding, apply equally to policymakers and researchers, as well as to many other stakeholders. Policymakers additionally have to contend with important constituents such as boards, state and local organizations, and influential parents who do not necessarily have in mind the interests of all students.

For example, a task force in one of Houston's poorest neighborhoods produced a report highlighting a substantial inequity in the student funding formula, which allocated significantly more funding for gifted and talented (GT) students than for economically disadvantaged students (Fifth Ward Education Task Force 2016). The report suggested changing the weighted pupil formula, which accounted for 90 percent of each school's budget and allotted a modest weight of 7.5 percent for low-income students but a much greater weight of 12 percent for GT students, who were disproportionately higher-income, white, and concentrated in specific schools. When this funding inequity was brought to the attention of the district's leadership, they acted upon it quickly, but they had to figure out a way to avoid provoking the influential parents of the higher-income, GT students. The acting superintendent's original proposal would have cut the amount of funding that schools received for GT students in half, but that was not politically feasible. The revised proposal therefore redirected funds for the poorest schools without touching the funding for GT students. The newspaper headline highlighted this choice: "HISD [Houston Independent School District] Chief Scraps Plan to Cut Gifted Student Funding" (Mellon 2016). After the headline and the first sentence, the rest of the article described the acting superintendent's plan to redirect $21 million to the poorest schools. The revised plan was later approved with a unanimous school board vote, and the subsequent headline read: "HISD Approves Spending Plan Favoring Schools with Most Low-Income Students" (Wermund 2016). Although redirecting $21 million is no small feat, it is not a sustainable solution given that the inequitable funding formula remained the same in order to appease the influential parents of GT students and avoid further white flight from the district, whose student body is only 8 percent white.

Another important interest that can supersede the interests of students is job security, which, for policymakers at all levels, is often tenuous: many policymakers must either be reelected or reappointed or have their contracts renewed. They are therefore under high pressure to perform quickly during their term in leadership, and they must please many powerful constituents, some of whom could expedite their termination. These conditions are important for accountability purposes, but they are not conducive to long-term planning or policies or interventions that might take years to produce desired results. Similarly, the pressure on many researchers, especially untenured faculty or researchers seeking career advancement, to produce academic reports requires that they pursue research questions that are interesting to the broader research community (and not necessarily to local decision-makers) and that their results be interesting or surprising (which can reduce incentives for replication or for publishing studies with insignificant results); for these researchers, the policy implications are often an afterthought. All of these interests make it difficult for education researchers and policymakers to work together effectively.

While education researchers and state and local policymakers struggle to connect in a meaningful way, vendors of textbooks, software, and curricula often do a much better job than academic researchers of disseminating research directly to decision-makers in school districts and state education agencies. Because that research, often produced and funded by these vendors of educational products themselves, is more likely to report favorable results (Borman et al. 2003), these local decision-makers need more access to independently produced, timely, context-specific research. Other sources of funding, such as federal agencies and private foundations, fund independently produced research, but their funding often does not support the cost of an effective partnership infrastructure. Many resources—

not just financial—are needed to bring together researchers and decision-makers to jointly develop a research agenda, build compatible research structures, and conduct and disseminate research findings in a direct and effective manner. Fortunately, the context for creating more meaningful connections between researchers and decision-makers is improving.

THE CHANGING CONTEXT

Despite numerous challenges to an effective connection between researchers and policymakers, several important changes have occurred since the release of the Coleman Report. Today's political context is quite different from that of fifty years ago and is primed for much better collaboration between education researchers and decision-makers, which I believe can more effectively reduce inequalities and inequities. These changes include: (1) increased emphasis on local decision-making, coupled with a nationwide movement among researchers, policymakers, and funders to create more meaningful and effective place-based partnerships; (2) changing institutional incentives for both academic researchers and leaders at state and local education agencies; and (3) technological advances in data science. These changes present a unique opportunity for improving the connection between research and policy and reducing educational inequities over the next fifty years.

The nationwide movement to create more meaningful relationships among researchers, policymakers, and funders has been in the making for several decades, but an emphasis on place-based partnerships did not begin until around 1990, with the founding of the Chicago Consortium on School Research (CCSR 2015). This model spread slowly at first, but quickly took off in the last decade as similar place-based partnerships between research institutions and local education agencies began to form in other large urban areas, such as the Baltimore Education Research Consortium (BERC), launched in 2006; the Research Alliance for New York City Schools, launched in 2008; the Stanford University and San Francisco Unified School District Partnership, launched in 2009; the Los Angeles Education Research Institute (LAERI), launched in 2011; the Houston Education Research Consortium (HERC), launched in 2011; the Education Research Alliance for New Orleans (ERANO), launched in 2013; and Shared Solutions in Philadelphia, launched in 2014. Although each of these partnerships has distinct features relevant to its local context, they share a primary aim to connect research and policy in a manner that promotes collective impact.

Along with the formation of these partnerships, a developing new field of research has added theoretical and methodological depth to partnership work, starting with Maureen Hallinan's (1996, 2011) plea for researchers to adopt a more practical approach in order to be more effective. Meredith Honig and Cynthia Coburn (2008) have helped researchers understand the different meanings of "evidence" and the complicated ways in which policymakers use it, and Anthony Bryk, Louis Gomez, and Alicia Grunow (2011) have promoted a problem-centered, sustained research infrastructure that cultivates a diversity of expertise so that research and development do not occur apart from an applied setting but rather through a "networked improvement community." In particular, Melissa Roderick, John Easton, and Penny Sebring (2012) argue that developing new roles for research is increasingly important as decision-making becomes more decentralized. All of these insights have helped to move the nascent field of research-practice partnerships forward, especially local place-based partnerships.

The spread of these partnerships and the accompanying development of the new research field reached a critical point with the passing of the Every Student Succeeds Act (ESSA) of 2015—the most recent reauthorization of the Elementary and Secondary Education Act (ESEA) of 1965. ESSA is in many ways a response to the lessons learned from the previous reauthorization, the No Child Left Behind (NCLB) Act of 2001. Among the lessons learned from NCLB was the need for a much stronger commitment to supporting the use of evidence in local decision-making. The evidence-based movement was already well under way in 2001, but recent developments would provide resources for research and evaluation as well as increase state and local power to act upon that evidence. Specifically, ESSA will:

- establish new resources to test promising practices and replicate proven strategies that will drive opportunity and better outcomes for America's students; and
- empower state and local decision-makers to develop their own strong systems for school improvement based upon evidence, rather than imposing cookie-cutter federal solutions, as No Child Left Behind (NCLB) did.

This commitment to the provision of resources for research, combined with increased state and local power to act upon that evidence, epitomizes the increasingly widespread emphasis on local decision-making, which is more conducive to collaboration between researchers and decision-makers.

National data provide useful benchmarks, but state and school district decision-makers want to use timely, context-specific evidence, based on questions they helped to develop. The national-level evidence provided by the Coleman Report may have been suitable for gauging the nation's inequalities and inequities, but it was not useful for local decision-making. The current evidence-based movement focuses on the power of evidence in local decision-making, which I believe is a more effective strategy for reducing inequality owing to the buy-in generated when local decision-makers and researchers collaborate on a long-term basis. In particular, local decision-making facilitates the development of a joint research agenda, which is an iterative process that requires extensive and frequent communication between local researchers and decision-makers. Most importantly, a jointly developed research agenda in turn increases the likelihood of aligning the timing of research with the timing of decision-making.

Another important change for researcher–decision-maker collaboration is taking place among the agencies and foundations that fund education research and education initiatives. Funders of education initiatives are more often stressing the need for external evaluations, and funders of education research are putting greater emphasis on the need for deeper collaborations with the education agencies involved. Funders are developing new requests for proposals that specifically require these types of collaborations to facilitate a thorough and strategic dissemination process that will directly inform decision-makers. Funders are also increasingly collaborating with one another to develop funding strategies that will enable them to accomplish more together than could be accomplished alone. For example, the Education Funder Strategy Group (EFSG), a group of about thirty foundations that meet quarterly, aims to create "systemic improvements in student learning and outcomes" by, among other goals, "building capacity and equity into the [public education] system to fully serve all students."[1] These foundations are leaders in a movement to support research that is not only rigorous but also impactful. This movement, which is spreading to other foundations, is critical for convincing researchers and decision-makers to work together in meaningful ways.

Unfortunately, the actors that have been slowest to join these important movements have been research universities. Although some research universities are developing criteria to recognize and reward applied research, there is still tremendous pressure on academic researchers to focus exclusively on academic publications, which can take years to produce and typically are not read by decision-makers. Most research universities place much less weight on other works that could convey information to decision-makers more directly, such as research briefs for school district leaders, newspaper articles for the general public, and presentations or research memos for state leaders. Furthermore, some academic publish-

---

1. See the mission statement of the National Public Education Support Fund as it relates to the EFSG at: http://www.npesf.org/education-funder-strategy-group (accessed June 28, 2016).

ers refuse to publish research that has already been publicized heavily. For these reasons, academic researchers have few incentives to invest a lot of effort in working with decision-makers through long-term alliances.

However, some universities are starting to recognize that reaching out to decision-makers can have many benefits, including more opportunities for securing funding (given the funders' strategies mentioned earlier) and an improved public image that attracts donors who value research with direct societal impact. Support from their university administration is crucial if academic researchers are to collaborate effectively with local decision-makers. For example, Rice University has been extremely supportive of my own efforts to collaborate with local decision-makers, including assistance in setting up formal partnerships, securing data-sharing agreements, and developing relationships with key leaders. If institutions like Rice take the lead in demonstrating to other institutions the value of this type of work, I believe that research universities can play an important role in changing the academic incentives for collaborating with decision-makers.

Advances in data science have been another crucial development in facilitating researcher–decision-maker collaboration. Although still an emerging field, these recent technological advances have much to offer education researchers that enables them to collaborate effectively with a variety of community partners as well as other researchers. Of particular use is the capacity to store extremely large amounts of data, from multiple databases that can communicate with each other, and in a manner that is secure yet easily accessible to approved users. Rice University recently invested $150 million in data science initiatives, and the Kinder Institute for Urban Research at Rice is building an urban data platform with spatial data architecture that will serve as a single access point for over 2,000 data sets maintained by the City of Houston, the Houston Independent School District, community organizations, and other partners.[2]

Not only are these data science developments enabling researchers and decision-makers to share data more easily and produce faster and timelier results, but they are also facilitating the development of new research methodologies and tools, such as machine learning, statistical learning, and better data visualization. With these developments in data science, state and school district leaders can store more information, including more granular data; they can more easily transfer sensitive data to researchers while minimizing security risks; and researchers can link more databases to open up new lines of research and apply new methodologies that require massive amounts of data. For example, many school districts had not been storing application data from job candidates who were not hired, owing to the cost associated with data storage. Without this information, researchers cannot study applicant pool changes over time or teacher selection, recruitment, and retention processes, which are associated with inequalities in student outcomes and are more challenging in some schools than in others (Jacob 2007). However, with improved and less expensive data storage technology, school districts can store unselected job candidates' information over a period of time. Furthermore, if school districts across a geographic region do this, researchers can study these processes across a regional job market, as neighboring districts often compete for job candidates.

These developments have created a context for researcher–decision-maker collaboration very different from the context of fifty years ago. The national movement to create more meaningful partnerships, the increased emphasis on local evidence-based decision-making, funders' initiatives to promote researcher–decision-maker collaboration, the changing institutional incentives for academic researchers, and the technological advances in data science have all created a context primed for a deeper

---

2. Jade Boyd, "Rice Announces $150 Million in Strategic Research Initiatives," Rice University News & Media, September 21, 2015, available at: http://news.rice.edu/2015/09/21/rice-announces-150-million-in-strategic-research-initiatives/ (accessed June 28, 2016).

and more effective connection between research and policy. I believe that the following approaches could seize this moment and reduce inequality over the next fifty years.

APPROACHES TO REDUCING EDUCATIONAL INEQUALITY

In response to the stalled progress in reducing educational inequalities and inequities, I propose three practical approaches that capitalize on the changes taking place that facilitate a more effective connection between research and policy. The three approaches focus on local, regional, and national measures to reduce educational inequities, and they all leverage a partnership research model. Local measures can help schools with high concentrations of disadvantaged students improve educational outcomes, regional measures can integrate schools and school districts in the long run, and national measures can support the development of local partnerships and facilitate work across partnerships.

Schools with high concentrations of disadvantaged students have become increasingly common and simply cannot continue to function in the same way. For example, students in these schools have lower access to teachers with higher value-added scores, which are associated with student achievement, especially in math and science (Lauen and Henry 2015). It is therefore important to understand how these schools function and how best to help students in very challenging contexts. At the same time, we must figure out how to disband the high concentrations of disadvantaged students in order for schooling processes to be more effective and, most importantly, to take up the work of reducing educational inequality.

Approach 1: Local Measures

Education researchers regularly interact with schools and school districts and even refer to these collaborations as "partnerships," but these collaborations typically are researcher-centered, are limited to the duration of a study or project, and yield academic publications that rarely benefit the schools involved (Turley and Stevens 2015). These collaborations are based on a *traditional academic research model,* which emphasizes researcher-developed questions, site selection based on those questions, and the dissemination of research findings primarily to other academics. As a result, academic researchers have limited involvement in informing policy and practice in school districts, and school district leaders have limited involvement in shaping research agendas at research institutions (Turley and Stevens 2015). In an effort to address this problem, research-practice partnerships (RPPs) apply a *partnership research model,* which focuses on developing a long-term alliance rather than a project-based collaboration, place-based research agendas that are developed jointly by researchers and decision-makers, and a dissemination process that prioritizes conveying information to decision-makers.[3]

There are many advantages to the partnership research model. Most importantly, this model is more likely to produce research that will actually be used by education decision-makers because that is its goal at the outset. To begin with, a jointly developed research agenda ensures that the research produced is relevant to the potential users of the research results because they play a direct role in developing the research questions. Developing an agenda jointly requires early and frequent communication, in the recognition that it is an iterative process that must include multiple perspectives and ongoing equal ownership of the agenda. Combining the expertise of decision-makers who can identify the most pressing questions with the expertise of researchers who can incorporate the broader literature produces research projects that are relevant and of great interest to decision-makers, most of whom will eagerly await the research results.

Another significant advantage to RPPs is that they produce local, context-specific research. Besides their lack of easy access to aca-

---

3. See William T. Grant Foundation, "Research-Practice Partnerships," available at: http://wtgrantfoundation.org/RPP.

demic journals, and the time to read them, an important reason why decision-makers do not use available research is that it is usually produced at a different location with which their district may not have much in common. Sometimes research sites are not identifiable in research publications, and even if they are identified and happen to have some similarities to local decision-makers' schools and districts, there is no guarantee that what worked at the research site will work elsewhere, given the ever-present problem of unmeasured factors. In addition, school district leaders must use the most recent data available because districts change rapidly, but by the time articles or books are published the data are several years old. For these reasons, local decision-makers are much more likely to make use of timely, local research because they can be assured that the evidence they are using is directly relevant to their context. This is particularly important for districts with high concentrations of disadvantaged students, in which schooling processes function very differently—an issue I return to shortly.

Another advantage of RPPs is that their dissemination process is much more effective. A common understanding of research dissemination among academic researchers is that it is unidirectional and occurs after the completion of a research project, but this is highly ineffective for local decision-makers. The dissemination process should be more like a two-way dialogue that begins before the study begins, continues throughout the course of the study, and culminates in a series of discussions about the study's findings, implications, and limitations (Tseng 2013). The joint development of research questions ensures that the research is relevant and of interest to the potential users, but the dissemination process continues throughout the study, as researchers and decision-makers meet regularly throughout the course of the study so that district leaders can respond to researchers' questions and researchers can inform them of what to expect before the findings are released—what is often referred to as the "no surprises" rule. For example, the Houston Education Research Consortium, the partnership between Rice University and the Houston Independent School District, holds weekly research team meetings that district leaders are invited to attend, either via videoconference or in person. After the completion of the study, researchers do not simply hand over a written report but meet with decision-makers to answer questions and discuss the study's main findings, limitations, and implications. This type of dissemination process requires a much larger time commitment by both researchers and decision-makers, but it yields better research and significantly increases the chances that the research will actually be used.

Finally, because RPPs are designed to be long-term, they have the advantage of facilitating important follow-up studies that help districts learn, for example, why an intervention did not work as planned. When an intervention does not work, determining whether the failure was due to an ineffective intervention or an effective intervention with ineffective implementation can be extremely challenging. Through long-term partnerships, researchers and district leaders can work together not only to study what works but also to learn how to make interventions work when they do not, whether by altering the interventions or altering the implementation of the intervention. For example, in its evaluation of a program for struggling readers using a regression discontinuity design, HERC found that it was not having the desired effect. The consortium recommended a change in the program's eligibility requirements in order to exclude the students near the test score cut-point, because there was evidence that the program was not helping these students. This change allowed the district to focus its resources on the students more likely to be helped by the program, and it allowed HERC to do a follow-up study to test the program's effectiveness for students in a different part of the test score distribution.[4]

By connecting research and policy in this manner, policymakers and researchers can work together to identify and implement effective tools for helping schools and districts with high concentrations of disadvantaged stu-

---

4. The HERC research briefs are available at: https://kinder.rice.edu/herc/.

dents. However, local efforts are not sufficient for addressing the larger need to improve economic and racial-ethnic integration, because segregation occurs primarily between rather than within school districts (Stroub and Richards 2013). As a result, efforts coordinated through regional and national measures are needed in order to disband high concentrations of disadvantaged students and help schools function more effectively. Improving economic and racial-ethnic integration is a necessary part of reducing inequality.

Approach 2: Regional Measures
Although local partnerships can produce work that informs integration policy, such as district magnet school programs that aim to integrate students, the level of integration they can achieve is limited by the fact that segregation occurs primarily between rather than within school districts. Kori Stroub and Meredith Richards (2013) estimate that almost two-thirds of multiracial segregation occurs between districts and only one-third occurs within districts. Furthermore, between-district segregation is highest in *fragmented* metropolitan areas, where a central city district is surrounded by a large number of smaller districts (Bischoff 2008). This means that significant changes in segregation can only take place at the regional level and that the greatest opportunity for change is in fragmented metropolitan areas.

There are clear patterns by race and socioeconomic status, for example, in my own region, the Houston Independent School District and neighboring Houston-area school districts. HISD, the largest district in Texas and the seventh-largest in the United States, is only 8.2 percent white, and 75.5 percent of students are economically disadvantaged, according to the 2014–2015 online district profile. In contrast, neighboring districts northwest of HISD are significantly whiter and less economically disadvantaged: 27.5 percent white and 49.7 percent economically disadvantaged in Cypress-Fairbanks; 40.9 percent white and 29.0 percent low-income in Katy; and 57.3 percent white and 24.5 percent economically disadvantaged in Tomball. Intradistrict efforts cannot integrate schools, especially if the district's student population is only 8 percent white, as is the case with HISD. Redistributing the few white students in HISD will not significantly alter the racial composition of the district's schools.

Local RPPs can play an important role in integration, but they must coordinate their efforts across partnerships, especially those in their region, in order to achieve macrolevel changes in segregation. School and district segregation matters a lot because a high concentration of disadvantaged students alters the functioning of campuses and districts (Rumberger and Palardy 2005). In schools and districts with high concentrations of disadvantaged students, teacher and administrator recruitment and retention is more difficult, course offerings are more limited, parent involvement is more challenging because of their limited time and resources, specialized programs that require parent organizing and fund-raising are nearly impossible, and remediating interventions are often ineffective owing to a lack of human capital, leadership stability, and other important resources. As long as these resources, through segregation, are concentrated in some schools and are deficient or completely lacking in other schools, efforts to improve educational outcomes among disadvantaged students are Band-Aid solutions at best. Band-Aids are helpful in the short term and should of course be utilized, but only in conjunction with longer-term regional solutions that aim to improve the integration of students.

There are some interdistrict collaboratives, such as in Rochester, Omaha, and Minneapolis (Finnigan et al. 2015). Some resulted from court orders or state laws, while others were voluntary, but regardless of their origins, these collaboratives have had very limited reach because they are choice-based and rely on the cooperation of suburban schools to provide student slots (Finnigan et al. 2015). Furthermore, these collaboratives are limited to districts and therefore lack the advantages of RPPs between districts and research institutions. In particular, regional RPP cooperation has the potential to inform region-specific decision-making to produce macrolevel changes such as improving economic and racial-ethnic integration. Intradistrict efforts cannot produce these changes, nor can interdistrict efforts without locally informed decision-making, based on timely, context-specific research.

Regional measures based on coordinated local RPP efforts are needed. Local knowledge can be synthesized at the regional level to produce measures to reduce inequality beyond what can be accomplished through local measures alone. Regional, interdistrict efforts informed by local RPPs can address a variety of regional equity challenges and guide actions such as those aimed at improving economic and racial-ethnic integration. Regional measures can address other equity challenges as well, such as the inequitable distribution of highly qualified and effective teachers. There are large differences between the qualifications of teachers in the highest-poverty and highest-minority schools—who are often inexperienced, out-of-field, or uncertified—and the qualifications of teachers in low-poverty and low-minority schools (Peske and Haycock 2006). Even when using value-added estimates in addition to experience and licensure exam scores, the distribution of teachers consistently favors economically advantaged and nonminority students in elementary, middle, and high schools, and these inequities are found at the classroom, school, and district levels (Goldhaber, Theobald, and Tien 2015). Districts may attempt to recruit and retain highly qualified and effective teachers, but an equitable distribution can only be achieved at the regional level because teachers compare salaries, bonuses, and work conditions across districts in their region. For these reasons, these types of efforts to improve equality of educational opportunity are best carried out through the regional cooperation of local RPPs.

Approach 3: National Measures

National efforts are needed as well. The number of research-practice partnerships at this level is increasing, but there are relatively few such RPPs, many are fairly new, and they are challenging to develop and maintain, as they must be structured to endure frequent leadership changes, funding fluctuations, and political swings. A national infrastructure could support the development of these partnerships, facilitate their communication and collaboration, and coordinate efforts to connect research and policy at the local, regional, and national levels. Several national efforts to support RPPs are under way. For example, the Institute of Education Sciences (IES) in 2013 began funding partnerships between research institutions and state or local education agencies to carry out research on issues of high priority for the education agencies. Private foundations have also increased their funding for research produced by these types of partnerships. In addition, the National Network of Education Research-Practice Partnerships (NNERPP) was launched in 2016 to support the development of these partnerships. Housed at the Kinder Institute for Urban Research at Rice University, NNERPP aims to (1) develop and share best partnership practices, (2) synthesize findings and build knowledge, (3) facilitate and produce comparative research, and (4) advance broader policies and system reforms. These tasks, which I describe in greater detail in this section, are prohibitive for RPPs working in isolation, but efforts coordinated through a national network are much more likely to succeed in connecting research to policy and practice and reducing inequality. Broader coordinated efforts will ensure that educational inequality is not only studied but also reduced.

First, NNERPP aims to *develop and share best partnership practices*. One reason why RPPs can be challenging to set up and difficult to maintain is that they require that participants have many skills in which researchers and district leaders typically are not trained. Although researchers often collaborate with other research institutions, it is unusual for them to collaborate with school districts in a long-term partnership, and these collaborations highlight the substantial organizational differences between research institutions and school districts. Members of these different institutions often are not fully aware of their extensive dissimilarities in terms of time lines, communication processes, and organizational structures, to cite only a few examples. Furthermore, when these partnerships are forged, it can be very difficult to maintain a proper balance of power between the partner institutions and the individuals involved.

Since most RPPs are fairly new, effective partnership practices have only recently begun to be developed and documented. There is much need for more in-depth information about how to develop and sustain these often precarious partnerships, such as how to handle frequent leadership changes and political swings, how to translate research into meaningful action, how to make communication styles more compatible, and how to deal with partnership fatigue. The next step for RPPs is to develop best practices for overcoming the barriers—erected by both researchers and district leaders—to using research evidence. For example, HERC researchers have significantly altered their research time lines in order to release research briefs prior to district budget decisions, and district leaders have altered their schedules in order to include research meetings to discuss evidence relevant to their decision-making. Information about the practices that improve the use of evidence is just beginning to be collected and documented. There is need for systematically collecting best practices from the full range of RPPs that now exist, and most importantly, there is great need for developing effective mechanisms for sharing this knowledge and putting it into practice.

Second, NNERPP aims to *synthesize findings and build knowledge*. Although local RPPs have the distinct advantage of enabling researchers to report findings directly to decision-makers in a manner that maximizes their utility, district leaders and researchers alike could also benefit from knowing more about the research practices and findings of other partnerships. Research produced by RPPs should be synthesized in a manner that enables researchers and policymakers from all over the country to strategically build on that knowledge and use it to develop solutions. National meetings give education researchers many opportunities to learn from one another, but there are few opportunities for district leaders to learn from one another, and even fewer opportunities for district leaders and researchers to learn from each other. Professional organizations target these two groups separately, but there are few organizations that explicitly aim to bring these two groups together in the context of research-practice partnerships.

Third, NNERPP aims to *facilitate and produce comparative research*. Although context-specific research is of great interest to local policymakers, the utility of this research cannot fully realized until the most promising policies and practices are tested in multiple locations in order to establish external validity and understand the conditions under which the findings apply. Simply determining whether or not something works is insufficient; it is necessary to understand why it works, and it is impossible to do so without testing it in different settings. Multisite comparative research is a powerful tool for identifying the range of contexts in which promising policies and practices are effective, for understanding the mechanisms by which they work, and for replicating findings.

Finally, NNERPP aims to *advance broader policies and system reforms*. Research produced in direct partnership between research institutions and school districts should be used to inform national policies as well as system reforms. Information obtained from RPPs is uniquely equipped to inform national agencies and interest groups, especially if it has been vetted through carefully coordinated comparative research and examined extensively by school district leaders who have actually implemented the programs of interest; these conditions can generate a higher level of buy-in and political will. Moreover, because this type of information has the greatest potential to improve educational equality, it should be shared directly with regional and national policymakers, including the U.S. Department of Education, the Council of the Great City Schools, the National Public Education Support Fund, the U.S. Department of Health and Human Services, the Forum for Youth Investment, state departments of education, and the Council of Chief State School Officers. A national network of RPPs could be an extremely effective vehicle for ensuring that research and policy are connected in a manner that reduces educational inequality.

CONCLUSION

I began by asking why the Coleman Report and the decades of education research that it influenced have not resulted in greater reductions in educational inequities. Especially in recent decades, educational inequities have not been reduced sufficiently and progress has stalled or even regressed by some measures. I attribute this failure in part to a significant disconnect between education research and policy. In this paper, I have described the conditions that produced this disconnect, as well as the political context that has impeded an effective connection between researchers and policymakers.

Despite these obstacles, I am optimistic about the next fifty years of education research. Several important changes since the release of the Coleman Report have created a more promising context for effectively connecting research and policy: (1) more emphasis on local decision-making, coupled with a nationwide movement among researchers, policymakers, and funders to create more meaningful and effective place-based partnerships; (2) changing institutional incentives for both academic researchers and leaders at state and local education agencies; and (3) technological advances in data science. In light of these recent changes, I have proposed three approaches to reducing educational inequality by focusing on efforts to connect research and policy at the local, regional, and national levels. Local research-practice partnerships can help schools with high concentrations of disadvantaged students improve educational outcomes, regional efforts can improve racial-ethnic and economic integration, and national measures can create an infrastructure that develops and facilitates work across partnerships and advances broader policies and system reforms.

The current political context is quite different from that of fifty years ago. Many obstacles to achieving educational equality remain, but today's context is much better suited for deeper and more effective collaboration between researchers and decision-makers. We must seize this moment and make every effort to connect research and policy at the local, regional, and national levels, for this is how we can ensure that the next fifty years of education research will have a greater impact than has been the case in the last fifty years and that it will play a more significant role in reducing educational inequities.

REFERENCES

Bischoff, Kendra. 2008. "School District Fragmentation and Racial Residential Segregation: How Do Boundaries Matter?" *Urban Affairs Review* 44(2): 182–217.

Borman, Geoffrey D., Gina M. Hewes, Laura T. Overman, and Shelly Brown. 2003. "Comprehensive School Reform and Achievement: A Meta-analysis." *Review of Educational Research* 73(2): 125–230. doi:10.3102/00346543073002125.

Bryk, Anthony, Louis Gomez, and Alicia Grunow. 2011. "Getting Ideas into Action: Building Networked Improvement Communities in Education." In *Frontiers in Sociology of Education*, edited by Maureen Hallinan. New York: Springer.

Chicago Consortium on School Research (CCSR). 2015. "UChicago Consortium on School Research." Available at: https://consortium.uchicago.edu/sites/default/files/uploads/UChicagoConsortium_Brochure_2015.pdf (accessed June 28, 2016).

Emmons, William R., and Bryan J. Noeth. 2015. "Why Didn't Higher Education Protect Hispanic and Black Wealth?" *In the Balance: Perspectives on Household Balance Sheets* (Federal Reserve Bank of St. Louis) (12, August). Available at: https://www.stlouisfed.org/~/media/Publications/In%20the%20Balance/Images/Issue_12/ITB_August_2015.pdf (accessed June 28, 2016).

Fifth Ward Education Task Force. 2016. "Empowering Educational Equity in Houston's Fifth Ward." Houston: A Fifth Ward Coalition of Churches. Available at: http://www.pleasanthillministries.org/files/uploads/documents/Task_Force_Report_-_For_Email_Purposes.pdf (accessed June 28, 2016).

Finnigan, Kara S., Jennifer Jellison Holme, Myron Orfield, Tom Luce, Sarah Diem, Allison Mattheis, and Nadine D. Hylton. 2015. "Regional Educational Policy Analysis: Rochester, Omaha, and Minneapolis' Inter-District Arrangements." *Educational Policy* 29(5): 780–814. doi:10.1177/0895904813518102.

Gamoran, Adam. 2001. "American Schooling and Educational Inequality: A forecast for the 21st Century." *Sociology of Education* 74 (extra issue): 135–53.

———. 2015. "The Future of Educational Inequality in the United States: What Went Wrong, and How Can We Fix It?" New York: William T. Grant

Foundation (July 11). Available at: http://wtgrant foundation.org/library/uploads/2015/11/The-Future-of-Educational-Inequality-Adam-Gamoran.pdf (accessed June 28, 2016).

Goldhaber, Dan, Roddy Theobald, and Christopher Tien. 2015. "The Theoretical and Empirical Arguments for Diversifying the Teacher Workforce: Review of the Evidence." The Center for Education Data & Research, University of Washington Bothell. Available at: http://www.cedr.us/papers/working/CEDR%20WP%202015-9.pdf (accessed June 28, 2016).

Hallinan, Maureen. 1996. "Bridging the Gap Between Research and Practice." *Sociology of Education* 69 (extra issue): 131–34.

———. 2011. "Improving the Interaction Between Sociological Research and Educational Policy." In *Frontiers in Sociology of Education*, edited by Maureen Hallinan. New York: Springer.

Honig, Meredith, and Cynthia Coburn. 2008. "Evidence-Based Decision Making in School District Central Offices: Toward a Policy and Research Agenda." *Educational Policy* 22(4): 578–608.

Jacob, Brian A. 2007. "The Challenges of Staffing Urban Schools with Effective Teachers." *The Future of Children* 17(1): 129–53.

Lauen, Douglas Lee, and Gary T. Henry. 2015. "The Distribution of Teachers in North Carolina, 2009–2013." Research brief. Consortium for Educational Research and Evaluation–North Carolina (August). Available at: http://cerenc.org/wp-content/uploads/2015/08/0-FINAL-Final-TQ-Distribution-report-8-6-15.pdf (accessed June 28, 2016).

Mellon, Ericka. 2016. "HISD Chief Scraps Plan to Cut Gifted Student Funding." *Houston Chronicle*, April 21.

National Center for Education Statistics (NCES). 2013. "Table 221.85: Average NAEP Reading Scale Score, by Age and Selected Student Characteristics: Selected Years, 1971 Through 2012." *Digest of Education Statistics*. Available at: https://nces.ed.gov/programs/digest/d14/tables/dt14_221.85.asp?current=yes (accessed June 28, 2016).

Peske, Heather G., and Kati Haycock. 2006. "Teaching Inequality: How Poor and Minority Students Are Shortchanged on Teacher Quality." The Education Trust, Washington, D.C. Available at: http://edtrust.org/wp-content/uploads/2013/10/TQReportJune2006.pdf (accessed June 28, 2016).

Reardon, Sean. 2013. "The Widening Income Achievement Gap." *Educational Leadership* 70(8): 10–16.

Reardon, Sean, Demetra Kalogrides, and Kenneth Shores. 2016. "The Geography of Racial/Ethnic Test Score Gaps." Working Paper 16–10. Stanford, Calif.: Stanford University Center for Education Policy Analysis (April). Available at: https://cepa.stanford.edu/sites/default/files/wp16-10-v201604.pdf (accessed June 28, 2016).

Roderick, Melissa, John Easton, and Penny Sebring. 2012. *CCSR: A New Model for the Role of Research in Supporting Urban School Reform*. Chicago: Consortium on Chicago School Research (February). Available at: https://consortium.uchicago.edu/sites/default/files/publications/CCSR%20Model%20Report-final.pdf (accessed June 28, 2016).

Rumberger, Russell W., and Gregory J. Palardy. 2005. "Does Segregation Still Matter? The Impact of Student Composition on Academic Achievement in High School." *Teachers College Record* 107(9): 1999–2045.

Stroub, Kori, and Meredith P. Richards. 2013. "From Resegregation to Reintegration: Trends in the Racial/Ethnic Segregation of Metropolitan Public Schools, 1993–2009." *American Educational Research Journal* 50(3): 497–531.

Tseng, Vivian. 2013. "Forging Common Ground: Fostering the Conditions for Evidence Use." In *William T. Grant Foundation: 2012 Annual Report*, 18–25. Available at: http://wtgrantfoundation.org/library/uploads/2015/10/Forging-Common-Ground.pdf (accessed June 28, 2016).

Turley, Ruth N. L., and Carla Stevens. 2015. "Lessons from a School District–University Research Partnership: The Houston Education Research Consortium." *Educational Evaluation and Policy Analysis* 37(1S): 6S–15S.

Wermund, Benjamin. 2016. "HISD Approves Spending Plan Favoring Schools with Most Low-Income Students." *Houston Chronicle*, May 5.